The

LOST BANK

THE STORY OF WASHINGTON MUTUAL—
THE BIGGEST BANK FAILURE IN
AMERICAN HISTORY

KIRSTEN GRIND

SIMON & SCHUSTER

NEW YORK   LONDON   TORONTO   SYDNEY   NEW DELHI

Simon & Schuster
1230 Avenue of the Americas
New York, NY 10020

First Simon & Schuster hardcover edition June 2012

SIMON & SCHUSTER and colophon are registered
trademarks of Simon & Schuster, Inc.

For information about special discounts for bulk purchases,
please contact Simon & Schuster Special Sales at
1-866-506-1949 or business@simonandschuster.com.

The Simon & Schuster Speakers Bureau can bring authors to your live event.
For more information or to book an event contact the
Simon & Schuster Speakers Bureau at 1-866-248-3049
or visit our website at www.simonspeakers.com.

Designed by Ruth Lee-Mui

Manufactured in the United States of America

1   3   5   7   9   10   8   6   4   2

Library of Congress Cataloging-in-Publication Data

Grind, Kirsten.
The lost bank : the story of Washington Mutual—the biggest bank failure in
American history / Kirsten Grind.
p. cm.
Includes bibliographical references.
1. Washington Mutual, Inc. 2. Savings and loan association failures—United States—
History. 3. Bank failures—United States—History. 4. Savings and loan associations—
Washington (State)—Seattle—History. 5. Banks and banking—Washington
(State)—Seattle—History. I. Title.
HG2626.S654W374   2012
332.3'20973—dc23   2011048587

ISBN 978-1-4516-1792-4
ISBN 978-1-4516-1794-8 (ebook)

For

STEVE GRIND

CAST OF CHARACTERS

WASHINGTON MUTUAL (WAMU)

EARLY YEARS, 1981–2004

LOUIS "LOU" H. PEPPER, chairman, president, and chief executive officer

KERRY K. KILLINGER, president, chief executive officer, and chairman

FAY L. CHAPMAN, partner at Foster Pepper PLLC and outside general counsel; in-house general counsel and chief legal officer*

S. LIANE WILSON, executive vice president, operations and administration; vice chair and chief technology officer

CRAIG E. TALL, vice chair of corporate development

WILLIAM "BILL" A. LONGBRAKE, senior executive vice president and chief financial officer; vice chair

LEE D. LANNOYE, executive vice president, commercial real estate; executive vice president, corporate administration and credit

DEANNA W. OPPENHEIMER, senior vice president, corporate relations and marketing; president, Consumer Group

M. LYNN RYDER, executive vice president of human resources

*Many executives and directors held multiple positions over the years. I've noted their starting and ending titles here and listed only those who play reccurring roles.

CRAIG J. CHAPMAN, Commercial Group president

JAMES "JIM" G. VANASEK, executive vice president and chief enterprise risk officer

CRAIG S. DAVIS, executive vice president, lending and financial services; president, Home Loans and Insurance Services Group

THOMAS "TOM" W. CASEY, executive vice president and chief financial officer

JOHN F. ROBINSON, executive vice president, regulatory relations

LATER YEARS, 2005–2008

STEPHEN "STEVE" J. ROTELLA, president and chief operating officer

TODD BAKER, executive vice president, corporate strategy and development

RONALD "RON" J. CATHCART, executive vice president and chief enterprise risk officer

DAVID C. SCHNEIDER, president, Home Loans Group

CHERYL FELTGEN, chief risk officer, Home Loans Group

JOHN P. MCMURRAY, chief credit officer; chief enterprise risk officer

ALAN H. FISHMAN, chief executive officer

NOTABLE DIRECTORS

STEPHEN "STEVE" E. FRANK, director; chair of audit committee; chairman of board; retired chairman, president, and chief executive officer of Southern California Edison

MARY E. PUGH, director; chair of the finance committee; founder, president, and chief executive officer of Seattle-based Pugh Capital Management

JAMES H. STEVER, director; chair of the human resources committee; retired executive vice president, public policy, U.S. West

ORIN C. SMITH, director; chair of the finance committee; former president and chief executive officer of Starbucks Corp.

WILLIAM G. REED, JR., director; chair of the governance committee; former chairman of Simpson Timber Company

DAVID BONDERMAN, director; cofounder, TPG Capital (formerly Texas Pacific Group)

WAMU EMPLOYEES

BRIAN MUELLER, lead financial analyst, Consumer Deposit Product Group

KEVIN JENNE, market research manager

MICHELE PERRIN, regional manager, Warehouse Lending Group

IRIS GLAZE, investor relations specialist; shareholder services manager

JPMORGAN CHASE & CO.

JAMES "JAMIE" DIMON, chairman and chief executive

CHARLES "CHARLIE" W. SCHARF, chief executive officer, retail financial services

MICHAEL J. CAVANAGH, executive vice president, chief financial officer

OFFICE OF THRIFT SUPERVISION
FORMER FEDERAL BANK REGULATOR

JOHN M. REICH, director

SCOTT M. POLAKOFF, deputy director, chief operating officer

DARREL W. DOCHOW, regional director, West Region

FEDERAL DEPOSIT INSURANCE CORP.

SHEILA C. BAIR, chairman

JAMES "JIM" R. WIGAND, deputy director, Division of Resolutions and Receiverships

STEPHEN P. FUNARO, WaMu dedicated examiner

OTHERS

DEBORAH "DEBBIE" T. KILLINGER, Killinger's first wife

BRAD AND BRYAN KILLINGER, Killinger's sons

LINDA KILLINGER (formerly Linda Cottington), Killinger's second wife

RAMONA JIMINEZ, WaMu subprime borrower

SARA VASQUEZ, WaMu subprime borrower

ADA AND LUIS OSORIO, WaMu shareholders

CONTENTS

CAST OF CHARACTERS   VI

PROLOGUE: OUT OF TIME   1

1. FRIEND OF THE FAMILY   9

2. REMOVE THE CORPORATE JETS   32

3. THE POWER OF YES   56

4. ALEXANDER THE GREAT   79

5. THE DARK SIDE   111

6. THE GROWING TROUBLE   146

7. SCENES FROM THE GREAT DEPRESSION   184

8. PROJECT WEST   216

9. THE FINAL HOURS   254

EPILOGUE: "BARELY A BLIP"   307

ACKNOWLEDGMENTS   335

NOTES ON SOURCING   339

NOTES   345

INDEX   369

OUT OF TIME

Always an early riser, Steve Rotella arrived at WaMu just before 7:00 a.m. on September 25, 2008. The autumn morning was cool and dark. The president and chief operating officer of the country's largest savings and loan bank was almost always among the first executives to show up each day.

Rotella lived with his wife, Esther, in a 7,200-square-foot house abutting a large cemetery in the upscale, trendy Seattle neighborhood of Capitol Hill. Each day Rotella climbed into his BMW and made the short trip downtown, easily navigating the now-familiar back roads to the office. He avoided Capitol Hill's main street, where a Starbucks glowed among the closed facades of dozens of bars and boutiques, and young hipsters in skinny jeans lined up in front of a popular sidewalk coffee stand. Even at this time of the morning, there would likely be traffic in that direction, although not nearly the kind of traffic he was used to in New York. Instead, Rotella drove directly downhill, along a street crammed with parked cars, condominiums, and apartment buildings on either side. To the west, he could see the jagged peaks of the

Olympic Mountains. As he paralleled the freeway, a large REI store loomed in front of him. When Rotella moved to the city three years earlier, he had promptly bought several thousand dollars' worth of outdoor gear at REI. He had been hiking just once.[1]

He pulled his car into one of the executive parking spots underneath WaMu's new skyscraper. The bank had built the multimillion-dollar office space two years earlier and shared part of it with the Seattle Art Museum. Rotella walked onto the executive floor and poured himself a cup of coffee. He usually avoided the giant Starbucks in the bank's lobby, believing it was overpriced. Sometimes, however, his assistant offered to run out and fetch him a latte.

By this time, the team of WaMu employees tracking the bank's deposits had already prepared the morning report. Because of the time difference, it reflected branch activity on the East Coast. Earlier in the week, the team had delivered a glimmer of good news. WaMu customers across the country had stopped pulling their money out of the bank at such a rapid pace. Daily deposit outflows now hovered around $500 million, down from a peak of $2.8 *billion* on one frantic day during the prior week. Rotella turned on his computer and scanned through the report for that day. He found more good news. People seemed to have calmed down and weren't withdrawing their money on the basis of rumors and speculation. They had come to their senses and were bringing their money back. The East Coast branches had seen a net inflow of several hundred million dollars. The media helped the situation. Newspapers reported that Congress had spent the previous night hammering out details of an unprecedented $700 billion bailout of the financial system, which was likely to help all banks, including WaMu. President George W. Bush had delivered his first-ever address focused just on the economy, pleading with the nation to bless the decision. If the bailout wasn't approved, Bush warned, Americans could be in for "a long and painful recession." "Our entire economy is in danger," he told the public.[2]

Even with the news that help could be coming, and even though customers' money seemed to be returning to the bank, Rotella didn't feel reassured. He felt uneasy. The halls of WaMu seemed far too quiet.

On the East Coast, the bank's newly appointed chief executive, Alan Fishman, had been desperately trying to sell the company. Rotella could count on one hand the number of hours he had spent with the New York banker since the WaMu board had moved him in two and a half weeks ago, ousting Kerry Killinger, the bank's longtime leader. Fishman was blunt, aggressive, and confident, the qualities that WaMu needed its chief executive to possess in the current situation. But what WaMu needed even more was Fishman's turnaround skills and his industry ties. Fishman needed to find a buyer for WaMu—or at least more capital—immediately. One of WaMu's government regulators, the Federal Deposit Insurance Corp., had just doled out an ultimatum that could potentially destroy the bank. If executives didn't find more money, or a willing purchaser, WaMu would land on a list of troubled banks—a scarlet letter that, when word leaked out, would terrify already anxious customers. WaMu had quietly lost billions of dollars in deposits over the last two weeks because of fears about its financial health. The bank likely wouldn't survive a "troubled" designation.

Fishman, along with several other executives and WaMu's investment banking advisers from Goldman Sachs and Morgan Stanley, had spent most of that panicked time fielding late-night calls from potential buyers, meeting with the buyers, and not sleeping. The buyers, including JPMorgan Chase, Citigroup, and Banco Santander in Spain, had in turn deployed dozens of representatives to scour WaMu's financial information in an online data room. Fishman, who regularly checked in with Rotella back in Seattle, reported heavy interest from the buyers. He soon expected to organize a deal.

But three days earlier, on Monday, the interested banks unexpectedly stopped calling, puzzling Rotella. On the East Coast, Fishman and his advisers couldn't get any answers from their chief executives, either. Now, on Thursday, the silence continued. Fishman and two other WaMu executives planned to fly back to Seattle, arriving that night. There was no point in staying in New York. It seemed no one wanted to talk to them anymore.

The silence continued throughout the morning of September 25, long after Rotella had finished his coffee, and into the afternoon. The day had turned gray and cool. Occasionally, bits of sunlight poked through the clouds, briefly casting shadows across the city. In Seattle, local weathermen called this phenomenon a "sunbreak."

Rotella, restless, sitting at his desk, called John Robinson, the bank's head of regulatory relations. Robinson played the middleman between WaMu and the two government agencies that oversaw its operations, the Office of Thrift Supervision (OTS) and the FDIC. Robinson wasn't in Seattle. By the luck of bad timing, he had flown to northern California the day before to attend meetings of the Federal Home Loan Bank of San Francisco, on whose board he sat. In the last week, the FHLB had been making a difficult situation even more difficult for WaMu. Scared about its own financial position, the FHLB was considering a much bigger haircut on the mortgages backing WaMu's line of credit, although it hadn't yet made a decision. WaMu relied on that credit to stay in business.

"John," said Rotella when he reached Robinson on his cell phone, "we're hearing rumors on the Street that JPMorgan is scheduling a press conference later today. Can you find out what's going on?"

JPMorgan was one of the banks that had been sifting through WaMu's data room, contemplating a possible purchase. But Fishman had reported that JPMorgan wasn't going to make an offer.

Robinson, also puzzled by the silence from prospective buyers, agreed.

"I'll try," he said.

Robinson ducked out of a meeting and found an empty conference room inside the nondescript bank building, on the edge of San Francisco's Chinatown. Once sequestered, he dialed the number of Darrel Dochow. Dochow, the regional director of the OTS's West Region, had overseen WaMu for years. He lived in a sprawling suburb outside Seattle and kept an office at the bank's headquarters. Always forthright, Dochow would surely tell Robinson if he knew something. Robinson called his office several times but couldn't reach him. He wasn't answering his cell phone, either.

Robinson proceeded up the chain of command, next calling Scott Polakoff, the deputy director of the OTS and Dochow's boss, in Washington, D.C. It was approaching 7:00 p.m. on the East Coast. Polakoff also didn't answer. Robinson left a message imploring the regulator to call him back. He returned to his meeting.

Not long after, Robinson felt his cell phone ring in his pocket. He picked it up and saw that the caller was Polakoff. He ducked back into the conference room.

"Scott?" he answered, after he had closed the door. "What's going on? I've been trying to reach Darrel, and Darrel hasn't gotten back to me. We're hearing rumors about a press conference this afternoon."

Polakoff paused.

Then he said, his voice strained, "I have some bad news for you."

"Go ahead."

"We are coming in to close you this afternoon."

Numbness gripped Robinson, but he continued to speak calmly.

"How much time do we have?"

"They'll come at six."

The Bloomberg machine on the credenza behind Rotella's desk hummed as Rotella waited for Robinson's call. WaMu's stock had closed that day at the dismally low price of $1.69 a share. But new reports from the afternoon showed relative improvement, and it looked as though WaMu would lose $600 million in deposits that day from the bank run. That was still a lot of money, but far less than on some of the days of the previous two weeks, and less than 1 percent of the bank's total retail deposits of $126 billion. The hemorrhaging of deposits appeared to have slowed. WaMu was still in a precarious financial position, but it no longer seemed so dire. The bank could survive.

Rotella's phone rang. He picked it up. It was Robinson.

"Steve," Robinson told him. "It's over. They're coming in to close us this afternoon."

The news stunned Rotella. "Is there anything we can do to put it off?" he asked.

"No," Robinson replied. "There's not any time left."

Just before 5:00 p.m. Pacific Time, Ada Osorio turned on the television in the family room of her house in Thousand Oaks, California, to catch the evening news. She was only half listening from the adjoining kitchen, focusing instead on making chicken casserole for dinner. Ada favored simple meals that didn't take too long to put together.

The casserole had only just begun to bake, the smell filling the three-bedroom property, when Ada heard a newscaster say something about "WaMu." Now the TV had Ada's full attention. WaMu had become so popular in the midsize city of Thousand Oaks—five branches had opened in as many years—that the Osorios had decided to invest. In the spring of 2007, when WaMu was trading at around $40 a share, they bought $100,000 of the bank's stock. Over the next several months, as the price of WaMu's shares dropped, the Osorios added another $100,000 to their investment. The money represented nearly all of the couple's savings since they had emigrated decades earlier, Ada from Costa Rica, Luis from Peru. They planned their budget, including expensive medication to treat Luis's heart condition, around their WaMu investment and its dividends. At their recommendation, the couple's two children also invested, although they didn't buy as much stock as their parents.

Over the preceding weeks, Ada and Luis, himself a former banker, had followed the news about WaMu. Much of the time it was hard to piece together what was going on. It seemed like a lot of bad news—the stock price kept falling, and now the company was up for sale?—but the Osorios continued to have faith. WaMu had survived both the Savings and Loan Crisis and the Great Depression, after all. Less than six months earlier, the bank had landed $7.2 billion in private equity from TPG, a group of seasoned investors. WaMu would pull through.

Ada stood in front of the TV, pictures of her family hanging on the walls. On CNBC, anchor David Faber, speaking with urgency, updated an earlier story: "JPMorgan is going to be buying more than just the deposit base of Washington Mutual. In fact, it is also going to be taking the assets on the bank's balance sheet as well, according to people close to the government side of this arrangement. Essentially, the OTS, the Office of Thrift Supervision, will be seizing Washington Mutual, delivering it to the FDIC, which is immediately going to deliver the deposits and assets and branches of the bank to JPMorgan Chase. JPMorgan is going to pay, I'm told, what may be more than $1 billion for the entire institution."[3]

As the report flashed to a yellow screen with the ominous question, "Wall Street Crisis: Is Your Money Safe?" Ada felt somewhat relieved.

She wasn't quite clear about the government's role, but it seemed that the new CEO had found a buyer for WaMu. The purchase price, if she had heard correctly, must be wrong. She didn't believe it was possible for someone to pay just $1 billion for a bank with $307 billion in assets.

The anchor continued, speaking over a graph showing JPMorgan's share price of $43.75, up 8 percent. "But they're not buying any of the stock. The equity holders are wiped out. The subordinated debt holders, the debt holders—wiped out."

In that moment, Ada knew, although she hoped she would later be proven wrong, that this was the worst news about her investment that she could have received.

Chapter One

FRIEND OF THE FAMILY

Not only will we succeed financially, we will succeed as human beings.
—Lou Pepper, speech to Washington Mutual employees

In 1951, Lou Pepper arrived in Seattle after World War II with no job prospects and lackluster interest from the law firms where he tried to find work. Now, thirty years later, he held the position of senior partner of a firm with sixty lawyers, a title that he, as a boy growing up in a farming town during the Great Depression, could hardly have fathomed. He had a lovely wife named Mollie and four children, almost all grown up. At fifty-seven, he was nearing retirement.

But now, in the summer of 1981, Pepper had a problem. He was beginning to realize, as he sat in a stuffy conference room at the Westin Hotel downtown, that the problem was about to become his own. Sitting around a boardroom table, as the July sun poured in through one of the windows, were an impressive array of men running Seattle businesses. Many of them would only grow more powerful over the next two decades. Among the men: an executive of Boeing; the head of the local power company, who would later represent the city's baseball team; and the president of a college, who would be elected a U.S. senator.[1]

The men went around the room discussing their schedules. All of them were busy. No one had time to run a scrappy little bank called Washington Mutual. As trustees,* however, they were in a desperate situation. The bank, after nearly 100 years in existence, was on the verge of failure. It was losing $5 million in capital a month, a rate that would put it out of business within three years, assuming the situation didn't get much worse.[2] Faced with this prospect, Washington Mutual's senior management team froze. Instead of finding ways out of the problem, they did nothing at all.

None of the trustees, and especially not Pepper, wanted to lose the bank. Pepper had developed a fondness for Washington Mutual. It had been his client for much of the last three decades at his law firm, Foster Pepper & Riviera.[†] He had spent countless billable hours working on its behalf. He remembered the first time he had walked into a courtroom sometime in the 1950s to file a foreclosure. The judge had looked down at him and said: "The one thing I know is that if you're here to foreclose a mortgage from Washington Mutual, you've done everything you can to help them save their home. My parents almost lost their house in the thirties and Washington Mutual made it possible for them to keep it."

It was one thing to work with a bank and another to run it, though. But as the trustees went around the table, Pepper was the only one of the prestigious group who could pull himself away from his day job. He was also the only one with experience in banking, even though he liked to tell people he didn't "know his ass from third base." As Washington Mutual's outside general counsel, he knew how to deal with the federal regulators in Washington, D.C., and had once outsmarted the Federal Deposit Insurance Corp. when it stood in the way of a merger at Washington Mutual. The *National Law Journal* rated him as one of the top twenty banking attorneys in the country.[3] "I will do this," Pepper told the board, "but only for six months."

The meeting ended. Pepper called his nephew, Bill Longbrake, who happened to be working with one of the regulatory agencies in

---

*Board members were known as "trustees" until Washington Mutual went public.
†After one more name change, the Seattle-based firm would ultimately be named Foster Pepper.

Washington, D.C. "I have never managed anything and I'm now the CEO," he told Longbrake. One of the trustees sent a letter to Pepper's children, explaining the situation. "They were totally confused," said Pepper later. "Dad's been a lawyer, now he's tied up with this other thing and this other thing is a thing that's losing a lot of money?" His wife Mollie's reaction was, in typical fashion, supportive. "There are a bunch of new people I'll get to meet," she proclaimed. Pepper's friends and family members sent letters. Several questioned his sanity. Others were supportive. "Save the bank," they wrote.

If there was one thing that Pepper did know instinctively, it was people. He knew that the employees of Washington Mutual would have two questions for him when he showed up the next day at its offices: "What the hell are you doing here?" and "What are we supposed to do?" Pepper decided to write a speech. He had the night after the trustee meeting to prepare. When he walked into the office the next morning, the chief financial officer quit. Pepper consulted with the head of the communications department about how to handle the CFO's resignation and his own arrival announcement. That person resigned as well.

With trepidation, Pepper called all the senior managers into the bank's small boardroom and gave his speech anyway. When he looked out across them, they looked back with uncertainty on their faces. No wonder. Not only was Washington Mutual in trouble, the whole banking industry seemed about to collapse during the summer of 1981. No one seemed to know what to do about it. Across the country, thousands of banks like Washington Mutual were losing money just as rapidly, and some were beginning to fail. Interest rates had shot up past 20 percent, forcing the banks to pay a high rate on certificates of deposit. At the same time, banks were receiving back only a low interest rate payment from loan customers, most of whom had 30-year fixed-rate mortgages. The difference between those two numbers was what caused Washington Mutual, and 80 percent of the banks like it across the country, to bleed so much money. Meanwhile, new customers, scared of the much higher rate, didn't want to take out a mortgage. The situation was so bad that Washington Mutual had stopped making mortgages for several months. Over the next few years, the federal government would step in and rescue more than four dozen banks.[4]

Washington Mutual had another problem: Hawaii. Its former president Wally Eldridge had decided Hawaii was the next frontier, promising several developers of large condominium complexes that Washington Mutual would supply the mortgages, to the tune of tens of millions of dollars. It was a promise the bank couldn't keep. In 1978, Washington Mutual had made the most money it had ever brought in during one year, ever: $18 million. Only three years later, it would lose $32 million.

Pepper stood at the head of the boardroom at Washington Mutual, all eyes focused on him. He held several sheets of paper on which he had scrawled his speech. He was nervous—this was his first time as head of a company. Usually, he kidded around with people as a way to make them relax. Sometimes people found his sense of humor a bit odd, but they usually just laughed along with him because he himself was laughing so much. This, however, was no time for joking. The managers were all worried about the potential collapse of their company. "They're probably wondering why I was chosen as CEO," Pepper thought to himself.

"I'm not a banker," he admitted to the group. But, he added, he had worked closely with the last four chief executives and, as a lawyer, had wrestled with the FDIC. He reassured Washington Mutual's managers that they were doing a great job. "I don't think we'll have to worry about operating this place," he said. Pepper wanted the bank to stick with its original mission, thought up 90 years ago by its founders. "We're going to be the best place for a person to put aside money for future use," Pepper said. "If there is something else our customers should have available to help them do that, we will try and provide it."

Pepper knew quite a bit about savings. He also knew that banks could become a scary business if not run properly. Born in a farmhouse in Illinois, he grew up in a town of 110, not counting his family, located between patches of forest, long stretches of fields growing oats, corn, and alfalfa and seven lakes of varying sizes. In Trevor (pronounced TREE-vor), Wisconsin, there were five major businesses where you could work if you weren't a farmer—the mostly vacant stockyards, the sauerkraut factory that opened only seasonably, a tile factory with sporadic hours, a blacksmith shop that later burned down, and an icehouse.

Dahl's General Store sold sugar and flour and some meat. Only the owners of the six local taverns made real money, and they all became less profitable after Prohibition ended. Some residents in Trevor had no jobs, although Pepper later recalled that no one paid attention to who received relief and who didn't.

For $25 a month, Pepper's family rented a two-story house adjacent to the railroad tracks that came with a barn and a chicken house. Pepper's mother ran the post office, conveniently located in the front room of the family's house. His father sold farm products and spices, door to door, around the county. Both parents had mastered the art of stretching money. Everyone's mother could repatch clothing, but Pepper's could repatch so well that it became hard to tell which had been the original garment. When the family went out occasionally for ice cream, it cost 25 cents because ice cream cost a nickel a scoop, and while there were six family members, Pepper's mother didn't like it. Only after the war did she claim to develop a taste for it. "A small town in the Great Depression is a great place to learn frugality," Pepper said later.

Pepper witnessed firsthand the perils of banking when, in 1932, his sister Ruth turned eighteen and planned to move to upstate Wisconsin to attend teaching college. That Ruth, as a woman, was going to college at all was unusual. Pepper's parents placed a high premium on education. They wanted all four children to go to college, including Pepper's three older sisters. When Ruth left, Pepper was an eight-year-old attending elementary school classes in a two-room schoolhouse, soon to become a one-room schoolhouse after county budget cuts. The eighteen kids in Pepper's school sat at individual desks and moved each year farther to the back of the room, as they grew taller and progressed in grades. Pepper liked the one-room schoolhouse because he could keep his ear tuned to the higher grades if he wanted and so could learn more, earlier.

Ruth, like her sisters, made money for her college tuition by waiting tables in the nearby homes of residents living on the lake. These people served dinner and lunch to tourists, or city dwellers on their Sunday drives. Ruth saved all the change she collected in tips to put toward her tuition of $21 a semester. She placed the money in Silver Lake State Bank, located about five miles away in the larger town of Silver Lake. One day Silver Lake State Bank shut down. It was one of thousands

of banks that abruptly failed during the Great Depression. Because
the government hadn't yet approved deposit insurance, Ruth lost everything. Not long after, another community bank across the border
in Illinois failed. This time the bank took with it the money tied up in
Pepper's grandfather's estate. In both cases, the banks' assets were liqui-
dated; some of the money was recovered, but only a portion.

In 1981, in the spirit of his upbringing, Pepper set about saving
money at Washington Mutual. The bank that Pepper inherited had
about $2 billion in assets and 35 branches scattered across Washington
State, mostly in the leafy neighborhoods of Seattle.[5] On average, Washington Mutual had added only one branch every three years for most of
the last century. "They were ponderous," said one former trustee and
board member. "Mostly they were poking along, doing fine." Inside the
branches, tellers waited behind long wooden counters, and customers
who wanted to take out a loan sat in chairs upholstered in mossy green
and faded gold undertones. Muted landscape paintings hung on beige
walls. Some branches were located in aging brick buildings; others were
outfitted with drive-through windows, the newest fad in banking. Banks
had only just started adding ATMs, and in fact, one of Pepper's more
notable jobs as Washington Mutual's general counsel had been to clear
the way for the country's first stand-alone, shared deposit machine, a
concrete and stone structure hooked up to a computer system. It took
up an entire air-conditioned room. Sometimes, if the temperature got
too hot outside, the ATM, or "Exchange," as it was called, would accidently spit out money, a kink that was eventually worked out.[6]

If the bank had aged, its customers weren't far behind. Most of
them were over fifty-five. Like Pepper, they had grown up during the
country's worst financial crisis. They were big savers. Many had taken
out their first bank account with Washington Mutual through a program the bank had launched in the 1920s, encouraging children to
learn about finances. Those students brought nickels and dimes they'd
collected to school, and a volunteer parent would gather the money
and bring it to the nearest bank branch. As they got older, those kids
became real customers who carried what was known as a passbook, a
ledger that looked like a slightly large passport and was common at
most banks. The Washington Mutual teller ran the passbook through a

cranky machine each time the customer deposited or withdrew money, stamping it with a record of the transaction. The machine broke down regularly. Washington Mutual executives often wondered how the bank would fare as its customers aged. What would happen when they died? "They'll leave their money to their kids," thought one senior manager at the time. "And their kids are not our customers."

Washington Mutual had earned a good reputation locally, but almost no one outside the Pacific Northwest had ever heard of it. That wasn't unusual. Most bank customers across the country kept money at smaller, local institutions. The financial giants, including the eventual Washington Mutual itself, didn't yet exist. The competition was the other community bank down the street. In the early 1980s, federal and state laws restricting interstate banking prevented financial institutions from expanding outside their home state, so there wasn't much potential to grow much bigger anyway. Washington Mutual was one of only about 200 banks that had assets of more than $1 billion, less than 2 percent of all banks. In 1994, the federal government passed legislation allowing bank holding companies to buy banks in other states—presuming the acquiring bank was healthy. Soon the number of banks with more than $1 billion in assets doubled.[7] And the banks would only grow much, much larger.

Pepper would eventually lay off about fifty employees at Washington Mutual to save money, but he first sent a memo to the entire staff. He hoped to signal that hard times were coming as the bank cuts costs, but he also wanted to raise morale. The memo reflected Pepper's personality: serious and teasing, in rapid and alternating succession. Without knowing it, Pepper also set in motion the thriftiness that would later distinguish Washington Mutual from its competitors.

The memo concerned plants. "All head office staff," Pepper wrote. "It is necessary to institute some austerity at Washington Mutual. We have started small by removing some of the lovely plants we had in our non-public areas and the big plants from the fourth floor offices."[8]

Washington Mutual's headquarters in downtown Seattle, a columned building with the bank's trademark *W* stamped on top, had only four cramped floors. The ground floor held the bank's largest branch, a grand space where an older, well-dressed greeter was stationed. The fourth floor was known as the executive suite, but that was a loose description. Employees referred to it as "walnut heaven" because the office walls were movable wood panels that could be rearranged if necessary. The panels reached from floor to ceiling and came with doors but not windows. Pepper, as the chief executive, had the best office. It had two real walls on one corner of the floor with two wide windows. On the rare clear day, Pepper could see Mount Rainier, Washington State's well-known volcano, fifty miles away.

"We now need to reduce the number of plants throughout the head office departments," Pepper continued in his memo. "The bank needs people more than a demonstration of its ability to grow ficus and palms. Our investment in them is equal to salaries of six employees for one year. If there is a plant in your work area that you've become attached to (or just sort of fond of) and it is marked for removal, you have several choices. 1. You can buy the plant at whatever the bank will get for it; 2. You can petition for a commutation of its sentence; remember, it must be both a wanted and a needed plant; 3. We can hold an appropriate farewell party for it. Can you think of other areas of cost cutting that don't hurt our services? Please let me know." Within a few days, employees had gathered the plants and piled them in a heap in the middle of the executive floor.

Six months passed, and then six more. After eighteen months, and two extensions of his law firm leave, Pepper resigned from the law firm and gave up pretending that he was only a temporary chief executive. In early 1983, he took Washington Mutual public, raising about $75 million.[9] It was, in his estimation, the only way to bring in enough money to save the bank. As a mutual bank, Washington Mutual was owned by its depositors, a structure not unlike that of a modern-day credit union. After it went public, Washington Mutual became a savings bank owned by its shareholders. (Both mutual and savings banks are known as "thrifts," because they deal with consumers, rather than businesses like commercial banks.) Pepper converted bank charters through a Washington State law that he himself had drafted as an attorney. The move also gave Pepper the flexibility to expand into other lines of businesses.

But money and flexibility weren't the only issues he faced. Pepper needed people to help him understand the increasingly complicated task of running a bank. Washington Mutual was now expected to invest in securities, hedge interest rate risk, and do "all kinds of things I didn't understand at all," Pepper said later. Banks had started hedging after the recent spike in interest rates, which pushed so many banks toward failure. If rates spun out of control again, the banks wouldn't lose as much money. They started buying securities backed by mortgages, or car loans or credit card loans, or other strange new products created by Wall Street. The income from those products would, theoretically, off-set any losses caused by fluctuating interest rates. Pepper wasn't alone in his confusion. Even the best accountants didn't fully understand the new secondary market. Until then, a mutual bank like Washington Mutual operated simply. It took customer deposits and made mortgages, and it could make only as many mortgages as customers brought in money.

Hiring wasn't easy. Even though it was no longer so sickly, Washington Mutual was still suffering. It had lost $19 million just before it went public.[10] Who wanted to work at a company that was losing so much money? It was the same question everyone asked Pepper when he took the job.

What Pepper didn't realize was that he himself provided the incentive. Would-be executives who interviewed at Washington Mutual found someone who looked like their grandfather, with a wide, shiny forehead, round glasses, and lots of white hair. While he swore occasionally, he spoke softly and considered himself shy, even though no one else would ever have described him that way. Pepper's smile stretched across his whole face, pushing out his cheeks and lighting up his eyes. He was lean, typically dressed well in a suit, and always gave a firm handshake. He asked thoughtful questions—"What's your philosophy on this?"—but also seemed sure of himself. When job candidate Liane Wilson came to interview to become the head of Washington Mutual's information technology department, Pepper told her that if she was selected for the job, he did not want her to use a new mortgage soft-ware program that had proved troublesome at other banks. Wilson was impressed not just that Pepper knew the details of the software program and that it hadn't lived up to expectations elsewhere, but that he knew what he wanted. "It's good to have strong leadership," Wilson thought. "He's not going to let you get away with a lot." She took the job, despite her reservations about the bank's financial position.

Bill Longbrake, meanwhile, lobbied to join Pepper as chief financial officer. After receiving Pepper's call for help in 1981, he flew to Seattle from Washington, D.C., and stayed on at the bank for several days before returning to work. Now he wanted in, permanently. Pepper knew he needed Longbrake, who had a doctorate in finance. But Pepper worried about nepotism—Longbrake was married to Pepper's niece. A board member eventually convinced him otherwise. "We can't afford your scruples," he admonished.

At about this time, a local investment banker called Pepper and encouraged him to hold a meeting with Murphey Favre, a securities brokerage in the eastern Washington city of Spokane. Pepper agreed. Kerry Killinger, one of the firm's shareholders, arrived at Washington Mutual's offices for the meeting. At thirty-one, Killinger looked barely old enough to roll a keg into a frat party. Pepper wasn't intimidated by his age, except possibly as it related to competitive sports. "I know enough that if he played squash, I wouldn't play him," Pepper thought to himself. Inside Washington Mutual's boardroom, Killinger told Pepper about Murphey Favre. The firm, as old as Washington Mutual, managed $400 million in assets across the "inland empire," the eastern half of Washington State.[11] The company ran top-performing mutual funds and offered customers financial advice. Washington Mutual, Killinger said, should consider a merger with the company. "You ought to buy us," he told Pepper.

Pepper was suitably impressed. Killinger, he thought, was a young man trying to sell an old company and was doing a great job at it. But Pepper's opinion of people selling securities wasn't great. "They scare the hell out of me," he said later. He thought many of them sold bad products for their own bottom line. Pepper didn't like anything in banking that he considered "goofy." Sometimes he would shoot down an idea from his team for that reason alone: "It's goofy." He believed in the adage "Never invest in a business you don't understand." Would Washington Mutual customers be safe investing in Murphey Favre's securities? Pepper came to think so, as the management of the company approved everything it sold. Murphey Favre also offered tax-exempt bonds, a type of investment free of federal income tax. Washington Mutual customers clamored to buy them, and Pepper knew that.

Pepper agreed to the merger—with a catch. He wanted Killinger to work at Washington Mutual. Killinger agreed. One of the board members asked Pepper, "You know he probably wants to be CEO, right?" Pepper replied, "It doesn't bother me."

The executives whom Pepper assembled were as unusual as they were smart. Few had ever worked at a bank. Lindy Friedlander, the new head of Washington Mutual's research department, held a PhD in biostatistics. Before she took the job, she had worked on a study for the University of Washington titled "Maximizing Compliance with Hemoccult Screening for Colon Cancer in Clinical Practice." She was looking at how doctors could get patients to take, and return, home medical exams. While she had no experience in banking, she could find out anything about customers. One day Pepper asked her if she could create a statistical analysis of deposits by the color of a customer's tie. "Yes," she replied, seriously. "Don't," Pepper told her.

Pepper did not gauge people's intelligence by their pedigree. Only a handful of people at Washington Mutual held advanced degrees. Some hadn't even completed college. Pepper knew from experience that a degree can sometimes mean nothing at all. "There are a whole lot of people out there that aren't getting the chance that they should," he said later.

Several of the new executives came from small towns and had survived the same sort of gritty, rural childhood as Pepper. Fay Chapman, who took over for Pepper as the bank's general counsel after he left, grew up in Gilroy, California, a dusty agricultural community that reeked of its chief export, garlic. Coworkers viewed Chapman as a sweet lady until she dropped the f-bomb in a meeting to make a point. "People don't believe me, but as each of us turned eight, my grandfather gave us all guns," said Chapman later.

They all dressed well, but not in the East Coast power-suit way. The men wore department store suits, and the women didn't always wear makeup. The number of women in itself was startling. In addition to Chapman, Liane Wilson, Lindy Friedlander, and Lynn Ryder, a longtime Washington Mutual employee who headed up human resources, Pepper had also hired a twentysomething named Deanna Oppenheimer in marketing and Mary Pugh, who had just graduated with an economics degree from Yale, to deal with the hedging and other confusing investments. The number of women at the bank would have been unusual even today. Twenty-five years ago it sparked multiple newspaper articles. "The past decade certainly has seen an increasing number of women moving into executive positions in the business world," noted the *Puget Sound Business Journal* of Washington Mutual's new hires.

Other employees tended to find some of the people Pepper brought in eccentric, or at least nothing like the stereotypical stodgy banker. "Lou Pepper pulled together a group of misfits," said one executive affectionately. Most of them would stay with the bank for the next decade or longer.

Employees at Washington Mutual grew used to Pepper's somewhat unorthodox leadership style. He didn't like to sit around, particularly not in his office. If he wanted to know what was happening at the bank, the last place he would find it, he reckoned, was staring out the window at Puget Sound. The other place he was sure wouldn't provide him with answers about actual operations was a report. "He didn't want to be fooled," explained Chapman, who also didn't care much for reports. "If you're an exec, and you sit in your office and you ask someone below you for a report, what do you think it's going to say? 'Things are going great! When do I get my bonus?'" Instead, Pepper wandered the hallways, stopping in at various departments. He would plop himself down on someone's desk, his leg hanging over the edge. "How are you doing?" he would ask. Or "I'm here to take your blood pressure," he would joke. Others called it "management by walking around." Executives felt comfortable wandering into Pepper's office as well.

Pepper didn't understand what "corporate culture" meant. He decided, "You shouldn't act like a CEO, you should act like whoever the hell you are." He encouraged executives to dress up on Halloween, bringing candy to the branches. He regularly ate in the cafeteria on the second floor with everyone else. He sat with the building's maintenance men so frequently that they presented him with his own work jacket. To employees, he really seemed like one of them. He said things like "Jesus Peesus" and transitioned nearly every thought with "but anyhow." "It was interesting times," he said later, of his childhood. "But anyhow." He often stitched together interesting anecdotes, or recited poetry, as a way of making an important point. This tic wasn't always successful at Washington Mutual. Once Pepper tried to fire someone, but the employee left the room believing he had been given a promotion. Another executive had to relay the bad news.

His background, which employees heard in bits and pieces, helped endear him to people. Pepper had enlisted in the Army Air Corps during World War II and graduated from cadet school in the summer of 1944. The Army trained him and his buddies to fly two types of combat planes and then shipped them to Hawaii, where they waited to relieve another group in Okinawa. But soon afterward the war ended. Pepper never fought anyone, and that was fine with him. At least he had managed to secure a free college education, through the GI Bill. Pepper wasn't sure what he wanted to do. He had previously enrolled in the University of Wisconsin as a science major. After the war, he opted for economics and then decided to get a law degree, too. "My dad had always admired lawyers," he said. "He had been on a jury and thought lawyers were swell." But when Pepper graduated at midyear, only one law firm in the state of Wisconsin had an opening for an associate. Someone else got the job.

Through the rain and the darkening evening, Pepper could see the rolling hills and the lights of the small downtown corridor as he drove into Seattle in December 1951. It looked huge to him. The Space Needle that would come to symbolize the city didn't yet exist, and the tallest skyscraper was a spindly tower that would one day be dwarfed by a flurry of construction. Pepper had inherited the family car and saved some money from the war. After law school, he had applied for jobs in Washington, D.C., where one of his sisters lived, and in a couple of other cities, including Portland, Oregon, and Los Angeles. No one was hiring. He didn't know anyone in Seattle but had stopped over there once during the war and liked how the city sat between lakes and the ocean, with a mountain range on either side. The managers of the dozen law firms he visited were nicer than those in other cities, but they had no jobs. Somehow he talked one of the local firms into hiring him temporarily. The firm needed someone to figure out if one of its clients, a national conservative talk show host, was about to get sued for libel. The firm's partners kept giving Pepper more work, until finally he had a permanent job. Washington Mutual eventually became his largest client.

By 1986—five years into his unexpected run as chief executive— Pepper had saved Washington Mutual. The bank made nearly $71 million that year. Its stock soared to a high of more than $26 a share, allowing the bank to increase its cash dividend by 50 percent.[12] One reason Washington Mutual was doing so well was that interest rates had dropped, luring customers to take out mortgages again. They arrived by the hundreds at Washington Mutual branches. The bank issued $467 million worth of mortgages that year, the highest volume it had ever produced, by far. While most customers still had a 30-year fixed-rate loan, adjustable-rate mortgages (ARMs) were becoming more popular. A typical ARM came with a fixed interest rate that automatically reset (usually higher) to the market rate after two or three years. Banks began making ARMs in the 1970s as another way to protect against interest rate swings. ARMs allowed banks to collect higher interest rate payments from some customers, offsetting the fixed rates paid by others. By the early 1990s, about 10 percent of homeowners held adjustable-rate mortgages, and customers were reporting problems. The banks were overcharging them in some cases. A federal government review reported that as many as 25 percent of the 12 million adjustable-rate mortgages in the United States in 1991 were "inaccurate." "Adjustable-rate mortgages are extremely complicated," warned a spokeswoman for the American Bankers Association at the time. "My advice to consumers is to take a close look."

Washington Mutual introduced its own, borrower-friendly loan. The bank wouldn't charge a customer more than a two-percentage-point increase when the loan adjusted. The bank also gave customers the unusual option of changing to a fixed-rate loan without going through the hassle of refinancing. "Is it good business practice to take advantage of the consumer's gullibility and give them less than the best terms they qualify for?" Pepper wrote later, in a book describing his management philosophies. "My personal feeling is that you should always give them the best deal. I further think that if you do, you will make more money in the long run."

With the bank no longer in any immediate danger, Pepper mulled over something less tangible: its culture. It was easy to offer someone a loan or a bank account, but couldn't customers find that at a dozen other different banks? Also, why would a teller choose to work at Washington Mutual over any other bank? Prompted by an employee, he gathered a group of people from various departments and gave them a vague assignment: figure out Washington Mutual's values. After a couple of months of deliberation, the committee reported back. The bank, its members decided, should focus on human value. Later, this included four areas: customers, coworkers, community, and the capital market (namely, shareholders). If any of those areas started to dictate the bank's operations more than another, or if the bank overlooked one group, that would signal a problem. Washington Mutual would concentrate on five values: ethics ("All actions are guided by absolute honesty, integrity and fairness"), respect ("People are valued and appreciated for their contributions"), teamwork ("Cooperation, trust and shared objectives are vital to success"), innovation ("New ideas are encouraged and sound strategies implemented with enthusiasm"), and excellence ("High standards for service and performance are expected and rewarded").

The exercise might have flopped, a victim of overzealous employee outreach. But perhaps because of Pepper, or maybe because he had pulled together a diverse group of people who weren't involved in the company's bureaucracy, Washington Mutual employees embraced the bank's new creed. The executive team framed the values and hung them in bank branches. They were printed in annual reports. Managers received faux baseball cards with their picture and Washington Mutual's logo on the front, and the values stamped on the back. The cards got traded back and forth. Working for the bank felt like being part of a very large, quirky family. Employees, with no irony, wore shirts that read "Washington Mutual cares about me." For Pepper's birthday in 1987, they dressed up, of their own accord, like the characters in *The Wizard of Oz* and performed an elaborate skit.

They called him down to the lobby of Washington Mutual's head-quarters and sat him down on a movable stage. With customers and intrigued tellers looking on, they pranced around wearing homemade costumes.

"I'm Glenda and I'm the WaMu witch," proclaimed one employee wearing a long cream dress and a tiara.

"I'm Dorothy," said another worker in a checkered dress and red high heels. "I'm a customer service representative and I'm looking for some enchantment in the way I deal with my customers." The idea of enchantment became a big deal at Washington Mutual after Pepper gave a speech instructing employees to think beyond products and services. "Let us be sure we leave room for an enchantment, a challenge, an experimentation—fun, far out, exciting things that may one day be our own mystique, our own mark—that sets us so far above the crowd that we won't be able to see it. Not only will we succeed financially, we will succeed as human beings," he said.

"You'll want to go to the land of corporate values!" announced the WaMu witch.

"Oh, where's that?" replied Dorothy as a larger crowd gathered in the bank's lobby.

"All you have to do is follow the WaMu road. When you reach the land of corporate values, go and see the great and powerful Lou!"

The skit, which involved Dorothy skipping circles around Pepper as the song "Louie, Louie" played, ended with everyone donning cutout paper masks of Pepper. Pepper, exceedingly entertained, received a new stamp with the acronym "G.P.L." Great and Powerful Lou. Long after Pepper retired, it became far more common to run into someone who had worked at the company for 15 years rather than 5. Few people wanted to leave.

Employees weren't the only ones in love with Washington Mutual. The bank had rehabilitated an old advertisement launched sometime in the 1970s proclaiming Washington Mutual the "Friend of the Family." The company hired an older, avuncular actor and dressed him up in Mr. Rogers–style cardigans. He became the face of Washington Mutual, assuring customers that the bank would take care of them. "Washington Mutual has always been a family bank," said the actor in one commercial, as a family smiled and passed around dinner plates. "We like to think of ourselves as specialists in family banking, from the smallest savings account up. Washington Mutual. Friend of the Family." Customers brought the bank more money.* Pepper could tell that the bank was growing. He spent a day sitting in the Washington Mutual branch near his house. He sat in the corner of the branch for a long time, and none of the customers recognized him or came over to greet him. They were all new customers.

By 1986, Pepper faced another problem, though: his succession. In three years, he would turn sixty-five. He had told the board, and promised himself, that he wouldn't stay on past retirement age. He figured he had two options: sell Washington Mutual, or find someone to take his place. While selling the bank wasn't ideal, it would have been a good time. Washington Mutual sat in a relatively strong position, even though another banking crisis was unfolding around it. This time banks were failing by the hundreds because of an energy downturn in oil states like Texas and Oklahoma, a commercial real estate bust in California and the Northeast, and an agricultural recession rippling through the midwestern states. In each region, banks had made loans that soured because of their region's respective downturn. Bank failures would surge to more than 1,000 during the Savings and Loan Crisis, the highest number since Pepper's sister saw her college funds evaporate.

One of the banks that failed early on was Continental Illinois National Bank and Trust Co., the largest financial institution in Chicago and one of the ten largest nationwide. "The Continental" had grown in the 1970s after its management team set an ambitious goal: to become one of the largest commercial real estate lenders in the United States. In just a few years, the bank increased its assets by more than 100 percent to $45 billion. Its stock price more than tripled, surging to $40 a share in 1981. Analysts, investors, and journalists heralded the management team and the bank's strategy.[13] One Salomon Brothers

---

*The executive team had a brief scare when they found out the actor had accepted a movie role on top of his Washington Mutual gig—what if it portrayed him in a not-so-friendly light? Luckily, the movie turned out to be *Planet of the Apes* and the team felt they could live with that. He was one of the apes and you couldn't see his face.

analyst described Continental as "one of the finest money-center banks going."

But the rapid growth led to problems. Continental had lent heavily to energy-related companies and charged much lower interest rates to entice businesses to take out loans. But when oil prices dropped, some of Continental's biggest clients started losing money, and thus Continental started losing money as well. When Penn Square, a huge bank in Oklahoma, failed, news spread that Continental was involved by as much as $1 billion with some of the speculative energy lending of Penn Square. The rating agencies downgraded Continental, one of the first signs of serious trouble. One reporter noted that the only difference between Continental and the *Titanic* was that the *Titanic* had had a band.

After Reuters ran a story suggesting Continental would file for bankruptcy, the bank's customers began withdrawing their money. Other banks stepped up with a $4.5 billion bailout package to help Continental, fearful of what its failure could mean to the industry. The money wasn't enough. The federal government had to decide: Was Continental too big to fail? It was the first time the description arose. (An acronym was born: TBTF.) If too many other financial institutions and companies were tied up with it, the bank's failure could spark an even bigger crisis. The government looked for another company to buy Continental but couldn't find one. Finally, it cobbled together a bailout package that included buying some of the bank's $400 million in bad loans and propping it up with capital. The government now owned 80 percent of the bank, a controversial move that sparked cries of socialism. At that point, Continental's 1984 downfall marked the largest bank failure in U.S. history.

Pepper had steered Washington Mutual away from these problems, refusing to listen to the siren call of analysts or shareholders. The analysts thought everyone should make more commercial real estate loans. Instead, Pepper started shrinking Washington Mutual's portfolio of them. He got out of one relationship with a broker in California who was funneling over commercial real estate loans. "Things began to get goofy" out in California, he said later. At one shareholder meeting, an investor stood up and demanded to know why Pepper wasn't as smart as the chief executive of another bank in Seattle, which was making more money. "We're doing what we think is right," Pepper responded.

"Shareholders can put their money wherever they want." By the next year, the bank in question had failed. At Washington Mutual's shareholder meeting, Pepper couldn't resist pointing that out.

To avoid commercial real estate lending—one of the biggest problems of the day—Pepper hired Craig Tall. Tall, who is actually relatively short, had never worked at a bank and had been brought in to sort out retirement planning. But Tall was, at heart, an entrepreneur. He convinced Pepper and the board to let him make some unusual acquisitions to bring in more money from other lines of business, including a travel agency. For several years, Washington Mutual customers could deposit money at a branch and then book a trip to Kauai at Mutual Travel. The ventures, to the surprise of some, made money.

Pepper decided to explore a sale of Washington Mutual, a possibility he had considered over the years. The only real candidate emerged in Minneapolis at Norwest, another savings and loan bank. But Norwest's eventual offer came in too low, and the deal fell apart. Next, Pepper hired a search firm to find a new president. He found one person whom he liked on the East Coast, but it was hard to persuade him to leave the financial power centers for a city known more for its growing fish and farmers' market than for its banks. Also, Pepper didn't really think that any of the people whom the search firm turned up were better than the executives he had already hired.

One day he called his senior managers into a conference room and told them that he had decided to create an "Office of the President." He would remain chief executive, chairman, and president, and he appointed not one, but two senior executives to assist him: Bill Longbrake and Kerry Killinger. The two men would split the duties of managing Washington Mutual, Pepper told the team. Other executives would report to one or the other. In any other company, the unusual move might have come with the high risk of creating fracture and sparking a backstabbing race for the president's position between Longbrake and Killinger.

But Pepper, although he favors long stories, is also direct. He never shied away from problems at the bank. He warned the management team, as they sat in the conference room, that he would tolerate no politics. "If any of you starts playing favorites, you'll be out of here,

forthwith," he warned. "This is a cooperative effort, not a competition."
The team followed orders. This unusual arrangement lasted for more
than a year, until Pepper chose Killinger as president. The decision
surprised Longbrake. He knew Pepper would retire one day, but he had
believed that the bank would be run jointly. He believed his strengths
would complement Killinger's. While both men possessed an excep-
tional ability to digest complicated financial reports, Longbrake—who
comes from a family of Presbyterian ministers and is a talented piano
player—believed he could run internal operations better. More wor-
risome for Longbrake was that Killinger, who had spent his career as
a money manager, tended toward the risky side. He thought about
Killinger's recent foray into junk bonds. Other troubled savings and
loan banks had started issuing debt to raise money. The bonds came
with a high interest rate because they weren't rated very high. One of
them came from Centrust, a savings and loan bank in Florida (whose
chairman would later be famously convicted of fraud). The banks were
in trouble and the risk of default was high. The banks started closing.
Pushed by national financial reform, the market collapsed. Washington
Mutual had to set aside $14 million to cover the losses on the bonds,
more than three times the amount of the previous year.[14] Earnings suffered.

When Killinger brought up the idea of investing in junk bonds, Pepper had seen it as a creative, relatively safe way to raise more money. He
appreciated Killinger's looking for ways to expand the business. Both
executives failed to anticipate the rapid downturn of the market. They
had no way of knowing that the government would pass new legislation
that would render those investments worthless. "They were not the best
thing we'd ever done," Pepper said later. "But it wasn't the worst thing
either." Longbrake, incidentally, was charged with cleaning up the bond
mess, which he eventually sorted out.

In Killinger, Pepper saw potential but not perfection. He viewed
himself the same way. Pepper was wooed by Killinger's intelligence.
Executives and board members quickly realized that if you handed
Killinger a report on any subject, or tried to explain something that you
found to be confusing, he understood it almost immediately and sometimes better than you did. On the off chance that he didn't, he would

ask half a dozen smart questions and then would understand. He had an uncanny instinct for spotting good companies. The mutual funds he had run at Murphey Favre always performed in the top percentile.

Killinger possessed an unflagging energy. His love of Washington Mutual seemed to parallel Pepper's. He often left home at 6:00 a.m., not returning until well after dinnertime. During lunch he ate a sandwich at his desk, instead of heading down to the second-floor cafeteria, which served casseroles and roast beef. One manager recalled that on several occasions, he shut the door of his office and ran rapidly in place or did push-ups. His two sons, Bryan and Brad, and his wife of twenty years, Debbie, got used to Killinger's absence. His sons often teased him that they planned to open an account at Bank of America or another competitor.

What Killinger didn't have a lot of, but Pepper thought he could develop, was charisma. Killinger was, at heart, an analyst, more comfortable with numbers than with people. He wore glasses that covered his face. His short brown hair was swept to one side in a comb-over. He was friendly and polite. He had a perplexing habit of never looking directly at you; his brown eyes would focus instead on the wall in the distance or the desk to the left. While Pepper would talk to anyone, an employee who stood alone with Killinger in an elevator sometimes suffered an awkward silence. Once, at a luncheon awards ceremony, Killinger sat a table with several Washington Mutual tellers and lower-level employees who were going to be honored. All the employees were nervous about Killinger's presence, so none of them spoke. Killinger didn't either. He focused on his food. Finally, one of the employees, who was taking a class to learn more about banking, broke the silence. "Where do you see the industry going in the next five years?" she asked him. Killinger's demeanor instantly changed. For the rest of the lunch hour, he rattled off his predictions. "We had the best discussion," the employee later recalled. She scribbled notes on napkins and later received a high grade on a paper she wrote on the subject. Pepper, meanwhile, had gotten both Killinger and Longbrake subscriptions to *The Atlantic Monthly* after appointing them dual presidents. He hoped that the narrative essays and fictional stories would offset all the financial reports they read.

Killinger had several other management flaws that worried Pepper somewhat, but he trusted the other executives he had appointed to make up for them. He hoped that after he himself left, they would serve as something of a life raft around Killinger. For one thing, Killinger was not particularly deft at reading people. He had called Chapman at the bank's outside law firm one day and asked her to come in for a meeting. Puzzled by the unscheduled request, she walked the short distance to the bank and showed up at Killinger's office. "I have a couple of real blind spots, particularly when it comes to some employees," he told Chapman. In not so many words, he was asking Chapman to watch his back. If a manager was taking advantage of him, or was out of line and he wasn't seeing it, would she please tell him? Chapman agreed and kept that promise for almost two decades. Killinger also delegated the role of assessing other people to his wife. He sometimes brought Debbie along to meet a competing chief executive or potential hire, just to get her opinion on the person.

On a snowy day in December 1988, the board of Washington Mutual appointed Killinger president. A year later he became chief executive and, several months after that, chairman of the board. Pepper kept a position on the board and an office at the bank, but he and Mollie left for a vacation on the Greek Islands after Killinger took over as chief executive. Pepper called his secretary once to ask how things were going. "Good," she replied, and then there was silence. "Well, what's going on?" Pepper asked. "Oh, lots of things." She paused again. Pepper caught on. "You don't need me anymore, do you?" he concluded.

Before he left, Pepper found an old certificate of deposit with a rate of 16.5 percent stamped on it. "Sixteen point five percent!" thought Pepper. The ridiculously high interest paid on the CD was a vestige of his first few years at Washington Mutual, when the bank had come close to failure. Now Washington Mutual ranked as one of the strongest banks in the Pacific Northwest, even during the Savings and Loan Crisis. Not only was it profitable, but it had grown from $2 billion in assets to $7 billion during the nine years of Pepper's tenure, and added fifteen branches.

Pepper framed the faded CD. Then he had a plaque made. He presented both to his new chief executive. The plaque read: "Whenever new troops arrived anywhere during World War II, the old troops greeted them by saying: 'You should have been here when it was really rough.'"[15] Always the jokester, Pepper wanted to remind Killinger that his job would be easy compared with the struggle that Pepper endured. It couldn't possibly get any worse.

Chapter Two

REMOVE THE CORPORATE JETS

Check your ego at the door.

—Kerry Killinger

In another life, Kerry Killinger might have been standing on a stage in an auditorium or concert hall, blowing air through tightly pursed lips, his hands fingering the valves of a trumpet. But instead, on a cold day in early March 1997, he stood hunched over a speakerphone with Craig Tall, both of them listening closely to the investment banker from Goldman Sachs on the line. They were hiding out in Washington Mutual's boardroom, the door closed.

"Kerry," admonished the banker through the speakerphone, "you have been waiting for something like this for five years."

Before he left, Lou Pepper had sold the bank's former headquarters, trading in "walnut heaven" for six leased floors of a 55-story skyscraper rising over the center of downtown Seattle. The boardroom and all of the executive offices were on the fifteenth floor, the highest of the leased space. Washington Mutual did not occupy the top floors of buildings.

Killinger's corner office, connected to the boardroom by a tiny bathroom, had an uninterrupted view of the Space Needle towering over the edge of downtown Seattle. Out of another window, he could look out across Puget Sound to the rows of houses dotting the skinny inlet of West Seattle. The views were just about the office's only luxury. A commercial-grade gray couch was pushed up against the wall, and a simple wooden table, where he and Tall usually spread out their work, sat in the center. Beige carpet covered the floor, and the desk, a simple design in reddish brown, was the same as those in the other executives' offices. Pictures of Killinger's two sons, and Debbie Killinger, sat on the shelves of a credenza. Later he would add a framed picture of himself and Warren Buffett. Once a year, Killinger went through every desk drawer and cupboard, throwing out any lingering clutter.

On one of the windowsills sat a small stuffed Energizer Bunny, a recent gift from Debbie. Next to that bunny was yet another one, this one customized for Killinger with a tiny trumpet hanging from its bright pink paw. One of the ad agencies trying to court Washington Mutual had sent it over after seeing the first one. Both referred to Killinger's seemingly unstoppable energy, which had earned him a nickname: the Energizer Banker.[1]

On the phone with Goldman, Killinger had a choice. If he ponied up more money, he would have a chance to buy the second-largest savings and loan bank nationwide. Washington Mutual would become the largest. *The very largest.*

"This is yours to lose," the investment banker warned the two executives.

Killinger looked at Tall. Tall looked back. Both had just arrived back in the office, straight from the airport.

Not a question passed between them.

That Kerry Killinger had ended up a banker at all was something of a hereditary fluke. He came from a family of skilled musicians, many of them trumpet players. His father, Karl Killinger, was a child prodigy. He gave his first solo cornet performance at age six and followed up that success with a live radio broadcast, the first of many, in the third grade. After serving in World War II, he started a 17-member dance band and bought an old bus for the band to travel in across the country. He painted "Killinger" in large letters across the side.

In Des Moines, Iowa, Karl Killinger patiently taught music at several of the local high schools. It was a position his own father—Kerry

Killinger's grandfather—had also held. After a quick nap in the afternoon, Karl Killinger performed with other local bands at high school dances and other functions across the state. Bands were a big deal in Iowa, so Karl Killinger and his family's name were well respected. One of Karl Killinger's high school bands performed during President Richard Nixon's inauguration; another became the first Iowa school band to perform in Hawaii, outside the continental United States.[2] Kerry Killinger's sister became a high school band teacher like her father and grandfather, and his youngest brother lived on trains while directing music for the Ringling Bros. Barnum & Bailey Circus, a job that Kerry Killinger's uncle had also held. (His second brother, like Killinger, bucked the family trend and became a laser physicist and, later, a professor.) Family events revolved around music.

At North High School, or "North," as it was called, Kerry Killinger held the coveted position of drum major, the leader of the marching band. Wearing an ornate tall white hat and a matching wool jacket and slacks, his vest draped with crisscrossing gold chains, Killinger marched his classmates onto high school football fields for halftime shows. Waving his baton, he led them in parades down the main streets of small towns burrowed among the cornfields outside Des Moines. At his direction, the marching band members would stop marching, or keep marching, or raise their instruments in song. His father, as the conductor, walked beside the band. After school, Killinger worked at a repair shop restoring musical instruments.

Debbie was an animated girl with strict parents, who got in frequent trouble for talking too much in class. She was skinny with long, straight brown hair, and she went to a junior high school on the other side of Des Moines. Debbie played her dad's cornet, but Karl Killinger, Debbie's music teacher, thought she should learn how to play the trumpet. He sneaked one of Kerry's trumpets over to Debbie, but she refused to put her mouth on it. It was owned by a boy, after all! When Kerry found out, he was similarly disgusted. The relationship would have ended right there, except that Debbie's friends dared her to ask Kerry to an upcoming dance. In turn, Kerry's friends dared him to accept. At the dance they realized they liked each other. Later, sitting next to each other in the same band class at North, they whispered back and forth so much that Karl Killinger gave them both Bs to teach them a lesson. Karl Killinger and his wife had also met while performing in their high school band.

Kerry Killinger lived an idyllic, Americana childhood, the kind that would soon give way to the more fragmented families of the 1970s. His family never moved from the two-story brick house where he grew up, a property with a wide front lawn that was the site of pickup baseball games. The house sat on a corner in the middle of a neighborhood with dozens of other brick houses, all lined with giant oak trees and bordered by wide sidewalks. The Killinger family wasn't rich. The home had one bathroom for a family of six and only two bedrooms. Karl had refinished the attic, creating two additional, smaller bedrooms. The Beaverdale neighborhood was considered more classic than the modern, post–World War II development where Debbie lived several miles away.

Kerry's mother stayed home with her kids. She ironed labels with Kerry's name on his clothes, including a madras plaid jacket that he loved and wore all the time. He would match it with striped shorts, dark socks, and loafers. He wore his hair in a straight line across his forehead. Kerry rarely got into trouble. If he did play a prank, it was something fairly innocent, like moving the parked car of a friend or toilet-papering his own house. Antsy, he hated to sit around. On top of all the music, he argued for the debate team, played tennis, and made it onto the school's winning basketball team. Kerry wasn't a natural athlete, so he practiced relentlessly to make up for that. He inherited his strong work ethic from his father. In his senior year of high school, an economics teacher refused to move his grade up to an A, from a B+, no matter how hard he studied. He just studied harder. The teacher gave in. The A pushed him into the top 3 percent of students at his high school.[3] He received a full scholarship to the University of Iowa.

Debbie and Killinger married young—he was nineteen and she was eighteen. She was already pregnant with their first son, Bryan. The couple drove three hours across the border of Illinois for the wedding. That way they avoided having the marriage certificate show up in the *Des Moines Register*. The simple ceremony, attended only by their parents, was held in the tiny town of Rock Island, on the shores of the Mississippi River.

The couple's first home was a brand-new 12-by-60 foot mobile home in Iowa City with white metal siding and three tiny bedrooms. Killinger had analyzed how he would finance the mobile home, deciding it wouldn't be a good investment to take out a loan from a bank. Interest rates on a mortgage in the early 1970s were high. Killinger instead drew up an investment proposal for his grandparents for a $6,000 loan with a 5 percent interest rate. He also charted the amortization of the loan over the duration of their investment, writing it all out by hand on a piece of paper. His grandparents lent the young couple the money and would be paid back in full, with interest. Each month, without fail, Debbie mailed a check with the loan payment and a letter updating her grandparents-in-law about the household. While Killinger attended school, Debbie stayed home with Bryan.

Killinger didn't have time to party in college. He took as many as 22 credits a semester and worked part-time repairing instruments, as he had in high school. He and a friend owned a duplex that they rented out for extra money. His grades were high. On one assignment, Killinger was asked to prepare an annual report for a faux detergent company, which had suffered in the last few months because one of its key ingredients had been banned by the government, forcing the company to substitute another ingredient in its recipe. The costly move sent the fake company into a tailspin. In more than a dozen pages, Killinger diligently updated shareholders on the efforts he was making to turn around the troubled detergent business. He attached detailed, hand-drawn charts, showing sales and production numbers. "Although the forced introduction of a C-free product depressed sales and earnings over the short run," Killinger wrote, "we look very optimistically to the ability of our new products to generate future sales and earnings." His professor awarded him an A+ and included a page-long note of praise: "Your company, with no exception, was well managed and, I do believe, confident of a sound future."

In five years, Killinger finished both his undergraduate degree and an MBA, with honors. Family and friends rarely heard him complain. When he was growing up, his family had shied away from any negativity, frosting every aspect of their lives with a thick layer of good cheer. "You could be sitting in a hurricane and somebody just got their leg crushed and they would write to the family and say, 'We're down in Florida and we're having a great time!'" said Kerry's son, Bryan, later. "If you have any faults you hide them—to a fault." Kerry's own parents supported and encouraged him. "You don't say, 'I can't,'" Karl would say. "You say, 'I haven't been able to do it yet.'"

In the kitchen of the Killingers' second house in Lincoln, Nebraska, the nicest one so far, Killinger got a call from the owner of Murphey Favre. He was twenty-seven and had been working for several years as an investment analyst at an insurance company, his first job out of college. The owner of Murphey Favre, a growing brokerage in eastern Washington State, asked if Killinger wanted to run a couple of mutual funds. The owner asked Killinger a few questions. "Where do you see yourself in the next five years?" Killinger replied, "In your job."

Killinger and Debbie were not the kind of couple who entertained often or went out—their only hobby was racquetball. In Spokane, they flipped houses. They specialized in run-down monstrosities in the small agricultural city's rough neighborhoods. Sometimes trash filled a house's backyard, or the basement was crawling with termites. Once the previous owners left behind several sticks of dynamite in an abandoned car. Usually the heat and electricity didn't work. Sometimes hookers lived there; another time a neighbor showed up carrying a gun. Debbie would work on the house during the day, with the boys in tow if they weren't at school. When Killinger finished, he would join her. They spent most weekends on the project of the moment. Killinger was usually in charge of electricity and plumbing, while Debbie handled the Sheetrock and also the details, like sewing homemade curtains. Bryan and Brad got paid to help, 10 cents an hour for Brad, the younger, and 20 cents for Bryan. Everyone shared in the profits if the house made money, as it always did. In the seven years the Killingers lived in Spokane, they renovated and sold five houses, each time putting in between $2,000 and $3,000 and making several thousand dollars. On one of their best flips, they bought a house for $3,750 and sold it for almost $18,000. Killinger used some of the proceeds to buy shares in Murphey Favre. He eventually became a majority owner, just as he had promised.

At Washington Mutual, Killinger was in his element. The bank, like the houses he had flipped, provided a blank slate. It was so small and had so much potential. He began buying other banks, small companies with branches hidden in the nooks and crannies of Washington State and with simple names like Frontier and Pioneer Savings and Old Stone. Each bank purchase brought a handful of branches, and tens of thousands of new deposits.[4]

Craig Tall, hired by Pepper in the 1980s, was in charge of finding potential "targets." He was a skilled, relentless negotiator, a fact that wasn't always apparent to those who didn't know him well. Generally soft-spoken and calm, Tall would once spend days hashing out the details of a bank merger following a complicated surgery to fuse his back. While the other bankers went off to hold private meetings, Tall, in pain, lay for hours in a break room in San Francisco until both sides returned to the table. Ultimately, Washington Mutual won the negotiation.

Tall also knew exactly when to stop negotiating and start drinking, dragging the other bankers off to dinner while the legal details were being settled. Usually he would have had the help of a big investment bank in New York, whose job it would be to match up companies. But big investment banks had no time for a small bank like Washington Mutual. Sometimes Tall flew to the East Coast to talk with them. Usually, he ended up calling other banks and asking to speak directly to their chief executive. It felt like going out on a lot of blind dates, some successful, others not. Tall partnered with Lindy Friedlander to research institutions. The two looked for banks that were in financial trouble, or whose chief executive didn't have a succession plan, or whose chief executive was getting a divorce and needed money, or that had any other sign of weakness. They made a list of those banks on a giant whiteboard and presented it to Killinger and the other members of the executive team at their weekly meeting, held each Monday morning. The team discussed all the acquisitions together and approved them together. It was a democracy. Everyone had a say.

In two years, Killinger orchestrated the purchase of eight little banks, adding close to $1 billion in assets. Washington Mutual grew to about $8 billion in size. In Oregon, Pacific First had run into trouble, and Washington Mutual bought its 129 branches, too. For the first time in Washington Mutual's 104-year-history, Killinger had doubled the bank in size. Washington Mutual wasn't located just in its home state anymore. Its branches blanketed Oregon as well. Killinger marched on, buying six more banks, at the rate of more than two every year, all over the West. Summit Savings Bank, four branches; Olympus Bank, eleven branches; Western Bank, forty-two branches; and on and on it went.[5] One bank manager left a bank after Washington Mutual bought it; he accepted a position at another bank, and Washington Mutual took over that bank as well. After this process repeated itself a couple of times, the manager recognized Washington Mutual executives when they walked into the bank's headquarters where he currently worked. "Oh, don't worry, these guys are okay," he told his coworkers.

By the mid-1990s, the bank that Lou Pepper had saved stood like a fortress in the center of a wide landscape of wreckage. The Savings and Loan Crisis had ravaged banks nationwide. Everyone was calling it the worst financial disaster since the Great Depression.[6] The destruction paved the way for a huge wave of mergers. Meanwhile, interstate banking laws that had prevented banks from expanding outside their home territory loosened as well. The country became a giant Monopoly board, with the stronger banks snatching up the smaller, weaker banks as quickly as they could. Several of the banks Killinger bought had been taken over by the government, or they would have been taken over, had Washington Mutual not stepped in to buy them. Banks were buying other banks so fast that, as a customer, it became hard to keep track of where you had put your money or even your bank's name. All the healthy banks were growing larger, transforming themselves into giant financial powerhouses with thousands of branches. The banks didn't just have several billion dollars in assets anymore; they had several hundred billion. In a cheeky reference to all the mergers, including its own purchases, Washington Mutual rolled out a new ad campaign, encouraging customers to "Merge with Washington Mutual!" The ad boosted checking accounts by 45 percent in just over a year.[7]

Even among all the other deals, Washington Mutual's shopping spree stood out. The bank had come out of nowhere. Who was this company? "It was definitely common for the big to get bigger," remarked one analyst later. "But Washington Mutual moved from the small camp into the big camp and then got even bigger. They were splashy, if not splashier than everyone else."

On the afternoon when Killinger and Tall received the phone call from the Goldman Sachs investment banker in early 1997, a mighty battle was under way in California. H. F. Ahmanson, the country's largest savings and loan bank, had just made a hostile bid to take over Great Western, the country's second-largest savings and loan bank, for $5.8 billion. The size of the potential deal—measured by assets—exceeded the total of the last 10 bank purchases Washington Mutual made.[8] Hostile takeovers were growing in popularity. Ahmanson had in fact hired the same legal team that Wells Fargo had just used to take over First Interstate Bank.

Ahmanson and Great Western were both headquartered in the suburbs of Los Angeles. Their hundreds of branches were scattered across California and Florida. For years, analysts had predicted one would buy the other. But there was no love lost between the two companies. They were fierce competitors. "If I used the word 'jaundiced,' that probably would have been charitable," said one Great Western executive about the relationship. Now, with its unwanted offer, Ahmanson sparked an all-out battle between the two banks. It ran an ad in the local papers, warning Great Western to "Begin Discussions with us NOW!" Great Western's response: "It's their shareholders' money. If that's the way they want to spend it, that's their business."[9]

The overture from Ahmanson left Great Western's chief executive, John Maher, with two options. He could give in and sell his bank to Ahmanson, or he could find another bank that he liked better to buy Great Western. He did the latter. This was fortunate, since Great Western had already landed on Killinger's most recent bank shopping list. Killinger and Tall figured they had several years to consider making a purchase before someone else bought the bank. That time frame had narrowed.

Killinger, Tall, and sixty other executives and employees flew down to Great Western's sprawling headquarters campus, located just outside Los Angeles in the San Fernando Valley. When Washington Mutual's team researched new banks to acquire, the members tended to travel incognito. They flew by the dozens into different cities on different flights, stayed in different hotels and sometimes in run-down motels, and checked in under assumed names. Often they would arrive somewhere in the middle of the night, and at least once they arrived in a blizzard. Their mission was to find out everything possible about the bank they might purchase. They weeded through thousands of loan records and financial documents for hours on end. Washington Mutual wanted to keep its negotiations secret until a deal was finalized.

At Great Western's headquarters, the executives spent a week inside a cavernous, warehouse-style room, where Great Western's financial information filled dozens of boxes. Each night the team members sat in a circle, perched on their respective boxes, sharing with the group what they had found. At the end of the week, they realized what Killinger and Tall already knew: Great Western would be a fantastic buy. There weren't any red flags in the documents. The bank's pile of bad loans from the recent California downturn was dwindling, and it was making money. If Washington Mutual bought Great Western, it would add 1,000 new branches and grow to almost $100 billion in assets, doubling in size again.[10]

There was only one problem. Washington Mutual had competition: Norwest. Both banks vied to be what is known in the business world as the "white knight" for Great Western. Great Western hadn't told Washington Mutual that it had a competitor, but Killinger and Tall had suspected that Norwest was also involved. Since Washington Mutual was now big enough that investment banks wanted its business ("They were visiting us now," said Tall), a handful of junior associates from Lehman Brothers called nearly every hotel in Los Angeles to ask whether Norwest's executives had checked in. Unlike Washington Mutual's, Norwest's executives were listed under their real names, a giveaway. The undercover work gave Washington Mutual a head start on the auction. Now that the bank knew its competition, it could try to figure out how much Norwest was likely to bid on Great Western.

A few days later Killinger and Tall sat in a conference room in the Los Angeles airport, trying to convince Great Western's board that Washington Mutual should buy their bank. They thought they had nailed it in the exhaustive three-hour presentation, interrupted only when Killinger accidently ripped his pants on the side of a chair (the pants were repaired in an embarrassing emergency sewing job). They hung out at their hotel all night, but they didn't hear anything back. They flew back to Seattle the next day, still uncertain. They had only just walked into the executive floor at Washington Mutual's headquarters when Killinger's assistant flagged him down. Great Western's investment banker was on the phone.

The Goldman banker told Killinger and Tall that Washington Mutual had to raise its offer by only $500 million to beat Norwest. If so, it would win the role of Great Western's white knight. The duo would have exactly one hour to come up with an answer. Killinger and Tall called up Washington Mutual's board, whose members had been waiting on standby for any word. They got the go-ahead. The executives raised their bid to about $6.3 billion, or $45.34 a share, and won.[11] Now Washington Mutual and Great Western were together battling Ahmanson for the vote of Great Western's shareholders. The shareholders would decide in an upcoming meeting whether to approve a deal with Ahmanson or Washington Mutual. Almost as soon as Washington Mutual's offer was made public, Ahmanson increased its own by $3 a share, to about $50. While that topped Washington Mutual, Ahmanson said its offer would be contingent on its share price.[12]

For the next three months, Killinger and Maher flew to dozens of cities across the country, pitching the investment funds that managed shareholders' money. Sometimes other executives from one of the two banks joined them, but mostly it was just the two of them. Ahmanson's chief executive, Charlie Rinehart, and his entourage also visited the money managers. Rinehart, admittedly, had not seen Washington Mutual coming, even though Killinger was not secretive about his plans to keep buying banks all over the country. Rinehart assumed Killinger would be too busy with another big purchase that Washington Mutual had just made in California: Keystone Holdings, the parent company of 220-branch American Savings Bank. American was Washington Mutual's first game-changing bank acquisition, and it had taken seven long months to hammer out the $1.7 billion deal.

Neither Great Western's nor Ahmanson's executives really knew what to make of Killinger or his executive team. They seemed close-knit, hardworking, and wholesome. They reliably held coffee meetings together every week. They got along. They were competent and straightforward and just . . . nice. You couldn't help admiring how they'd hustled across the West Coast, buying almost every bank in their path.

On the other hand, the Great Western and Ahmanson executives thought they were better than Washington Mutual. In their opinion, the bank wasn't as advanced—it made mortgages and opened checking accounts and that was about it. Washington Mutual had no flair, they thought. Their different headquarters cities said it all. Seattle, understated, down-to-earth, and bike-friendly, was like the coffee shop guitar player to Los Angeles's money-fueled, sun-bleached rock star. In Los Angeles, everything was just flashier. Californians also carried more debt to fuel their purchases, as Washington Mutual soon found out. Customers in California bounced way more checks than consumers in other states. "We viewed ourselves as superior to them, but so what? They were the buyers and we were the sellers," the head of Great Western's mergers and acquisitions team later recalled.

Kerry Killinger himself puzzled the other executives. He was not like many of the bankers they knew, the showboat guys with dapper suits and white shoes. Killinger was not slick. He watched *Beavis and Butt-Head*, the crass MTV cartoon about two teenage boys making teenage boy jokes. Sometimes Washington Mutual executives would catch him and Debbie snickering about the show as they traveled on business. He also seemed to like his bank, and not in the normal way of bank chief executives who saw their institutions as giant, personal cash cows.

Every six months Killinger visited each bank branch. He started this trend at Debbie's suggestion, when the couple was in Palm Springs at a meeting. (Debbie had also, on at least one occasion, directed one of Killinger's speeches by giving him hand cues that the audience couldn't see.) At first Killinger was hesitant about the branch visits. "What would I say?" he asked Debbie. But then he shook hands with the manager and saw her face light up. Making conversation slowly became easier after that.

In each meeting with shareholder representatives, Killinger and Maher would walk into the conference room or office and shake hands with the representatives from the investment houses. These companies invested money for much larger clients like pension funds, insurance companies, and mutual funds. They were not the typical Washington Mutual investor, who was more likely to be similar to the bank's customers. Maher, intense, direct, and crackerjack smart, had worked as a managing partner at Lehman before taking over Great Western. He knew what to say, and how to say it, to convince the investment houses that they should approve a merger of Great Western and Washington Mutual. He was a practiced speaker, often talking extemporaneously. When Killinger spoke, he tended to read directly from a prepared script, rarely straying from the pages. He spoke drily but to the point. Killinger, however, convinced just as many people with his earnestness. "He didn't strike you as sophisticated, but he struck you as someone who would take care of your money," said one Great Western executive who was along for several of the visits. Noted *Fortune*: "Those who heard him were converted to WaMu worship."

The shareholder representatives would often ask what Killinger planned to do with Great Western's corporate jet. The plane was a sore point for shareholders. It cost Great Western hundreds of thousands of dollars a year. This question placed Killinger in an awkward position. He had no intention of keeping the corporate jet, but he also didn't want to criticize Maher's use of it, particularly with Maher sitting right next to him. The two men had, in fact, used the plane to make their rounds of shareholder calls, but only because they sometimes traveled to several cities in one day. "No, no," Killinger would tell the representative carefully, after the question was posed. "I don't think we'll be availing ourselves of the corporate jet."

Killinger, like Pepper before him, ran Washington Mutual on a tight budget. The entire bank ran an internal communication system called Whiz, which cost only $2,000 to install. Even as other companies switched to e-mail, Washington Mutual stuck with Whiz. "It was very, very cheap and it lasted forever because we ran it for a long time," said Liane Wilson, who was in charge of technology. She always asked Killinger for better updates, only to be told the bank couldn't afford them. So there was no way Killinger was going to allow the banks he purchased to keep their perks. The executive team canceled country club memberships and corporate credit cards and sold company cars. The team shuttered sweeping executive suites, which were almost always located on the top floor of a building. The plants were out, as were the corporate jets and the executive chefs. Killinger and his team always flew coach on commercial airlines. "Check your ego at the door," he would regularly tell employees, or "Frugal is sexy."[13] With an annual salary of $560,575 and a bonus of $372,900, not including stock options, Killinger was making the most he had ever made at the bank. But he was still making about $500,000 less than the previous Great Western chief executive. He did, however, own more than twice as many shares in his bank as Maher. Even small corporate perks made him uncomfortable. For a long time, he would not allow his executive assistant to buy him lunch. On the days he didn't have outside meetings, Killinger took the elevator down to the bustling lobby of the bank's headquarters building, where he always bought half a turkey sandwich on wheat and a cup of soup (never the kind with a cream base, as he watched his weight) to bring back up to his desk. His assistant finally convinced him to turn over the duty, mostly because people he knew kept stopping him to chat along the way. A quick trip to the deli would turn into an hour he didn't have.

The Killinger household operated similarly. There was little extravagant spending. Debbie joined Killinger on business trips carrying Cup Noodles and instant coffee in her suitcase. When Bryan, their older son, wanted to buy his first car, Killinger went to a big lot that sold repossessed cars and picked one out for him. After that car broke down for good, Killinger offered to pay half of a $3,000 down payment on a second used car. When Brad turned old enough to drive, Killinger gave in and bought him a new car, but only after Debbie tallied up all the repair bills on the used cars and showed him that those costs outweighed the purchase of a new car. Both Bryan and Brad worked after school, either running paper routes or working behind the counter at Burger King or Domino's Pizza.

Killinger owned a Mercedes, but it was used and kept breaking down. He also owned an Oldsmobile, which the family referred to as "the banker mobile." Each year the family took a ten-day trip to Hawaii. Usually Killinger worked. On one occasion, he held a conference call in the middle of the night, hiding out in the bathroom of the hotel room (the family usually stayed at the Holiday Inn), sitting on the toilet so as not to wake up Debbie. By this time, analysts had estimated Killinger's worth at about $100 million.[14]

The family's house might have been considered posh. It was located in the same expensive neighborhood as the lakefront home of Microsoft billionaire Bill Gates, with only a couple of miles and a swanky golf course separating the two properties. But Killinger and Debbie had rescued the six-bedroom house out of foreclosure when they first moved to the city in the early 1980s. The house had been trashed. It had a leaky roof, none of the light switches worked, and almost everything, inside and out, was painted brown. The previous owners, in dire financial straits, had sold all the dirt in the backyard. The lawn had become a giant mud pit covered in ankle-deep water. Killinger and Debbie carpeted and repainted, replaced the roof, and expanded the master bedroom. "He was not a downtime guy," said one close friend of Killinger. "Even if he had downtime and he was home, he was constantly looking for projects to do or things that needed to be taken care of."

As Killinger worked on the Great Western deal, he and Debbie were in the middle of renovating the kitchen. Executives at the bank, calling with some concern or another about the merger, heard hammers banging in the background during the conversation. Killinger once drove to the opening of one of Washington Mutual's new call centers with dirt under his fingernails, although this was unusual. Killinger cared strongly about appearances. They bought the house for $215,000 in 1983. By 2008, it was valued at about $2 million. Even when the Killingers had finished remodeling, however, the house looked respectable but average. It was the kind of house you might find in any upper-middle-class neighborhood. The walls were painted white with the occasional piece of framed art, mostly reprints. Each room was sparsely decorated. They bought some new furniture when necessary, but other pieces came from the mobile home in Iowa City, or from one of the houses where they had lived in Spokane.

Charlie Rinehart, Ahmanson's chief executive, tried to sway Great Western's shareholders to approve a merger with his bank. He pointed out that Washington Mutual's executives were largely inexperienced. "We have better systems to make mortgages to consumers," he would argue. "These guys have never been through a downturn. They don't know how to screen customers to make sure they will pay back their loan." In California, the real estate market hurtled through much higher highs, and much lower lows, than nearly anywhere else in the country. Ahmanson had just survived one of those disastrous lows. In Seattle, the real estate market was much more stable, protecting Washington Mutual's executive team from the wild fluctuations. "You can't tell how good anyone is at underwriting when housing prices are going up," Rinehart said later. Only during a severe economic downturn, he believed, did it become apparent how well a bank was making mortgages. He also tried to attack Washington Mutual's forecasts, specifically the amount it claimed it would make when it bought Great Western. The numbers were "absolutely unprecedented" and "absurd," Rinehart said. For a while, Rinehart convinced at least some of the analysts of the benefits of his own company's hostile takeover plans. "I thought he did a heck of a job," crowed one Smith Barney analyst after a Rinehart presentation. "I'd give him six (out of six) on artistic impression and a 5.8 on technical merit. He was very believable."[15]

But Killinger, even without the Wall Street flamboyance, was dazzling. Shareholders loved how down-to-earth he seemed. Analysts and investment bankers were dazzled by his brilliance, his ability to discern the best deals, and his timing. He had bought eighteen banks in seven years, and not one of those banks had been a lemon. Washington Mutual's stock price climbed, and the bank posted a healthy return on assets. "We thought he was a superstar," one analyst later said. "He was the vision and his team was the operation. It was the perfect blend." Another analyst remarked, at about the time the Energizer Bunnies started showing up in Killinger's office, "I'm not sure this guy ever goes to sleep at night."[16]

The war over Great Western intensified. Washington Mutual and Great Western jointly took out a full-page advertisement in *The Wall Street Journal*, declaring their merger "A SUPERIOR COMBINATION IN EVERY WAY." The ad continued, "THIS IS A *SUPERIOR* MERGER WITH A *SUPERIOR* PARTNER FOR *SUPERIOR*

VALUE." And then: "AHMANSON AND ITS INFERIOR PRO-POSAL—A LOSING PROPOSITION IN EVERY WAY." Ahmanson fired back the next day with its own full-page advertisement. "DO NOT ALLOW YOUR INVESTMENT IN GREAT WESTERN TO BE PUT AT RISK," the headline declared in an even larger, more warlike font.

Killinger and Tall couldn't tell if they were winning or not. At this point, because the offers were based on fluctuating stock prices of Great Western and Ahmanson, they were both worth about the same, $6.7 billion.[17] Moreover, Great Western's board members might suddenly change their minds about the whole thing, adding another dimension of uncertainty. There were so many people involved in four straight months of mud-slinging that Tall held up to seven conference calls a day. He made sure all the public relations people were responding to the latest Ahmanson attack and that all the investment bankers and lawyers were kept up-to-date. The decision would come to a head soon, when shareholders of Great Western would vote hours before their annual springtime meeting.

But suddenly Rinehart backed out. A court ruling had thrown a wrench into Ahmanson's plans. The bank wouldn't be allowed to delay the shareholder meeting, as it had anticipated, so its efforts to take over Great Western were thwarted. Rinehart had been planning on the extra time to rally more shareholders. He couldn't increase his bid, as it would dilute the value of the existing shares.[18] As quickly as it began, the fight ended. "WaMu," predicted one analyst, "is going to be a Goliath."[19]

The thing about acquisitions, Washington Mutual's executive team found out, is that if you do enough of them, it doesn't matter if the other company is really small or really big. Buying banks had turned into another line of business. Negotiating a deal worth several million dollars wasn't too different from one worth multiple billions. "It really became just zeros at the end of a long number," said Tall, who almost always wore a tailored black shirt on deal-making days. Washington Mutual now controlled a big chunk of the West Coast. It was the largest mortgage lender in Washington, Oregon, and California. Its market capitalization across the country, the value of its shares, had increased in just five years to $16 billion from $1.2 billion. During each of those last five years, the bank had made money, pulling in a profit of $482 million the year it bought Great Western. It had branches in Boston and Miami and Salt Lake City and in many smaller towns in between.[20] One Washington Mutual manager who had worked on the mergers was wandering around a balmy, palm-tree-lined small town in Florida, whose name he couldn't recall, when he looked up to find himself standing in front of a Washington Mutual branch. For a second, the manager was puzzled, staring at the bank's logo. "What is Washington Mutual doing in Florida?" he thought. Not until that moment did the impact of all the hours and hours he had worked, buried in his office in Seattle, become apparent.

Killinger got the most public attention, but an executive team that had become shrewdly adept at acquisitions abetted him. Someone jokingly drew a picture illustrating how Washington Mutual digested its new purchases. The drawing, gleaned from the children's book *The Little Prince*, showed a long snake that had just swallowed a giant elephant. The snake's stomach was a round ball, indicating the elephant inside. The stomach was labeled with Fay Chapman's and Liane Wilson's names, because they were the two most involved behind the scenes. As outside general counsel and, later, chief legal officer, Chapman handled the legal details while Wilson took care of the technology side. At the top of the long head of the snake was Tall's name, because he was negotiating the deals. The head of the snake had two eyes and was labeled "Kerry." He was the face of the deal, the one who spoke to the chief executives and the media and flew to branch openings. In the French children's story, the child narrator draws the picture of the snake and the elephant and passes it around to adults, who all believe it is a drawing of a large, lumpy hat. Only the Little Prince views the drawing as the narrator intended, as a reptile that has swallowed its prey.

The scariest part of a bank merger is combining the two computer systems, each controlling millions of bank accounts and hundreds of thousands of pages of mortgage information. It's a delicate combination, like trying to mesh together two bowls of spaghetti, as one observer noted. The situation is rife with potential mistakes. During the national merger frenzy of the 1990s, mistakes were even more common. Wells

Fargo tried to combine the systems of First Interstate in only a few months. Some customers had trouble with their deposit balances; others couldn't make their credit card and mortgage payments online.[21] Then, as Wells Fargo tried to transfer nearly a thousand First Interstate branches into its own system, some customers' accounts disappeared. Customers abandoned the bank and Wells Fargo wrote off $150 million to cover the problems.[22]

Early on, when it became apparent that Killinger wasn't going to stop buying banks, Liane Wilson put together a detailed process for how Washington Mutual would absorb its new purchases. This process is a key ingredient in any merger. It is also, arguably, the least sexy job. Under Wilson's direction, each department at Washington Mutual had a representative who would come up with his own merger plan for his respective department at the other bank. That group of people became known as Washington Mutual's A-Team. *A* stood for *acquisition*, although the reference to the 1980s television show was not lost on the leadership team. In one episode of the action series, revolving around a group of ass-kicking ex-Army men, one character famously cackles, "I love it when a plan comes together." When Washington Mutual purchased a new bank, the A-Team would arrive at the bank and spread out, each person taking over a different division.

Rail thin with coiffed white hair, Wilson was pragmatic, commanding—"I could be a real bitch during integration," she said later—and good-humored. She laughed loudly when one of her direct reports showed up on a merger weekend wearing a gas mask from the local army-navy surplus store. He was making fun of Wilson, who often conducted business while on a smoke break.

Early in the transition of one bank at Washington Mutual, a help line suddenly lit up with calls. Customers had been trying to use a phone line in Florida to access their accounts. Now that phone line wasn't working. One of the bank's vendors had screwed up. "Get more people at the help line," Wilson barked. "Get the problem fixed." The issue was resolved. "There were no glitches at Washington Mutual," one analyst later noted.

The crux of the transition took place over one tense weekend, so customers wouldn't notice a change at the branches. Wilson dispatched thousands of workers to each new branch. Those workers changed out all the ATMs and other equipment. This work often happened over a long weekend, so for most of the 1990s, none of the Washington Mutual executives had a long weekend or, often, any weekend at all.

On Presidents' Day weekend in 1998, Wilson sat in her office, examining a stack of paperwork. The A-Team was about to convert all of Great Western's technology. About six months had passed since Washington Mutual had bought the bank. Due to Great Western's size, and therefore the risks, Wilson had staggered the work over three upcoming weekends. Now she carefully made sure that all the details had been thought out.

She glanced up to find Killinger standing in her doorway. He looked as if he had a big secret. He had driven several miles from his house into the city. Even though it was a holiday, he wore slacks and a blazer. Wilson was also dressed up, as was everyone else working that day. Killinger didn't believe in the trend toward casual workplace dress. "Business got casual when dress got casual," he sometimes said.

"You won't believe the call I got this weekend," Killinger said.

"Huh?" Wilson replied, distracted.

"It was very, very interesting," he said. He had her attention.

"Are you going to tell me, or are you going to keep me in suspense?"

"I don't know if I should tell you this, but you're sitting down," Killinger said. "The call was from Charlie Rinehart."

"What!" Wilson exclaimed.

"Yeah," Killinger said. "They want us to take a look at them."

Wilson stared at Killinger, astonished.

"Kerry," she said. "You can't be serious." She reminded him that she was, at that moment, reviewing the plans to convert the systems of the biggest bank Washington Mutual had ever acquired. And that merger had come after the two previous biggest bank purchases in Washington Mutual's history. Her head was full of deadlines and details and a million scenarios that could go wrong. Now Killinger was proposing another purchase, one that would be Washington Mutual's biggest ever.

"Well, we're going to have to talk about this," Killinger said.

• • •

In any merger, combining the culture of the two companies is a little like trying to integrate two families after a second marriage. Neither side is sure of the other. Making it work is almost as important as meshing together the computer systems. Killinger and his team would solve this problem by wiping out the leadership team at the acquired bank. On the rare occasion when they offered a higher-level executive a job, it was at a much lower salary than that executive had been making. At other times the executive would make much more by leaving the new company, since a change in control usually invoked a golden parachute. Killinger didn't want to pay the new executives more.

Washington Mutual, new employees soon found out, wasn't run like a top-down organization. There was a lot of communication. Whenever a deal was announced, Killinger and the leadership team would arrive at the new bank's headquarters and meet with the management team. They circulated a "transition newsletter" for the new employees to keep them up-to-date. As soon as they knew how many people they were going to lay off—the immediate concern of all employees—they announced the number without delay.

Killinger didn't inspire the same kind of team building that Pepper had, but he believed strongly in maintaining the culture of the bank. The corporate values remained in place, and had been narrowed down to three main adjectives: Fair, Caring, and Human. Killinger worried that affecting the culture might get in the way of financial results.[23] Once, as he was giving a speech at an off-site manager meeting, a Washington Mutual employee interrupted him. The employee handed Killinger his trumpet and band jacket. Perplexed, Killinger put on the jacket, grabbed his trumpet, and joined what turned into a musical procession, marching through downtown Seattle from the Hilton Hotel to the bank's headquarters. Passersby stopped to watch, while drivers craned their heads out of car windows or honked. When his brother later traveled through town with the Barnum & Bailey Circus, Killinger joined him on stage for a brief performance. He kept a trumpet in the office. In the evening after most people left, you could sometimes hear him tooting on the horn. He preferred jazz.

But Killinger had few close friends, in part because the bank took up so much of his time. Even the people who should have known him best didn't, really. Killinger was aloof and sometimes guarded. Many found him to be emotionless and not empathetic. "Kerry went to college and got his MBA and all that, but it was like he didn't pick up the intellectual elements around a university," said one executive who worked closely with him.

Charlie Rinehart and his board of directors had realized something. Being a good bank no longer sufficed. If Ahmanson wanted to survive among the new banking giants, particularly in California, it had to be big. Running a bank is a little bit like running a grocery store. It's a business with thin margins, where companies make money by selling a lot of something to keep costs down. "If your loan system costs $1 million and you write one loan, it just cost you $1 million to write that loan," Rinehart said. "You have to make up for it in volume." But Rinehart, whether he wanted to make loans or sell bulk carrots, no longer had a way to grow Ahmanson, at least not as rapidly as the competition. Washington Mutual had bought all the other banks that could have made his own bigger. Rinehart knew something else as well. In California, customers banked at Bank of America first, followed by Wells Fargo, Ahmanson (which operated as Home Savings of America), and, in the number-four spot, Washington Mutual.[24] Rinehart knew that his company's number-three position was worth a lot of money. "In reality, this is ridiculous," Rinehart said later. "But it was the mantra from the analysts. You had to be in the Top Three. WaMu would have to pay a big price to get us."

He called Killinger. And Washington Mutual bought Ahmanson. The $10 billion deal was the largest in Washington Mutual's history and the biggest so far among American savings and loan banks.[25] On the same holiday Monday when Rinehart called Killinger, the executives held an impromptu meeting about whether they could handle buying another massive bank. They decided they could. In just 13 days, the two banks put together a deal. There was a strange moment when Killinger and Tall flew to Los Angeles to meet with Charlie Rinehart and his team to hash out the details. They walked into the conference room and saw the men whom they had spent months battling. Everyone was cordial, although the general atmosphere was strained. "It was like suddenly marrying your sworn enemy," Tall said later.

Washington Mutual was now the seventh-largest financial institution in the United States. It had more than 2,000 branches and more than 30,000 employees scattered across the country. Pepper had left Killinger a bank with 50 branches and $7 billion in assets. Now Washington Mutual had $150 billion. "In the last three years, we've done what no other bank in history has done," Killinger told an interviewer. He wasn't referring just to the acquisitions. Washington Mutual had introduced a concept to its customers known as "free checking"—checking accounts devoid of fees. While many other banks closed as many accounts as they opened, Washington Mutual enticed average office workers or housewives to bring in their money. (It made money by charging those customers overdraft fees when they bounced checks.) The popularity of free checking forced WaMu's competitors to grudgingly follow suit. "We don't believe in 'free,'" grumbled one Bank of America executive before his bank introduced the product.

For Pepper's fiftieth anniversary of living in Seattle, the group of employees whom he had hired in the 1980s gathered to celebrate with him. They ate lunch, drank champagne in Killinger's office, and marveled at how far the bank had come in just ten years. Recently Pepper had traveled with the executive team to New York, where Killinger rang the bell of the New York Stock Exchange. Washington Mutual now traded under the symbol "WM." Pictures from the trip show the team huddled in front of the storied Stock Exchange building on a cold December day. Later they would wave a giant Washington Mutual flag from between the stately columns, which were wrapped with red and white stripes in honor of the holiday season. Inside, in the middle of the busy trading floor, Pepper, Killinger, Tall, Wilson, Deanna Oppenheimer, Fay Chapman, Bill Longbrake, and several other executives gathered for a photograph. They put their hands together between them, just as a sports team might after winning a big game. They all smiled. Pepper had a description for this rare sort of moment, which he later wrote about in his book: "Once in a while in a business or group, the stars all line up right, the moon is in the right house, times are excellent—people are all happy, everything is going along perfectly. That is 'Camelot.'"[26]

Proud of the management team he had created, Pepper wrote a speech and handed it out to the executives at his anniversary gathering.

"This hiring," he wrote, "was my contribution to WaMu. What has happened since I retired is beyond belief. I doubt if any business since maybe Henry Ford's has grown any more rapidly. So, measured on an economic scale, you have been an absolutely, unbelievably stellar team." He continued: "The truly glorious thing in my mind is that you have demonstrated that nice people can win. My good fortune in hiring you was not just your intellect or your energy or your dedication but that each of you is a nice person. So, as I start my second 50 years, I thank you for making me look so good."[27]

At about this time, one of the local analysts who had closely covered Washington Mutual since the 1980s wondered if Killinger would have to adjust his style. As head of a much larger bank, Killinger faced higher expectations, especially from the bank's shareholders and analysts. Both groups would expect him to continue his boy-wonder routine, pulling in even larger profits. "The demands are a lot tougher," the analyst noted.[28]

Killinger admitted that he probably wouldn't be able to visit all the branches every six months anymore. But he did not plan to change his hands-on management style. "So far he has demonstrated this remarkable ability to . . . keep the bank on course," said one of the longtime board members. Tall also defended Killinger. "We all get forced to make adjustments," he told a reporter, "but I don't think you fundamentally change who you are. I don't think Kerry's going to change who he is."

Chapter Three

THE POWER OF YES

I wouldn't lend some of these people money to buy a bicycle, never mind a house.

—account executive at Long Beach Mortgage,
a subsidiary of Washington Mutual

To reach Washington Mutual's legal department, Fay Chapman had to leave her office and the secured executive floor, walk down the hallway past the women's bathroom, and wait for an elevator to take her up to the next floor. She didn't consider this trip a hassle. She traveled between the two levels even if she didn't have a specific meeting scheduled. She liked to stop in on her employees just to see how things were going.

On this day in the summer of 2003, however, Washington Mutual's chief legal officer had a purpose as she pushed the button for the seventeenth floor. She got off the elevator and walked directly over to the desk of one of her employees, another lawyer who worked with Long Beach Mortgage, the subprime lending subsidiary of Washington Mutual. The employee had called Chapman with a problem.

Over the last few months, he had grown concerned about the loans made by Long Beach. He didn't think the mortgages were meeting the underwriting guidelines that Long Beach had promised its customers—investors across the world who were buying securities packed full of the loans.

The compliance department at Washington Mutual had just completed an internal quality review on a group of mortgages Long Beach had made in the first quarter of 2003. It had turned up some troubling information. Of more than 270 loans sampled—a fraction of those made at Long Beach during the year—40 percent were deemed unacceptable because they contained some kind of "critical error."[1] *Critical error?* Long Beach's "credit management and portfolio oversight practices were unsatisfactory," the report concluded.

Long Beach, and therefore Washington Mutual, was potentially selling products with different ingredients from what it had advertised. Bad ingredients, perhaps. And the products, securities packaged with subprime loans, were a global product. Investors clamored to buy them. Each time Long Beach representatives turned up at the American Securitization Forum's popular annual conference in Las Vegas, they ignored the seminars and spent 12 hours each day, for three days straight, meeting with eager investors instead.

After Chapman talked to the employee, she spoke to a second, and then a third. All three voiced the same concern. She walked out of the legal department, took the elevator down to her own floor, and marched directly into Killinger's office. The executives had learned long ago that the best way to bring Killinger an issue was in a one-on-one meeting. He avoided confrontation. He would ignore e-mails and avoid phone calls until a problem resolved itself on its own. On one business trip to the East Coast, he had fielded a frantic-sounding call from someone back in Seattle. When he hung up, the manager accompanying him had asked about the problem. "The natives are restless in the office," Killinger replied. "I'd rather see if they can work it out themselves. I hate this stuff. It's better that I'm away."

In Killinger's office, Chapman demanded a meeting to discuss the Long Beach issues. She didn't like people to sugarcoat problems for her, so she certainly wasn't going to do it for anyone else. She also could be persuasive, sometimes in an unusual fashion. Once, in a heated negotiation, she had abruptly thrown a stack of papers at a government official who stood in the way of one of Washington Mutual's bank deals. After she flung the papers, she stormed out of the room, leaving behind a startled table of bankers. The move sped up the negotiations.

At Chapman's insistence, Killinger agreed to a meeting about Long Beach. The company, once considered an insignificant acquisition because of its small size, now seemed much more significant. But four years earlier, when the executives had decided to buy it, Long Beach had almost been an afterthought. It had only about $328 million in assets, a sliver of the tens of billions of dollars that Great Western and Ahmanson had added to the bank's holdings.

In the spring of 1998, the first time Craig Tall brought up the possibility of buying Long Beach, the executive team had been at an all-day retreat in a conference center on Seattle's waterfront. Tall hadn't brought it up with any real seriousness. Long Beach wasn't even on the day's long, action-packed agenda. "It would make a good investment opportunity," he said of the small mortgage company.

Tall always looked out for potential investments, constantly evaluating which banks to buy next. Recently, his hunt had grown to include subprime lenders. Washington Mutual had never before made those types of mortgages. A borrower who takes out a subprime loan is someone who has racked up debt or has never had a credit card, doesn't make much money, or possibly doesn't pay his bills on time. A subprime borrower cannot qualify for a regular, prime mortgage. Because the borrower is more unreliable, the whole business is much riskier for the lender. Subprime borrowers are much more likely to stop paying their loans.

The business was potentially lucrative, though. Because subprime borrowers got charged much higher interest rates and also higher fees on their loans, the lender could make more than on a normal loan, assuming the loan did not go into default. A subprime borrower might hypothetically have a mortgage with a 12 percent interest rate, versus an 8 percent interest rate for a prime borrower. As with other types of mortgages, the lender could sell the loan on the secondary market to investors, making even more money. If a homeowner did default, someone else would have to worry about it.

At the time when Tall started hunting, subprime lending had become a faddish trend. All across the country, but especially in California, companies formed to make these loans. Larger banks had jumped on board. In just three years, the number of subprime lenders tripled, reaching

more than 200 by 1997.[2] Washington Mutual wanted to stay competitive. Buying a subprime company had another, less-talked-about
benefit: it quieted local community organizations. Each time Washington Mutual purchased a bank, there was almost always an outcry
from activist groups about how little money the bank loaned in poorer
neighborhoods. Under the requirements of the federal Community
Reinvestment Act, Washington Mutual had to lend a certain amount of
money to these groups. In 1998, Washington Mutual was in the middle
of a ten-year, $75 billion commitment to make loans to lower-income
groups and minority borrowers.

Tall conferred with Killinger, and the two had agreed that rather
than start up a subprime lending division at the bank, it would be much
easier to buy a subprime lender outright.

Tall soon realized that subprime lending companies were a lot different from the other banks Washington Mutual had bought. The executives all seemed shadier, and the accounting fishier. He came close to
signing a deal to buy a company in California called Aames Financial,
but he got a bad feeling. He had, by this time, learned to trust his instinct when making deals. (He had once decided how much to pay for
a bank by writing down several prices on a piece of paper and pulling
them out of a hat—the one he chose was the winning bid.) He backed
out of the Aames deal at the last minute, even though Washington Mutual's board of directors had already approved it. "There were just too
many parts that didn't feel right," he said later.

That was when Tall discovered Long Beach, headquartered just
outside Los Angeles among the rows of strip malls and crisscrossing
freeways. Disneyland was less than 10 minutes away. Long Beach had
72 offices across the country and was profitable. It was also growing
rapidly. In 1998, its parent company, Long Beach Financial, had funded
$2.6 billion worth of mortgages, nearly $1 billion more than the previous year.[3] Long Beach, like other subprime lenders, wanted to expand
but found it hard to raise capital to do so. Selling was the next best option.

As soon as Tall raised the possibility of buying Long Beach at the
executive retreat, Lee Lannoye objected. Lannoye had sat on Washington Mutual's executive team through most of the 1990s and headed up

several divisions at the bank, including corporate property management. More recently he had spent months on the merger of Great Western. He had laid off the executive chef and shuttered hundreds of thousands of square feet of office space in Southern California. He had overseen the sale of the Jaguars and the Cadillacs that Great Western executives used to drive around Los Angeles, and he had helped negotiate John Maher's severance contract. Maher had asked for extra trips on the bank's corporate jets so he could fly up north to the Bohemian Grove, an upscale, invitation-only men's club located on the Russian River in northern California, or down south to the exclusive PGA West golf club near Palm Springs. Maher was fond of the Wild West and his entire office had been decorated with John Wayne–style art, which he was allowed to take with him when he left.

Lannoye had a major problem with Long Beach Mortgage, which he now voiced to the other executives sitting around the conference room table. He believed that acquiring Long Beach would turn Washington Mutual into a predatory lender. If subprime loans were more profitable, wouldn't there be a misguided incentive to keep making those loans over others? And if that happened, wouldn't borrowers who could have qualified for a regular loan get stuck with a subprime loan instead? Such borrowers would end up paying a higher interest rate and more money than was necessary. It didn't seem like the "Friend of the Family" thing to do. While Washington Mutual had adopted a different marketing campaign by this time, many of its customers and shareholders still remembered the popular slogan. "Minority borrowers with good credit might be charged higher rates," Lannoye argued. The Department of Justice had just accused Long Beach of this very practice: charging higher mortgage rates to minorities. The case had been settled for $4 million.[4] Lannoye was so opposed to the Long Beach purchase, and so vocal in his opposition, that executives dropped the subject before any further discussion ensued.

Several months later, at another all-day executive retreat, Tall brought it up again. Again, Lannoye shot down the idea. He wasn't the only one who had qualms. Liane Wilson didn't think the purchase fitted in with Washington Mutual's long-term plan. Fay Chapman also was concerned. So far, she had voted no on a Long Beach acquisition.

A disciple of Lou Pepper, she lost sleep over any business decision that might be too risky. "Fay has always had a healthy skepticism about any endeavor," said one executive later. Chapman has short, wispy hair, and a comforting smile, but her expression can turn pointed if she harbors doubt about something someone is telling her. But Chapman also believes that subprime loans play an important societal role. When she was thirteen, her parents had moved from the town of Gilroy ("Garlic Capital of the World") to the coast of central California—and struggled to find financing on a new house they wanted to buy. Her father was an engineer, but the bank considered him too old to get a loan and he didn't make enough money. Her mother was a stay-at-home mom. Her family eventually bought the house through the unusual practice of seller financing, in which the seller of the home acts as the bank, and the buyer makes monthly payments. This was long before subprime lenders even existed. "There are people who borrow from these types of companies and they're not bad people, they're just poor," Chapman said later. "How are they going to get on the rising escalator of home prices?" She added: "Some of my closest friends would disagree with me on this."

Craig Chapman finally convinced her, the last time the executives discussed the Long Beach purchase at a meeting in 1999. Craig Chapman, who is not related to Fay Chapman, comes from a similar hardscrabble background. He grew up in a large, blue-collar family in upstate New York. Fay Chapman didn't always agree with him. He was a salesman and she a lawyer, but they had common childhoods. "As he and I used to say, 'We grew up with the people who took out these kinds of loans,'" Fay Chapman said. Craig Chapman had spent seventeen years working at Household Finance Corp., one of the largest subprime consumer lenders nationwide. Tall had hired him to run a Washington Mutual subsidiary based in Florida called Aristar, which the bank had inherited from Great Western. Aristar was a smaller version of Household Finance. The division made consumer loans with high interest rates to borrowers who couldn't afford the several hundred dollars to buy a refrigerator or a television. It was, essentially, a hard money lender. At one point, a significant number of the loans at Aristar were collateralized by guns. Before Craig Chapman took over, Aristar had been floundering. Moody's Investors Service had downgraded the company, expressing concern over its "uncertain strategic direction" and "a diminishing position in the extremely competitive consumer finance industry."[5] Craig Chapman now ran the division successfully. He made sure that loans met a high standard.

At the executive team's regular Monday meeting, Craig Chapman gave a presentation, running through the operational details of a Long Beach purchase. If Washington Mutual bought Long Beach, Craig Chapman would be in charge of it. The executives sat around the boardroom table, with their own individual take-out lunches in front of them. (The general attitude: Why should our shareholders pay for our lunch?) By this time, in mid-1999, the price for Long Beach had tumbled as the subprime industry had crashed. A debt crisis in Russia had squeezed the secondary market for subprime loans, forcing many of the lenders out of business. Another change: Lee Lannoye, the most vocal opponent of the purchase, no longer worked at the bank. He had been forced into retirement by Killinger as part of a company reorganization.

Craig Chapman, in his presentation, assured the group that Long Beach Mortgage would remain small, making up just a fraction of Washington Mutual's overall loan portfolio. He would look after the company closely, just as he did with his hard money lender, Aristar. After all, Aristar was much larger than Long Beach, and it hadn't faced any serious problems. "The point was, 'Okay, this is just another line of business,'" recalled Fay Chapman later.

Killinger had remained quiet about Long Beach, but he supported the idea of buying a subprime company and ultimately favored purchasing it. He typically didn't voice his opinion until the end of a discussion, preferring to let everyone else slug it out, listening carefully, and making a decision only if the group didn't reach consensus. If the discussion was about an acquisition, he also wanted to see the research on the company before he made up his mind. He was not a spontaneous decision maker. During the Ahmanson acquisition, the negotiations over the price of the company had escalated, with the Ahmanson executives driving for more money than Killinger was willing to pay. Killinger, at the very last minute and under intense pressure, had had to decide on his own whether to pay the higher price. It was the kind of moment he avoided. "He was really agonizing over that decision," Lannoye said.

Once Killinger made a decision, he didn't want any crying about it. He didn't dwell on the past.

The executives, despite various misgivings, agreed at the meeting to buy Long Beach. The Washington Mutual board approved the $350 million deal. The bank announced it without fanfare.[6] Washington Mutual had just spent the last several years dazzling the country with its megapurchases. By comparison, this new company barely increased its size.

In the end, Fay Chapman supported the acquisition. For several years, she had no real occasion to regret her decision. Then she received that phone call.

Long Beach Mortgage had started out like Washington Mutual, as a small, plain vanilla bank. Its founder, a successful, self-made California developer named Roland Arnall, would later become an ambassador to the Netherlands, a well-known philanthropist, and a billionaire. But in 1979, he decided to open a bank. The bank would help bankroll his real estate deals.[7] He called it Long Beach Savings and Loan.[8]

For most of a decade, Long Beach operated no differently from any other thrift. It took customer deposits and made mortgages. In the late 1980s, Arnall and his management team discovered a critical gap among the companies providing financing to home buyers. Two types of customers needed home loans: those who could qualify for a normal mortgage and those who couldn't. Those who couldn't had no choice but to borrow from hard money lenders at high interest rates. Often they couldn't get a loan at all. A borrower went either to a hard money lender or to a bank. No option existed in between. To fill the gap, Long Beach started making subprime loans, referred to then as B paper loans, or loans to borrowers with poor credit. Lenders like Long Beach could charge a lower interest rate than hard money lenders, because Wall Street firms bought the mortgages to securitize into bonds and sell to their own investors in a new secondary market.

The culture at Long Beach started to change as soon as the executive team began hiring salespeople by the dozens. Many of the existing employees found these new people to be louder, more brazen, and generally more aggressive than everyone else. "It was like going from

Nordstrom to the ninety-nine-cent store," said one former employee later. The bank's profits exploded, reaching $14.1 million in 1989 from $2.8 million just a year earlier.[9]

Long Beach was among the first to start making subprime loans, but larger banks soon followed. The competition for prime loans had grown, making it hard for banks to make as much money on them. Within several years, subprime loans made up 5 percent of all new mortgages nationwide, or $38.5 billion. By the late 1990s, that number had grown to $140 billion, or 10 percent of all new loans.[10] The new subprime companies found fertile territory in Southern California among largely minority neighborhoods. A lot of residents were immigrants with no credit history and low-paying jobs. Others just couldn't qualify for a normal mortgage because housing prices were so high.

Subprime loans suffered criticism, and warnings of fraud, but they also filled a government-mandated need. Minority borrowers could qualify for them, and minority homeownership rates had become the big issue of the day. Banks that avoided lending to minorities could be accused of "redlining," knowingly depriving them of services. "In those days, everyone was saying, 'Why aren't you lending in the inner city?'" said one former Long Beach executive. "If you didn't, you were redlining." In 1995, the Clinton administration rolled out an ambitious plan to boost homeownership from 64 percent to 67.5 percent, adding 8 million new homeowners within five years. President Bill Clinton announced this plan flanked by a young couple who had just purchased their first home but had struggled to get financing. "This is a big deal," the president said at the announcement. "This is about more than money and sticks and boards and windows; this is about the way we live as a people and the kind of society we're going to have."[11] Fannie Mae and Freddie Mac, the giant government-sponsored entities that purchased the bulk of mortgages from banks, announced that they would ease up credit requirements. The Clinton administration was pressuring the agencies to make loans to minority and low-income borrowers at a time when lenders wanted to make more subprime loans.[12]

By the mid-1990s, Arnall found himself in the middle of an expensive divorce. Already he had turned Long Beach Savings and Loan into a mortgage company, abandoning its thrift charter and the oversight of

the federal Office of Thrift Supervision. He pulled his executives together and told them that he planned to sell a portion of Long Beach—
the wholesale division—to help fund the proceedings. In the wholesale
division, Arnall's subprime salespeople, known as account executives,
didn't actually deal with customers. Their job was to find loans to fund
from independent mortgage brokers scattered across the country. A
customer visited a broker, and the broker found the best mortgage rate
from any number of lenders, including Long Beach. A Long Beach account executive, meanwhile, tried to make sure the broker sold him the
loan. The account executives did this by offering the most money back
in return for the loan (which the brokers didn't have to disclose to their
customers) as well as using old-fashioned sales tactics: cold calling, repeatedly and persistently, brokers in their territories. Brokers would also
call the Long Beach salespeople and let them know what sort of mortgages they had available, rattling off statistics like menu items: "I have
a single woman, FICO score 620, no money down . . ." Long Beach's
wholesale division could accumulate millions of dollars of loans without
ever talking to a borrower, a big difference from the retail lending that
Washington Mutual was known for.

Long Beach Financial spun off from its parent company and went
public, raising $162 million from investors.[13] Arnall continued running
the other private company, building it into another subprime business
called Ameriquest Mortgage. Despite problems in the industry, Long
Beach had made $30 million in 1998, up 20 percent from the year
before and up 200 percent from the year before that. On paper, nothing about Long Beach seemed particularly unusual. The company had
a batch of bad loans from customers who had defaulted or gone into
foreclosure, but every bank, and particularly subprime lenders, recorded
bad loans every year. Long Beach's volume wasn't unusual. In its annual
reports, the company reported strict guidelines for making mortgages.
Those guidelines limited how much borrowers could leverage themselves. The company wouldn't allow loans with a higher loan-to-value
ratio than 85 percent; this meant that customers had to have at least
15 percent of their own money (or equity in their homes, or a second
mortgage) in the transaction. They also couldn't borrow more than
$500,000. Long Beach forced borrowers with the worst credit histories

to put more money in up front and also charged them higher interest rates.[14]

Soon after the acquisition, Long Beach employees discovered that Washington Mutual executives weren't sure what to do with their company. They took Long Beach private. They planned to keep Long Beach's managers. The division started losing money, in large part because interest rates rose nationally, whittling away the profit it could make on each loan. Craig Chapman flew down to California to meet with the Long Beach managers and asked them what they planned to do to make the company profitable again. He wanted them to ratchet back costs to save money. The managers had another idea. "We want to increase volume," they told him. Chapman didn't agree with the strategy. Shortly afterward most of the managers quit or were fired. The division was meshed together with Aristar and, from the employees' perspective, left alone. Chapman was in Florida, and he was also running Washington Mutual's commercial division. The bank's main regulator, the federal Office of Thrift Supervision, wasn't tasked with Long Beach's oversight. Since Washington Mutual made Long Beach a subsidiary of its holding company, the state of California was supposed to regulate it. Most subprime companies avoided federal oversight, as they weren't considered part of banks.[15] "I think they forgot that they bought us," one Long Beach employee later said.

Eventually, the bank did take over one part of Long Beach: the servicing division, which dealt with the borrowers. The executives made the move to cut costs but soon realized their flawed thinking. Subprime borrowers are not regular borrowers. They need reminders to pay their mortgage every month. If they are late, they have to be called right away, not thirty days later. Long Beach Mortgage had a long room packed full of customer service representatives whose sole job was to call Long Beach customers. The calls started at 6:00 every morning and rolled throughout the day, into the evening, and on weekends. "On the day you get your loan, you get a welcome call from the person who's going to be your collector," said a lawyer working on Long Beach's securitizations. "Three days after you miss a payment, you get another call." Lumped together with the borrowers who regularly paid their mortgage on time, Long Beach borrowers got lost in the shuffle.

Still, Long Beach continued much as it had for the last decade. Its hundreds of account executives fanned out across the country, finding mortgage brokers to funnel millions of dollars in subprime loans. The account executives funded loans on the basis of guidelines they received from Washington Mutual's headquarters. The guidelines weren't much different from what they were before. They dictated how much money borrowers had to have at closing or how high their credit score had to be to qualify. If a loan from a broker didn't meet these guidelines, Long Beach account executives weren't allowed to fund it. A mortgage broker might ask for an exception on a loan that didn't fit the guidelines.

Then the guidelines at Long Beach started to loosen. Washington Mutual had become the country's largest savings and loan bank. Killinger, who believed the bank should be the best at any business line it entered, now wanted Washington Mutual to become the biggest mortgage lender nationwide. He announced bold plans to grab 20 percent of the nationwide mortgage market share, more than four times the amount Washington Mutual had held in 2000.

At about the time when he started talking about this goal, Killinger also changed the company structure, though this change was barely mentioned in one of the company's financial filings. He divided Washington Mutual into three different units, or silos, making each silo its own autonomous business. The president of each silo was now responsible for how it performed. Killinger had moved much of the power of the company from a centralized group of people at the bank's helm—his longtime executive team—to the division heads. While some of those people remained in leadership positions, the new structure effectively wiped out the cohesion of the team, long a factor in Washington Mutual's success. Increasingly, the Home Loans Group became the voice in Killinger's ear, dictating the direction of the company.*

Craig Davis, who had a long career in the mortgage industry, was in charge of that division. Killinger had kept him on board after WaMu's acquisition of American Savings Bank in California. The decision to keep Davis, along with many of his direct reports, was controversial

---

*Washington Mutual's mortgage division was renamed several times over the years, but it's referred to by its final name, the Home Loans Group, throughout this book.

among Washington Mutual's executive team and senior managers. The bank almost never kept executives from other companies. As a result, Davis found the reception at WaMu chilly. He took over a mortgage division that was an afterthought at a company focused primarily on its retail branches. That changed. Davis was a skilled, driven salesman, and he took over the Home Loans Group, to the exclusion of almost everyone else. "Our goal is clearly to be the nation's number-one home lender," Davis declared at a 2001 event, echoing Killinger's goal. Washington Mutual rolled out a new advertising campaign called "The Power of Yes." It was initially meant as a reference to the many services the bank offered its customers, and the message was clear: Washington Mutual would issue a mortgage much faster than any other lender, with approval almost certainly guaranteed. A new commercial showed a quirky borrower named Paul who was having a bad day until he got approved for a home loan at Washington Mutual. After that nothing irked him, not a giant pot of scalding hot coffee spilled on top of him and not a bowling ball smashed into his groin. "The uncertainty of getting a home loan made Paul irritable," the voiceover on the commercial boomed. "Then he went to Washington Mutual. Thanks to their flexible lending rules, Paul got a quick approval. Now he's always in a great mood."[16] Another commercial showed a man digging through a pile of garbage, trying to find an old pay stub to prove his creditworthiness. "WaMu can make getting a mortgage easier," the voiceover explained. "The Power of Yes" then crossed the screen.[17]

With Davis at the helm of the Home Loans Group, "everything was a lot more Hollywood," said one loan consultant. Indeed, the "Power of Yes" campaign premiered at the Academy Awards. At the division's annual sales meeting, known as President's Club, Davis and his team flew in actors to a renovated sugar refinery on the island of Kauai, where they performed *The Rocky Horror Picture Show*. They required Washington Mutual employees to dress up and sing along. The group decorated a large convention center in Atlanta to look like the inside of a revival tent, complete with massive speakers and two giant video screens. They flew in a gospel choir from Los Angeles to play in between speeches. The choir, swaying back and forth onstage, sang, "Let me feel the power, 'The Power of Yes,'" to the tune of Aretha Franklin's song "Spirit in the Dark." Meanwhile, an "evangelist" in a white suit strode back and forth among the crowd of 1,500 Washington Mutual salespeople who had flown in from the eastern half of the United States. The "evangelist" carried a microphone and praised the bank's mortgage products. He would lean back, look up, and shout, "WaMu-lujah!"[18] Noted one Washington Mutual executive who worked with him: "The only thing Craig liked better than sales was planning the next party."

In just one year, between 2000 and 2001, the number of single-family mortgages WaMu made tripled, reaching $155 *billion*. The bank had amassed a servicing portfolio of $500 billion in home loans across the country. It wasn't the largest lender yet, but it was getting close.

Inside Long Beach Mortgage, competition to make more subprime loans intensified. The loan-to-value ratio increased, reaching 90 percent or sometimes 95 percent, which meant a person with terrible credit could buy a house with only 5 percent of his own money involved. Usually the borrowers weren't even putting money down; they were just refinancing repeatedly, sucking the equity out of their homes with each new loan they took out. Long Beach account executives started making more "stated income" loans, in which borrowers had only to tell the account executive what they made, with no proof. Stated income loans (which also were called NINA loans, for "No Income, No Assets") weren't a new invention. They had been used sparingly, usually for the self-employed and those without a consistent pay record.

Many subprime borrowers, including those who had loans through Long Beach, got a "hybrid adjustable-rate loan." They took out either a 3/27 (a loan with a fixed interest rate that adjusted after three years and kept adjusting every six months for 27 years after that) or a 2/28 (essentially the same product, but instead of adjusting after three years, it adjusted after two and kept adjusting for 28 years).[19] The rates adjusted higher, but homeowners could refinance. Home prices were rising rapidly, at the rate of about 10 percent a year nationwide. In several of the southern cities where Long Beach made loans, homes appreciated as much as 16 percent a year.

Everyone at Long Beach was well compensated for the loans he or she made. The higher the volume, the higher the pay. If an account executive made a handful of mortgages worth about $800,000, he would make $3,200, or 0.4 percent of that amount. But if he brought in $5 million, he would collect $30,000, or 0.6 percent, plus an additional $30 for every loan.[20] (WaMu intended that last, smaller amount to cover expenses for account executives, like cell phone bills and client lunches.) Some account executives funded $5 million in a single month, the equivalent of, say, 10 houses. Others funded upward of $20 million a month, the size of entire neighborhoods.

Long Beach wasn't unusual. Salespeople in the business got paid well for making subprime loans, double or sometimes triple the amount that they got paid if they made a prime loan, because the demand for sub-primes on Wall Street was so high. Salespeople slipped their own managers (who didn't make large commissions) under-the-table bonuses for pushing their loans through the system. The managers, in turn, came to expect those additional payments. If they didn't receive these bonuses each month, they complained. "They would say, 'How am I going to make my car payment?'" recalled one account manager at Long Beach. "You basically had to do it." Some managers weren't comfortable with this under-the-table pay structure, which meant they lost the best sales-people and, thus, more money. One manager at a Long Beach office in Southern California went so far as to refuse to push through a sales-person's loans after that particular account executive stopped making the under-the-table payments, blackmailing the salesperson into paying him. Many of the salespeople drove Porsches and Mercedes and lived in gated communities perched high among the foothills of Los Angeles County. Their houses overlooked the smoggy city and the worn neigh-borhoods where they made loans.

The mortgage brokers, the people talking with the actual custom-ers, made money by selling mortgages to lenders like Long Beach, and again, the more they sold, the more money they made. Their own ranks had swelled in the last decade and a half from 7,000 independent of-fices nationwide in the late 1980s to 53,000.[21] They were everywhere: in strip malls sandwiched between nail salons and liquor stores, in office complexes that needed paint jobs, and sometimes in the living rooms of people's houses. The majority of all subprime loans across the country were made through these brokers. Local governments imposed little regulation. In California, a real estate agent could broker a loan without even applying for a separate license. As one loan officer put it: "Any Joe Blow could go out there and get a license."

The Long Beach sales team did not let Kerry Killinger down. By 2003, the subsidiary made $11 billion in loans, nearly four times the amount Long Beach had been making when Washington Mutual bought it.[22] Washington Mutual had become the fourth-largest wholesale lender of subprime loans nationwide. All the other subprime lenders had grown right along with it. New Century Financial, also based in Southern California, had become the country's largest wholesale subprime lender, with $24.5 billion in loans.* That amount was nine times the volume it had made only four years earlier.

In no time at all, Long Beach's mortgage applications looked unbelievable. Someone who was self-employed claimed to have $30,000 in the bank, but a call to the bank revealed he had only $15 in his account. Construction workers, teachers, and maids all somehow made thousands of dollars a month more than they should have. "Did I ever check to see if a maid was really making $6,000 a month?" said one Long Beach account executive later. "No." At other times a person's rent was listed as higher than it should have been, indicating an ability to pay a higher mortgage rate. The 5 on a FICO score had been changed to a 6. Fraud became commonplace, and not just at Long Beach. It had become so routine at subprime lenders that no one on the ground floor found it particularly surprising anymore. Some of the mortgage brokers kept templates on their desktops of bank statements that they could change, on their own, to fit a borrower's need. Borrowers, meanwhile, used Wite-Out to alter sections of their mortgage application if it had been denied. "Whatever you had to do to close a loan, that's what was done," a loan officer at Ameriquest told the *Los Angeles Times*.[23] "If you had to state somebody's income at $8,000 a month and they were a day-care provider, who's to say it wasn't?" Ameriquest, Roland Arnall's company, had grown to become the largest subprime lender in the country. But its loan officers falsified lending

---

*This ranking doesn't encompass all subprime loans; it covers just those made by wholesale lenders like Long Beach Mortgage.

documents, misled borrowers about the terms of their loans, and made up borrowers' income. "It was like a boiler room," said another loan officer at Ameriquest. "You produce, you make a lot of money. Or you move on. There's no real compassion or understanding of the position they're putting their customers in."

Many of the subprime borrowers weren't homeowners at all. They were house flippers who wanted to make money by buying real estate and selling it off, quickly. A salesperson at the subprime company Nova-Star recalled one customer who wanted to buy a second house, describing it as his primary residence. Even during those days of loose credit, many lenders shied away from investors. They were generally more likely to default, particularly if they already owned a home. To prove that he wasn't an investor, the customer told the NovaStar salesperson that he owned a junk-hauling business. He needed a big yard to park his junk-hauling truck. The customer's broker sent over an appraisal, showing an obviously doctored photo of a large truck, shrunk to fit in the garage of the house. "We turned it down," said the salesperson. "But 21st Century Mortgage did it."

In one case brought to Fay Chapman's attention, a Long Beach account executive in Los Angeles scheduled a closing with a borrower named Jose Flores. Flores, according to his mortgage application, was a fifty-six-year-old landscape gardener. When Washington Mutual ran the credit check on his Social Security number, it discovered that Flores was dead. "We said, 'Well, this is probably not going to happen,'" said Chapman. But two days later, the mortgage broker showed up at closing with a guy who looked to be in his twenties and introduced him as Jose Flores. "Excuse me," said one of Chapman's employees in the legal department who handled the file, "but we don't think this is the Jose Flores that applied for the loan. The Credit Bureau says that he's dead." "Well," replied the mortgage broker, "what do you need?" "We need some evidence," said Chapman's employee. "Why should we believe him?" The next day Jose Flores returned with evidence. He produced a sheet of notebook paper on which he scrawled: "I don't understand why the Credit Bureau thinks I'm dead. I'm right here. Jose Flores."

At Long Beach, the account executives had a name for that type of fraud. They called it "bad fraud," implying unbelievable fraud that wasn't executed well by the person involved. It wasn't always clear who had lied: the borrower, the broker, or the salesperson buying the loan from the broker. It didn't matter. "Whatever was out there, we just took it," said one Long Beach account executive.

When Jim Vanasek, Washington Mutual's chief risk officer, referred to subprime loans, he added wryly, "The world is a very dark and ugly place." Vanasek, who was in charge of making sure the bank didn't take too many risks, also hated "The Power of Yes." He hated it so much, in fact, that later, at an annual bank retreat, he made the unusual move of cautioning a room full of managers about careful lending. He waited until everyone was finished rallying about "The Power of Yes" and then told the crowd, "'The Power of Yes' absolutely needs to be balanced by the 'The Wisdom of No.'"[24] Killinger also believed in cautious underwriting. In the executive team's weekly morning coffee meetings, he warned that the bank should be careful about how it made loans. But he relayed this advice in a closed-door room to higher-level executives, who were more than a thousand miles away from the epicenter of subprime lending.

Long Beach account executives weren't stupid. Many of them knew they were making loans that borrowers had almost no chance of paying back. "I wouldn't lend some of these people money to buy a bicycle, never mind a house," said one account executive. Said another: "I don't think anyone was trying to screw anyone, we were all just trying to make money." And out there was this vague notion of Wall Street, and Wall Street wanted to buy these loans. "I thought they must know something I didn't," said the account executive. "They all have MBAs and PhDs, and I just thought there was some variable that I didn't get."

Long Beach off-loaded the loans in two ways. It packaged them up and turned them into securities with the help of an investment bank, or it sold off batches of whole loans to investors. In either scenario, WaMu scattered the mortgages across the world. They usually ended up in the portfolios of a pension fund or a hedge fund with its own set of investors.

To sell off the loans, Long Beach typically accumulated a group of mortgages and compiled their attributes. Did the homeowner have a fixed-rate or adjustable-rate mortgage? (It was usually adjustable—the

volume of adjustable-rate mortgages at Washington Mutual was growing substantially.) What was the borrower's credit score? How much
of a down payment did he make? The investment banks then fought
among each other to come up with the best deal structure, essentially
figuring out how they could chop up all the loans and reorganize
them into types of bonds that would bring in the most money from
investors. All the investment banks wanted to buy from Long Beach, as
subprime loans brought more money than did prime loans. Each deal
had different levels of risk called tranches; a security rated highly by
one of the rating agencies was theoretically the safest for the investor.
A lower-grade investment meant the risk was much higher, but so was
the return. Investors got paid when the homeowner made loan payments. Back then, few people worried about what would happen if a
homeowner didn't make payments. They worried that the homeowner
would refinance, paying off the loan too soon. To make sure that didn't
happen, lenders sometimes charged borrowers a prepayment penalty.

Long Beach, like every lender that turned its loans into securities,
had to attach representations and warranties to each deal, documentation assuring everyone involved that it had packaged the bond with the
types of loans it had promised. If the loans weren't what Long Beach
had promised, investors could force Long Beach to buy them back.
Long Beach employees in the lender's tiny capital markets division flew
around the world, meeting with the investors who would ultimately
own the bonds to sell off the securities. As part of those presentations,
Long Beach went over its process for making loans and also relayed its
guidelines. But it was unusual for anyone sitting in those meetings to
look at an actual Long Beach mortgage file or talk to a real borrower.
Investors based decisions on statistics and on grades given by the rating
agencies.

In the two years after Washington Mutual bought Long Beach, the
bond deals rolling out of the subprime lender and into the hands of
investors weren't particularly large. They ranged in value from about
$400 million to $700 million, and Long Beach offered one every quarter. Then the demand from Wall Street grew. "It took off like a freight
train," recalled one lawyer who worked on Long Beach's securities. The
investment banks dictated the market, and their investors had little

interest in buying 30-year fixed-rate loans. The Long Beach deals grew larger and came together about once a month. Long Beach's subprime loans became so popular that the company frequently committed to selling off millions of dollars of mortgages before the homeowner had signed any paperwork. That expectation, which was communicated to the Long Beach account executives, only increased the sales frenzy. The entire market for mortgage-backed securities took off, surpassing $1.8 *trillion* in 2002, an increase of more than 200 percent in just two years.[25] Long Beach soon funneled mortgages into the largest subprime security deal the market had seen so far, a $4.1 billion bond that catapulted the problems of all the mortgages Long Beach had been making into the hands of someone else. This system spread risk: if one homeowner defaulted, it wouldn't affect an investor holding a security made up of hundreds of mortgages. Washington Mutual earned $1.4 billion selling its mortgages, an increase of $400 million in just one year.

The call from Fay Chapman's employee working on the securities came in the summer of 2003, as Long Beach's factory churned out more bonds. Chapman, by her own description, is not wired the way everyone else is. She is mildly dyslexic, as are several members of her family, although she didn't discover her dyslexia until she was older and one of her daughters was diagnosed. She is the kind of person who can look at a picture of a box and then, with no trouble, identify from several choices exactly how that box would look if someone flattened it. "People who think normally have a hard time with it," she said. She had once taken a job at a Mercedes-Benz dealership where her boss gave her the menial task of sorting car parts. All the tiny pieces of the car came with different serial numbers that had to be organized. Chapman loved it. "It made sense to me," she said. She considered staying on at the dealership but turned to a career in law instead. She was a strong advocate of her legal team at Washington Mutual, a role she continued to play even after she left the bank. Her staff felt comfortable confiding in her.

After the call, Chapman sat in a meeting with Killinger, Craig Davis, and Davis's deputy, Tony Meola. By this time, Killinger had moved Long Beach from under Craig Chapman's direction to Craig Davis's oversight in the Home Loans Group. Because Long Beach was a lender, it made sense to place it under Davis's control. The division had already been having problems when Davis took it over a year earlier. Rumors had bubbled up to WaMu's headquarters about loan fraud in the small subsidiary. Although Fay Chapman didn't know it, Long Beach's securitizations over the last three years ranked among the worst-performing deals in the country.

In Washington Mutual's executive conference room, once the door closed, Chapman did not mince words. "I want to shut down the Long Beach securitizations," she said.

She told the group about the concerns of the other lawyers on her team. She recounted the issues they had seen with the securities, and how she didn't think the mortgages met the standards advertised to investors. Long Beach, Chapman said, might not be accurately portraying what it sold.

Right away Davis and Meola promised to take care of any problems. "We'll fix it," they assured her.

Chapman wasn't convinced. "I want to see for myself that it's fixed," she said. She didn't trust Davis and Meola to take care of the problem. ("I definitely made it confrontational," she said, later.)

If Long Beach were closed, however briefly, it would cost the company a lot of money, Davis and Meola argued. "You can't shut us down."

Chapman listened with frustration. "Look," she said. "We are not going to do any Long Beach securitizations until I'm satisfied the sales documents are true."

Davis and Meola resisted. They did not want Long Beach shut down. They would fix the problem.

Chapman could take it no longer. "We're not going to do it, we're just not!" she screamed.

At this point, Killinger, who had stayed silent through the discussion, interjected. "That's it, guys," he said. "We're not going to do anything more until Fay is satisfied." Chapman was mildly surprised and also gratified. But she was still worked up. She got up and left the room.

Immediately, Chapman launched a review of Long Beach's loans. In Southern California, she assembled a team of Washington Mutual appraisers, lawyers, and three different contracting companies, a total of about a hundred people. The team rented out two large conference rooms at a hotel blocks away from Long Beach's headquarters. They rented an additional ten rooms at the same hotel, just to store all the loan files. A moving truck hauled dozens of boxes from Long Beach's offices to the hotel, driving back and forth across a busy intersection and down a quiet side street until 2,200 boxes were spread across the ten rooms. The team rifled through thousands of loan files, ten hours a day for the next three months. Each evening the legal head of the investigation FedExed a CD of the day's results back to Seattle. What the team found was astonishing.

A homeowner's loan file was a mess of paperwork that often fell apart at the mere touch, papers flying free across the carpeted hotel room floor. Some files were missing crucial pieces of information like an income statement, or they contained information that shouldn't have been there at all, like the deed of trust, which should have been filed with the local government. Page two of someone's loan paperwork was in another person's file, and that person's file was missing pages four and six. Only half of the 22,000 loan files had been scanned into a computer. The remainder existed in paper form only. For each mortgage, Long Beach representatives should have gone through a checklist, making sure everything about the home had been recorded: Had someone checked the property to make sure the bathroom worked? Had the house had an appraisal? "These properties are all sorts of crap; some of them are mobile homes parked in a neighbor's backyard," Chapman said later. "No one was making sure the conditions had been met." Long Beach employees, it turned out, had been writing mortgages the way they might scribble a grocery store list.

By the end of three long months, Chapman's team had reviewed 4,000 mortgages from Long Beach. Of those, only 950 were deemed good enough to be sold to outside investors.[26] The rest were basically garbage. Even more troubling, several hundred loans had so much paperwork missing that Long Beach wouldn't have been able to foreclose on a borrower in default. It wasn't even clear who owned the mortgages anymore. While the issue of mortgage ownership would years later become a massive nationwide problem, it had so far received no attention. The early Long Beach problems were unreported and went unnoticed by the public.

Chapman's whole review process had been a huge hassle to Long Beach's account executives. They couldn't push loans as quickly. Their files had been taken and volume decreased, eating away at their salaries. "They were incensed," said one of the reviewers. "They didn't understand why they had been shut down." The pipeline transferring securities to investors backed up to the tune of about $1 billion a month while the review continued.

After Chapman's team finished, she and Craig Chapman set up what amounted to a war room for Long Beach at Washington Mutual's headquarters in Seattle. Killinger transferred Long Beach back under the control of Craig Chapman, who had, by this time, moved to Seattle. Aristar, the hard money lending division he had been heading up, had been sold. The two Chapmans appointed managers for each of Long Beach's lending areas across the country. Every day, at 2:00 p.m., everyone would gather in the war room in Seattle and listen as each manager, by teleconference, reported on the loan problems for the day. Every single loan moving out of Long Beach was reviewed, and every mistake identified. The legal team held each mortgage to a checklist. They wouldn't approve it unless each file included everything on that list. Craig Chapman compiled all the errors and frequently presented them to Washington Mutual's board of directors.

Each team of account executives at Long Beach received its own underwriter, a move designed to add more oversight. The under-the-table commissions stopped, briefly. Some account executives still tried to push through bad loans, but those files didn't make it past the war room. The securities rolling out of Long Beach received passing grades; they were sold again. For two years, they performed no worse than anything else on the market—they were not great, but not terrible either.

Long Beach had grown larger than Washington Mutual had planned, but it still represented only a small part of an enormous bank. And now, in late 2003, the division was under control.

Chapter Four

ALEXANDER
THE GREAT

This is a company that does not make major mistakes.
—Kerry Killinger

In June 1999, Kerry Killinger turned fifty. Debbie threw an elaborate surprise birthday party for the occasion, after carefully saving money outside the family's strict budget over the preceding years. She rented a conference center on Seattle's waterfront and hired an ad agency to create a jingle that she burned onto CDs titled "Kerry Killinger Unplugged," which served as the party invitations. The two-minute jingle had a catchy, oft-repeated chorus: "Kerry is fifty, Kerry is fifty, Kerry's big, big, big, big fifty!" She invited 250 people, including the Washington Mutual board members and executives, dozens of other high-level managers at the bank, and prominent city and business officials. "Don't dress up, just come on and get down," the jingle instructed them.

The guests streamed into a banquet hall lined by life-size cardboard cutouts of Killinger's likeness. The multiple Killingers wore light shirts and ties and smiled at the guests from behind oversize wire-rimmed glasses. Guests received Killinger pins. If the pin tilted one way, it showed a smiley face; in the other direction, the picture showed Killinger's face scrunched into an unflattering but funny expression. You couldn't tell from looking at it, but Killinger had been using a weed eater when the picture was taken.

To lure her husband to the surprise event, Debbie told him they were attending a party honoring someone else. She had hung fake signs announcing that person's celebration all around the conference center. When Killinger walked into the darkened banquet hall to the chorus of people shouting "Surprise," he was completely surprised. Food stations scattered across the room offered beef and fish and sushi. The outside deck featured a cigar bar. A long white sheet cake with raspberry filling was decorated with gilded gold edging and a large frosting bow. On stage, an MC introduced the Spinners, a popular soul band that played into the night as guests danced. Waiters wore neon glow-in-the dark necklaces and glasses. Debbie called Washington Mutual's executive team onto the stage. In unison, they serenaded Killinger with the jingle featured in the invitations: "Kerry is fifty, Kerry is fifty, Kerry's big, big, big, big fifty!" Everyone laughed and clapped along. An overwhelmed Killinger smiled and appeared to be having a good time.

Not long afterward Killinger called Liane Wilson into his office. Wilson had been at the party—she had worn a backward hat and the Kerry Killinger weed-eater pin and had belted out the jingle on stage. Killinger asked her an uncharacteristic question: What should he do if he was having trouble at home? The question surprised Wilson. It was typical of Killinger to ask other executives for advice, but it was uncommon for him to reveal anything personal. Wilson herself had been divorced, so she had some perspective on marital problems. Still, she stumbled to answer. Everyone at the bank knew and liked Debbie. In a way, everyone felt loyal to her. Many of the executives believed she helped keep Killinger grounded. She was not enamored of the lifestyle that is afforded a CEO's wife—she rarely visited Killinger at the office, and she didn't particularly like to travel with him on business. She preferred sweats and a T-shirt to the dressy clothing required at events that she often had to attend. Usually she compromised with loose-flowing black pants and a black shirt. She fulfilled her role for the good of Killinger's career and the bank. She and Killinger had been married for thirty-one years. In those three decades, she had missed only two of the dozens of events that required her presence. Since she had never had a career and her two sons had long since grown up and left home, her life was Washington Mutual, just as Killinger's life was Washington Mutual. Each day she waved to him from the front door of their house as he left home. Each evening when he wasn't away on business, she waited for him to return.

Wilson thought about Killinger's question for a moment. Then she told him, "Kerry, you have to do what makes you happy." She wasn't sure if it was the best advice, but she believed it. She didn't know what problems Killinger faced, nor did he tell her. Some of the executives thought that Killinger and Debbie were drifting apart. He was always gone on business. He also seemed to care more about accessories that didn't interest his wife. He mentioned wanting to buy a second house, possibly on the water, and a boat. He started carrying business leadership books around the office. "What do you think a real company would do in this situation?" he would ask the executives sometimes.

The trouble at home had started before his fiftieth birthday party. Debbie, inexplicably, got sick with several different problems, some of which her doctors couldn't diagnose. She had ulcers and couldn't eat. She lost forty pounds and slept all the time. She had a fever that would appear and persist. She kept making trips to the hospital for tests, until she had been there about twenty-five times. As Killinger worked long hours, she hired a car service to take her to the hospital.

Debbie drank on occasion, but she began to drink heavily as the unexplained health problems continued. As Christmas neared in 1999, she realized she needed help. She made an appointment at the Betty Ford Treatment Center in the desert of Southern California and spent twenty-eight days getting treatment. During that time, Killinger visited once. He stopped returning her calls.

When she arrived back home in February 2000, after the hired car picked her up at the airport, she knew something was wrong. "I wasn't going to tell you the night you got home," ventured the man who had scrawled long notes of admiration in her high school yearbook. He told her he wanted a divorce. Debbie left the house and walked around the block. When she got back, Killinger made her promise not to say anything. He didn't want to tell anyone until after the annual shareholder meeting. He didn't want the news affecting Washington Mutual's stock price.

The shareholder meetings were Killinger's chance to impress. Once a year for an entire decade, he stood in front of the growing crowd of attendees to relay the news of the previous year's stunning growth. Killinger cared so much about Washington Mutual's stock that he later had the bank's quarterly performance printed out and framed in the bank's conference room. He hung a copy in his office. Some of the executives later joked that he slept with a printout under his pillow. Killinger liked to remind people that Washington Mutual's stock had delivered greater returns than the S&P 500. In 2000, Washington Mutual would report record earnings of $1.8 billion and asset growth of more than 760 percent in four years. The few complaints at the annual shareholder meetings involved food and beverages. Once, one of the shareholders wondered why the bank didn't serve coffee before the meeting instead of after it ended.

That April Debbie sat through the meeting, as well as the dinner with the bank's board of directors at an upscale city club the night before. She usually planned the dinner, helping to organize a gift if one of the directors happened to be leaving. She knew who ate which foods and who didn't.

Two weeks later Killinger filed for divorce. Under "Allegation Regarding Marriage," the reason given was vague.[1] The divorce papers said simply: "This marriage is irretrievably broken." Debbie had asked if there was another woman involved. Killinger assured her there wasn't. "We are two different people," he told her. Killinger moved out of the family house and soon rented a three-bedroom condo, facing one of Seattle's more popular beaches. During the summer, during the precious few weeks a year when the sun appeared in Seattle, hundreds of residents and tourists descended on Alki Beach, Rollerblading and biking on the path in front of Killinger's new condo, eating clam chowder at the time-worn seafood bars down the road, and sunbathing on the sand. Once a year, a fraternity of men dressed as pirates sailed a stately tall ship decorated with skull and crossbones flags into the bay. The faux pirates would pretend to pillage the crowd, which had gathered to watch the annual tradition.

By January 2001, the Killingers' divorce was final.[2] The couple reported about $70 million in assets, including the value of stock and stock options, retirement plans, and bank balances. The money was spread across more than twenty different Washington Mutual accounts, with only several thousand dollars held at other banks. Debbie received about $37 million—more than half of the couple's wealth. She kept the house, the Mercedes, and a Jaguar Killinger had bought for her. The cars were worth $28,000. Killinger took the remainder of the money— $33.6 million—and a Lexus and an Acura, together valued at $38,000. From the house, Killinger took only his table saw, his motorcycle, and several WaMu mementos.

About eight months later Killinger married Linda Cottington, also a native of Iowa. He had met Cottington a couple of years earlier. Both were active members of the national Federal Home Loan Bank system. Killinger sat on numerous national and local boards, including America's Community Bankers, Alliance for Education, and Washington Roundtable. Cottington was trim, blond, and about nine months older than Killinger. She had been married to Tom Miller, Iowa's long-serving attorney general. Together the couple had one son, then a teenager. In addition to serving as vice chair of the board of the Federal Home Loan Bank of Des Moines, she had worked as a regional managing director of consulting for the national accounting firm Deloitte & Touche and served as a vice president of Mercy Hospital Network, based in Des Moines.

Debbie suspected that Killinger had been seeing Linda in the last few months of their marriage. Killinger, always a regular exerciser, had intensified his workouts. He pounded out miles on the StairMaster before he left for work. The rattling of the machine woke Debbie each morning. Sometimes he followed that up with a run on the treadmill. He lost weight. He started wearing more cologne. He sent furtive e-mails when he thought his wife wasn't paying attention. Phone records showed lengthy conversations to unknown phone numbers, which Debbie later discovered belonged to Linda. One of those conversations happened after a difficult family meeting about her drinking problem on Christmas in 1999.

Debbie found out everything she could about Linda, even hiring a private investigator. She kept this knowledge secret, even after the Killingers filed for divorce. She waited to confront him with it. A couple of months after the divorce was finalized and before Killinger remarried, he stopped by the house on his way to Europe. He was traveling with the Greater Seattle Chamber of Commerce, on whose board he sat. Killinger told Debbie that he planned to stay longer to meet up with someone he had met, a woman who was long divorced. Debbie asked her name. Killinger told her it was Linda but would not reveal her last name.

"It's too soon for that," he said.

"Is it Cottington?" Debbie asked.

Killinger stared at her. He showed no emotion whatsoever.

"Are you sure she's divorced? How's her son, Matt?" Debbie continued.

Killinger just kept staring at her.

Shortly after that conversation, in May 2001, a short article in the *Des Moines Register* announced Cottington's divorce.[3] The article said that Cottington would be moving to the West Coast to "accept a new position" but gave no further details. The article, quoting a statement released by Cottington and Miller, said that the two "continue to be good friends."

Killinger married Cottington on a beach in Hawaii on the day after Thanksgiving. The ceremony was small and private. On the following Valentine's Day, the new couple rented a richly decorated Spanish ballroom at a hotel in Seattle—with luxurious drapes framing long windows, and an ornate chandelier hanging from the 20-foot ceiling—and invited several hundred people for a black-tie reception. By this time, many Washington Mutual employees had met Linda. Killinger had brought her into the bank on the way to a Mariners baseball game on a summer afternoon. It was too soon for anyone to get to know her. But several employees and managers wondered whether a new wife might change Killinger or perhaps even distract him.

The bank purchases had not stopped. Killinger turned his attention to mortgage companies. In 2001, he spent about $16 billion and bought three of them: PNC Financial Services Group, Bank United, and Fleet Mortgage Corp. The three companies together boosted the pile of loans WaMu serviced nearly 400 percent, to $378 billion. By buying Bank

United, WaMu inherited 155 new branches in Texas. It had snapped up
the companies as interest rates dropped and homeowners rushed to refinance their mortgages. Washington Mutual was in the perfect position
to take advantage of the boom. The volume of refinancing at the bank
had jumped more than 500 percent during the year, and refinancing
would continue at a frenetic pace.[4]

Increasingly, Killinger had become intent on expanding to the
East Coast, home of the country's largest and most powerful financial
institutions. Washington Mutual had few branches east of the Mississippi River. Killinger studied the market and found that 28 percent of
customers in New York and parts of Connecticut and New Jersey were
ready to switch banks.[5] Those customers, said Killinger in a conference
call to analysts, found the service they received "fairly austere." In New
York, "people don't care about people—it's just about profits," Killinger
added. In early 2002, Killinger paid $5.2 billion for Dime Bancorp., a
savings bank with $28 billion in assets and 260 branches and loan of-
fices across New York. Washington Mutual took out giant billboards
in Times Square declaring, "The Power of Yes. Whatever your dream
home is, we have your loan." The billboards came with life-size cutouts
of houses. The bank decorated taxicabs—and Yankee Stadium—with
ads. Washington Mutual bought out Broadway's theaters for a day and
gave the seats to the city's teachers, many of whom later opened new accounts.[6] Quipped one New York hedge fund manager about Killinger:
"There are some who think he has a size complex."[7] Bankers thought
the concept behind Washington Mutual was strange. Free checking?
"We scratched our heads—how do they make money off of that?" one
New York banker later recalled. "Then we realized, 'Oh yeah, they're
doing it by charging overdraft fees.' That's like you book a room at the
motel that's cheap, and you find out the minibar is still expensive. Young
people and poor people love it. They started getting all these customers
and drove everyone to free checking."

Washington Mutual wasn't just expanding by buying companies
anymore. The bank had started a new initiative whereby it entered a
new city and opened several dozen branches all at once. These weren't
just any branches. Deanna Oppenheimer, one of Lou Pepper's hires
who was now in charge of WaMu's retail bank, came up with a concept

called Occasio. *Occasio* means "favorable opportunity" in Latin. The Occasio branches looked nothing at all like the branches of Pepper's generation. WaMu called them "bank stores." Inside the Occasio store, khaki-clad employees greeted customers from a "concierge" desk, directing them to what WaMu called a "teller tower." At the teller tower, WaMu employees carried touch screen devices and stood next to the customer as he deposited or withdrew money. At one end of the Occasio branches, which had been designed by the same company that built Disney's retail stores, was a play area for children called "WaMu kids." Cartoons played on repeat on a widescreen TV. The bank sold WaMu Action Teller Dolls, a line of Barbie-inspired dolls all wearing Washington Mutual gear and toting various accessories. For $19.95, customers could purchase the female African American teller, or the white male teller, wearing shiny brown loafers and a sweater vest emblazoned with a Washington Mutual logo. "How closely does Action Teller resemble a real bank service rep?" questioned *The Wall Street Journal* in a story about the dolls. "His box says he's a 'team player,' 'super friendly,' provides 'hours of fun' and is 'non-toxic.' You decide."

WaMu debuted its first Occasio branches in Las Vegas, where it opened five new locations. In the first few months, those branches opened twice as many checking accounts as usual, and twice the amount of deposits flowed into the "stores." "We had new customers waiting in line for our doors to open," Oppenheimer reported at the time. "It's the first time I'm aware of that a bank entering a new market received a reception like that."[8] WaMu opened 20 more in Las Vegas. In Phoenix, it opened 26 new branches, followed by 43 in Atlanta, 20 in Denver, and about 60 in Tampa, all by the end of 2002. This strategy was all part of Killinger's plan to open 250 stores annually in what he called "a fairly aggressive expansion period."[9] WaMu deemed those cities "fast-growing urban markets" where the bank had not been located previously. In Chicago, WaMu announced plans to open 70 stores within a year, paying little attention to critics who warned of the competiveness of Chicago's consumer banks. Killinger, undeterred, told analysts he planned to open as many as 150 branches in the Windy City over the next several years, although he acknowledged, "Chicago is a huge undertaking."[10]

At a financial services conference hosted by Lehman Brothers in 2003, Killinger laid out his grand vision for Washington Mutual.[11] He wanted to create a bank that would serve the average person, offering the best products to the middle class. "What we are is a retailer of consumer financial services, creating a whole new model that has never been seen in this industry," he told the crowd. "I think it's going to be comparable with what we saw when Wal-Mart redid the broad middle mass-market retailing and how they changed the whole world. I think it is going to mirror what Starbucks did in the coffee business, what Costco did in warehouse merchandising and what you are seeing with Home Depot."

He continued, as slides showing the bank's stellar performance flipped behind him: "Five years from now, if we've done our job correctly, we will have established the leading national franchise focused on the consumer. It is not a bank. It is not a thrift. It's not a mortgage company. It's an integrated financial services company going after the mass consumer market."

Killinger, with his aw-shucks demeanor and his five-year plans, had become America's favorite banker. Since he took over as WaMu's chief executive in 1990, his arrival on the banking scene in the 1990s, his popularity had only grown. In 2001, the national trade publication *American Banker* pronounced him "Banker of the Year," a title that had earlier gone to the famous financier Sanford "Sandy" Weill and would later (twice) go to Weill's protégé Jamie Dimon, the chief executive of JPMorgan Chase. "He's one of the more driven people I know," said one investment banker in the flattering profile that accompanied Killinger's award.[12] "He really wants to be a winner in the industry, but he doesn't come across as a grab-you-by-the-throat, or arrogant kind of guy." The article relayed: "Associates say that, though WaMu has changed a lot under Mr. Killinger, he has not. He has learned to delegate more, but he still relies on that inner circle of senior executives who for the most part started at WaMu when he did, and who now run many of its divisions." Lou Pepper, quoted in the article, said, "There's no ego in the man. He's just the same as when I first met him."

Few would describe Killinger without mentioning his ambition. He was "brash and ambitious" or "relentless, aggressive, analytical and ambitious—all with a winning personality."[13] "What he lacks in flair, Mr. Killinger more than makes up for in drive and ambition," wrote *The New York Times*.[14] Said one analyst, "Since he took over in 1990, his stock is the best-performing issue among banks and major thrifts. He has made a lot of people wealthy."[15] Said another: "Kerry Killinger's credibility on Wall Street is unquestioned."[16] One of the analysts likened him to an empire-building Greek king: "He's the Alexander the Great of the thrift industry."[17]

Washington Mutual's earnings topped $1 billion in the first quarter of 2003 for the first time in the company's 114-year-history, in large part because the bank was furiously making home loans.[18] Owners of the stock rejoiced. Their dividend rose to 30 cents a share. The bank, now the country's largest savings and loan, had amassed $268 billion in assets. It had more than 3,000 branches and ATMs and 50,000 employees. It ranked 94 on the Fortune 500 list, up from the 398th position six years earlier. "We are getting to a size where people are saying, 'God where did these guys come from?'" Killinger boasted to a *Forbes* reporter.[19] In another interview he claimed, "This is a company that does not make major mistakes. We do that by learning daily lessons."[20] WaMu took out a half-page ad in *The Wall Street Journal* touting its stock. The ad showed a cartoon of a woman putting on lipstick, with the message: While lipstick colors are mere fads, owning shares of WaMu will "look good on anyone."[21] Shortly after the ad ran, the bank's stock reached an all-time high of $45 a share.

The young investment analyst who had walked into Lou Pepper's office years ago began to disappear. Killinger dyed his hair darker and got corrective eye surgery. He no longer hid behind his oversize glasses. Debbie Killinger had always dressed him in blazers and suits, although not the overly expensive kind. Now Killinger, looking svelte, took to wearing sleeker, trendier clothing, much to the amusement of the other executives. "Are you on your way to the clubs?" Craig Tall joked when Killinger showed up at work one day wearing a black cashmere sweater.

Killinger, who had steadfastly refused to fly private planes, began to use them after all. The board of directors passed a resolution allowing it. If Killinger flew commercial, it would pose a security risk, the directors believed. Washington Mutual bought a five-year timeshare in three midsize business jets. Each plane cost $1 million during the life of the contract. Every month the bank paid an additional $14,000 for each of the planes, presumably for maintenance. Each time Killinger flew anywhere, it cost about $700 in fuel costs and about $2,500 each hour the plane spent in the air. It wasn't unusual for Washington Mutual to shell out a couple hundred thousand dollars each month in plane costs. The cost to the company was not detailed for shareholders. NetJets, the timeshare company WaMu used, described one of the planes, a Cessna Citation X, as "the world's fastest midsized business jet." It had a 24-foot cabin and large cushy seats, as well as a refreshment center stocked with sandwiches and drinks. This was hardly the picture of corporate excess; many executives at larger investment banks and finance companies traveled on much bigger planes. Often their companies owned these planes.

Killinger was oddly protective about Washington Mutual's leased jets. He didn't want other executives to use them. If others wanted access, they had to provide a clear reason why they couldn't fly commercial. Executives weren't sure whether Killinger felt this way because he worried about the cost or because he believed only the CEO should have the benefit of a private jet.

Whatever the reason, Killinger began using the planes frequently.

He embarked on a nationwide road show to hold "brand rallies" for Washington Mutual's tens of thousands of employees in various cities. He crisscrossed the United States, stopping in Stockton, California, Florence, South Carolina, and Jacksonville, Florida. He would eventually participate in more than fifty rallies in a dozen cities, hosting as many as three hour-long shows each day. He brought along an entourage: a new executive assistant hired to aid him on these trips and often his new wife, Linda. Linda and Killinger usually sat together at the front of the plane, talking quietly or laughing. Since his second marriage, Killinger seemed much more relaxed. His family had stopped worrying as much about his health. "Killinger was smitten," said a close business associate. "He was like a little kid."

Linda sometimes brought along Como, the couple's new Havanese, a fluffy white toy dog named after the northern Italian lake where the couple had vacationed. Como the dog and Linda were frequently by

Killinger's side, something WaMu executives and employees weren't used to. Killinger had initially seemed embarrassed about the purchase of a dog that could fit in a large handbag. Later he appeared to get over it. He told *Fortune*, "It's important for leaders to do whatever it takes to connect with their employees. For example, when I visit our financial centers, I'll have my wife with me and often we'll have our eight-pound dog, Como. It really breaks the ice because so many people have had experiences with pets."[22] Not everyone was fond of Killinger's pet. Said one investment banker who worked closely with him: "He always had that damn dog Como with him, which he treated like a child."

Killinger hosted the first brand rally in early 2002 outside Chicago, in Downers Grove, a small town located an hour and a half from the even smaller town where Lou Pepper had grown up. Hundreds of WaMu employees, now known internally as "WaMulians," poured into a conference center to hear Killinger speak.* (The WaMulians, incidentally, had a nickname for cash. They called it "wamoola.") Often they had just joined the bank from another that WaMu had acquired.

The presentation had been carefully choreographed. Killinger would walk on stage and pump up the audience with news of the company's strong financial position and enviable brand name. "Our story began all the way back in 1889," Killinger would tell the audience, "when WaMu was first established to help Seattle residents rebuild their homes after a huge fire wiped out a large part of the city." As he read from a prepared script, his voice boomed across the concert-style venue.

Behind him, an enormous slide showed the company's core values, little changed since Pepper's group framed them in 1987. He elaborated on the values (Fair, Caring, and Human) to include "Ethics, Respect, Teamwork, Innovation, Excellence." In Killinger's script, an italicized note under "Ethics" reminded him to "stress above all others." So Killinger told the crowd, "It's important that the highest degree of ethical standards be maintained throughout the company. The stakes are

---

*Washington Mutual was officially rebranded as "WaMu" in 2006, despite earlier market research that showed some customers didn't like the name. In California, customers thought "WaMu" sounded too much like "Shamu" the giant killer whale that lived at the Sea World amusement park in San Diego.

simply too high. The collapse of Worldcom; Enron; Arthur Anderson, combined with several recent high-profile CEO abuses, have all contributed to a $4 trillion loss in stock market value. I have developed a zero-tolerance policy toward any form of dishonest or otherwise unethical behavior in our organization—and on that point, there's no room for compromise." Killinger was defiantly ethical, sending off a check to Microsoft after the company tried to give him a free WebTV, a new product that connected a person's television to the Internet. "There's just right and wrong," Killinger said in a later interview.[23] "You just have to be centered about what the right thing is." He told *Fortune*: "Regarding ethics, I try to do the right thing and use the test of 'Am I comfortable with having my mother read this in tomorrow's newspaper?'"

At the brand rally, Killinger would tell employees about his aim to turn WaMu into a "category killer" like Disney or Wal-Mart or Southwest Airlines. "Look at these names," he said, as they flashed on the screen. "They're examples of what we call 'category killers,' that's to say, companies which have managed to set themselves apart from their industry competitors." Another slide came up, proclaiming: "You are the brand!" "It's not unrealistic," he told the audience, "to think the WaMu brand could become a category killer within a relatively short period of time. Look at what Starbucks was able to do in the beverage industry."

Employees applauded, but WaMu staff and consultants in attendance could tell the presentation was missing something. It overemphasized financial details, and Killinger himself seemed a little rusty, despite directions provided him on his script. "Romance the room," the script reminded him. Or: "Compare other financial services companies with WaMu (e.g., male-dominated; cold; arrogant; money-hungry; would kick the dog; versus warm, friendly people who you've invited over for a barbecue)." The sound system crackled with unknown problems.

Following his presentation, a pair of entertainers would take the stage, revving up attendees with skits and antics. The two men weren't WaMu employees, but everyone thought they were. They wore the trademark WaMu branch outfit: khaki pants and a collared T-shirt with the bank's logo. They imitated various famous performers—Elvis, Bob Dylan, John Denver—and crooned WaMu-themed songs.

"I think I did it again," sang one of them, wearing a blond wig and strumming a guitar in an imitation of Britney Spears and her hit song, "Oops, I Did It Again."

> *I made you believe we're more than a bank.*
> *Oh, baby*
> *We are worthy of trust*
> *But don't take ourselves too serious*
> *'Cause to be oh so human*
> *That is just what makes us WaMu*
> *Oh Kerry, Kerry.*

During "Who Wants to Be a WaMoolian-aire?" the entertainers shouted out questions to the audience, game-show-style, all related to the company's brand. One of the last questions: "Kerry Killinger has said *this* WaMu brand promise will last? A. Until we are a 'category killer.' B. As long as he's CEO. C. Thru [*sic*] WaMu's 200th anniversary. D. Forever." The correct answer was D., "Forever."

Somewhere between Irvine, California, and New York City, Kerry Killinger hit his stride. At a hotel conference center in Milwaukee, spotlights illuminating the stage, he stopped using his script. He spoke freely, using his hands for emphasis as he stood on the podium, smiling just as he would have smiled if he were speaking to someone he knew instead of a room full of several hundred employees. When the entertainers jokingly made fun of him after the performance, cameras panned the room and showed Killinger, standing off to one side of the stage, laughing just as hard as the audience. Back on stage, as part of the entertainment portion of the event, he waved his hands and yelled, "Yeah, baby!" in an imitation of Austin Powers. The crowd roared with laughter, some attendees wiping tears from their eyes.

During one late spring brand rally, held in a steaming conference room with no air conditioning in eastern California, an employee standing in the audience fainted in the middle of Killinger's speech. A murmur traveled through the crowd. On stage, Killinger could tell that something was wrong. He stopped talking as other employees gathered around the woman, who had woken up and appeared to be fine. The song "Taking Care of Business" filled the auditorium, the same song that had played when Killinger walked on stage at the beginning of the event. One of the entertainers had turned it on again to distract the agitated crowd. Without pause, Killinger started shaking his arms and legs in a hilarious white man's dance. Right away, a female employee in the audience, unprovoked, jumped on stage with him, and together the two started dancing, bumping hips as the audience went wild. The fainting woman was forgotten as the music died down. Killinger hugged the employee after their impromptu performance, and she walked off stage to more applause. "At that point," said one of the entertainers who observed all this, "Kerry Killinger was pretty much a rock star."

Afterward, when Killinger walked off stage, an admiring throng of employees would surround him, some waving limited-edition Killinger bobble-head dolls, others asking for autographs. Almost all wanted a picture. Some couldn't believe they worked at a company—a bank, even!—that was just so cool. Killinger glowed. If he needed any proof that he had created a great place to work, here it was, on the admiring faces of his employees. One attendee gushed in a thank-you note to him after a rally, "I hope you know what an incredible impact you have made on my team. We are very lucky to have you."

After each event, Killinger typically rushed to another employee meeting or a media interview or a lunch with a local politician or community group. His assistant booked little downtime on these trips. Killinger wanted his schedule full. Days began right after breakfast and lasted through the evening, including several rallies. A town car would whisk Killinger and his crew between various appointments. Once, as Killinger left a rally, someone else's limousine was parked in front of the conference center. He was annoyed. "What if the employees see that?" he said. "They'll think it's ours." He climbed into his own town car, which delivered him and his crew back to the corporate jet.

For the better part of two years, as WaMu's Home Loans Group grew, as the bank bought up new mortgage companies, and as Long Beach's account executives churned out loans laced with fraud, Killinger was out of the office. His nonappearance at headquarters became a sore point for executives and managers. Many had become disenchanted with their longtime leader. Killinger had always served as the face of

WaMu, trusting his team to run the operations. Now the bank was much larger, and his absence was more noticeable.

Killinger's compensation at WaMu escalated rapidly. In 2003, his salary of $1 million was $400,000 more than that of Deanna Oppenheimer, the next-highest-paid executive. Killinger's annual bonus increased to $2.9 million, up from $1.5 million four years earlier.[24] In total, Killinger made about $12 million a year, counting his retirement benefits, stock awards, and options.[25]

In Seattle, he and Linda bought property just north of the city, in an exclusive gated community on a high bluff overlooking Puget Sound. The couple tore down the existing house and replaced it with a 4,400-square-foot home designed by a well-known Seattle-based architecture firm known for its high-end, contemporary design. The multimillion-dollar home adjoined a golf and country club. The Killingers bought a second house in Palm Desert in Southern California, a $2 million property located next to another golf course.[26] The Palm Desert house, however, was only a transitional home until the couple found a better property. Instead of leasing a boat for a couple of weeks a year, as was his habit, Killinger bought his own.

At WaMu, plans were under way for a new, $300 million skyscraper that would house the bank's headquarters. The 42-story building would tower over downtown Seattle. The exterior design, influenced by the Embarcadero Center in San Francisco and Rockefeller Center in New York, would be constructed with a combination of beige stone and glass. As the glass reflected the sky, it would take on a bluish tint. Together, the two colors conjured up images of a WaMu branch employee in his standard khaki pants and blue-collared shirt, intentional color choices. Construction on the building began in 2004, and employees moved in two years later.

Inside the new skyscraper, WaMu would trade in most offices in favor of cubicles, but not traditional cubicles. Rather than having hard walls, the new WaMu cubicles would come with high walls and sliding glass doors (which employees would nickname "shower stalls"). The "stalls" would be spread out, with shared common areas in between. "The idea was, if we could have most of the employees in one location, I could drive the culture I wanted—a common culture," Killinger told a reporter. A WaMu building planner added: "Having people sit in private offices with big oak desks is not who we are." Killinger and the other executives, however, would retain their offices, to be housed on the thirty-second floor of the new building. Killinger remained steadfast in his belief that the executives should not take up a building's top floor. As a result, no other department wanted to move into the prime office space either. Eventually WaMu moved the community relations department to the top level. Killinger's office on the thirty-second floor was the largest. It would look palatial because of the open design, although its square footage was about the same as that of his former office. The building's plans called for a buffet-style dining room and an outdoor garden, as well as a lounge with indoor and outdoor fireplaces. On top of the skyscraper, employees could walk around on meandering footpaths overlooking the city on a 20,000-square-foot patio.[27]

Killinger figured the cost of the skyscraper would be offset by the $15 million a year that the bank would save on leasing office space. WaMu's 5,000 employees in downtown Seattle worked in a dozen different buildings. They would now be located in five buildings, but mostly in the new one. The bank also devised an unusual, and somewhat complicated, deal with the neighboring Seattle Art Museum, the city's largest museum. The museum wanted to expand but didn't have enough money for it. WaMu paid the museum $27 million and in return received the land just next to the museum as well as a parking garage across the street. As WaMu built its skyscraper, the museum expanded its own space. As another bonus, WaMu agreed to lease eight floors of the museum's new 16-story building for $5.8 million a year until the museum grew large enough to occupy the whole space. City officials and the museum heralded the somewhat odd marriage. The museum would not have been able to expand without WaMu. Several members of Killinger's family took to calling the new space "Kerry's building."

The "band of misfits," the longtime executive team that Lou Pepper had assembled more than a decade earlier, began to disperse. The breakup began with Liane Wilson. Like everyone else, she was exhausted following the merger spree of the 1990s. In her 15 years at WaMu, she had overseen the complicated integration of more than 20 companies.

But that wasn't the real reason for her departure. She disagreed with Killinger's decision to turn each of WaMu's business lines into a separate silo. She noticed that Killinger had come up with the idea at about the same time he started carrying around a copy of the best-selling business leadership book about General Electric, *Jack Welch and the GE Way*. The introduction claimed that Welch ran "the most powerful business enterprise on Earth." Chapter 1, titled "Embrace Change, Don't Fear It," explained to the reader: "Welch, the tomorrow-driven leader, loves change. He finds it exciting, daring, imaginative. Thinking about change, he argues, keeps everyone alert and on their toes."[28]

In spite of Welch's wisdom, Wilson had lobbied against the structural change at WaMu. She had tried several times to talk Killinger out of it. She believed the change would make it much harder for anyone to figure out what was going on in each of the units. The executives would no longer be making decisions based on consensus. As a chief executive, Killinger was much better at devising the company's five-year-plan than focusing on operational details. In Wilson's view, echoed by others on the executive team, there would be much less oversight in this new structure. She worried in particular about giving so much power to the Home Loans Group.

Killinger, a good listener, listened each time Wilson relayed her concerns. Occasionally he explained his reasoning: "We're just too big." When Killinger finally presented the structural change at a board of directors meeting in the summer of 1999, Wilson saw she had lost the battle. She told Killinger she would retire. He did not want her to leave and convinced her to stay, at least until the company completed its dreaded Y2K technology conversion. She stayed a strained two years, seeing many of her fears play out.

Around the time of Wilson's departure, Craig Tall was working out at a hotel gym in Tampa, Florida. He and Craig Chapman had spent the day driving around the city, visiting the offices of Aristar, the hard money lending division that WaMu had inherited several years earlier. Now Tall had a break before the two were scheduled to meet for dinner. At the gym, Tall began to feel poorly. His back and neck flared with pain. Several months earlier, that same feeling had led to a small heart attack. Tall had received several stents in his arteries but returned to work with little delay. This was, after all, the same man who had negotiated a bank deal after a surgery to fuse his back.

That day Tall left the workout room and called Chapman from the hotel. "I think I need to go to the hospital," he said grimly. Chapman drove Tall to the emergency room. The doctors performed a series of tests late into the evening and delivered bad news: Tall needed open heart surgery, right away. But Tall wanted to return to Seattle and his own doctors. Chapman got on the phone and called Killinger. Could the executives use WaMu's NetJets account to book a private plane back to Seattle? There was no way Tall could travel on a commercial airline in his fragile condition, Craig Chapman explained. Killinger hesitated. "I don't know if we can get a private plane down there," he said. After several minutes of discussion, it seemed to Chapman that Killinger either didn't want them to use the plane or couldn't decide whether to let them. So Chapman found a phone book and arranged for one himself, making sure he chose the least costly option. (Tall would long believe that Killinger arranged for the plane.)

The ordeal was not soon over. Back in Seattle, Tall suffered a complication from the surgery and spent most of the next three weeks in a medical-induced coma. After he left the hospital, six months passed before he could walk around the block. He knew he couldn't handle his job at WaMu alone. He hired Todd Baker, a former lawyer, to head up mergers and acquisitions. Baker took the lead on all the mortgage purchases that followed, while Tall took a backseat role.

During this time, Tall grew concerned about the rapid pace of mortgage acquisitions. He lobbied unsuccessfully against the purchase of HomeSide Lending, the U.S. mortgage unit of National Australia Bank Limited. The purchase had been carried out in two separate transactions that ultimately added another $130 billion to WaMu's loan servicing portfolio. Tall hadn't been in favor of the second phase of the purchase, which gave WaMu full ownership of HomeSide. Tall, Killinger's closest ally next to Fay Chapman, didn't think Killinger favored that particular acquisition either. Increasingly, however, the executives running the Home Loans Group called the shots at WaMu. "The mortgage division became very market share driven," Tall said later. "It was this momentum that was unstoppable."

Tall took a leave from WaMu and enrolled in a month-long program at Harvard Business School called "Odyssey: School for the Second Half of Life." The intensive training, billed by its instructor as giving people ages forty to sixty-five "the tools and understanding to make and sustain change at midlife," proved revelatory for Tall.[29] "My life had been invested in WaMu," he said later. "What WaMu had become was a large part of who I was. I just had to figure out if I could keep my own identity and leave." The program gave Tall the confidence to walk into Killinger's office and announce his departure. He resigned from the executive committee but agreed to remain as an adviser, a decision that bothered some of the other executives. They felt Tall was getting paid for not doing much work at all. Over time Tall's opinion became less and less important to Killinger.

Bill Longbrake, meanwhile, had remained at WaMu, even after, to his frustration, Pepper chose Killinger for the top job. In the mid-1990s, Longbrake had briefly returned to Washington, D.C., accepting a position as the FDIC's CFO. But in little more than a year, he returned to WaMu. He had not enjoyed his position at the federal regulatory agency, and the person hired to take his place at WaMu hadn't worked out. When Longbrake returned in 1996, he told Killinger that he would remain CFO for only five years. Those five years ended in 2001. "I thought, 'This is no fun,'" Longbrake said later of the position. "It had become too stressful." Killinger put Longbrake in charge of managing the bank's risk instead. Longbrake did that for two years, until he received the first of two terse e-mails from Killinger, who sat only three offices away. It informed Longbrake that Killinger had decided to combine WaMu's risk management function under Jim Vanasek, stripping Longbrake of the responsibility. Longbrake, like Tall, stepped into an advisory role. A year later Killinger sent Longbrake a second e-mail, telling him he was no longer welcome to participate on the executive committee.

Killinger hired a batch of new executives and senior managers, a move that muddied WaMu's corporate culture. The new executives held multiple advanced degrees and came from high-powered companies that Killinger admired. The new CFO, Tom Casey, had a long history at General Electric, where he was a vice president and chief financial officer of its insurance subsidiary. To the WaMu senior managers who had spent years creating and working for the bank, the new people seemed to have little respect for the company. They held no attachment to WaMu, the older managers thought, and wanted only to churn out a profit. But to the new executives, WaMu seemed like a ten-year-old kid playing dress-up. It had all the attributes of a big bank, but it didn't act its age. WaMu, thought the new managers, was filled with a bunch of people who had no idea what they were doing. Some even believed that of Kerry Killinger himself. Several new managers started not-so-discreetly calling the old ones "legacy losers," a jab made worse when the name callers formed their hands into an L-shape and pressed it on to their forehead. Many of the old managers retired.

The multibillion-dollar mortgage companies continued to stack up, waiting for someone to remember that they had been purchased and mold them into the larger bank. An unprecedented rush to refinance mortgages was under way nationwide. WaMu wanted to take advantage of it. *The integration of all those other companies can wait* was the general attitude around the company. *Let's make more loans.* In no time at all, WaMu was making mortgages on not one but at least *twelve* different loan software programs, none of which related to another.[30] For Liane Wilson, this practice was the stuff of nightmares. Through the 1990s, she had worried about the potential for these problems.

It didn't take long for WaMu's borrowers to realize something had gone wrong. Homeowners who paid their mortgages each month received notices that they were in default. WaMu had never assigned anyone the task, after a new acquisition, of picking up those customers' mortgage payments. Homeowners had been sending out checks that got stored in security boxes, which were never inspected. The payments sat there for weeks, unprocessed. WaMu thought the borrowers just weren't paying.

As Killinger embarked on his nationwide brand rally tour, dozens of customers began filing complaints. Several hundred were filed in Texas alone. The Texas attorney general's office launched an investigation.[31] One series of complaints alleged that WaMu had failed to service customers' mortgages. Not only did the bank lose payments or process them incorrectly; it then charged customers fees for its mistakes. WaMu responded that it had made "certain errors in servicing some of plaintiffs' loans" but added that "the errors have been corrected and . . . reflect nothing more than mistakes that will, from time to time, occur in the ordinary course of any enterprise." Craig Davis pointed out to a reporter that WaMu had made five acquisitions in 18 months while handling the largest refinancing boom in history. "There were a lot of things hitting at the same time," he said.[32] WaMu was now the country's largest servicer of mortgages—with a portfolio of more than $700 billion—and the second-largest originator. In three years, WaMu's home loan volume had shot up 400 percent to $274 billion.[33]

Davis and the Home Loans Group had been working on something that, they believed, would revolutionize the mortgage industry. The revolutionary idea was an expensive mortgage software program called Optis, which WaMu said meant "best." The program, initiated at about the same time the bank adopted the "Power of Yes" campaign, would allow salespeople to make loans as quickly as possible, even over the Internet. Dozens of WaMu employees from across the country worked on the new program over the course of several years. At one point two years into the project, the Home Loans Group grew so cocky about its ability to deliver the software that it dismissed the outside tech company collaborating on the project.[34]

The project kept getting delayed in favor of making more loans. The system was also full of bugs. Optis could process mortgage applications, but it had trouble underwriting and closing loans. It couldn't handle the volume of mortgages that WaMu hoped to push through. "It was very cumbersome," said one of the WaMu employees who worked on Optis for more than three years. "We didn't actually think it was going to speed anything up." Because the Home Loans Group had ownership of the project and it was carried out within that silo of the bank, some WaMu managers and executives didn't know the extent of the problems. Others who offered help were turned away.

WaMu abruptly announced plans to dismantle the project. One employee likened the decision to "killing your firstborn." The bank ended up charging off $150 million related to its failure. "The abandonment of Optis 0.2 represents a significant management/technology failure,"

WaMu's federal regulators noted in an exam report that year. Publicly, WaMu was much more vague about the cost of the failed program, or whether it had eliminated the program at all.

In light of the failure of Optis, the problems with borrowers' mortgages, and the turmoil at Long Beach, Craig Davis retired. For the next two and a half years, the Home Loans Group, the largest and most unwieldy division at WaMu, would operate without a dedicated leader. Killinger briefly transferred the division under Deanna Oppenheimer's direction but then moved it again under Craig Chapman's oversight. Chapman was also managing WaMu's commercial division, as well as Long Beach Mortgage.

The problems at WaMu continued. Like other lenders, WaMu had been hedging its mortgage servicing rights, or MSRs, to protect itself from changes in interest rates, as a kind of insurance. Mortgage servicing rights are valuable. They represent the fees earned for administering the mortgage after it has been packaged, turned into a security, and sold to investors. WaMu wanted to keep working with its customers, even though it had sold their loans. To protect the value of the MSRs, WaMu bought various derivatives to offset the effect of whipsawing interest rates. The process, as Lou Pepper discovered when the bank began hedging in the 1980s, is fraught with complications. One WaMu senior manager working on the hedges compared it to building a computer chip in a dust-free room. "If there is one little bit of dust," said the senior manager, "you can sneeze and drop $300 million on an MSR portfolio." Said another executive: "If there has ever been a voodoo accounting system, it's that."

The model WaMu used to build its hedges was antiquated, and the bank wasn't hedging using the right mix of derivatives. The crucial formula didn't work. This was true at a number of other banks as well, but the size of WaMu's mortgage portfolio caused it to stand out. The hedging model, said the senior manager working on it, was in "a terrifying state." The model wasn't built well enough to handle the rush of homeowners trying to refinance their mortgages.

WaMu's patchwork of systems for making mortgage loans did not help. A homeowner would lock in a low interest rate through a WaMu loan officer, but before WaMu's arduous loan processing system could recognize the rate lock, the rate might increase, dramatically. WaMu still had to honor the customer's lower rate. "It was a real piece of sloppiness," said the WaMu senior manager. The bank announced that it expected its mortgage banking income to swing from a profit of about $1.3 billion in 2003 to just several hundred million dollars in 2004. The bank laid off more than 13,000 employees and closed 100 home loan centers,[35] although Killinger promised that the bank would still manage to open 150 new home loan centers over the next two years. Shareholders filed a class action suit against WaMu, Killinger, and other executives in federal court in Seattle, alleging that it was "materially false and misleading for defendants to claim that Washington Mutual maintained a unique business strategy that would allow the company to achieve growth and profitability." The suit cited Killinger's public statement about becoming "the Wal-Mart of consumer finance."

The company that did not make major mistakes had now made several, all in the span of a couple of years. The media, the analysts, and the shareholders, after lauding Killinger for so many years, turned against him. A *Fortune* article under the headline "What Went Wrong at WaMu" proclaimed: "Washington Mutual built itself into America's biggest mortgage bank almost overnight. But this year, POW! Profits are getting hammered and the CEO is apologizing to Wall Street." A piece in *The Economist* stated bluntly, "WaMu has suffered more than other banks because it is run badly."[36] One analyst pointed out that Countrywide, then the second-largest mortgage bank nationwide, had not suffered the same problems as WaMu. "Isn't it time to get this company sold?" questioned the analyst. "This is way, way, way too painful. You guys have proved that you can run an excellent retail bank. You can't run a mortgage company."[37]

The criticism devastated Killinger. He half-jokingly wondered if the board might fire him. But this was his only outward sign of angst. No one ever knew what he was thinking. Publicly, Killinger attempted to soothe in his typically calm fashion. In a conference call to investors, he apologized for the poor financial performance of the Home Loans Group. "I know many of you are unhappy," he said. "I understand your concerns. As a substantial shareholder, I am not happy, either."[38]

From his retirement, Lou Pepper occasionally wrote Killinger letters of advice. The former chief executive and board member sent a particularly blunt note after the mortgage problems erupted at WaMu. Pepper suggested Killinger hire a chief operating officer, a move Killinger had long resisted, despite WaMu's size. "You don't hire a COO until you're ready to retire," he liked to say. Even after fourteen years as chief executive and sixteen years as president, Killinger didn't want to relinquish either position. Pepper, in the letter, advised him to hire someone smarter than himself. In his estimation, doing so was a true sign of an executive who knew what he was doing.

"You seem to have resisted getting a COO and I hope you are over that now, as your distraction with national and international obligations have you away far too much," Pepper wrote. "You really could have used someone watching the nitty-gritty for you in the last couple years. Had you done so, you would still be a hero.

"But a caution if you have decided you need one now. You must get someone who is in the top one half percent on the capability scale. You have not been too lucky in the recruiting department and I think you must start fresh on recruiting. With all due respect, you do not have the help in recruiting you need. And, you have to steel yourself to hire someone smarter than you. This will be hard for you, as you have not done that so far. My greatest and perhaps only strength was in hiring people smarter than I was."

Pepper's letter continued: "I also really worry about optimism. While you must be optimistic, there are times when the worst-case scenario must be shown. These are times when there is great stress, with substantial unknowns out in the future. Isn't this one of those times? If it is, and I submit that it is, there is no alternative but to give the worst case to the decision makers or later be in an untenable position of failing to make full disclosure. If you make full disclosure you may lose money, but failure to do so has much worse penalties. Much, much worse.

"There is one other piece of advice you won't necessarily relish, but I wouldn't be me if I didn't tell you what it is. You are involved in a serious cost-cutting effort. You should start with the page in your proxy that has the five highest paid. Reduce it by several million, and not just across the board cuts, but aimed clearly at performance—maybe all down a little bit, but some a lot more than others. Naturally, you as

CEO and COO, take the biggest hit, but if you are serious about saving the place, you will show that either it will be saved, or you will take a hit with the rest of the folks that work there, especially as the problems are not their doing. Are you real enough to do that? I think you are. Oh, that's hard! Why did I have to bring that up?"

He ended the note: "This is all said with the greatest respect and affection for you, Kerry. I have always been proud of you. But, I have seen tough situations in the past. I have seen the reactions to them, and I have seen the results. My advice to you here is based on all of those observations."

Killinger ignored Pepper's last bit of advice—his own salary climbed steadily. But he eventually acquiesced to the idea of hiring a chief operating officer. The other executives, WaMu's board, and the bank's federal regulators all pressured him. The bank hired a search firm. In the summer of 2004, the firm turned up Steve Rotella, the president and chief executive of JPMorgan Chase's home lending division. Rotella was among the second tier of executives whom the search firm had contacted. It had first tried to hire more senior people, but they had had little interest, in large part because the WaMu board couldn't guarantee a speedy succession to chief executive. It was unclear to the candidates when, or even if, Killinger would ever step down.

Rotella had worked in banking for more than two decades, mostly in the mortgage business. He had moved up at JPMorgan Chase through a series of promotions until he landed in the position of president and CEO of its mortgage unit, Chase Home Finance. Over the years, the division had grown, in part through acquisitions. It was among the largest lenders nationwide. Like every other mortgage business, Chase Home Finance had been making plenty of money until the refinancing boom slowed. Earnings had plunged 45 percent in the first six months of 2004 compared with the previous year, in part because Chase was losing money on its hedging, just as WaMu was.[39] Still, Rotella was well respected. "He was a very senior, seasoned quality operating manager," said one former JPMorgan executive who worked closely with him.

But Rotella's recent relationship with JPMorgan had been rocky. The company had just bought Bank One in a massive $58 billion deal that created the second-largest bank nationwide, behind Citigroup.[40]

As part of the merger, Bank One's chief executive Jamie Dimon became president and chief operating officer of the combined JPMorgan Chase, and he would soon move into the chief executive position. At the time WaMu's headhunters approached Rotella, Dimon had started to clean house in a process that critics later called the "Dimonizing" or "ethnic cleansing" of JPMorgan Chase. Some former JPMorgan executives, unhappy with the new leadership at the bank, began to leave. Dimon and his crew didn't think Rotella was a team player, while others considered him arrogant. Rotella, and other executives from the old JPMorgan Chase, weren't happy with the new management, either. One likened Dimon and his team to "a cruel, vindictive pack of wolves." Rotella hadn't been looking when WaMu came calling, but he wasn't sorry to go. The feeling was mutual on the part of Dimon and Rotella's new boss at JPMorgan, Charlie Scharf.[41]

Rotella grew up on Long Island with a sister and two brothers in a two-bedroom house that his parents still own. His father was a custodian and his mother a homemaker. His father's highest salary was $12,000 a year. Rotella put himself through college on a scholarship at the State University of New York by working full-time at a grocery store. He continued working as he got his MBA from the same college. After school, he landed at a consulting firm and later at Chemical Bank. Chemical Bank merged with Manufacturers Hanover Corp., which merged with Chase, which merged with JPMorgan. All the while, Rotella held on to his job.

In an industry known for its big personalities, Rotella is understated. He is short, with graying hair, thick eyebrows, and an olive complexion. He is even-tempered and speaks confidently, without much trace of an accent. In that way, he is like the people of Seattle, many of whom tend to be passive and guardedly friendly. Rotella is friendly, but he is also blunt. Bluntness is unusual in the Pacific Northwest, where people like to err on the side of politeness. "Seattle Polite" is a widely described phenomenon. After nearly two decades of working at a large New York bank, Rotella is adept at navigating corporate politics. His critics would go further, saying he is a skilled underminer. In this way, he contrasted with Killinger, who was brilliant at reading numbers but often naive about internal politics. Rotella had never been to Seattle. When, at age fifty-one, he had his interview with Killinger in the summer of 2004, it was the first time he had visited the city.

The interview had not gone well, or at least Rotella thought it had not. Rotella met Killinger at WaMu's headquarters and spent two hours talking with him in a conference room. Killinger hardly looked him in the eye. During the meeting, as Rotella spoke about his plan to address some of WaMu's problems, and his own merits, Killinger wrote notes on a yellow legal pad, his fist tight, his head down, concentrating. Rotella had no idea what the CEO of the country's largest savings and loan might be writing. He flew home and told his wife that he probably hadn't gotten the job. He didn't feel that he had connected with Kerry Killinger.

Rotella was wrong. Killinger had liked him—it was just hard to tell. In one-on-one meetings, Killinger sometimes did spend more time writing notes than interacting with the person in front of him. After a series of interviews with executives and directors, Killinger offered Rotella the job. Killinger gave up his long-held title of president, and Rotella became president and chief operating officer. After the announcement, Deanna Oppenheimer resigned. Both she and Craig Chapman had wanted to be president. The two executives had been widely viewed inside and outside the bank as potential successors to Killinger. Killinger told Oppenheimer that she wouldn't get the position. He thought she was a terrific marketer but didn't have a firm enough grasp on the financials, a view echoed by other WaMu managers. Oppenheimer announced that she would be leaving to pursue other interests.

After working at WaMu for nearly two decades, Oppenheimer had a big following. Not only had she helped revolutionize the industry with free checking, she had driven the much-replicated Occasio branch concept. She is charismatic and supportive. Her former employees still speak of her in hushed, flattering tones. Her going-away parties lasted a week. Barclays in London soon hired her to head up its own retail bank. Later, after she turned around that division, she was promoted to vice chairman of Barclays global retail bank, where she oversaw operations in fifty countries. An industry trade magazine pronounced her the second most influential woman in banking—in the world.[42]

After her departure, the breakup of Pepper's group of executives, the team that had long been described as the secret ingredient in WaMu's success, was nearly complete. The group had supported Killinger from behind the scenes for more than a decade. Only Fay Chapman remained an active member of the inner circle.

A corporate fissure had formed between the executives at WaMu, and if it had had a name, it would have been "Steve Rotella." His arrival widened enormously the divide between the old, fun-loving bank and the hard-charging financial behemoth that WaMu had become. "Steve Rotella," noted one longtime manager later, "was very polarizing." WaMu's old guard believed that Oppenheimer should have been promoted into Rotella's position. They resented his arrival. That a conference room was torn down to afford him a larger office only added to the antipathy. They didn't like that Rotella hired dozens of JPMorgan Chase employees, who were generally more aggressive. Rotella, in fact, poached so many people from his previous employer that JPMorgan threatened to sue. The New York bank was later accused in a lawsuit of stationing undercover "moles"—including Rotella—at the company ("corporate espionage," the complaint against JPMorgan alleged).[43] The president's new hires became known internally as "Rotella's Club."

On the other hand, the new guard at WaMu viewed Rotella as a savior. He was a real New Yorker banker, the one who would rescue them from this small-minded company that operated like Disneyland—lots of splashy, grand ideas and dress-up time on Halloween but little substance. "There were quite a few nice people there," said one of the more recent hires. "But they were Peter Principled. They had gotten to a level that was beyond them." Killinger still insisted that executives dress up on Halloween, as had been Lou Pepper's long-standing tradition in the 1980s. Rotella refused, as did chief financial officer Tom Casey, who came from General Electric. Casey and Rotella got along from the start.

One of the executives joked that the problems at WaMu ran so deep, and through so many departments, that it required a 12-step program to come to terms with them. Rotella, as a new executive, had arrived on step one. "Steve is a much more reserved person," said one of his direct reports, comparing him generally with other, more outspoken leaders. "A lot of people read that incorrectly as standoffish and arrogant." Even so, Rotella didn't shy away from dealing with the bank's problems or hide out in his office. He was a hands-on manager who liked to get involved in the details. Indeed, he encountered issues so severe and so numerous that he repeatedly reminded senior managers that he had inherited a mess—a constant refrain that pushed another manager to sass him during a conference call, "Yes, we know you've inherited a mess."

There were smaller issues. Thousands of PCs ordered on the cheap had languished in a warehouse, losing value. One of WaMu's data centers happened to be located directly on the San Andreas Fault. But there were also well-known larger problems, like the twelve different software systems trying to make mortgages all at once. Killinger's controversial corporate structure change, the one that had sparked Liane Wilson's resignation, created odd multiples of the same position in each business silo. Rotella found people doing the same jobs, or trying to do one job, inefficiently.

Several months earlier Killinger had sent WaMu's board of directors his annual memo, outlining WaMu's new five-year plan. He wanted the bank to grow by about 10 percent a year, reaching $500 billion in assets by 2009.[44] He still planned to open 250 new branches a year. "Kerry was consumed by WaMu being a 'growth company,'" said one investment banker who worked with him later. "It was an obsession almost."

Killinger told Rotella not to worry too much about the retail bank. "The retail bank runs itself," he said. In some ways, that was true. But many of the branches that WaMu had opened with spectacular fanfare in Chicago, Atlanta, and other cities were losing millions of dollars. WaMu didn't know it right away—there wasn't a sophisticated tracking system in the branches. In the Chicago area, WaMu had accumulated more than 160 branches,[45] but many of them were located in strip malls with no drive-through windows. No customer enduring an icy Chicago winter wanted to get out of his heated car to walk into a bank. Real estate agents in the city joked that WaMu, trying to dominate the market, had snatched up any sort of lease at all, regardless of location.

This assertion was unfortunately true. Killinger had bragged that

WaMu could open a new branch for $1 million or less, compared with about $4 million normally,[46] but the cost saving had to come from somewhere. Often it came from the cheaper leases. "Some people thought we were a finance company, because we were in a strip mall," said one retail bank senior manager later. WaMu eventually shut down about 50 branches in Chicago. It did the same in other cities where it had expanded rapidly: Tampa, Phoenix, and Atlanta. "If you're trying to open thirty locations at once, the odds are you'll get one or two A sites, a bunch of B sites, and even more C sites," said one WaMu manager who managed the bank's properties. "Patience in real estate is the answer." But there had been no patience. Now dozens of branches weren't making enough money, even as the bank opened new ones.

Rotella rented a bus and went on a branch tour with several of the retail branch executives. He instructed the team not to pick locations in advance—he wanted to pop in with no warning. Many of the branches, the team soon found out, were in disarray. Distracting paper signs, like fading community announcements, cluttered the walls. In one particularly large branch outside Seattle, Rotella and his team walked in and asked for the manager. In time, the branch manager strolled down a staircase from the second floor. Rotella asked the manager to show them the upstairs. Grudgingly, the manager agreed. On top of the staircase, the team discovered a steaming cup of coffee and a cigarette tray. Golf balls and clubs littered a long hallway. They had interrupted the branch manager in the middle of his play time. Rotella yelled at the startled man, warning him to clean up his act. Once outside, the WaMu team walked around the block, pretending that they had left. They then returned to the front of the branch where, through the window, they could see the manager at his computer, watching ESPN.

All of this was fixable, though. Rotella and several other executives convinced Killinger to stop building new branches and then to close more than 150 locations that weren't making any money.

The real problems were in the Home Loans Group and its wayward stepchild, Long Beach Mortgage. Later, in an e-mail to Killinger, Rotella summed up the bad feeling he'd gotten when he first learned of the problems in that division. "I said the other day that HLs (the original prime only) was the worst managed business I had seen in my career. (That is, until we got below the hood of Long Beach.)"[47]

By the time Rotella arrived at WaMu in December 2004, many of the operational issues in the Home Loans Group had been exposed. The public and shareholders knew about the problems.

But they didn't know the half of it.

Chapter Five

THE DARK SIDE

I'm a little nervous about it. I have this feeling of impending doom. It's almost too good to be true.

—WaMu Option ARM customer

By 2003, with the "Power of Yes" campaign broadcasting into every corner of the country, WaMu's Home Loans Group had earned an internal nickname borrowed from *Star Wars*: the Dark Side. Home loan volume at the bank had grown astronomically over the last several years under Craig Davis. Now the group had another plan to increase market share.[1] It wanted to push sales of Option Adjustable Rate Mortgages, otherwise known as Option ARMs.[2]

The Option ARM was WaMu's most profitable, and most confusing, mortgage product. It was an adjustable-rate mortgage, enticing borrowers with a teaser interest rate as low as 1 percent for the first month. After that, the loan had a floating interest rate based on an index. The borrowers would see their payment amount change as the index jumped or fell—usually the payment would be higher. Not to worry: the Option ARM allowed homeowners four options each month for paying their loan. They could pay the full amount; they could pay an even higher amount to get rid of their debt in fifteen years instead of thirty; they could pay just the interest on the loan and not the principal; or they

could make a "minimum payment" that covered only some of the interest, and none of the principal. If the borrowers chose that last option,
however, the interest that they skipped paying would be added to the
loan's principal, increasing the amount of money they owed in the long
run. The customer would be holding what's known as a negatively amortizing mortgage.[3]

After five years, the Option ARM would "recast," and the borrower
would have to make a normal, full mortgage payment each month—a
much higher amount than the "minimum payment" option.* Through
the strange witchcraft of modern mortgages, a homeowner with a
$400,000 loan and a $1,333 monthly payment would hold a $432,000
loan with a $2,786 monthly payment. Historically, someone who was
self-employed, or whose income fluctuated throughout the year, took
out an Option ARM. The borrower—an actor, for example—could
theoretically pay more when he had money, and less when he didn't.
While an Option ARM wasn't a subprime loan—it wasn't typically
made to borrowers with bad credit—it was almost as lucrative to WaMu
and other lenders. WaMu could also sell off its Option ARMs, like the
mortgages rolling out of Long Beach, to outside investors, who could
turn them into securities to be sold again.[4]

Option ARMs weren't new at WaMu, at least in its recent history.
The loan had been a flagship product at American Savings Bank, the
first large California bank WaMu purchased in the mid-1990s, and the
bank where Davis had worked previously. WaMu just kept making them
after it bought American Savings. American Savings also introduced
WaMu to the concept of "originate-to-sell," selling off loans on the secondary market for a higher profit.

In the summer of 2003, Kevin Jenne, a manager in WaMu's market
research department, received an intriguing assignment from the Home
Loans Group: figure out the allure of Option ARMs. How could the
division better market them to customers? Jenne was a longtime WaMu
employee who had remained after WaMu acquired his Oregon bank

---

*The loan might recast sooner if the borrower kept accruing unpaid interest by choosing
the minimum payment option. WaMu capped this amount between 110 and 125 percent
of the normal loan amount.

in one of Killinger's first purchases in the early 1990s. He was a self-described "30-year-fixed guy" and knew almost nothing about Option ARMs. At WaMu, the market research department operated like an independent agency, serving the various divisions within the bank. Jenne had never really worked with the Home Loans Group before. It was fairly isolated from the rest of the company, and Jenne thought of its employees as "those people over there." Soon he found himself moderating a series of focus groups with WaMu customers in Orange County and Illinois. The thirty-one people who attended the dual sessions had two things in common: all of them held Option ARM loans, and few, if any, understood what that meant.

Jenne listened patiently as, over and over again, the borrowers described what they believed to be their loan terms. They had gleaned startlingly few details about their loans from the mortgage broker or the WaMu loan consultant who had helped them through the process. Most of them knew they held adjustable-rate loans. They also thought the loan was cheaper than a regular mortgage, because they didn't have to pay as much each month. Approval hadn't been a hassle, the customers said—WaMu had required little paperwork or income documentation. That's where their knowledge stopped. "From their perspective, it was a low payment loan, and that's all it was," Jenne said. "No one understood the option thing."

Some of the borrowers in the focus groups were first-time home-buyers, still awed by their new ability to capture the American Dream. Recently, President George W. Bush had announced plans to increase minority homeownership by 5.5 million people, piggybacking on the goals of his predecessor, President Bill Clinton. "We want people owning something in America," Bush declared at an expo in New Mexico. "That's what we want. The great dream about America is, I can own my own home, people say."[5] The focus group borrowers, some of them members of minorities, were effusive about their buying power. "They had been told by so many people that they couldn't afford one," Jenne said. Now they could.

Few of them understood what negative amortization meant, or that it could make their debt grow in the long run. Some people mistakenly referred to it as "reverse amortization," while others just called it "tacking it on at the end."[6] Even though they couldn't explain it, the customers mostly thought it wasn't a good idea. Didn't that mean they would somehow be falling behind? Borrowers, WaMu noted in a follow-up report, found negative amortization to be "a moderately bad or very bad concept." The report also noted: "No one mentioned that price appreciation would likely overcome any negative amortization, particularly in Southern California where real estate prices have increased substantially over the past several years."[7] Rising home prices meant that borrowers could just keep refinancing their mortgage over and over again, avoiding the major pitfalls of the Option ARM.

The handful of Option ARM borrowers who owned investment properties didn't necessarily understand negative amortization, but they realized the benefit of appreciation. The investors had taken out Option ARM loans, waited six months for their property to increase in value, pulled out the equity, and taken out another Option ARM. With that second Option ARM, they bought yet another investment property and repeated the cycle again until some held multiple Option ARMs from WaMu. (One of these prolific borrowers was featured on WaMu's glossy annual report.)

Half an hour into the first session with borrowers in Orange County, Jenne could tell that quizzing these people on their loan terms was futile—they didn't know their loan terms. He got up, excused himself, and left the room. The borrowers remained seated in comfortable chairs around a conference table, cookies and juice laid out in front of them. Jenne walked into another room at the sterile interrogation facility, behind a two-way mirror, where two mortgage production employees from the Home Loans Group had been observing the discussion. These two employees had initiated the research. "I don't think we're asking the right questions," Jenne told them. The questions he had put together seemed useless. But the mortgage employees disagreed. They wanted him to ask about indexing, even though the customers barely understood interest rates. "Find out what the index means to them," they instructed Jenne.

Jenne's job was to act as an impartial interviewer. He obligingly returned to the room. He asked the group of borrowers: "How does your interest rate change?"

No one responded.

"It changes, right?" Jenne probed.

The borrowers looked around the table at one another. Finally one said, "Yeah, it changes."

"I think it's indexed," offered one woman.

"Yeah, yeah, indexed!" agreed another. They had answered a question correctly!

"Well, what's it indexed to?" Jenne asked.

Another long, awkward pause ensued.

"My loan is indexed to the Nikkei," proclaimed one borrower.

"Your mortgage is based on the Japanese stock market?!" Jenne thought to himself. "Of course I didn't say that," he said later. "But I'm going, 'Oh, my heavens.'" Strangely, in another focus group, in Illinois, another borrower also believed his loan was indexed to the Nikkei. Jenne never discovered where borrowers had received that information.* "I don't think they were being told this by someone," said Jenne. "I think that the only index they had heard of, like on TV or something, was the Nikkei. It was just bizarre."

The borrowers did seem worried about the loan terms. One of them said, "It's really scary to me what's going to happen in five years." Another echoed the same sense of foreboding with a slightly more compressed time frame. "Something terrible happens in three years." Said a third borrower: "I'm a little nervous about it. I have this feeling of impending doom. It's almost too good to be true."[8]

On the other hand, the borrowers seemed comfortable in their ignorance. "Despite their lack of understanding, participants were almost universally happy with their loan choice," the report noted.[9] They could make lower payments each month and get a new loan before the higher payments kicked in. Two women who had endured costly divorces reported that paying less made it possible for them to stay in their homes. "I could either get this loan or sell the house," remarked one borrower.

---

*WaMu's Option ARMs were indexed to either the 11th District Monthly Weighted Average Cost of Funds Index (COFI), which is derived from the interest expenses reported each month by the members of the Federal Home Loan Bank of San Francisco in Arizona, California, and Nevada, or the Monthly Treasury Average (MTA), which is a 12-month moving average of the monthly yields of U.S. Treasury securities.

The Home Loans Group wanted Jenne to recommend ways to market the Option ARM. So Jenne and his team noted in their follow-up report that the best way to off-load the product onto customers was to tell them little about it. That avoided the problem of complicated loan terms and words that no one understood. "Focusing on the right 'need to know' information is critical to developing more Option ARM sales. Participants seemed easily overwhelmed by the product details," the report concluded.

Helpfully, the WaMu borrowers suggested replacement names for the Option ARM, which was considered a marketing problem. Option ARM sounded more like a complicated software program, or a dangerous surgery perhaps. "Flex ARM!" one borrower said. Others threw out "Less Stress Loan" and "Flex-ability." One customer thought it should be called the "Chinese Menu Loan," because "you can choose what you want."[10]

Jenne moderated another handful of focus groups, this time with WaMu's loan consultants and outside mortgage brokers. One of the first groups met in a rough neighborhood of North Hollywood. The facility was much smaller and darker than usual, with video cameras hanging in odd locations, paneling instead of soundproof walls, and shabby tables and chairs. Jenne realized halfway through the meeting that he was conducting an interview in the middle of a movie set, specifically a pornography studio. No matter, the WaMu salespeople were just as excited about the Option ARM as they would have been anywhere else. Jenne had chosen people who made hundreds of Option ARMs a year. Many of those loans were refinances. The salespeople, extroverted and excitable, bubbled over talking about the mortgage. They got paid each time they refinanced a loan. "This is a great loan for me, because I can refinance my customer once a year," said one loan consultant. Another replied incredulously, "You wait a year? I've had this guy for a year and a half, and I've refinanced him three times!"

But the salespeople complained that the Option ARM could sometimes be a hard sell. Their customers didn't understand the mortgage and, therefore, didn't want it. Mostly borrowers wanted a thirty-year fixed-rate loan, just like their parents'. It was easier to just give them what they wanted. "Everybody comes in and says, 'What if interest rates go up 12 percent tomorrow and I lose my house?'" said one WaMu loan consultant. "Everybody has these extreme unrealistic scenarios that they think can happen. There is a lot of paranoia out there."[11]

The other problem was money. WaMu paid its thousands of loan consultants the same commission on a thirty-year fixed-rate loan as on an Option ARM. In that case, why not just give the customer the thirty-year fixed-rate loan he wanted? Mortgage brokers were in a similar position. When selling a WaMu Option ARM, they faced a cap on commission, which they hated. They could get around the cap if they charged a prepayment penalty, but none of the brokers wanted to do that. If the brokers raised rates even slightly in the midst of a home lending frenzy, that would drive away the customers who repeatedly refinanced their homes. Those borrowers would just go to another, cheaper broker.[12] The salespeople considered whether a higher commission might encourage them to make more Option ARMs, even if the Option ARM wasn't necessarily the right mortgage for their customers. Yes, it probably would, the salespeople concluded. But they didn't explore that problem.

Many of the salespeople had coworkers who didn't believe in the Option ARM. These people wouldn't sell it because they found it bad for customers. "You're going to have to change the mindset of a lot of the consultants," one salesperson warned. This negative thinking, however, could be wiped out through training, Jenne later noted in his follow-up report. Many salespeople didn't understand the characteristics of the mortgage. They didn't know how to sell it, or even how to broach the subject with a customer. "If the loan consultant doesn't ask the right questions, you'll never know what [the customer] is willing to do," one salesperson pointed out. Indeed, the group noted that the Option ARM could be good for all kinds of homebuyers: investors in rental property, the elderly, and the overly indebted. Take a borrower in the last group, for example—someone who had tens of thousands of dollars in credit card bills but still wanted to buy a house. Why not give that customer an Option ARM? That way, the salespeople reasoned, the borrower could make lower monthly payments and use the money that he was "saving" to pay down his other debt. (Never mind that the borrower's debt would be increasing with an Option ARM loan.) "If they were using a fixed-rate loan," the follow-up report pointed out, "they would not be able to do this because they would be required to make principal payments each month."[13]

One loan consultant offered up a simple way to tell if reluctant salespeople needed more training on the true benefits of an Option ARM loan. Ask them this question: "An elderly lady with a low, fixed-income needs to choose a mortgage loan that will best meet her needs. She could get a fixed-rate loan with a monthly payment of $1,400, or an adjustable-rate loan with a payment of $1,100. Which loan should you sell her?" The right answer was, of course, the lower monthly payment. Who wouldn't want to save $300 a month?

Jenne got the feeling that the employees from the Home Loans Group weren't happy with the research. They micromanaged their way into the report writing, making sure that some of the findings didn't come off as quite so negative. During the research process, Jenne thought about how the Option ARM had the potential to alter the long-standing relationship between a bank and its borrowers. He reflected on the word *mortgage*, which is derived from Latin and French words meaning "death pledge."[14] For decades, the rules of lending dictated that customers held a long-term contract with their bank. If they didn't pay, the bank would come calling. In that well-respected relationship, Jenne noted, the bank held the obvious upper hand.

But now WaMu and many of its competitors allowed borrowers to choose their own terms and trusted that they would choose correctly. The borrower decided when to pay and how much. Jenne had just observed firsthand the borrowers WaMu trusted, as well as the salespeople who would sell to those borrowers. Jenne came to believe that the Option ARM wasn't just a bad idea—it might be evil. "After a while, I lost that feeling," Jenne said. "Then I came back to it later on. And then I thought, 'No, no. This product is definitely evil.'"

Whether or not Kerry Killinger saw Jenne's research on America's hot new mortgage product—and it's likely that he didn't see it—WaMu doubled its annual Option ARM production to $68 billion in one year.[15] By early 2005, WaMu promoted the loan as its "signature mortgage."[16] It made up more than 25 percent of all the mortgages WaMu made or purchased.[17] Two years earlier Option ARMs had been a much smaller fraction of that total. Meanwhile, fixed-rate mortgages, the kind that everyone's parents had received, the kind that WaMu had made for more than a hundred years, had lost their majority ranking. They now made up less than a third of all mortgages at the bank.[18]

WaMu wasn't alone. An entire country of lenders had shifted toward short-term lending, a change blessed by Federal Reserve chair Alan Greenspan in, oddly, a meeting of the Credit Union National Association. Credit unions had steered clear of offering unusual mortgage products, in part because their charters prevented them from doing so. "Homeowners clearly like the certainty of fixed mortgage payments," Greenspan told the group of credit unions.[19] But, he added, homeowners "might have saved tens of thousands of dollars had they held adjustable-rate mortgages rather than fixed-rate mortgages during the past decade." "American consumers might benefit if lenders provided greater mortgage-product alternatives to the traditional fixed-rate mortgage," Greenspan said, without suggesting specifics.* A national survey came out, revealing that a third of Americans who had purchased a home in the last several years used some kind of "creative mortgage option," such as an interest-only payment option, or miss-a-payment mortgage. (That last choice wasn't offered by WaMu.) Of the homeowners surveyed, one in five had bought a home that was considered out of his price range.

Some banks began offering Option ARMs or other adjustable-rate mortgages for the first time. Others, like WaMu, simply turbocharged their existing product line. IndyMac, a midsize California mortgage lender, shifted its mortgage product mix just as WaMu did, cutting its prime loans and doubling its adjustable-rate volume, including Option ARMs.[20] Golden West Financial, another California-based lender operating as World Savings Bank, made Option ARMs almost exclusively. The company's $119 billion loan portfolio had increased as, the bank noted in its 2005 annual report, "there has been an industry-wide

---

*Greenspan later backpedaled on this statement, telling *The Wall Street Journal*, "I did not mean to disparage the 30-year self-amortizing mortgage. I thought I was focusing on a narrow segment of prospective households who didn't like either adjustable rate mortgages currently in place or the 30-year fixed and that they might like something slightly different which would be a variable maturity mortgage."

increase in the origination of option ARMs, our principal mortgage product for the past twenty-five years. The increase had been facilitated by the emergence of a secondary market for the product."[21]*

Indeed, lenders had no problems off-loading Option ARMs to investors on the secondary market, just as they had been able to sell subprime mortgages. The demand was so high that WaMu sold off 70 percent of its Option ARMs in 2005, significantly more than in the previous year.[22] WaMu got paid nearly six times as much for selling an Option ARM as it did for selling a fixed-rate loan (109 basis points versus 19 basis points). Subprime loans fetched an even higher price (150 basis points).[23]

By now, WaMu was packaging and selling billions of dollars of mortgages. The bank had discovered that it was far more lucrative to cut out the middleman—the investment banks—and bundle securities on its own, opening an office in New York to handle the trading. In just three years, WaMu's mortgage-backed-security volume doubled to $73 billion, earning it the number-two position of all companies nationwide churning out high-risk bonds. WaMu even outpaced the investment banks: Lehman, Bear Stearns, Goldman Sachs, and JPMorgan Chase. Only Countrywide would best WaMu in this practice. The bulk of WaMu's securities received stellar grades from the rating agencies, which were tasked with measuring their riskiness.

The bank counted Fannie Mae and Freddie Mac, the government-sponsored entities that had earlier bought Long Beach bonds, among its largest customers. Long ago the federal government had founded these agencies with the goal of increasing mortgage lending and, thus, homeownership—Fannie Mae during the Great Depression, and Freddie Mac thirty years later. If banks could sell off their mortgages, they would have more money to fund new ones, rather than just relying on customers to bring in deposits. But by 2005, after initially avoiding risky loans, Fannie and Freddie had become just as market-share-obsessed as the rest of the industry. The two entities had begun buying up or insuring large quantities of high-risk loans from lenders like WaMu.[24]

---

*Golden West, however, was a portfolio lender; this meant it did not sell its Option ARMs on the secondary market like WaMu.

Eventually, Fannie and Freddie would together buy $500 billion in loans from WaMu, more than a quarter of every dollar in loans WaMu originated.[25]

Another big customer was Goldman Sachs. Between 2004 and 2008, Goldman collaborated on at least $14 billion in loan sales and securitizations with WaMu and Long Beach Mortgage.[26] WaMu's relationship with Goldman was murky. Not only was the giant investment bank buying securities and loans from WaMu; it was also helping to package some of the bank's securities (about 6.5 percent of WaMu's total issuance between 2004 and 2008). Later, Goldman provided investment banking advice. Historically, investment banks were supposed to help advise companies on mergers and acquisitions, or help them find new capital. But that relationship had grown tenuous, in part because of the 1999 repeal of the Depression-era Glass-Steagall Act. Before it was repealed, the act limited the conflicts of interest at banks because it prevented them from running too many types of businesses.

WaMu executives harbored suspicion that Goldman was taking advantage of the bank. "I don't trust Goldy on this," Killinger later wrote in an e-mail, debating whether to hire the investment bank as an adviser. "They are smart, but this is swimming with the sharks. They were shorting mortgages big time while they were giving [Countrywide Financial] advice." In at least one instance, Goldman was betting against a subprime security made of Long Beach loans that it had bought from WaMu. The performance of the security was so bad, however, that Goldman's dual bets—on the one hand, that the security would lose money; on the other, that it wouldn't—ended up canceling each other out, said a person familiar with that particular trade. "It was a wash," he said.

By mid-2004, Killinger faced a dilemma. He wanted to keep growing earnings, and thus the bank's stock price, but that wasn't going to happen by making fixed-rate mortgages. Fixed-rate mortgages weren't making much money. WaMu had been able to make a lot of thirty-year conventional mortgages in the past. Interest rates had been so low that customer demand was high. Now interest rates were creeping up again, and demand had waned. Killinger knew that the bank was making the most money off of subprime and adjustable-rate mortgages. After the hedging debacle, when WaMu had lost hundreds of millions of dollars because of unchecked interest rate swings, analysts had been pressuring the bank to start taking more risk on credit—mortgages—rather than on rising and falling interest rates.

There was no better way to do it than making riskier loans. These kinds of loans came with higher interest rates that adjusted at different times, allowing WaMu to hedge against the fluctuating rates of its own funding sources.* The real risk was if the borrower defaulted on the loan. What's more, WaMu's federal regulator, the Office of Thrift Supervision, had just criticized the bank for its haphazard subprime lending. "WMI continues to increase its exposure to subprime borrowers without an enterprise-wide, clearly-articulated subprime lending strategy," OTS examiners wrote after its annual exam.[27]

At an executive team meeting, Killinger presented a new five-year plan for the bank. He called it WaMu's "higher-risk lending strategy."[28] Not only would WaMu increase its production of Option ARMs, but Killinger wanted to make more home equity loans and more subprime mortgages out of Long Beach. Home equity loans allow customers to borrow against the equity built up in their houses through rising home prices.

Nearly 60 percent of the loans WaMu made were already of the risky variety that Killinger outlined in his plan.[29] The bank, incidentally, did not classify Option ARMs as "higher-risk loans" because they were issued to prime borrowers who theoretically had better credit scores. It did, however, consider loans made with no income verification or "stated income" as risky. Before, WaMu's Home Loans Group had expanded rapidly without much thought to profit. Rather than make mortgages in new markets nationwide, Killinger planned to increase profit in areas where WaMu was already located.

Most members of WaMu's executive team supported Killinger. Briefly,

---

*Large, publicly traded banks always have to take some kind of risk if they want to make money, and finding a balance between various risks is what makes a good bank. If WaMu had, for example, continued to make 30-year fixed-rate loans to high-quality borrowers, it might have suffered from market risk, when its own borrowing rates exceeded the amount it was receiving back from borrowers. That was the very problem affecting many banks in the early 1980s.

they considered other ways to grow earnings. They could expand the commercial division, making loans to businesses instead of consumers—but the idea never gained traction. They could lob off the mortgage division and sell it—but no one liked that idea. Without a mortgage division, WaMu would have had to expand into a different business line. Otherwise, the bank would just be hoarding customers' deposits with nowhere to invest them. WaMu would shrink. "It would be financially devastating," said Craig Chapman, one of the executives who agreed with Killinger's plan. Even ever-suspicious Fay Chapman, who had been stuck cleaning up the recent mess at Long Beach Mortgage, didn't oppose Killinger. She was skeptical, but she thought through the strategy and, much as she had with Long Beach Mortgage, concluded that these types of mortgages could be made correctly. She believed that Jim Vanasek, WaMu's chief risk officer, could keep the bank on the right track by limiting the different categories of risky mortgages WaMu made, "which is why everyone signed on," said Craig Chapman.

Vanasek, who once likened subprime loans to "a very dark and scary place" and who had since earned the nickname "Dr. Doom," took a stand against Killinger's new direction. Over the last several years, Vanasek's work had become increasingly impossible. He was the chief risk officer, in charge of balancing risk, at a bank that was loading up on it. His division had withered as a result of cost cutting at the bank. He handled this challenge by attempting to turn his department into a fortress into which no lenient lending policy would be allowed to pass. He had little sympathy for the needs of the salespeople. As a result, he battled constantly with the Home Loans Group and its executives. He had tried with little success, for example, to limit the number of stated income loans WaMu made. But because Killinger refused to settle arguments, Vanasek often lost. The salespeople were much more persuasive, and they were the ones making money.[30]

In 2004, Vanasek met with Killinger alone. He told Killinger that he had a brilliant idea. As mortgage lenders across the country increasingly churned out poor-quality loans, why didn't WaMu advocate just the opposite? Vanasek urged Killinger to take out a full-page advertisement in *The Wall Street Journal*, a big, splashy ad, decrying all this ridiculous lending and urging companies to adopt responsible practices. "I thought he could stand out as the leading mortgage executive if he could blow a whistle and say, 'Enough is enough,'" Vanasek said in later congressional testimony. But changing direction would mean forfeiting market share and profit. Killinger cared deeply about market share. He kept making plans to diversify and build up other lines of business outside mortgage lending, only to change his mind and switch direction again. He never took action on Vanasek's suggestion.[31]

Killinger presented the new "higher-risk lending strategy" to WaMu's board of directors.[32] Within a year, the bank planned to expand its portfolio of high-risk loans more than 40 percent to $45 billion. The bank expected that this strategy might also increase the number of borrowers who would default, causing bad loans, and therefore losses, to rise. But those losses could be controlled. The board approved the new direction.

On a wet Saturday morning in the fall of 2004, a group of parents watched their teenage daughters bash it out on the soccer field. It was the sort of weather the Northwest is known for, gray and unrelenting. The parents wore high-end, hooded rain jackets and thick fleeces. Their children, part of an exclusive soccer club, ran through scrimmages on a field located just off Lake Washington. Yachts perched on the water's edge. The kids were covered in mud, but that wasn't unusual during soccer season.

On the sidelines of the soccer field, two fathers struck up a conversation about banks. One of the fathers was William Dunnell, the longtime owner of a small investment advisory firm in Seattle. His business was located not far from one of WaMu's first branches, in a middle-class neighborhood that once housed Nordic fishermen and had since grown into a trendy enclave of bars and restaurants. Dunnell, because of his line of work, had been following financial news regularly. He had heard some disturbing secondhand stories about some of the shenanigans in the mortgage business, stories about crazy loans that didn't seem possible. It wasn't the kind of story he had seen anywhere in the mainstream media. "I even had a guy call me up and say, 'Have you thought about getting into recommending mortgages?'" Dunnell said later. "He had this new thing where you can take all the equity out of your house in an interest-only loan and put it into a life insurance policy. He even gave me a CD on it." Like many others in Seattle, Dunnell had borrowed money from WaMu. He had a simple, thirty-year fixed-rate mortgage. He had recently refinanced it.

The other father was Todd Baker, WaMu's executive vice president for corporate strategy and development. Dunnell knew that Baker worked at WaMu, but during all the weekend mornings they spent by the side of the soccer field, Baker had almost never talked about the bank, and he rarely spoke of the industry, either. Today, however, Dunnell wanted to know what Baker thought of Tom Brown, a fiery hedge fund manager who ran a blog called Bankstocks.com, which analyzed the largest consumer banks. "Attention Bank of America shareholders and employees!" Brown wrote in one typical, ruthless attack. "The individual running your company, Kenneth D. Lewis, is an egomaniac set on enriching himself at your expense, by using your equity (and, employees, by putting your jobs at risk) to cobble together as large a company he can get away with. Ken doesn't care how unwieldy your company is. Or what businesses it's in. Or how fast it grows, or how profitable. He only cares that it be *big*."[33] Dunnell asked what Baker thought. Baker's assessment of Brown: "He's okay."

In the middle of the discussion, Baker paused. An odd expression passed over his face as he looked down at the shorter Dunnell. "If the housing or mortgage markets slow down," Baker said of WaMu, "we're fucked." Dunnell, startled by the unexpected comment, nodded but didn't reply. He turned his attention back to the soccer field, where the girls kept on playing.

By this time, WaMu's Home Loans Group had been tainted by "The Power of Yes." "We joked about it a lot," one loan consultant later told *The New York Times*.[34] "A file would get marked problematic and then somehow get approved. We'd say: 'O.K.! The power of yes.'" Borrowing a playbook from Long Beach Mortgage, WaMu loosened its underwriting. A flyer circulated through the company's hundreds of loan offices across the country. "A thin file is a good file," it read. Rather than ask for a bank or income statement, one WaMu loan manager in San Diego took pictures of a mariachi singer and a gardener as proof that the borrowers, both claiming six-figure incomes, held jobs. This particular manager later admitted that he had been abusing methamphetamines, according to the *Times*. Coworkers saw drug paraphernalia on his desk. "We had this expression: 'Loan consultants don't work for WaMu. WaMu works for loan consultants,'" said Jenne, the market research manager. "They'll sell what they want to sell."

In the face of an unstoppable sales force, the bank's underwriters, the people in charge of making sure loans met all criteria for approval, were rendered useless. FICO scores slipped further, and Option ARM borrowers got approval for loans based on the minimum payment option, not on the higher amount they would have to pay.[35] Stated-income loans grew dramatically. Half of all the bank's subprime loans were made to borrowers who didn't provide documentation. The same was true for 70 percent of WaMu's Option ARM borrowers and *90 percent* of all home equity borrowers. In a later congressional hearing, Senator Ted Kaufman (D-Del.) repeated these statistics out loud, then repeated them once more. "I keep saying these numbers over again because I hope they're going to change," he remarked drily.[36]

WaMu's underwriters would deny loans, only to have upper management reverse the decisions, doling out "exceptions." Loan consultants bartered with them to approve their loans, offering kickbacks. In Atlanta, an underwriter warned her coworkers to make it obvious that the loan had been originally denied and to cite the reasons. That way, if the loan file came into question later, the underwriter could easily identify the problem. "CYA," the underwriter told her coworkers. "'Cover Your Ass.' Just don't say this is right." But the people checking the loans had become a worthless dam in a river littered with debris. In an internal memo, Melissa Martinez, one of the senior vice presidents in WaMu's risk department, instructed risk managers to "shift (their) ways of thinking" away from acting as a "regulatory burden" on the company's lending operations and toward being a "customer service" that supported WaMu's five-year growth plan.[37]

There was something else influencing WaMu's loan consultants: Countrywide Financial. Countrywide, the biggest national home lender, managed to come out just ahead of WaMu in nationwide mortgage market share, even though WaMu was three times its size.[38] In 2003,

WaMu ranked as the number-one servicer of mortgages in the country, but it remained the number-two originator of home loans, the real prize title, behind Countrywide. (In one celebrated quarter, remembered well internally, WaMu beat Countrywide in this ranking.) By 2005, WaMu had fallen to the number-three position in both categories, once again behind Countrywide. But in one ranking, WaMu had managed to beat its closest competitor. While Countrywide had also increased its Option ARM production, WaMu had increased its more.

WaMu had, in fact, considered buying Countrywide several years earlier. Craig Tall and Kerry Killinger had flown down to the lender's headquarters in Southern California, a Mediterranean-style villa at the foot of the Santa Monica Mountains. They had met with Angelo Mozilo, Countrywide's storied chief executive. Over the preceding three decades, Mozilo had painstakingly built Countrywide into the country's largest home lender. The son of a Bronx butcher, he possessed the sort of over-the-top, bankerlike characteristics that made him seem even more outlandish in comparison with Killinger, the reserved son of a high school music teacher. "If you ever stop trying to make your division the biggest and the best, that's the day you die!" Mozilo once exclaimed.[39] An Italian American who tanned easily, Mozilo drove fancy cars and wore nice suits, unbuttoned shirts baring his chest, and gold chains. Killinger would later refer to the Countrywide chief executive in an e-mail as the "great orange-skinned prophet from Calabasas."[40] The deal between the two companies hadn't worked out. By one account, Mozilo insisted that he would run the combined lenders if a merger took place, a demand that Killinger opposed. By another account, Killinger couldn't get comfortable with Countrywide's hard-charging culture. And by yet a third account, Mozilo just wasn't interested in the deal.

Killinger wanted to beat Countrywide, and that goal trickled down from WaMu's headquarters to the company's thousands of loan consultants, who were reminded, in e-mails and in meetings, of the lender's threat. WaMu bought Long Beach just after Countrywide started its own subprime division—hiring a former Long Beach executive to get into the business[41]—and Countrywide had also started making more high-risk loans. If Countrywide dropped its teaser rate on one type of mortgage, so did WaMu.[42] When WaMu started up its capital markets

division, it hired executives from Countrywide. "Whatever Countrywide did, WaMu wanted to do, too," recalled one loan consultant.

When Steve Rotella arrived, he took control of the Home Loans
Group. He and Craig Chapman didn't get along from the start; Chapman wanted to leave as soon as he didn't get the position of president
and chief operating officer, but complicated contract negotiations kept
him from leaving. In the meantime, Chapman thought Rotella was
weakening Chapman's leadership by relaying important information
only to his direct reports. Chapman often refused to work with the new
president, and Rotella didn't think Chapman was being transparent
about some of the inner workings of Long Beach Mortgage.[43] Chapman
tore through Rotella's patience. After trying for months to get along, in
part because Killinger had called Chapman his "best operator," Rotella
recommended to the board of directors that they get rid of him.

Chapman resigned, and Rotella later wrote to Killinger in an e-mail,
"In hindsight, I would have pushed him out sooner."[44] Rotella began
moving in his own people. He hired David Schneider to head the division; Schneider was a young, up-and-coming executive who had made
a name for himself as chief financial officer and, later, head of the retail
bank at Old Kent in Michigan, then moved up once more to become
president and chief operating officer of CitiMortgage in St. Louis.
Schneider appeared headed for banking stardom when WaMu hired him.

Schneider's employees found him quite different from his predecessor. He wasn't as intense as Chapman, who had often paced back and
forth at meetings and sent e-mails in all caps. "EXCELLENT! Bring it
on!" Chapman wrote in one 2004 missive regarding a new home loans
campaign he called "GOING ON THE OFFENSIVE."[45] During a
sales meeting related to operational changes, Chapman kept telling
his team, "You don't like it? There's the door." One meeting attendee
counted the number of times Chapman used this phrase during the
hour-and-a-half gathering: twenty-one. By contrast, Schneider was polite and unremarkable, both in his management and in his appearance.

The Home Loans Group increased the commission that loan consultants received for making Option ARMs. Subprime loans, home equity loans, and adjustable-rate mortgages all fetched more money than
30-year fixed-rate loans. Just as the earlier focus groups had predicted,

more pay for Option ARMs meant more salespeople made them. For making an Option ARM loan on a $300,000 house, they earned a commission of $1,200, versus a commission of $960 for a fixed-rate loan. Just as at Long Beach, that rate increased as the salesperson made more loans.[46] "These loan officers are being tossed out there saying, 'Go get all this stuff. We're going to pay you through the nose. We don't care how dangerous it is,'" said one saleswoman. "I would do $400 million in straight-up conventional loans and that would be just a third of my paycheck, maybe a quarter. The money was in Option ARMs."

The whole thing had an eerie, Stockholm Syndrome quality to it. Some salespeople knew they were making bad loans but continued to make them anyway. "It's like an abusive relationship," said one Long Beach sales manager. "You don't know how bad it is." Added another loan consultant: "We all just got lost in this rolling rock down this long hill." Others were pressured to do it by their supervisors. "I swear 60 percent of the loans I approved I was made to," one WaMu underwriter later told *The New York Times*. "If I could get everyone's name, I would write them apology letters."[47]

WaMu had been transformed into a loan clearinghouse. Like a giant vacuum, it sucked in mortgages from all kinds of places and spat them out to investors in one form or another. It purchased billions of dollars in subprime loans through other lenders—Ameriquest, in particular. WaMu still made home loans to customers in person, as it had since its founding. But now, more than 100 years later, WaMu also had thriving correspondent and wholesale divisions. The difference between the two was in who provided the money for the loan. In the wholesale division, WaMu funded loans through tens of thousands of mortgage brokers across the country, just as at Long Beach Mortgage. This setup was a cheap way for WaMu to accumulate millions of loans. Closing a loan through the wholesale division cost the bank only $1,800, about 65 percent less than if a customer got a loan through a WaMu employee.[48] WaMu saved this money because it didn't have to process the customer's application. In the correspondent division, an outside lender funded his own loans and sold them to WaMu. In this way, the bank was buying loans from its own competitors. Both ways of accumulating loans were perilous. Since the salespeople making the loans weren't employees, WaMu had no control over them. "There's heroin and then there's black tar heroin, and that's what that was," one WaMu executive later observed. In 2005, about 70 percent of the $208 billion in loans that WaMu originated came through the correspondent and wholesale divisions.[49]

As all these loans passed between different companies and people, everyone made money. A lot of money. Consider the job of Michele Perrin, a WaMu employee in the bank's new warehouse lending division in Southern California. WaMu inherited the division through its 2001 purchase of Bank United, where Perrin worked. The division grew into one of the largest in a national market once estimated at about $200 billion.[50] For all intents and purposes, Perrin's job was to make sure the flow of mortgage money never ceased. In the warehouse division, she and her team lent money to outside lenders so they could make more home loans, selling them back to WaMu in the correspondent division. WaMu would then frequently sell those loans again, either to Fannie Mae or to Freddie Mac, or to the Wall Street banks.

Perhaps because Perrin is an avid scuba diver—pictures in her house in Orange County show her swimming with a thirty-two-foot whale shark in Hawaii and a six-foot moray in the Red Sea—she conjures up images of fish when she thinks about the nation's complex mortgage machine. In Perrin's mind, the mortgage banker, or broker, who worked with the customer represented the tiny fish, which then got swallowed by a bigger fish (WaMu), which then got swallowed by an even bigger fish (the investment banks, or Fannie Mae and Freddie Mac). "The bigger fish are going to just keep swallowing the mortgages," Perrin said.

However you envision it, Perrin's division provided billions of dollars in loans to other companies across the country—often companies also making risky mortgages. In 2004, WaMu's second-largest client in the warehouse lending division, with an outstanding loan balance of about $400 million, was Taylor, Bean & Whitaker, one of the country's largest privately held mortgage lenders. A federal grand jury would later convict its owner, Lee Farkas, of running a $2.9 billion fraud scheme. He was sentenced to 30 years in prison and ordered to pay $38 million. In this way, WaMu helped fuel an entire industry. (This trend also worked in reverse: Goldman, for example, provided Long Beach Mortgage with a $2 billion credit line, the largest of Goldman's accounts in 2006.)

Unlike some of her coworkers, one of whom had a career as a professional singer, Perrin had spent the better part of two decades in the mortgage trade. At WaMu, she was known as the "Billion Dollar Baby." On December 14, 2004, a summary report came out, detailing the amount of advances outstanding to all the mortgage companies that WaMu's warehouse division was funding, ranked by salesperson. Perrin's portfolio exceeded $1 billion in loans, a stunning amount. By the following year, Perrin—who was paid on a complicated commission structure based on net interest income—had doubled that amount. She was now making more money than many of WaMu's senior executives, some of whom were earning compensation in the low seven figures.

WaMu subjected Perrin and her team to the same sort of values training that Killinger and the other executives brought to each bank they had acquired in the 1990s. But as the mortgage acquisition pace quickened and the number of WaMu employees ballooned, the indoctrination to WaMu's culture had become forced. The bank instructed Perrin and her coworkers to read the inspirational book *Who Moved My Cheese?* This is an allegory of four mice—Sniff, Scurry, Hem, Haw—and their reluctance to let go of their old cheese and search for new, better cheese. "It is mind numbing," said Perrin, who detested the book. "On one page, there's a picture of a chunk of Swiss cheese and it says, 'Movement in a new direction helps you find new cheese.' I was like, 'Why don't you just shoot me?'" Regardless, Perrin had to write a book report on *Who Moved My Cheese?* for her team's internal newsletter. She concluded in her page-and-a-half-long report: "I know that I would like to be a Sniff or a Scurry, to see the changes coming and jump into action, but I will more likely be a Haw, hanging back and mourning the Old Cheese a bit before heading out to find the New Cheese. But I will not be a Hem, stuck at the empty Cheese Station, indignant that the Cheese has moved."

When new employees seemed not to have adjusted, WaMu hired an actual blues band to help them write their own songs about how they felt about change. Each team of songwriters had to stand up on stage and perform their made-up blues song. "I got the mean down, low down lack-of-communication blues," Perrin and her team sang. "They were feeding us beer at the back of the room," she said later. "Some of the groups were literally falling down on the stage."

Despite its elements of ridiculousness, the "culture training" bonded employees to each other and to the company. Employees still believed strongly in the culture of WaMu. In some ways, it could explain why Perrin sat across from one of her mortgage bankers in 2005 and pleaded with him to start making Option ARM loans, even though she knew Option ARM loans were probably the worst product on the market. Perrin later recalls the incident with some anguish, but there was reasoning behind it at the time. "Selling loans in the secondary market was perceived as a one-way door," she said later, of Wall Street. "We originated the products and it was like a big black hole—as long as they kept asking for more, we kept making them. People didn't think it made a lot of sense, but, heck, it's their own funeral."

One young mortgage banker who lived in San Diego was nice and recently married and had founded his own growing company. Each month he lost millions of dollars because of his refusal to make Option ARMs. "The other guys were making hand-over-fist more money than him," Perrin said. Because he lost money each month, while everyone else reported record profits, he risked losing his funding from WaMu. If he recorded a loss for more than two months, Perrin would have to drop his line of credit, a move that could shut him down. "We had this whole credit department that's watching all these customers," Perrin said. "They were not allowed to lose money." So Perrin went out to talk some sense into the man.

She tried, over and over, to convince him that he had to make Option ARMs. "I was begging him to do it," she said. But the lender refused. "Michele," he told her. "I will not originate an Option ARM mortgage. It's not the right thing for my customer." For two straight years, he never recorded a profit, and he never changed his mind. Somehow Perrin managed to keep his funding.

Nothing seemed quite as surprising to Perrin as Kerry Killinger himself. The stark contrast between the well-spoken, gracious WaMu chief executive whom she met and saw speak several times at company events, and the obvious recklessness of the people at the bank buying, selling, or making mortgages, astonished her. It didn't seem like all this could possibly coexist at the same company. "Kerry Killinger," she observed, "was like a sweet old lady who owns a giant rottweiler."

Killinger's higher-risk lending strategy depended on a housing market that would never slow down, but faint whispers that such a drop might be coming were being heard across the country. On a spring day in 2005, Lou Pepper sat in his car at a railroad crossing at a small seaside town in Washington State. Pepper and his wife, Mollie, had years earlier bought a farmhouse abutting an Indian reservation on the edge of Anacortes, about an hour and a half north of Seattle. The farmhouse, perched above the cold waters of Puget Sound, reminded Pepper of his childhood home in the Midwest. It had dark green and maroon trim, a wide front porch that overlooked the water, and an adjacent barn, which served as a workstation and a garage. Pepper hired someone to clear a half-acre's worth of sprawling blackberry bushes from the backyard, and he had planted rosebushes and fruit trees in their place. He drove around the property on a small golf cart.

Pepper waited as a train towing cars filled with lumber passed through. He counted for a long time as car after car moved slowly down the tracks. He couldn't be sure, but he assumed the lumber had been freshly cut in Canada and would move down the coast to California, where it would feed the building frenzy under way. Pepper counted about 70 cars, more than he had ever noticed travel through the area at one time.

Back in his office, on the second floor of the farmhouse, Pepper typed out a letter to Killinger.* "Some few years ago, you and I talked, Kerry, about the Dot Com Bubble," Pepper wrote. "We concluded that it would not last long enough to cause enough inflation in the real estate market to threaten the bank. We were right on that one. Now there is a different problem, which I am sure all of you are aware of, and that is the speculation in single-family homes. This, I am sure, is a threat to the bank that you cannot avoid, as you are in the business in a big way. I

---

*Pepper's letter is addressed "Kerry and Friends," but it is unclear to whom he sent it in addition to Killinger.

am astounded at the extent of the speculation and the flurry of building
going on to take advantage of it."

WaMu now made the highest proportion of loans to real estate investors and second-home buyers.[51] Nationally, nearly a quarter of all
homes sold in the previous year had been purchased by people who had
no intention of living in them.[52] (During the Great Depression, WaMu's
then-chief executive had declared, "Our job is not to get in the real estate business. It is to stay in the banking business and make friends.")[53]
In his letter, Pepper reminded Killinger and the other executives about
the problems he had faced with speculative condo development in Hawaii when he arrived at the bank more than two decades earlier. While
WaMu, at that time, had endured the problem, Pepper noted that other
banks had not been so lucky.

"What might you do?" Pepper wrote. "Well, I sure would get rid of
non-owner occupied loans, prime or subprime, as there is no real reason
to hope that the amateurs or pros owning those in this market will do
anything but walk away at the first hiccup. What is the penalty now for
dumping them? I don't know. But isn't your first loss the best loss when
you see danger?"

He went on, "I would bet that there will be greatly increased expense
when the bubble starts deflating and delinquencies increase. Is it likely
that they will increase? Yes, I would say it is inevitable. And with the low
or no equity position of many of the borrowers, the chance of foreclosure is really substantially higher than it has been in any period in my
time at this business."

Pepper acknowledged that WaMu's stock price had floundered over
the last two years. After reaching its all-time high of $45 at the end of
2003, it now hovered between $40 and $45 a share. But an attempt to
make more money by taking on riskier loans was likely to be only "short
term happy, but long term really dangerous."

"Needless to say, I am merely pointing out what appears to me to
be a real likely big problem," wrote Pepper. "You have the ability to
quantify the risks I see and then take deliberate action to avoid them
to some degree at least. I see the likelihood of the problem to be great
enough to really hunker down and ride out whatever storm this latest
folly brings."

And with that, Pepper ended his letter: "Boy, am I glad to be writing this and not among the people it is addressed to!"

Even without Pepper's wisdom, Killinger had recognized that the astonishing growth in housing could not be sustained, even as he pursued an incongruous strategy of making mortgages that relied on the housing market's upward momentum. Just after WaMu's board approved the "higher-risk lending strategy," Vanasek e-mailed Killinger about some of the problem's facing WaMu's risk management team.[54]

Killinger replied: "I have never seen such a high-risk housing market as market after market thinks they are unique and for whatever reason are not likely to experience price declines. This typically signifies a bubble."

"I could not agree more," wrote Vanasek, who had already been warning his team about the possibility of a housing bubble. "All the classic signs are there and the likely outcome is probably not great. We would all like to think the air can come out of the balloon slowly, but history would not lean you in that direction."

A panel of U.S. senators later questioned Vanasek about this exchange at a congressional hearing.[55] The inconsistency in WaMu's strategy perplexed the senators. "How do you account for the fact that somebody has seen a bubble, and by definition, a bubble is going to burst, and then their corporate strategy is to jump into the middle of that bubble?" Senator Tom Coburn (R-Okla.) asked.

"Well, frankly, that is quite hard to answer with anything that would satisfy you," Vanasek replied. "I can only say that at that point in time, the conventional mortgage, a 30-year mortgage, yielded very little, so the company was constantly concerned about the reaction on Wall Street to earnings and profitability and therefore pursued these strategies in the face of that." A longtime manager who worked closely with Killinger later offered this assessment of him: "He's not a theoretical speculator. He's anchored in reality. But the problem was, reality was going to flip on its head."

Acceptance about the housing market's invulnerability was pervasive. It originated at the top levels of government and trickled down from there. In the fall of 2005, Ben Bernanke, on the verge of a nomination to become the next chairman of the Federal Reserve, dismissed the idea of a housing bubble. The 25 percent increase in home prices over the previous two years, he told a congressional committee, "largely reflect[s] strong economic fundamentals," like job growth. Bernanke expected that "a moderate cooling in the housing market, should one occur, would not be inconsistent with the economy continuing to grow at or near its potential next year."[56]

The National Association of Realtors, meanwhile, distributed pamphlets to the general public, reassuring homebuyers about the remote potential of a housing bust. "There is virtually no risk of a national housing price bubble based on the fundamental demand for housing and predictable economic factors," the country's largest association of real estate agents wrote in a 2005 Q&A on its website.[57] The agency's chief economist, David Lereah, told Gwen Ifill in an interview on PBS *Newshour*, "I don't like to use the word 'bubble' because bubbles burst."[58] Lereah published a book: *Are You Missing the Real Estate BOOM?* The subtitle: *Why Home Values and Other Real Estate Investments Will Climb Through the End of the Decade—and How to Profit from Them.* Lereah, citing 20 years of experience as a "real estate/banking economist," observes in the book: "Too many households do not own enough real estate property. And of those who do, many do not realize the many ways they can leverage their investment and increase their stake in the real estate boom." He advises: "In most cases, real estate is the largest financial purchase a household ever makes. It needs to be treated as an investment similar to stocks and bonds."[59] A year later Lereah revised the title of his book to read, more confidently: *Why the Real Estate BOOM Will Not Bust—and How You Can Profit from It.* And underneath: "How to Build Wealth in Today's Expanding Real Estate Market."[60]

In both years, the cover shows a house floating in the sky and a family on the ground, looking up at it.

In the summer of 2005, problems reemerged at Long Beach Mortgage. For three years the subsidiary had grown exponentially, and WaMu's subprime volume had more than tripled during that time, reaching $35 billion.[61] Nationwide, subprime lending had reached a feverish volume of about $800 billion, representing nearly a quarter of all new mortgages.[62] At Long Beach, the oversight that Fay Chapman and her team put in place after the exhaustive legal review had come unglued. Long Beach's managers had been given full rein at the company and had whittled away at policies preventing out-of-control lending. Loan standards relaxed. Even as Long Beach's account executives funded more mortgages through brokers, the WaMu subsidiary operated with little fraud protection. One Southern California Long Beach sales manager, in fact, tried to point out problem loan applications at the division. She created a spreadsheet charting the false information for her managers, only to be told after several months that "there were inconsistencies," but they couldn't be confirmed. The sales manager, who had worked for years in a fraud department at another subprime lender, had even submitted a borrower's original credit report along with the blatantly doctored version. "The fraud department did not know what they were doing," said the sales manager later. "They blamed it on the credit reporting agency."

Long Beach homeowners began missing mortgage payments. Some borrowers never wrote even a single check to pay off their debt. (Of those delinquent loans, 99 percent could have been prevented, a later internal review concluded.) As the defaults grew, the investors who had bought the loans demanded their money back. In no time at all, Long Beach had to repurchase a full $837 million worth of bad loans, at a loss of more than $100 million to WaMu.[63] Rotella fired Long Beach Mortgage's management team and moved its oversight under Schneider. The division became a subsidiary of the bank—not WaMu's holding company—a switch intended to increase oversight. But the problems only continued.

As Rotella tried to sort out the many problems in Long Beach Mortgage and the Home Loans Group, he also tried to figure out how to make both groups profitable. He e-mailed Killinger, telling him he thought the Home Loans Group needed to focus "on organic growth" of home equity loans and subprime mortgages.[64]

Killinger replied: "Regarding Longbeach [sic], I think there is a good opportunity to be a low cost provider and gain significant share when the industry implodes." He added: "It makes sense to leverage the home loans distribution channels with subprime, home equity and Alt A." Alt

A was another type of mortgage aimed at borrowers with less-than-perfect credit

Rotella agreed, noting that "we did these kinds of analyses all the time at Chase, which caused us to run as fast as we could into home eq, alt a, subprime (our investment banking brethren stopped us from going too far there)." He continued: "I feel strongly that where we need to land is a new home loan unit that includes prime, heq and subprime. It is a far superior model."

Just a week after this exchange, Killinger expressed concern in an earnings call about overheated housing markets: "We are keeping a very watchful eye on this situation and believe that we may be entering a period of industry shakeout, in both the prime and subprime sectors."[65]

All the while, WaMu's Option ARM customers behaved as the earlier focus groups had anticipated. Each month tens of thousands of them received their mortgage statements, and each month most of them chose the "minimum payment" option. At the end of 2005, nearly half of the loans in WaMu's $70 billion Option ARM portfolio were negatively amortizing.[66] WaMu customers had avoided paying $316 million in interest, up from just $19 million a year earlier.[67] WaMu booked that interest as earnings, which meant that the bank, in accordance with national accounting standards, was making money off of borrowers not paying down their debt. Andrew Leonard, a writer at Salon.com, took notice and remarked darkly: "That's Enron economics, folks, and we all remember what happened to that company." (Leonard also noted that "Negative Amortization" would make a terrific name for a punk band.)

Across the country, lenders that made large numbers of Option ARMs reported the same phenomenon. Seventy percent of borrowers nationwide were paying the minimum amount each month. Golden West Financial, the large Option ARM lender, reported $160 million in unpaid interest, up from $27 million in one year. Its chief executive reassured a reporter that its lending practices were disciplined. It wouldn't get into trouble, he said. The only risk would be a broad decline in home prices, in which case, the executive pointed out, all mortgages would suffer.[68]

WaMu, incidentally, avoided disclosing exactly how much interest its borrowers hadn't paid but appeared to change that stance after Jesse

Eisinger, then a reporter at *The Wall Street Journal*, pointed out its lack of transparency.[69] WaMu, like Golden West, brushed off the risk of the Option ARMs, noting in its 2005 annual report that "credit risk usually diminishes when housing prices appreciate."

Each year, as it had done for more than two decades, WaMu held an elaborate, multiple-day celebration, honoring the most prolific mortgage salespeople across the country. The event was called President's Club. To become a member of President's Club and receive an invitation to the swanky getaway, salespeople had to have funded millions of dollars of home loans during the previous year. WaMu posted loan volume rankings on its website, increasing the pressure on employees to beat their peers. "Where do you rank?" wondered one President's Club advertisement titled "Yes you can!" "What can you do to take your business to the next level? Your management team is here to help."[70] Managers of home loan centers across the country cheered their salespeople on with milestone incentives and encouraging e-mails. Each office tried to beat the others' monthly sales goals and ensure that all it own employees made it to President's Club. Read one such e-mail from the manager of a home loans center in northern California: "Less than one week and we have a long way to go to hit our 440M! Scott is out front with 8 fundings Friday and 79 MTD [month to date]—looks like he'll make the *100 Club*! Cyndi is currently in 2nd with 6 on Friday and 65 MTD followed by Maureen who funded 7 on Friday and has 60 MTD. This one might get a little crazy before 2 p.m. on Thursday! *Let's see who can fund daily double digits this week!*"[71] The three people mentioned in the e-mail made more than 200 loans in three weeks. "Here's a tip for getting to President's Club," one repeat attendee wrote from Oregon, as part of the advertisement for the event. "Make it once and bring your wife. She will make sure you never miss it again!" Said another attendee: "My husband still can't believe the way we were treated."

The mortgage industry regularly threw splashy sales events. But in recent years, WaMu's President's Club parties had become increasingly spectacular, each event more over-the-top than the one the year before. One reason for the seven-figure festivities, the incentives, and the pandering was that WaMu worried about losing its salespeople to other companies. Nearly every other bank and home lender in the market, not just Countrywide, paid a premium for riskier home loans. If the salespeople could collect more money somewhere else, why wouldn't they? They had no allegiance to WaMu.

The Home Loans Group usually held President's Club in Hawaii or another tropical location like Puerto Rico or Cancún, and always at an expensive hotel or conference venue. Hundreds of WaMu salespeople flew in from all areas of the country, especially from Arizona, Florida, and California, where houses couldn't go up fast enough. Each night the salespeople arrived in their hotel room—all expenses paid—to find gifts on their pillows such as iPods or boutique chocolates or digital cameras. Throughout the long weekend, the bank held rousing sales sessions, but mostly people hung out on the beach or played golf. They took helicopter rides or excursions around whichever tropical paradise they were visiting. "You were treated like some kind of dignitary in a country full of people who worshipped you," said one repeat attendee. The crux of the event was a black-tie awards dinner, an outlandish affair that typically devolved into a night of after-hours partying, filled with drinking and sex. Managers often danced on tables.

At David Schneider's first President's Club, held in early 2006 in Maui, someone had chosen the Academy Awards as the theme of the awards dinner. The salespeople, women in thin-strapped dresses and expertly styled hair, men in tuxedos and bow ties, streamed into a windowed conference center perched over the Pacific Ocean. In keeping with the theme, the attendees walked in on a long red carpet, partitioned off by ropes, behind which WaMu-hired photographers snapped photos like paparazzi. The salespeople posed for pictures in front of a hanging white backdrop with the "President's Club" logo stamped across the front. A cavernous banquet hall was richly decorated to fit the occasion. Deep red, gauzy fabric crisscrossed the wide ceiling and hung along the walls. Dozens of tables had been set up across the room with little space in between them. At the front, a concert-style stage held a podium and several giant TVs so the attendees in the farthest corners could still follow the program. An elegantly dressed waitstaff circled with wine.

Just before 7:00 p.m., the lights in the room dimmed. A voice-over announced Schneider, who walked onto the stage. The attendees applauded.

"Thank you ladies and gentlemen, and welcome to this very special awards evening," Schneider said, reading from a script.[72] "Wow, could you feel the energy and excitement tonight out on the red carpet? Talk about star power!

"But don't worry," he continued. "I'm told that the age-old tradition here at Washington Mutual is 'What happens at President's Club, stays at President's Club.' And who am I to mess with tradition? . . .

"I want to pay special homage to all of you astonishing returning champions of President's Club. You multiple award-winning superstars clearly lead our entire industry as the standard others can only attempt to match. You folks really do make this feel like the Academy Awards tonight because everywhere I turn I see another star of another box-office sensation. And so to you, the greatest collection of talent I've ever had the good fortune to address, I promise an evening of fast-moving fun, celebration, and tribute in ways old and new."

This year Schneider had a surprise for President's Club attendees. "What could make a night like this more special than having one of the most recognizable, accomplished, and beloved celebrities on the planet emcee it? I can't think of anyone more perfectly suited than Earvin 'Magic' Johnson. He embodies this year's President's Club theme, 'Dare to Dream.' Ladies and gentlemen, here he is—the one, the only . . . Magic!"

WaMu had recently announced a partnership with the former basketball star turned businessman to encourage lending in lower-income communities. WaMu and Johnson planned to build several new branches together.

"Good evening, everyone. It's great to see you all again looking so fine and impressive everywhere I turn," Johnson said. "President's Club . . . it's kind of like the NBA All-Star game. Everyone there is an all-star, so you all start out as the top people at what you do."

Johnson explained how the bank would be handing out awards to its top-performing salespeople. He introduced Steve Rotella, who, now that he had become president of the company, attended the events along with Kerry Killinger. Both spoke to the audience, and both handed out awards. Killinger, who had no background as a mortgage peddler, seemed out of place amid all the partying. While he gamely went along with everything, he stuck out like a parent at a heavy-metal concert.

"Thank you, Magic Johnson," Rotella said, taking the podium. "Wow! Never in my wildest fantasies did I think I'd get to say, 'Thank you, Magic Johnson,' as part of my job. I guess that's just another way Washington Mutual is helping to deliver the American Dream. But when it comes to delivering the American Dream, I am in absolute awe of you people. Even under the most difficult of environments—especially under the most difficult of environments—the cream truly does rise to the top, and that's what President's Club means to me."

The highest-volume loan officers took turns walking up on stage and accepting a handcrafted glass statue, which essentially served as an Oscar. Some of the salespeople who received awards had made it to President's Club twenty years in a row. Others had funded hundreds of millions of dollars in loans in one year. In one Southern California home loan center, a duo of loan officers known for their taste in expensive cars made more than $1 billion in loans during the year, the equivalent of more than 2,000 houses. "They battle evil competitors— and sometimes underwriters—to get the best loans for customers," said Tony Meola, the manager in charge of mortgage production, when announcing the team's award. Another loan officer, who had worked for WaMu for more than fifteen years, funded $1 billion of loans in 2005, on his own. "If we had a Walk of Fame, his star would be on it," Meola announced. "He has earned not just a place, but rightfully an entire wing on WaMu's Hall of Fame."

Meola's next award recipient was Tom Ramirez, a WaMu loan consultant who had become a mortgage lender legend in Southern California. Ramirez worked out of WaMu's office in Downey, a largely Hispanic neighborhood of cracked sidewalks and graffiti-marked homes, east of downtown Los Angeles. WaMu called the Downey office a Community Fulfillment Center, the bank's name for home loan branches that served minority communities. Those centers often used even looser guidelines for making loans, allowing lower credit scores and less income documentation. Ramirez specialized in Option ARM lending. While he didn't take out billboards with his face painted on the front, as many mortgage salespeople did, he was an expert marketer. He often attended important local events. Most of the local salespeople knew Tom Ramirez or at least had heard of him. While many found him nice and personable, they also harbored jealousy for his extraordinary loan production.

He had pioneered a program that allowed real estate agents to collect referral fees for sending clients to WaMu.[73] Those agents made 1 percent off the total loan cost, which the borrower paid at closing. (Whether the borrower knew this remains unclear.) Real estate agents loved the idea. They arrived in Downey from all over Los Angeles County with loan applications. Because the program proved so successful, WaMu expanded, filling a neighboring building with more loan processors.

At WaMu, Ramirez, who was sometimes called "Tommy" by executives, also had a stellar reputation. Loan consultants from around the country knew his name, aspiring to bring in as much business. Killinger had singled him out for praise, lauding his work with minority borrowers.[74] Rotella held meetings with him and his Downey team and criticized executives in the Home Loans Group for failing to implement the team's demands. Ramirez and his loan consultants wanted to approve borrowers with lower FICO scores, bypassing a senior underwriter's approval, and allow assets to count on a loan application, even if they weren't yet in a customer's account. By counting money in a bank account before it was deposited, for example, a customer might qualify for a loan even if the money ultimately didn't show up. Rotella didn't think Ramirez's demands were unreasonable. "I met them last year and I was so impressed, I suggested we use them to spawn similar operations in Hispanic communities across the U.S., if possible using them to model, train, and certify the work," Rotella wrote in a glowing e-mail about Ramirez and his team, which also questioned Schneider for failing to meet the group's demands.[75] "Frankly, not much has happened," Rotella wrote. "We should fall all over ourselves to have a business segment that attracts minorities, is almost all Option ARMs, is not price driven, delivers great quality and is oriented toward the average guy, our market."

For 17 straight years, Ramirez had received one of the highest honors at President's Club, the number-one loan consultant. He had funded more units than any other WaMu office nationwide. In 2005, he made more than 2,300 mortgages, a feat announced that night at President's Club. To achieve that astounding rate, Ramirez would have had to make more than six mortgages a day, every single day during the last year, including weekends and holidays. Of course that was impossible. Ramirez achieved that volume because a team of junior loan consultants and associates made mortgages in his name. That was a common practice in the business.

"In our world of superstars, he is bigger than a Brad Pitt, George Clooney, or Tom Cruise. He's at the Henry Fonda, Burt Lancaster, John Wayne legendary status," Meola said in announcing Ramirez's award.

Several months earlier a disturbing internal report had come out about the quality of the loans made in the Downey branch, as well as that of another Community Fulfillment Center in the neighboring East Los Angeles city of Montebello.[76] For three years, rumors had circulated at WaMu about fraud in the two locations. But fraud is hard to prove, and it's even harder to prove in a company atmosphere where sales trump all else. Schneider later presented a faux diagram of WaMu's corporate structure, labeling each tier: "SALES." "We are ALL in Sales," it read.[77]

In the summer of 2005, WaMu launched a review of the mortgages made in Downey and Montebello. The review found an "extensive level of fraud," as was later noted in an e-mail circulated among management.* Among the hundreds of loans that borrowers had received from the Downey office in the previous two years, nearly *half* contained fraud. At Montebello, fraud rates exceeded 80 percent. All of it, the reviewer wrote in the e-mail, was "attributable to some sort of employee malfeasance or failure to execute company policy."[78] The fraud was outrageous, even in the age of bloated incomes on mortgage applications and false bank statements.

---

*In later congressional testimony, Rotella said he had not been told about the fraud report on Downey and Montebello, and it wouldn't be brought to his attention until 2008. If "there indeed was fraud, believe me, significant action would be taken," Rotella said. Schneider also claimed not to have seen it.

On one loan application, everything about the buyer was made up, including his Social Security number, his income, his assets, and his credit reference letters. The buyer had tried—and he would have been likely to succeed if not for the review—to include a house in Mexico as collateral on his mortgage from WaMu. "The credit package was found to be completely fabricated," the review concluded. "Throughout the process, red flags were overlooked, process requirements were waived and exceptions to policy were granted." On another loan, a buyer had refinanced his three-bedroom investment property, and within a year, the value had jumped 90 percent from $322,000 to $610,000, even though nearby homes sold for about $400,000 (which would still represent a sizable appreciation rate of almost 25 percent). During the year, the three-bedroom house had somehow grown in size. The description of the property had also changed, despite no apparent construction. Someone had altered the details of the property to inflate the value of the home.[79]

The fraud report had come out not long before President's Club, yet here was Tommy Ramirez, the top producer not only in the Downey office but in the country, walking up on stage to shake Killinger's hand and accept his trophy. Of loans that had been referred to Ramirez, 58 percent contained fraud,[80] a rate that one WaMu executive would later describe as "eye-popping." Luis Fragoso, another high-volume loan consultant at the nearby Montebello office, posted a fraud rate of 83 percent for loan referrals. He also was honored at President's Club.

"No one in history has put more people into their first home," said Meola, up on stage. "Please put your hands together for an extraordinary man, Tom Ramirez!" The audience cheered. In 2005, WaMu made $3.4 billion in profit.

Chapter Six

THE
GROWING TROUBLE

Bye, bye, mortgage banking guys. You made money when it was sunny, but the well has gone dry.

—Song written by WaMu employee Michele Perrin,
to the tune of "American Pie"

Lights lowered, the room grew dark. On stage at the Anaheim Convention Center in California, two giant flat-screen television panels blazed to life behind Kerry Killinger. Within moments, the faces of different WaMu employees filled the dual screens, their voices reverberating across the wide space. Clips of the employees, all espousing WaMu's corporate values, played in a rapid montage.

"We're bringing something of value and something different."

"I care so much about our customers."

"We're one big happy family."

"I'm building myself; I'm feeding my soul."

*"The sky's the limit. If someone's willing to give a piece of their heart and their life, there's really no limit to what you can do."**

The video—*The WaMu Way*—had been Killinger's idea. One of his executive assistants produced the six-figure endeavor, and it premiered at WaMu's annual State of the Group meeting in early 2006. WaMu

---

*This platitude was delivered by Luis Fragoso in WaMu's Montebello branch.

held the massive get-together each year to update its employees on the state of the company, a play on the U.S. president's annual State of the Union address. But the event was known as a giant pro-WaMu rally. Thousands of employees from across the country attended, and WaMu rented a large convention center in Seattle, or sometimes California, to hold everyone. The bank usually hired someone famous to speak. One year Ellen DeGeneres held a mock talk show. After the values video finished playing, Colin Powell, the former U.S. secretary of state, was next on the agenda. Killinger always made a big entrance. Once he rode in on a Segway. Another year he donned a space suit and was lowered onto the center of the stage.

Not long into the values video, Killinger appeared on screen, standing against a white backdrop. His cheeks were rosy, and his hands sliced the air. He spoke emphatically.

"I don't think there's a single institution in this country as well positioned as Washington Mutual is today. We want to build something that's so unique, that has such great opportunity for employees and our customers and our communities and our stockholders—that no other company in this country can possibly match. What really matters to me, when I come to work every day, is that I'm making a difference to the client, because that's really the bottom line."

Killinger held a sign that read "CEO" upside down until—whoops!— he realized his "mistake" and turned it around. He smiled at the camera. The video cut to Steve Rotella, wearing his usual open blazer. Rotella chuckled as if he had just heard a great joke. He addressed the camera.

"One of the key reasons I came here a year ago after being with another company for eighteen years is the value of this company. I think it's different and I think it's important and I think it's powerful. I would not have been as interested in joining Washington Mutual if the values were something that were just words up on a bulletin board, and that's true at a lot of companies. It's not true here."

The video lasted several minutes and was nearly finished when Lou Pepper appeared on screen. He sat in an office chair, against the same white backdrop as the other executives. His legs were crossed and his arms folded. He delivered his advice gruffly, without his trademark smile:

"Be nice to one another. Work hard at your job, work smart at your job,

try hard, always be pleasant. You'll succeed in business and you'll succeed as a human being. That's a nice way to live your life."

Unless they knew him personally, none of the thousands of attendees at the State of the Group gathering would have guessed that Pepper had been annoyed as he shot the video. WaMu's corporate values, which Pepper had tasked a group with creating two decades earlier, had changed. Instead of just "Fair," "Caring," and "Human," two new attributes had been added to WaMu's longtime creed: "Dynamic" and "Driven." On the video, WaMu employees had spoken of the new values.

"We're driven; we love to compete."

"We love to win."

When Pepper arrived at WaMu's headquarters, where a car waited to take him to the video shoot at a nearby studio, he asked for a dictionary so he could look up the definition of *driven* or *drive*. The negative connotations of the word dismayed him. Merriam-Webster offered up several definitions of *drive*, including "to impart a forward motion by physical force" and "to frighten or prod (as game or cattle) into moving in a desired direction." During the short drive to the studio, Pepper complained repeatedly about the new values. "It sounds like something you would do to cattle," he told Killinger's assistant, who was heading up the project. The assistant listened, but his mind was on the project. He was racing to get the video finished on a tight deadline and had already surpassed the budget. "I was just like, 'I need to get this video done,'" the assistant later said.

At WaMu, Lou Pepper had become like the Ghost of Christmas Past. While everyone knew of him, few of the new executives and employees had met or spent any time with him. For years, Killinger had provided him an office, even after Pepper retired from the board of directors in 1997. But in WaMu's recent move to its new skyscraper, Pepper no longer had a place. When he visited—and his visits became much rarer after his executive team broke up—the new employees treated him respectfully, but after he left, they tended to roll their eyes at his long-winded stories and vexing advice. "Bless his heart, everyone had heard his stories not once, but twice," one longtime employee said. "It was very busy; it wasn't the old WaMu."

Pepper's book had just come out—the one he had written about his thoughts on leadership. In retrospect, the book reads like a well-written warning manual. He advised companies to offer products only if they are good for customers. "You may make a quick buck selling a high mark-up product, but you also start the clock running on your demise," Pepper wrote.[1] The new executives and managers paid little attention. While the book was in production, the project had caused grumbling around WaMu's headquarters. "There was a lot of work and expense involved," said one employee who worked on it. Pepper tried hard to avoid the pitfall of the old boss getting in the way of the new one. He offered up occasional suggestions, only to be largely ignored. Killinger humored him but didn't take him into his confidence. And as for the values—not many people on the executive floor cared if WaMu was considered "human" or "driven" anyway. "I thought that was a smoke-screen," said one executive later. "Why don't we admit we're business guys and do the right thing for our shareholders? It was just happy horseshit." Added another executive: "The old culture could not have survived the growth of the company."

After Rotella was hired, Pepper wrote him a long e-mail, trying to explain, in a circuitous way, the history of WaMu and its culture. The e-mail was a jumble of Pepper's fond memories and anecdotes. He relayed the story of a longtime branch manager whom he admired because of her tenacity and devotion to customer service. "In California, where she went several times, she found the folks happy to have us and eager to learn," Pepper wrote. "Her experience in New York was remarkable. She said she was helping a sort of grumpy customer, and he finally said, 'I don't want any more of this West Coast Nice.' She said she just broke up laughing and the startled customer soon joined her and all went well. Oh, she was a piece of work. Ideal as a trainer. I am sad she retired." This tale was classic Pepper. It focused on human nature. He loved to point out good deeds carried out by those around him. He admired his daughter for answering the phone one day and helping out an older caller who had dialed a wrong number.

Rotella, who was busy, eventually stopped writing back.

Suffering from health problems and weary from battling the growth of high-risk loans, Jim Vanasek, WaMu's chief risk officer, retired. In the spring of 2005, in one of his last attempts to change the company's direction, he wrote a memo to WaMu's executive committee. If the bank continued to make high-risk loans, he warned, the results could be disastrous for the company. "My credit team and I fear that we are considering expanding our risk appetite at exactly the wrong point and potentially walking straight into a regulatory challenge and criticism from both the Street and the Board," Vanasek wrote.[2]

His warning went unheeded. In early 2006, David Schneider gave a presentation to WaMu's board of directors. The president of the Home Loans Group announced his plans to shift from "low-margin business" to "high-margin products." High-margin products were defined as home equity loans, subprime loans, Alt-A loans, and Option ARM loans. A prime, thirty-year fixed-rate mortgage was considered a "low-margin" product. Within two years, Schneider wanted to increase WaMu's home loan volume by about 12 percent to $232 billion by pushing high-risk loans. He planned for 80 percent of WaMu's home loan portfolio to consist of these kinds of mortgages, up from about 50 percent at the time of the presentation. Subprime, for example, would double to $70 billion, or 30 percent of all home loans. Fixed-rate loans would shrivel further, to just 2 percent of the portfolio. While Schneider's plan was a continuation of Killinger's "higher-risk lending strategy," it called for much larger increases in these kinds of mortgages.[3]

After Vanasek left, Killinger hired Ron Cathcart, a Canadian who had worked at Bank One and Canadian Imperial Bank of Commerce. Cathcart shook up enterprise risk management. He installed a chief risk officer in each division of the company, and that officer reported both to Cathcart *and* to the head of the business unit.[4] WaMu employees jokingly referred to this dual reporting as "double double." Cathcart wasn't in favor of it—he wanted all the risk officers to report to him—but the bank had undergone a long review. The executive team and directors approved the new structure. While the move theoretically increased the amount of oversight at WaMu, it also made each business unit's risk officer more beholden to that division's growth. Cheryl Feltgen, the new chief risk officer of the Home Loans Group, faced annual performance reviews based in part on the volume of loans produced; the higher the volume of loans, the bigger pay raise she received in the coming year.[5]

The structure change ended up draining power from Cathcart, who oversaw risk for the entire company.

Cathcart also took a different approach with the Home Loans Group. Whereas Vanasek had waged war against the division's executives, Cathcart tried to work with them. This tactic met with mixed results. While he demanded to see fraud reports and noted numerous problems, Cathcart sometimes appeared too lenient. When federal regulators tried to impose national guidelines on high-risk loans, Cathcart suggested in an e-mail in early 2007 that the Home Loans Group hold off unless the bank had to report changes "for public relations" or "regulatory reasons."*[6]

Feltgen wrote a year-end letter summing up the accomplishments of the Home Loans Group's risk management team, noting Schneider's shift to high-margin products. She wrote to her employees: "You have partnered successfully with the business units of Home Loans in pursuit of our collective goal to drive profitable growth with the right balance of risk and return." Quoting a phrase from Schneider's new internal growth campaign, she added: "Recognize that 'we are all in sales,' passionately focused on delivering great products and service to our customers." Cathcart replied, "Great letter."[7] Feltgen would later describe Cathcart as "not well respected," adding that he didn't have a strong voice. Schneider, in contrast, possessed both these qualities.[8]

Halfway into 2006, with Schneider's strategy firmly in place, something strange happened. For the first time in eleven years, the median price of existing homes nationwide *declined*. The 1.7 percent drop was the second-largest year-to-year decrease in home prices since the National Association of Realtors started keeping track thirty-eight years earlier, in 1968. Home sales, which had started falling several months earlier, plummeted almost 13 percent from the previous year.[9]

The steep drop brought all sorts of speculation from economists and bankers and analysts. Was the dreaded end to the housing bubble here?

---

*A person familiar with Cathcart's thinking later said he was concerned with how borrowers might be affected by the changes and didn't want the bank to publicly release anything that wasn't well thought out.

Or was this just a "correction," a euphemism used by real estate agents and Wall Street to describe falling home prices? *The Wall Street Journal* surveyed industry leaders and found varying levels of optimism. David Lereah, the chief economist for the National Association of Realtors (whose book had just come out with the new title *Why the Real Estate BOOM Will Not Bust*), gave an upbeat assessment. He called the "price correction" a welcome development. "The price drop has stopped the bleeding," he said. "Sales have hit bottom. Sellers are finally getting it. I am confident the housing sector is picking up."* The most negative take on the news came from a small economic consulting firm called Naroff Economic Advisors. Naroff offered this prediction: The "decline is likely to continue as the supply of homes, measured in months, reached the highest level in over thirteen years. With inventories so high, there is a lot more adjustment before the existing home market hits bottom."[10]

In December 2006, on a Monday night after work, Todd Baker, WaMu's executive vice president of corporate strategy and development, was catching up on some reading. Two stories in *The Wall Street Journal* caught his attention. At 9:00 p.m., he typed out an e-mail to Killinger, Rotella, Schneider, and the other members of WaMu's executive team. "It's subprime day at the Wall Street Journal," he wrote, copying and pasting both articles in the e-mail.[11] The first one, "More Borrowers with Risky Loans Are Falling Behind," was perhaps the most disturbing. It claimed 2006 was on track "to be one of the worst ever for subprime loans." About 80,000 borrowers who had taken out subprime loans at lenders such as WaMu and Countrywide and New Century, and whose loans had been turned into securities, were behind on payments. "We are a bit surprised by how fast this has unraveled," said the head of UBS's asset-backed securities research in the article. The 2006 subprime borrowers were apparently going into foreclosure at a faster pace than in previous years.[12]

---

*In 2007, Lereah would leave the National Association of Realtors (he said of his own accord), to take another job. His unrelenting optimism earned him several nicknames, according to *The Wall Street Journal*, including "Mr. Liar-eah" and "Baghdad Dave," after the Iraqi information minister Mohammed al-Sahaf, who was known as "Baghdad Bob," due to his pro-Iraq press briefings during the U.S. invasion.

In the second article, the *Journal* wrote that more subprime lenders wanted to sell their companies but were having a hard time finding buyers.[13] H&R Block wanted to off-load its subprime unit, Option One Mortgage. Roland Arnall's Ameriquest, the company that Long Beach Mortgage had spun out of a decade earlier and that had later turned into a subprime mortgage "boiler room," was up for sale.

Ron Cathcart also received Baker's e-mail with the *Journal* stories, and he forwarded it on to his team later that night. He called out a particularly disturbing paragraph tacked at the bottom of one of the articles: "An analysis by Merrill Lynch & Co. found that losses on recent subprime deals could be in 'the 6% to 8% range' if home prices are flat next year and could rise to the 'double-digits' if home prices fall by 5%."

"What do our numbers show?" Cathcart asked his team in the e-mail. The inquiry turned up troubling information, reflected in an Excel spreadsheet. "Our 2006 Long Beach securities have much higher delinquency rates early in their life than the 2003 to 2005 vintages," Cathcart's employee reported. If housing prices declined 5 percent a year for four years, losses might indeed climb into the double digits.

At about the same time, Tom Casey, WaMu's chief financial officer, attended the annual Lehman Investors conference in New York and returned with bad news. "He says equity investors are totally freaking about housing right now," wrote the managing director of WaMu's trading office in an e-mail, summing up a meeting with Casey. "He asked how we could prepare for this."[14]

WaMu had to get rid of as many risky mortgages as possible. If the housing market continued to cool, two things would happen. Home prices would drop, and many borrowers would owe more on their loans than their houses were worth. Their mortgages would be "underwater." Without price appreciation, buyers wouldn't be able to refinance adjustable-rate loans, so they would be left paying at a much higher rate. For WaMu's Option ARM borrowers, this scenario was "something terrible happens in three years." Since many of WaMu's borrowers held some kind of adjustable-rate loan, and since they couldn't afford the higher rate (WaMu had often issued mortgages based on the lower one), the bank would face a massive wave of defaults and foreclosures. Subprime loans were at an even higher risk. Those borrowers already had bad credit, and fraud had permeated Long Beach Mortgage. WaMu would face losses on those loans, as no one else would want to buy them anymore. Casey instructed WaMu's trading division to look at off-loading recent batches of subprime and Option ARM loans.

Even as concern grew, Killinger wanted to explore a purchase of Ameriquest, an acquisition that would have flooded WaMu will billions of dollars in additional subprime mortgages. "They don't ring a bell at the bottom," Killinger liked to say, implying that smart companies make deals at just the right time. "He really thought we could get in and buy assets cheap and buy businesses cheap," said one WaMu executive. Even Cathcart, the person in charge of WaMu's risk, floated the idea of buying Ameriquest in early 2007.[15]* Ultimately, the deal didn't work out. WaMu looked at buying a subprime auto loan business but ended up purchasing Providian, a subprime credit card company.

In early 2007, Ramona Jiminez, her husband Gerardo, and her mother Maria began looking around East Los Angeles for a house. Jiminez, who had years ago moved to California from Mexico, was thirty-two years old and came from a large family. She had four children, the oldest fifteen, and several siblings who had their own spouses and children. She had never before owned a house. For years her family had rented apartments in El Monte, an industrial neighborhood in the San Gabriel Valley. In El Monte ("Welcome to Friendly El Monte" read the city slogan), tortilla trucks drove down potholed streets and ruined cars were stacked up on parched lawns. The air smelled of exhaust from the millions of commuters driving across Highway 10 toward the city of Los Angeles, and dust rose up from all corners of the parched neighborhood. El Monte was only 20 minutes away from Downey, where Tom Ramirez and his team made Option ARMs by the hundreds.

Jiminez and her husband hired a real estate agent to help them find a house. They wanted to stay in El Monte, and they wanted their entire extended family to live there together. Although this house was

---

*WaMu regularly bought loans from Ameriquest through its correspondent division. Although WaMu didn't detail those loans in its public filings, the mortgages were reportedly faring better than those that were originated out of Long Beach Mortgage.

Jiminez's first, she wasn't as exuberant as many first-time homebuyers. Her thinking was practical. She had a large family, and they needed somewhere to live. She didn't know whether home prices were falling or rising in El Monte. She couldn't recall hearing President Bill Clinton or President George W. Bush or anyone else talk about the joys of minority homeownership.

For several weeks, Jiminez drove around the streets of East Los Angeles with her mother and husband and real estate agent. One day they pulled up in front of a property that would hold the whole family. The one-story house was beige with white trim, but the paint was cracking and streaked in some places with dark stains, as if a storm had swept through and permeated the walls with water. Inside, the house had two small bedrooms and a kitchen not larger than a closet, all of which seemed to have been cobbled together and then ignored since the construction four decades ago. The walls and the floor and the cupboards, once seemingly a brighter white, now appeared dull. A dirty window overlooked the street, where dozens of other houses looked just like this one. In the back of the 3,300-square-foot property—what had attracted Jiminez and her family—three other homes were squished together in a row. The fourplex was separated from the worn neighborhood by a square patch of lawn with a couple of scraggly bushes, and by a waist-high iron fence that locked and slid open only with some maneuvering of the latch. The property was listed at $875,000. All sixteen family members could live there.

Jiminez didn't have to visit a bank to get a loan. A real estate agent in California could take care of financing as well.[16] Jiminez and her husband had low credit scores, 580 and 615, respectively. But Jiminez's mother, who would also be listed on the loan, had recently sold her own house in Los Angeles after Jiminez's father died. That sale had netted $200,000 for a down payment. Jiminez's husband worked at a construction company in Orange County. For the last several years, there had been no shortage of work as the company built houses by the hundreds in high-end subdivisions.

The family had to fill out little paperwork to get a loan. "It was cut and dried," Jiminez said later. She spoke fluent English, but she didn't understand the details of her mortgage. She knew she was paying only the interest rate on her loan, and that it would cost $4,330 a month. The agent had told her that the mortgage was variable, which Jiminez understood meant the rate would adjust. But she wasn't sure when that would happen, or how much more she would pay. "A lot of people questioned me," Jiminez said. "Why did they give you that loan?" She didn't have a good answer. The agent sold Jiminez's loan to Long Beach Mortgage, now owned by WaMu. WaMu would service Jiminez's mortgage, but the bank packaged it up into one of its last bond deals, a subprime security called, cryptically, WAMU Series 2007-HE4.[17] Without her knowledge, investors scattered around the world now bet that Jiminez, a thirty-two-year-old housewife with four children and a FICO score of 580, would keep paying the mortgage on her rundown property in El Monte. (Other investors were betting against it.) They were also betting that homeowners who took out the other 2,479 mortgages in the $440 million bond deal would pay back their loans as well. Eighty percent held adjustable-rate mortgages. Nearly 40 percent lived in California.

One of the other homeowners in the bond lived less than half an hour away from Jiminez and her family, just outside the crime-ridden neighborhood of Compton. In 2003, the year Sara Vasquez bought her three-bedroom house, Compton's law officers recorded 548 burglaries, 43 murders, and 1,021 reported cases of aggravated assault.[18] Still, Vasquez and her husband loved the kidney-shaped pool in the backyard and had taken out a loan for the property through a mortgage broker. They received an Option ARM, although they didn't know it—they just knew that their interest rate was 1 percent and they paid $800 a month. It was cheaper to own a house than to rent an apartment. Soon, however, their mortgage payment shot up to $3,000 a month. "There was a lot of wording on those documents I didn't understand," she said later. Vasquez, who was thirty-one and worked at a nearby detention facility, refinanced her mortgage. In the meantime, she had a baby and divorced her husband. WaMu bought her $425,000 subprime loan. In the bond, everything was based on numbers and averages. Investors knew that the average FICO score was 613, with the lowest at 470 and the highest at 812. They didn't know that Vasquez's kidney-shaped pool had become a deteriorating eyesore ("We thought it was great to have a pool, but you need a lot of stuff to keep it running"), or that Jiminez's family couldn't afford a telephone.

WaMu's subprime securities had already begun to go bad by the time the subprime security deal comprising Jiminez's mortgage came together. Long Beach Mortgage paper "is among the worst performing paper in the market in 2006," wrote the head of WaMu's capital market division, David Beck, in an internal e-mail.[19] In one bond deal, nearly 20 percent of the borrowers had missed loan payments. In another, packaged by Goldman Sachs, WaMu provided 1,534 Long Beach loans, some of which later became delinquent.[20] Goldman wrote to WaMu, complaining about the bank's bad loans: "As you can imagine, this creates extreme pressure, both economic and reputation, on both organizations. The investors are demanding answers, decisive action, and resolution."[21] Noted one employee working on WaMu's bonds: "Structured finance works. The problem is if you put junk in, it stops working."

WaMu's need to off-load risky loans intensified. Beck sent out an e-mail to several WaMu executives, including Schneider and Rotella, labeling it "high importance." He had to figure out how to get rid of $433 million in Long Beach loans that hadn't yet soured but were "second liens," which meant that they held a junior position on a loan behind another lender. If the borrower went into foreclosure, WaMu would be paid last or in many cases not at all. "The performing second lien investor base is in disarray," Beck wrote, "and for all intents and purposes distributing credit bonds backed by subprime second liens is not a viable exit strategy."[22] The window to sell loans to investors began to shut in late 2006. Now, in early 2007, it was closing further. Option ARM borrowers had started to miss payments, and WaMu wanted to get rid of a large chunk of them before they soured. Cheryl Feltgen communicated this desire in an e-mail with an all-caps subject line: "URGENT NEED TO GET SOME WORK DONE IN NEXT COUPLE OF DAYS."[23] Feltgen wrote that WaMu could still make money by selling the Option ARMs. In California, home prices were falling further and mortgage delinquencies were growing, but somehow investors weren't paying attention. "The market seems not to be yet discounting a lot for those factors," Feltgen wrote. Even Killinger, not typically involved in the details of mortgage transactions, offered his opinion, encouraging

executives to sell off as many Option ARMs as possible. WaMu packaged about 1,900 of the delinquency-prone Option ARMs, worth about
$1 billion, into a security. None of the materials sent out to investors
disclosed WaMu's internal process for picking mortgages that might
default. More than 85 percent of the bonds received the highest grade
from the rating agencies. Three years later over half of the mortgages
would be delinquent and a quarter would be in foreclosure.[24]

None of this turmoil seemed to faze WaMu's Capital Markets Group,
which had ballooned to 200 employees, with offices in New York, Los
Angeles, Chicago, and Seattle. The division presented plans to package
and sell Collateralized Debt Obligations (CDOs), a type of security
whose popularity had grown over the previous five years and which was
even more complicated than a regular mortgage-backed security. CDOs
were packaged with any kind of debt, causing the authors of a later book
about the financial crisis to describe them as "asset-backed securities on
steroids."[25] WaMu wanted to package its CDOs with home equity loans,
credit card debt, and slices of mortgage-backed securities. It also wanted
to sell synthetic CDOs (made up not of actual mortgages but of bonds
made from mortgages held by someone else) and hybrid CDOs (which
were made of a combination of the two). WaMu saw it as another way
to off-load risk. The bank ultimately didn't start a CDO division.

At this point, the overall volume of home loans WaMu was churning
out had decreased. By the end of 2006, it had dropped more than 20
percent from the previous year to $158 billion, and by the end of 2007 it
would drop another 37 percent. By that time, it would have fallen nearly
75 percent from its height in 2003. WaMu's mortgage production numbers were in line with those of banks nationwide. Fewer homeowners
were applying for mortgages.[26] WaMu's Option ARM lending fell, as
did its subprime volume. The Home Loans Group sold off $140 billion
in servicing rights to Wells Fargo, sold another chunk of $22 billion in
mortgages, and started to lay people off.

Still, the bank held a potent mix of high-risk loans. More than half
of its mortgages were Option ARMs, and about 15 percent were subprime.[27] The Home Loans Group didn't plan to stop making them,
either. In its "2007 Product Strategy" report, the division again outlined

its intent to keep pushing risky loans, including Option ARMs and sub-prime.[28] Even as David Schneider closed several of the Community Ful-fillment Centers, he wrote in an e-mail, "It is critical I emphasize that WaMu remains committed to the subprime business. I believe there is continued opportunity for us to offer subprime products to our custom-ers through all our distribution channels and drive profitable growth in this business."[29] Schneider asked his production manager how soon the group could double subprime loan origination. Killinger meanwhile told the *Puget Sound Business Journal* in Seattle that, while WaMu was cutting back on subprime lending, he planned for it to remain an im-portant part of the bank. "At this point," he said, "we will actually try to be more optimistic in growing our [subprime position]. You just need to be careful and do it in a very prudent manner."[30]

At President's Club that year, the partying continued. A mere six days after Feltgen sent her "URGENT" e-mail about offloading Option ARM loans, WaMu's salespeople gathered at the Grand Hyatt Hotel in Kauai, a lush property with sundecks, hot tubs, and waterfalls. Music filled one conference room as a group of loan consultants swiveled around to face the audience of rowdy salespeople.[31]

"I like big bucks and I cannot lie," they sang to the tune of Sir Mix-a-Lot's "Baby Got Back."

> *You mortgage brothers can't deny*
> *That when the dough roles [sic] in like you're pontin' your own cash*
> *And you gotta make a splash*
> *You just spends*
> *Like it never ends*
> *Cuz you gotta have that big new Benz.*

The Kick-It Krew, as they were called, danced as the song lyrics ran on two giant screens. The cleverness was endless, with Botox and ski trips to Aspen and "nips and tucks" substituted in place of Sir Mix-A-Lot's lyrics.

> *So players ["Yeah!" they yelled]*
> *Players ["Yeah!"]*

Do you love to make big bucks? ["Hell yeah!"]
Well, be bold ["Be bold!"] Be bold! ["Be bold!"]
Be bold and make big bucks
Make me big bucks.

Undeterred by the problems in the mortgage industry, WaMu's salespeople had something else to celebrate at President's Club. Recently Countrywide had floundered, sacrificing nationwide market share in Option ARMs to WaMu. Countrywide still maintained the number-one position, with 27 percent of Option ARM production, but WaMu, at a close number two, would soon steal that title. The Home Loans Group's recent "Product Strategy" report outlined WaMu's commission structure. Option ARMs would continue to net the most pay based on mortgage volume.[32]

In a darkened room at President's Club, a mock funeral for WaMu's biggest competitor began.[33] A band played upbeat music as one loan consultant walked on stage. "Please not now," he said, waving off the band. "That's the wrong feel for this moment."

The music shifted to a somber melody. "That's better, thank you," said the loan consultant, faking distress. "Brothers and sisters of the Home Loans fraternity . . . it is my sad responsibility today on this otherwise joyous occasion to be the bearer of tragic news. For this day, we have lost one of the true legends in our industry."

Four pallbearers wearing black clothing and sunglasses walked on stage, carrying a giant coffin with "Countrywide" etched into the side. They set the coffin on a pedestal.

"So many of us warned the dearly departed about the risky—and some may say reckless—behavior they engaged in. Throwing money around like Paris Hilton and selling products they don't really know or understand.

"But still the shock of their demise takes us by surprise. I guess we should have suspected something when they had their Option ARM amputated. They just couldn't stop the bleeding."

As the service continued, the music switched to a familiar tune as the loan consultant kept talking: "Na, na, na, na, na, na, na, na, hey, hey, hey, goodbye!"

". . . Borrowers across the nation will all be better served with simpler banking and more smiles! And some really scary and dangerous people won't be on the street anymore. To tell you the truth, I never really liked them anyway. All of a sudden, the dark cloud over the mortgage world has been replaced by blue skies and sunshine!

"And all of us will make more money and have more fun. So I guess the news really wasn't as bad as I thought it was, because it makes us want to say: 'Na, na, na, na, na, na, na, na, hey, hey, hey, goodbye!'"

In just six months, WaMu's bad loans jumped 45 percent. By June 2007, the bank held $1.7 billion worth of delinquent subprime loans and $750 million in mortgages that had gone into foreclosure.[34] Even during the height of WaMu's home loan production in 2003, the bank had not recorded so many bad loans. WaMu was not alone—other banks also posted higher levels of souring mortgages. Some borrowers, and not just WaMu customers, were still making their credit card payments, even as they stopped paying their mortgages. Historically, when a borrower was in financial trouble, he would stop paying every other bill first. He missed a mortgage payment only if all other avenues of saving money were exhausted. Now the longtime trend reversed. Borrowers had never been able to afford the mortgages in the first place.

The loans were becoming even harder to off-load. In the first half of the year, WaMu lost $202 million on subprime mortgages it had planned to sell. All the while, the value of the loans deteriorated.

As part of his annual strategy session, Kerry Killinger wrote a rather grim memo to WaMu's board of directors. "For the past two years, we have been predicting the bursting of the housing bubble and the likelihood of a slowing housing market," he wrote. "This scenario has now turned into a reality. Housing prices are declining in many areas of the country and sales are rapidly slowing. This is leading to an increase in delinquencies and loan losses." Indeed, the Federal Reserve Board predicted that "the correction of the housing sector [is] likely to continue to weigh heavily on economic activity through most of this year— somewhat longer than previously expected."[35]

Over the years, WaMu's board of directors had often been warned about the possibility of a real estate market crash. Ever since Bill

Longbrake had been relieved by a terse e-mail of his executive team duties, he had holed up in his office at WaMu, churning out long reports
on the economy and the housing market for the bank's directors. The
rest of the time he spent as a loaned executive for the Financial Services
Roundtable, the national industry group in Washington D.C., whose
members came from the largest financial services companies across the
country.

A true academic, Longbrake left no detail unanalyzed in his 30-page
reports, cramming them full of information. He would offer up a macro
view of the economy and the housing market. But in 2005, at about
the time Lou Pepper was counting train cars full of lumber passing
by, Longbrake became worried enough to write a warning in one of
his reports. He noted that risk in residential lending, WaMu's primary
source of business, was growing. It would be wise to monitor that risk,
he wrote, and come up with strategies to deal with it.

Longbrake's nervousness about the housing market could be traced
back to 2003, long before anyone thought much about the possibility of a crash. At WaMu's annual State of the Group meeting that
year, he voiced his concerns. After telling a series of jokes ("My first
job was working in an orange juice factory, but I got canned" and "I
became a professional fisherman, but discovered I couldn't live on my
net income"), Longbrake presented a slide show to the hundreds of
attendees, outlining the risks in the housing market and the effect on
WaMu. He had highlighted "Potential for a Single Family Real Estate
Price Bubble." Then, in finance-speak, he predicted what would happen in the next several years. Customers, unable to make much money
on the stock market, would invest in homes instead. "The consumer,"
Longbrake told the group, "has found that small increases in housing
prices, given the substantial leverage that is much greater than ever was
possible in the stock market, can lead to large gains in home equity." At
the same time, refinancing a mortgage would become easier for the customer, as would taking out a home equity line of credit.

"The bubble then builds through a reinforcing cycle of rising home
prices and rising consumer confidence. This leads to an increase in
the demand for investor properties and second homes, which, in turn,
places further upward pressure on home prices."

Longbrake wasn't the only one worried. In a late-2006 report to the board, Cathcart elevated "residential real estate and mortgage market exposure" to the second-highest risk level. In later congressional testimony, Cathcart said WaMu's board was responsive when he presented risks to the company. But he wasn't aware if the board ever imposed consequences on executives for not following through on problems.[36]

Killinger himself was sounding warnings, although one manager who sat through almost every board meeting in the years before 2008 couldn't recall a time Killinger used the word *bubble* to describe the housing market. Killinger also spoke constantly of the "irrational mortgage lenders," which he believed were likely to face problems at the first sign of a downturn. The "irrational mortgage lenders" were companies that did nothing but make mortgages, unlike WaMu, which had a large retail bank.

WaMu's board was a mix of longtime Seattle business leaders ("local yokels," noted one critic) and executives from across the country with little hands-on banking experience. This scenario was not unusual. Corporate boards are frequently made up of well-known executives who don't have extensive knowledge of the industry they oversee. In theory, this setup provides a company with access to expertise that transcends all industries. A board member of a growing big-box store, for example, might have no experience ordering crates of diapers and cranberry juice, but he might be skilled at acquisitions. Only one of WaMu's board members had true banking experience: Mary Pugh, the chair of the finance committee. Pugh was one of Pepper's hires in the 1980s, a young Yale graduate who had been tasked with figuring out the new, complicated developments in the banking industry. She had also been the chair of the long-ago committee that Pepper put together to develop WaMu's corporate values. Her face was memorialized in a black-and-white sketch from the 1980s, showing all the faces of the values committee members. Pepper keeps the sketch in his home office. Pugh left the bank in 1991 to open her own money management firm and then returned as a director eight years later. She still runs Pugh Capital Management.

Other WaMu board members included Orin Smith, the chief executive and chairman of Starbucks from 2000 to 2005; Tom Leppert, the mayor of Dallas; and Steve Frank, the former president and chief executive officer of Southern California Edison, the giant electric company. Director Charles Lillis had founded LoneTree Partners, a private equity firm based in Colorado; director Phillip Matthews was the chairman of Zodiac Marine Holdings, a worldwide marine products supplier; and Regina Montoya served as chief executive of New America Alliance, a Texas-based organization that promotes the economic advancement of the American Latino community. Director William Reed had sat on WaMu's board for *38 years*; he was one of the longest-running board members in the country. At one point, Reed also sat on the boards of other Seattle-based companies: Microsoft, Paccar, and Safeco Insurance.

WaMu board members were among the highest paid in the country, second only to Goldman Sachs's board. The lowest-paid WaMu director, Montoya, made $127,000 in 2007. The highest-paid, Frank, earned $274,000. All directors, with the exception of Killinger, received a combination of stock and option awards, a base pay of $60,000, and a $1,200 fee each time they attended a board meeting. In 2007, the bank met 11 times. Each year the directors received a $6,000 cash retainer for attending meetings. WaMu paid $750 for each telephone conference. Committee chairs were paid thousands of dollars extra. As WaMu's "lead independent director," Frank earned an additional $25,000, a yearly fee that was increased in 2007 from just $5,000.

Killinger, as chairman, had always held enormous sway over the board. In his first decade as chief executive, he wowed the directors. Each year WaMu's earnings grew, and its stock price marched steadily higher. "I had nothing but good to say about him," said one former board member. "He was one of the brightest people I have ever been around." Over the last several years, the board had grown used to Killinger's stellar performance and had been lulled by it. Several board members known for their toughness left. The current group of directors leveled criticism infrequently, and as Cathcart later pointed out in his congressional testimony, board members rarely punished executives for wrongdoing. They sat through numerous audit reports and internal reviews detailing fraud in WaMu's subprime mortgage division. They had approved Killinger's higher-risk lending strategy.

For his part, Killinger presided over the boardroom as if it were a theater, with everything scripted and approved in advance. Before board meetings, he spent hours reviewing the materials that would be presented. He worried about what would be said. Executives and managers sometimes felt pressured to spin harsh news, polishing language that sounded too disturbing. WaMu executives rarely spoke to board members outside meetings. At WaMu's board meetings, as in most management situations, Killinger liked to avoid confrontation.*

But while WaMu's directors heard about the housing market, they received few details about the bank's mortgages and its borrowers. In part, that was because WaMu had made little effort over the years to track complex data. It was another one of those mundane tasks—like the multiple loan underwriting systems—that the bank ignored as it grew. The problem was most noticeable, not surprisingly, in the Home Loans Group, where no one had a good way to measure loan-to-value ratios or whether a customer already had a mortgage—or even ten or fifteen—with the bank. Employees erased files in the data collection system and replaced them with new ones. They stored files electronically in hundreds of different places, none of them easy to locate. When a borrower applied for a mortgage with limited documentation, no one kept track of which kind of documentation he or she had provided.

Each division of the bank had a different way of defining a county. For example, WaMu had no uniform description of Los Angeles County, where a large number of its borrowers lived. County demographics were not presented with any granularity or consistency. The board, for example, never saw charts detailing the population drain in Southern California and the influx of immigrants with low-paying jobs. This demographic was increasingly WaMu's customer base in Southern California. When WaMu sold off a bad loan, it didn't trace the borrower or the property once the relationship was severed. That meant that WaMu had little historical information on the life of its mortgages. Data were sometimes so inconsistent that the risk management team

---

*At Countrywide, by comparison, the company's directors frequently called executives outside the meeting, asking questions about the lender's activities. Board reports were almost never reviewed ahead of time, and managers presented controversial data without the prior blessing of chief executive Angelo Mozilo, or the other executive team members.

later took to drawing skulls and crossbones on reports, a warning that no one should make assumptions based on the information inside.

In June 2007, even as Killinger wrote to the board of directors about declining home prices "leading to an increase in delinquencies and loan losses," and even as the bank carried $1.7 billion of past-due subprime mortgages, he reaffirmed WaMu's aim to keep making higher-risk loans to capture more market share. He announced this intention at the board's annual strategy session, held at an upscale conference center south of Seattle, which Killinger had built for off-site WaMu gatherings. An executive in attendance recalled that only one board member, Steve Frank, questioned Killinger's presentation. Frank asked whether the bank should be increasing credit risk "at this stage in the cycle." The large subprime lender New Century Mortgage had just gone bankrupt.

Soon afterward another internal audit circulated about Long Beach Mortgage.[37] It was the third investigation into the beleaguered subprime division in just four years. It too called out Long Beach for its unsafe lending practices. "Repeat issue," the WaMu report noted. Separately, AIG, the international company insuring WaMu's mortgages, discovered its own problems.[38] From a sample of loans at WaMu, AIG identified seven—and later a total of twenty-five—that contained fraud. The loans had been made in Montebello, the same Community Fulfillment Center in Los Angeles that had been written up two years earlier, along with the Downey branch. AIG complained, but WaMu ignored the insurer, prompting AIG to file a formal complaint with the state of California. That action sparked another internal WaMu review nearly a year later, but no apparent resolution.

Earlier in the year, David Schneider altered Long Beach's pay structure to try to clean up some of the problems at the division. Each month a credit review team selected four mortgages and based the underwriter's pay on the quality of the loans. Sales managers saw a similar commission change. If too many borrowers didn't make their first payment, the sales manager's bonus would be cut. If the loan did go into first-payment default, the sales manager had to take the unusual step of talking to the borrower, something he had never before had to do. Each month the Long Beach employees received lists of loans that had gone into default. They fastidiously called each customer to see what had gone wrong. There were rumors that the account executives out in the field would soon be forced to do the same thing. "We basically had shifted from being sales managers to credit risk managers," said one Long Beach sales manager. "It was a tough, tough transition for a lot of people. They had never done anything like it." On the heels of yet another negative Long Beach audit, the Home Loans Group rolled out more changes to try, once again, to fix the problems at Long Beach. The division built a template ("Underwriter Decision Summary") that would help employees remember what they needed to see before they approved a loan: a sufficiently high credit score and income, for starters. WaMu would no longer make subprime loans if the bank couldn't verify a borrower's income.

At about this time, Kevin Jenne, the WaMu market research manager who had years earlier led the Option ARM focus groups, was called into a meeting with the Home Loans Group at WaMu's headquarters. As he listened, several managers in the mortgage division expressed their newest concern: subprime loans had a marketing problem. How could the Home Loans Group rebrand the mortgages so they would be more attractive to customers? Jenne looked around the room, trying to read people's expressions. He harbored serious doubt about this new assignment. "Wasn't the subprime market falling apart?" he thought. Ben Bernanke, the chairman of the Federal Reserve, had told the Senate Banking Committee that losses from subprime loans could top $100 billion nationwide.[39] Jenne felt like asking, "You don't really mean this, do you?" But instead, he waited for the meeting to end. Then he discreetly suggested to his team: "Maybe we should slow this down a little and see what happens next."

Jenne and his team stalled. Several weeks later, in late July 2007, the subprime market collapsed. Fear had been growing for months, and now the failure of two hedge funds run by Bear Stearns terrified investors. The hedge funds had bet on subprime loans.[40] The effect of their collapse was dramatic. The rating agencies downgraded subprime securities like those made by Long Beach. Long Beach accounted for only 6 percent of the securities issued in 2006, but it received 14 percent of the downgrades. Any exit strategy for selling subprime loans had disappeared. Investors abandoned them. Lenders such as WaMu had to hold on to them and take the losses that followed.

In WaMu's warehouse lending division, Michele Perrin watched as her clients began to falter. Within months, all but five of twenty-six mortgage lenders she worked with would collapse. One of WaMu's largest clients, an Arizona-based lender called First Magnus Financial Corp., filed for bankruptcy. The U.S. Department of Housing and Urban Development would later conclude that First Magnus had been offering illegal kickbacks to entice mortgage brokers to funnel over loans to the company.[41] Its father-and-son management team spent so much money running the company that "even the most pampered and precocious movie star would blush," a bankruptcy trustee later concluded. When First Magnus failed, it left more than $1 billion of loans that it couldn't sell to WaMu. The circular, interconnected nature of the country's mortgage market, which Perrin had once likened to fish, had helped everyone make a lot of money. Those days had ended.

Perrin and her coworkers in Southern California were told by WaMu's headquarters that it would take some time for the bank to sort out the future of the warehouse lending division. The division still had about $7 billion in loans outstanding. "We couldn't talk to our customers and tell them that anything was wrong," Perrin said later. "We sat in our offices and shook." When she first arrived at WaMu, Perrin had been tasked with writing a song about communication, with the help of a hired blues band. Now, with her sense of good humor still intact and with nothing else to do, Perrin wrote her own song, to the tune of "American Pie." She called it "Bye-Bye Mortgage Lending Guy."

> *A long, long time ago,*
> *I can still remember*
> *How the refis used to make me smile*
> *And I knew if I had my chance*
> *That I could make a big paycheck*
> *And maybe I'd be happy for a while*
> *But February made me shiver*
> *With every program I'd consider*
> *Bad news on the doorstep*

We couldn't clear one more stip. *

I can't remember if I cried

When I read about poor Countrywide

But something touched me deep inside

The day mortgage lending died.

So bye-bye, mortgage banking guys

You made money when it was sunny

But the well has gone dry.

Them Wall Street boys were on a crack-induced high

Singin' this will be the day you all die.

This will be the day you all die.

By the end of August 2007, WaMu still hadn't made a decision. Perrin and her coworkers gathered for a sales meeting at the Gaylord Texan, a lavish convention center and resort between Dallas and Fort Worth. A climate-controlled glass atrium protected guests from the brutal Texas summer heat, and a 600-foot lazy river wound around the property, "like a moat," thought Perrin. The meeting was held as a way for warehouse division employees to give updates on their clients and deliver plans to grow their business. The meeting was also a chance for the employees to meet their new boss, David Beck. Beck, who also ran the Capital Markets Group at WaMu, had recently been given oversight of Perrin's division.

Each employee was required to stand up in front of a group of about thirty people and present the status of his or her accounts. As Perrin's turn neared, she grew nervous. Beck sharply criticized each employee before her, skeptical about the health of WaMu's clients. The negative attitude was a big departure from previous meetings. Suddenly, Perrin felt as if someone had swung an ax in between her eyes. She had begun suffering from migraines several years earlier, in part because of the frenetic pace of her job. Pain erupted in her head. She leaped from her seat at the front of the conference room as another employee continued his presentation on stage. But she didn't make it to the bathroom before she threw up.

---

*A "stipulation," or required item to complete a loan file, is like a request for further documentation.

That night Perrin, shaky but stable with the help of prescription drugs, joined her colleagues and direct manager at one of the hotel's upscale restaurants. Everyone heckled her about the earlier incident, joking that she couldn't handle her liquor from the night before. Then the rowdy group fell uncharacteristically silent. "What the heck is going on?" Perrin asked her manager finally, echoing the thought on everyone's mind. Beck's negative reaction during the presentations surely didn't bode well for the group's fate. Perrin's manager paused. Then he looked around the table. "I believe that this is the end," he said. Everyone stared back at him. Perrin began to cry.

Three weeks later WaMu officially announced its plans to shut down its warehouse lending division, as well as its correspondent division. It would soon get out of wholesale lending as well.

WaMu's bad loans stacked up higher, reaching $5.5 billion in the fall of 2007—more than double the previous year's amount.[42] Subprime borrowers weren't the only ones missing payments—everyone was. Across the country, foreclosures soared, increasing nearly 100 percent compared with the previous year. WaMu still made money, but only a paltry $184 million that quarter. A bright spot was the $345 million it made off Option ARM borrowers, who continued to rack up debt by choosing to make the minimum loan payment each month. WaMu set aside almost $1 billion to cover the growing mortgage problems. Despite it all, the worsening national crisis cemented the board's trust in Killinger and his management team. Killinger had said the "irrational mortgage lenders" would fail, and now they had failed. One of WaMu's board members told a reporter, "I'm enormously supportive of management."[43]

In WaMu's market research department, Jenne and his team no longer worked to make risky loans look good. Instead, they had to figure out how to get borrowers to pay back their mortgages. The first step was getting them to answer the phone. "The collections department was calling these people eight to ten times a day, on their cell phones, at home, in their offices," Jenne said later. "No one was answering." Jenne and one of his coworkers soon embarked on a nationwide delinquent homeowner tour, visiting the families that couldn't make their mortgage payments. They wanted a broad sample of people, so they found a few community groups—the kind that advertised ominously on billboards, "ARE YOU AFRAID OF LOSING YOUR HOME?" These groups directed them to errant borrowers. Jenne now saw, in person, that WaMu had not been the only lender enamored of Option ARM or subprime mortgages.

He brought a video camera. He sat on people's back porches, in their kitchens, and in their living rooms, trying to find out what had gone wrong. He and his coworker interviewed dozens of borrowers, all of them shocked by an event that they believed was never supposed to happen—the fall of the housing market. In Chicago, Jenne filmed a mother and father who had been renting an apartment in a neighborhood full of gang fights and violence. The couple had saved for years to buy a house. They wanted to move their three boys to a better neighborhood. When they bought a house, with a mortgage from the California lender IndyMac, the two parents felt rich. They started buying their boys new clothes and presents. Their credit card debt skyrocketed. No matter—the family's new house was appreciating in value, rapidly. They took out a home equity loan. "The father thinks this is great," Jenne said. "He says, 'I'm in way better shape now!' Then he runs the credit cards up again, and then goes and gets another loan. That's okay, because the home is worth double what it had been."

The husband and wife in Chicago, at the request of Jenne, dug around the house for a while and located their mortgage statements. They were four months behind on payments. They had an Option ARM loan, but they didn't understand it. All they knew was that their loan amount had increased each month from $1,200, an amount they could barely afford, to $3,500, which they couldn't pay. If they moved, their boys would be yanked out of a good school and transferred to one in the ghetto. Jenne asked the couple to explain the mortgage statements. "The woman pointed to the minimum payment option," Jenne said. "And she said, 'Well, this is our loan payment right? The small one?' And we just got this sick feeling in our stomachs." The parents, even though one of them handled bookkeeping for a large hotel chain, hadn't realized they had a choice of payments. Of course, the borrowers in Jenne's long-ago focus groups had also been confused about this option. WaMu had ignored their confusion.

In the middle of the discussion, the couple's phone rang. It was IndyMac, trying to collect its money. The couple looked at each other, frightened. "Can you pick up the phone and talk to them?" Jenne asked the husband, tilting his camera toward the phone. He heard only one side of the conversation.

"Yeah. Well, no I don't. No, I haven't got it . . . Well, how much do you want? . . . I haven't got that! I'm going to make it up . . . No! No, no, look . . . You can't yell at me like that!" The husband slammed down the phone. "Whenever I talk to them," he told Jenne, "they yell and scream at me and cuss and want their money." After the interview ended, Jenne turned off the camera. He felt choked up. He noticed that his coworker had red-rimmed eyes. He grabbed the mortgage statement and explained to the borrowers, years too late, what it meant to have an Option ARM mortgage.

Jenne and his coworker arrived back at WaMu headquarters with more than 80 hours of footage, a raw and merciless documentary on high-risk lending. This was far more research than WaMu had undertaken on its borrowers before they took out mortgages. "There were people who were lying and there were people who were hiding things, but there were a whole lot of people who were just terrified and didn't know what to do," Jenne said of the homeowners. He whittled the tape down to several short clips and played the abbreviated video for David Schneider and several employees in the Home Loans Group. He chose one clip in which a mortgage broker in Florida, who had bought six investment properties with loans from different banks, sat in an armchair next to a stack of bills. All of the man's mortgages were delinquent. He picked up WaMu's late payment notice from the pile, glanced at it, and exclaimed to the camera, "They want to negotiate, but what do I have to negotiate about?" He crumpled the letter and threw it aside. The footage startled Schneider, as it did everyone at WaMu who saw it. He ordered Jenne and his team to begin working on a friendlier approach to collections. WaMu did not want the borrowers' homes back.

Jenne didn't visit Ramona Jiminez or Sara Vasquez in East Los Angeles, but both had stopped paying their mortgages as well. Jiminez's husband had lost his job in the construction industry. Her brother had died of cancer, and since he had been living in one of the homes on her property, she had lost another source of income. Companies promising loan workouts started calling Jiminez. "It was weird," she said later. "These people were trying to help us, but they wanted $9,000."

One day, as Vasquez sat at her job at the county jail, she began to feel strange. The pressure on her had been growing for months. She could no longer afford the house with the kidney-shaped pool in Compton. After losing her previous job, she had been unemployed. She was raising a toddler on her own. She had started using food stamps. She had begun missing mortgage payments. Now she felt her heart racing. She thought she might faint. "I'm having a heart attack," she thought. She left the jail, planning to drive to the hospital. As she crossed the street to her car, she began to hyperventilate. The doctors diagnosed her problem: an anxiety attack. It would be her first of many.

The delinquencies of both Jiminez and Vasquez contributed to a fast-growing rate of default in the WaMu securities that their mortgages had been meshed together to make. Within several years, the subprime securities that WaMu had packaged during 2006 and 2007 would suffer unprecedented default rates as high as 42 percent and losses as high as 65 percent.[44] The securities had frequently received the top grade from the rating agencies. WaMu had been able to off-load the risk of mortgages held by people like Jiminez and Vasquez, but now it had contributed to losses suffered by investment banks, hedge funds, pension funds, and other investors around the world.

Through the growing turmoil, Kerry Killinger remained upbeat. The optimism born from a childhood of avoiding negativity coursed through him. He told investors in a conference call in the fall of 2007: "I'm very pleased with how we've managed the company during this period of stress."[45] At Lehman's annual investor conference, just after Lehman shut down its subprime lending unit, Killinger told the audience, "This, frankly, may be one of the best times I've ever seen for taking on new loans in our portfolio."[46] He said that WaMu would add "some $20 billion in loans to its books this quarter, increasing its loan portfolio by about 10 percent." Noted Drew DeSilver, a *Seattle Times* business reporter, about Killinger's performance: "He might as well have quoted Baron Rothschild, the 19th-century financier who reportedly said the best time to invest was 'when blood was running in the streets.'" A former WaMu employee stopped by for a visit at the bank and found Killinger calm, almost relaxed. When he spoke about WaMu, he did so without a hint of anxiety. "I'm pretty confident about how things are shaping up," Killinger told the former employee. "Don't be nervous about what you're hearing."

Killinger often wanted to talk about his new house in Palm Desert, a $6 million spread abutting an exclusive golf course that cost $250,000 to join.[47] He and Linda now spent most weekends in California. They took full advantage of the company's corporate jet timeshare, increasing their trips to visit family and friends around the country. Killinger counted Dick Fuld, the chief executive of Lehman, among his acquaintances, and the couple sometimes flew to Fuld's Idaho hideaway for the weekend. "He would just wax poetic about getting invited to things like Davos," said one WaMu executive, referring to the World Economic Forum in Switzerland, which Killinger had twice attended. "It was really cool for him to talk about a meeting with Bernanke and Greenspan." In three years, the Killingers spent about $200,000 traveling on the corporate jet, a cost that was charged to the bank. At the end of 2007, the board of directors forced him to reimburse WaMu for his personal use of the plane.

Killinger's salary had grown dramatically. When it reached its peak in 2006, he had made $21 million in one year, including a collection of stock options worth $3.9 million at the time, retirement benefits, stock awards, and a $4 million bonus. The next year, the year of the subprime market collapse, Killinger's salary had been halved. He didn't receive a bonus that year. But he still brought in $11 million. In five years, he had made nearly $80 million.[48] He was among the highest-paid executives in the country. Rotella was also paid well. In 2006, he received a $3.7 million cash bonus, more than the fiftieth percentile of his pay grade. "That level of compensation was necessary to recruit Mr. Rotella when he joined us as a mid-career senior executive from one of our competitors," WaMu noted in the public documents it filed outlining pay.

Killinger's optimism did not uplift the other executives—it chilled them. They were increasingly disturbed and perplexed by the way he handled the bank's problems. Outwardly, WaMu had to project calm, to the public and to its shareholders. But internally, the executive team wondered why Killinger hadn't yet launched into crisis mode. He didn't seem to grasp the magnitude of what was happening around him. He was like a small boy watching a house being engulfed by flames, as hundreds of firefighters rushed back and forth around him, trying to put it out. Robert Williams, WaMu's treasurer, tried repeatedly to persuade Killinger to cut the bank's shareholder dividend. WaMu had always paid its investors generously, but Williams believed that the bank needed to set aside money to handle the rising pile of souring loans. Killinger was hesitant. He thought that if WaMu had a lot of cash on hand, it would become a takeover target. He also hated to disappoint shareholders. Williams won the argument.

The other executives turned to Rotella, who, as a result, took on more of Killinger's responsibilities. Killinger had trouble making decisions, so Rotella began to make them for him. He met with Killinger more frequently, asking about his own role at WaMu. Rotella wanted more authority—people needed decisions. He also wanted to know whether he would ever have a chance at Killinger's position. What did Killinger think about Rotella's future at WaMu? He wrote Killinger a long e-mail, asking him if they could have a talk about "some specific items" that "revolve around broadening and strengthening our relationship, which I think has been very good, but can and should move to an even higher level at this crucial time.

"At the same time," Rotella typed on his BlackBerry, "I would like to get more insight about the future for me. I think these two things go hand-in-hand very nicely. I look forward to a quick meeting of the minds. I want nothing more than to lock arms and drive the company with you and win, and to move forward personally at the same time."

Killinger, ignoring the subject of Rotella's future at WaMu, responded positively. Rotella had become a trusted adviser, but Killinger had no intention of stepping down. "We ultimately need to tell folks to get on the train or get off," Killinger wrote back. "The key dynamic for you and me is to be in sync and to be united in telling the players to join us or leave." The players, in this case, were the other members of the executive team. Rotella's concern about his role at the company went nowhere.

Killinger continued to shy away from the problems. After an executive meeting in early 2008, Cathcart asked to speak with him privately. The chief risk officer had just been told that the Office of Thrift Supervision planned to downgrade the bank's health rating. State and federal regulators score banks on the basis of an internal, closely watched rating known as CAMELS. The acronym CAMELS stands for Capital adequacy, Asset quality, Management quality, Earnings, Liquidity, and Sensitivity to market risk. Under this system, banks are ranked on a 1 to 5 scale, with 1 as the highest, best rating. Each bank also receives an overall score, which everyone cares about most. While the ratings aren't public, they're important because they determine how much scrutiny a bank faces from the government and how much it can borrow from its own lenders. In the last decade, WaMu had scored an overall rating of 2. But in the face of its growing loan problems, the OTS planned to drop its score to 3.

After everyone else left the room following the executive meeting, Cathcart delivered this news to Killinger. "I just wanted to let you know that the OTS is downgrading us," he said.

Killinger stood up from the conference room table. "I don't like to hear bad news," he said.

"It's my job to deliver bad news," Cathcart replied.

But Killinger was already walking out the door.

WaMu was tarnished. In just a year, its stock had plummeted 60 percent, wiping out billions of dollars in market share. The bank stopped making subprime loans altogether. By that time, Long Beach Mortgage had been recognized as the second-worst subprime lender in the country, just behind New Century Mortgage. In some cities—Stockton, Denver, and Sacramento—Long Beach beat out other lenders for the highest number of mortgages in foreclosure.[49] WaMu announced that it would lay off about 3,300 of its 50,000 employees nationwide. The bank planned to close more than half of its 336 home loan centers.[50]

The bank's mom-and-pop shareholders used to call WaMu for an occasional chat, happy about the bank's performance. Now they called constantly, demanding to know when the results would improve. The person answering their calls was Iris Glaze, who worked in WaMu's investor relations department. Glaze had worked at the bank for seventeen years—she started the same month as Killinger—and she was an exuberant worker. She knew everyone's name. She is less than five feet tall ("Look down at the ground if you're looking for me," she advises people at large events), and she lives in a small white house with purple shutters. Framed pictures of irises hang on the walls. She called people "sweetie," told friends she "loves them to pieces," and liberally hugged coworkers, including Killinger himself. Many of the bank's employees continued to believe in Killinger's leadership.

Glaze was steadfast in her love of the bank. For years, she had organized WaMu's shareholder meetings. She remembered when a woman stood up during the question-and-answer session and declared, "Kerry, I want to thank you for my life. If not for my dividends I would be dead." Killinger did not inquire why the woman would have died, but the whole team loved the compliment. "Everyone was so happy at those shareholder meetings," Glaze recalled. Many of the shareholders she talked with regularly were local, older investors who had bought in when WaMu first went public in the 1980s and were extremely proud that they had held on to their stock so long. One man called Glaze before each earnings report came out, inquiring if it had yet been filed.

Over time Glaze had observed the changing culture of WaMu, in part through her attempts at socializing. She used to flit between departments, saying hello to people and inquiring after their health and children. On her cube wall, she stuck pictures of her coworkers and their kids. After a while, it seemed as though everyone was too busy to talk. She used to drop in on Killinger, but now she found his door frequently closed. "I always wanted to have a potluck," Glaze said later. "There were so many ethnic groups at the bank—we had a guy from Eritrea! But there was no interest. They were all too busy." Years earlier Glaze and her team would order fried chicken from a nearby takeout restaurant, laughing among themselves over a shared lunch.

More recently, Glaze had learned the careful art of not saying anything at all. Investor relations was in charge of the glossy language on WaMu's annual reports. The group had to find ways of saying bad things in a good way. "You couldn't say the sky is green," Glaze said later. "You had to say the sky is not blue." At about the time the subprime market collapsed, Glaze began fielding calls from enraged shareholders. Soon the shareholders filed lawsuits. Three were consolidated into one large class action suit, led by a pension fund in Canada.[51] The suit alleged that the bank hadn't properly disclosed the extent of its risky lending. In hundreds of pages, the complaint, which named Killinger, Schneider, Rotella, Casey, Cathcart, and WaMu's directors, outlined WaMu's out-of-control lending culture, citing interviews with dozens of anonymous salespeople.*

Then WaMu slashed its dividend. When the cut came in late 2007, after Williams's insistence, it was huge. Shareholder payout dropped almost 75 percent a share, to just 15 cents. WaMu publicly announced the change, but Glaze hadn't considered that some shareholders might not have heard about it in advance. She fielded a call from a sobbing ninety-two-year-old woman. "I didn't get a notice," said the woman. "There must be some mistake." Glaze explained patiently, "No, sweetie. There's no mistake." "You don't understand," the woman replied, sobbing. "I live on my dividends."

In November 2007, Andrew Cuomo, New York's attorney general, filed a lawsuit against eAppraiseIT, the company WaMu used to handle its appraisals.[52] In the suit, Cuomo accused WaMu of pressuring appraisers to inflate home values, and alleged that eAppraiseIT and its parent, First American, had yielded to WaMu's demands. Between 2006 and 2007, eAppraiseIT conducted 260,000 appraisals for WaMu, earning $50 million in fees. By forcing higher appraisals, mortgage companies could close more loans. The practice had become common in an industry addicted to volume. Faulty appraisals helped grow the housing bubble, as they helped push price appreciation.

Preemptively, WaMu's legal department, headed up by Fay Chapman, had started looking into the appraisal problem at WaMu before Cuomo announced his suit. When the news broke, Chapman volunteered to take on the internal inquiry into the bank's appraisal practices. She happened to be in New York, at a legal training seminar, so she instructed her team back in Seattle to begin working on the issue.

---

*This lawsuit was later settled out of court for $205 million in 2011, months before the trial would have started.

Chapman had been operating on autopilot at WaMu. Years earlier she hadn't stood in the way of Killinger's higher-risk lending strategy. She had thought the bank could handle the limited risk. She hadn't anticipated the arrival of new executives, or that there would be an even greater push to make those kinds of mortgages. But by now the problems at WaMu had reached such epic proportions that Chapman reconsidered. It had come to her attention that a loan consultant in Florida had made a second mortgage to O. J. Simpson, despite a giant court judgment against him. "I just about blew my top," Chapman recalled later.[53] Chapman had long believed that the entire housing market was about to collapse—not just drop a few percentage points in some tropical locations but truly collapse. She could see the bad loans on WaMu's balance sheet, and she felt that the drop was coming, but she couldn't necessarily explain why. "It seems kind of stupid, but I thought maybe it was woman's intuition," she said later.

One night in early 2007, Chapman went into Killinger's office and told him about her fears. "Kerry, for the sake of a lot of the people who stayed here and have been loyal to you—you need to sell out," she advised. She knew that JPMorgan Chase in New York had been sniffing around the bank. "You need to get out while you can get something for this bank." Killinger listened but ultimately brushed off her concerns. She tried talking to David Schneider, telling him that the Home Loans Group should stop making the riskier types of loans to subprime borrowers.* Schneider told her, "We're going to keep making them because people are buying them." She regularly got into shouting matches with Tom Casey, the chief financial officer, most recently over what constituted a subprime loan. Casey's view was narrower than Chapman's. "As an attorney by trade, she just wanted to be open kimono about everything," said one of the other executives, who regularly sat in between the arguing Chapman and Casey. "Casey wanted to manage the message." Chapman sounded increasingly paranoid, like the guy shouting about the end of the world on a busy street corner. "Fay was the only

---

*The Home Loans Group did eventually stop making two kinds of subprime loans before the division was shut down.

one saying 'don't,'" said another executive. "There were times when she overused that card." She was the last of Killinger's loyal supporters—the group of people appointed by Lou Pepper to serve as a life raft around him. In meetings, Chapman took to playing games on her BlackBerry, her head down. Sometimes she doodled on her notepad.

Chapman also had a strained relationship with Rotella, epitomizing the rift between WaMu's old guard and the new leaders. Rotella would later publicly claim that he tried to cut back on higher-risk lending and clean up the subprime division, but Chapman believed that he embraced the bank's strategy, and that he allowed many of the problems in the Home Loans Group to continue. Unbeknownst to Chapman, WaMu's main federal regulator at the Office of Thrift Supervision, Darrel Dochow, was also suspicious of Rotella's actions. He wrote— "confidentially"—in an e-mail to his supervisor that he believed Rotella was "using the appraisal issue to undercut/move out general counsel Faye [sic] Chapman, who has challenged him in the past." Dochow noted that Rotella pushed to use third-party appraisals "and continues to downplay the various business units' failings."[54]

The legal training seminar ended several days after the WaMu appraisal investigation erupted. Chapman flew back to Seattle. She was concerned about the status of the legal team's investigation. During a conference call with Killinger, Rotella, and several other executives, she began to suspect that the investigation was being taken out of her control. She was right. While she was gone, Rotella had been in to see Killinger. Rotella had discovered that the legal department had been looking into the appraisal issue before it was announced, and he found this unacceptable. As president of the company, he felt he should know of any problem arising at the bank, particularly if it involved a high-level, public lawsuit. Other managers felt the same way; they thought Chapman should have elevated the problem to the board.

Chapman, meanwhile, didn't think the legal department had tried to hide prior knowledge about Cuomo's investigation. One of the attorneys in her department had reported on it at a meeting attended by David Schneider. What Chapman hadn't said, however, was that the legal department was looking into Schneider and Cheryl Feltgen, the chief risk officer of the Home Loans Group, to see whether they had played roles in the faulty appraisals.*

Right after she returned from New York, Chapman went to see Killinger in his office. "Legal isn't going to be in charge of the investigation any longer," Killinger told her. "You have to step away from it." As Chapman listened, astonished, Killinger told her that the bank would now investigate the legal department, to determine whether any cover-up had occurred. Feltgen, meanwhile, would be placed in charge of the internal appraisal investigation. It was a decision that Killinger had agonized over for a long time.

"You've got to be kidding!" Chapman exclaimed. She was furious. She felt that Killinger had just chosen Rotella over his longtime confidante. Even worse, he had put Feltgen in charge of the investigation, when the investigation was into the appraisal review group, the very division that Feltgen headed up. "I just couldn't believe it," Chapman said later.

She resolved to be patient. She knew she had a temper. She had always been able to reason with Killinger, and he had always trusted her advice. Chapman thought there had to be a way to make Killinger realize his mistake.

She started off slowly, questioning him once again on his decision. But before long, she grew frustrated. His answers were vague. He couldn't give her a solid reason why she was being pulled off the investigation.

"They told me not to talk to you about it," Killinger said.

"Who's 'they'?" Chapman demanded.

Killinger wouldn't tell her. Chapman thought he was defending Rotella and possibly other executives in the Home Loans Group.

Against her better judgment, she yelled at him. It was the only thing she could think of to try and get through to him.

---

*The status of Chapman's internal investigation after she left is unclear, but the outside law firm hired by WaMu eventually found no merit in the allegations levied by Cuomo. Rotella later fired Feltgen as a result of the appraisal issue, as well as the lawyer on Chapman's team who reported to the Home Loans Group.

"Steve just wants your job!" she shouted at one point. Chapman had no direct knowledge of this—she had just guessed, correctly.

"I'm sure Steve only wants what's best for the company," Killinger replied. Eventually, Chapman could see that her words weren't having any affect. As they rained down on him, he sat there, impervious.

Chapman realized that she couldn't stay at WaMu. She had put up with a lot—the long-ago company structure change, the dead borrowers at Long Beach Mortgage, the change in Killinger—but this development was too much. She couldn't sit by and watch her own department investigated, while the necessary investigation was swept aside.

Killinger asked to see her one last time before she left. In his office, she sat across from him, just as she had hundreds of times. The Energizer Bunnies, once prominently displayed, had been moved to the back of a closet. Killinger and Chapman had both devoted their careers to WaMu. They had grown up at the bank, together. Killinger had only just been appointed president that day in the 1980s when he called Chapman into his office. He had asked her to watch his back, and she had. Now the worry lines on both their faces had stretched considerably, right along with the fractures in the company.

Chapman could tell that Killinger felt bad about the circumstances. In his own way, he tried to apologize. He assured her that the announcement of her departure would make it clear she had left of her own accord. She could just return to Foster Pepper, he reminded her.

Chapman disagreed. There was no work for her at the law firm. It had been years since she worked there. "You don't know what you're talking about," she told him. She accused him of destroying her career.

Killinger didn't respond. Once again the discussion went nowhere.

A brief statement announced Chapman's retirement in late 2007, with few details. Her own attorneys worked out a settlement with the bank. She received pay of about $1 million, and over the next two years, she was scheduled to receive consulting fees of $2.7 million. None of WaMu's board members, whom she had known for years, called to ask why WaMu's longtime chief legal officer had resigned in the middle of a growing financial crisis. "I felt like I had failed," Chapman said later. "People had faith in me. But I couldn't overcome it."

Over the weekend, Chapman brought in her husband, her oldest daughter, and her daughter's 120-pound Newfoundland dog to help clean out her office. WaMu's headquarters was silent and dark. They filled boxes with framed photos of Chapman's daughters, legal books, and the many glass cubes etched with the names of the WaMu acquisitions that Chapman had worked on over the years. The cubes had been a gift from the investment bankers working on each deal. Chapman was selective. She took only the cubes bearing the names of the banner deals of the 1980s and 1990s: Pacific First Bank, Great Western, and WaMu's long-ago IPO.

To relieve her anger, Chapman walked. She walked miles around the tree-lined streets of her neighborhood, a well-to-do community of older houses owned by academics from the nearby University of Washington. She walked up and down Seattle's steep hills and along a mossy street that wove through a wooded park. She downloaded classic literature from Audible.com, listening for hours to the well-known stories she had once read as an English major at UCLA, the *Iliad* and *War and Peace* among them.

Chapman lost weight, and her family worried. Still, she couldn't let go, and her anger wouldn't abate. She never spoke to Killinger again. He approached her at a cocktail party several months after she left. She turned away.

Chapter Seven

SCENES FROM THE
GREAT DEPRESSION

I just want people to calm down. Have a little faith.

—Kerry Killinger

Benaroya Hall is a plush, popular event facility located in downtown Seattle. A tall circle of windows rises high above its circular lobby, and its auditorium seats 2,500 people, usually concertgoers who have come to hear the Seattle Symphony. Inside the auditorium, hundreds of gold-colored seats rise in tiers above the ground floor, surrounding a deep stage. The building is named for one of its largest donors, Jack Benaroya, a well-known philanthropist and civic leader in the Pacific Northwest.[1] Not one for self-aggrandizing, Benaroya reportedly had to be convinced to put his name on the $120 million facility when it was built in the late 1990s. Outside its doors, next to a memorial for the Korean War and a small waterfall trickling over granite, a dedication is carved into stone steps. It is a quote from Plato: "Man was not made for himself alone."

On a chilly Tuesday in April 2008, hundreds of investors poured into the lobby of Benaroya Hall for WaMu's annual shareholder meeting. WaMu often held its shareholder meetings at the performance hall. The bank's name is still etched on one wall, indicating its donor status. Over the years, as WaMu grew, the security the bank required had increased. Shareholders walked past dozens of guards waiting at the doors. Bomb-sniffing dogs had earlier made rounds. The attendance was higher that day than what WaMu had seen at any of its annual meetings, ever.

The shareholders, many of them older and dressed in jeans and sweaters and faded blazers, milled about, talking among themselves. They clutched paper coffee cups and cookies. Some of them spoke to the dozen local and national reporters who had shown up for the occasion, venting anger and anxiety, the journalists quickly scribbling quotes on their notepads. Others gave television interviews, the cameras trained on their angry faces. WaMu employees also gathered, including retirees from the bank. They, too, were heavily invested in WaMu stock. Everyone waited anxiously.

WaMu's headquarters building was located across the street from Benaroya Hall. The bank's executive team and its board members usually made the one-minute trip on foot. But on this day, many of them piled into hired cars in WaMu's parking garage. The cars pulled out of the garage, drove all the way around the block because of a one-way street, and, several minutes later, delivered the executives into the parking garage beneath the facility. They did not want to confront the company's investors.

That day WaMu reported a first-quarter loss of more than $1 billion, on top of the $1.9 billion it had lost in the final quarter of the year. Twenty-six billion dollars in market value had been wiped out as WaMu's stock plummeted more than 70 percent. The bank's stock was trading at around $11 a share. The shareholder dividend had been cut to one cent.

In its annual report, WaMu described the confluence of severe economic problems it faced.[2] Home prices continued to fall, particularly in California and Florida, where the majority of WaMu's mortgages were located. In some areas, they had dropped as much as 30 percent. The number of homes on the market nationwide ballooned and credit constricted, making it hard for prospective buyers to get a loan. Foreclosures, already high, rose even higher. At WaMu, they doubled over the year. It was developing into one of the worst housing downturns in decades, possibly even since the Great Depression. "Faced with these unfavorable conditions," WaMu noted, "an increasing number of borrowers, including those with adjustable-rate mortgages that repriced upward at the expiration of their fixed rate periods, have defaulted on their loans, thereby contributing to an increase in delinquency rates."

The bank revealed that 75 percent of its Option ARM mortgages were made using limited documentation from the borrower—"consistent with mortgage industry underwriting practices," WaMu wrote. As a result, those borrowers were much more likely to default. The Home Loans Group had debated how to deliver this blow to shareholders. One employee noted in an e-mail, "It is important that language found in the 10K be balanced, accurate and not provoke emotional reactions from the reader."[3] The sentence in the report read: "A significant portion of Option ARM loans in the company's portfolio were originated using limited documentation and have a higher risk of default than fully documented loans." Cheryl Feltgen, the chief risk officer in the Home Loans Group, sent an e-mail to David Schneider, the head of the division. "I think we should delete the word 'significant,'" she wrote. "While it is true that a majority of the loans on the books are low doc, that is a mixture of borrower requested and lender granted low doc, so I think it is misleading to say that all low doc loans have a higher risk of default."

"I agree 'significant' is too strong," Schneider replied.

To deal with the rising pile of bad loans, WaMu hired a new chief credit officer from Countrywide in late 2007. John McMurray* had initially resisted moving over to WaMu, but the bank promised him "a safe island in the storm." Contrary to those reassurances, the problems at WaMu made Countrywide seem like a church holding a bake sale. Not long before the shareholder meeting, McMurray made a presentation to WaMu's board of directors, outlining an even bleaker situation than shareholders read about in the year-end report. Killinger allowed him to deliver his thoughts, but he preceded McMurray's report with

---

*McMurray later became a whistleblower in the Securities and Exchange Commission's lawsuit against Countrywide's Angelo Mozilo, telling the government in a deposition that he had warned the lender about loan problems and recommended better disclosure to shareholders.

a preemptive explanation of the bank's position. For perhaps the first time, the board saw, in detail, WaMu's perilous concentration of mortgages in the states hit hardest by the housing crisis. McMurray included a series of charts and graphs illustrating home appreciation in different California markets growing sharply, then falling. In one breathtaking slide, he showed that WaMu's home equity loans represented *1,366 percent* of the bank's total equity. That startling percentage was colored red. And 90 percent of those loans, although it wasn't mentioned in McMurray's presentation or WaMu's annual report, were made to borrowers who didn't provide income documentation. WaMu easily ranked as the largest home equity lender. The company with the next highest volume had only half as many loans. WaMu had no disaster plan, so if a giant earthquake leveled California and all those borrowers tried to draw down their home equity loans, the bank could run out of money.

Increasingly, it looked as if the country were heading toward a financial crisis. As Killinger would soon point out in the annual meeting, two hundred mortgage lenders had gone out of business. Countrywide had just been forced to sell itself to Bank of America at a discount. WaMu's faux funeral for the mortgage lender had been right on the mark. Financial companies that bought securities backed by mortgages had suffered a collective $180 billion in write-downs. Wachovia, Fannie Mae, Freddie Mac, Lehman Brothers—all had raised, or were trying to raise, billions of dollars in capital. Only weeks earlier Bear Stearns, the once-mighty investment bank, had nearly collapsed. JPMorgan Chase bought the company for just $2 a share* in a deal backed by the government. The purchase price was a fraction of what the stock had been worth twenty years earlier. The press had used adjectives such as "stunning" and "shocking" and "watershed" to describe the monumental event. "This is like waking up in summer with snow on the ground," one Wall Street attorney observed in *The New York Times*.[4]

As Iris Glaze in WaMu's investor relations department could attest, shareholder angst at the bank had been mounting for months. It reached a fever pitch after WaMu announced its annual pay plan. The bank would be rewarding executives *without* calculating huge losses

---

*Later revised to $10 a share.

from expenses related to foreclosures or from loans that had soured. WaMu executives would be paid handsomely, while shareholders suffered from the bank's inept business decisions. And despite what Killinger would later call "an extraordinarily difficult year," WaMu still held its expensive annual President's Club party. A month and a half before the annual meeting, salespeople flew to Paradise Island in the Bahamas. The mood at the upscale resort was noticeably more reserved than usual. Thousands of loan consultants had been laid off in recent months. The attendees at the American Securitization Forum's annual conference, held in Las Vegas in early 2008, also were gloomy. The ranks of people working on mortgage-backed securities had been slashed. In just a year, the conference turned from late-night parties that rendered everyone hungover and happy to the atmosphere of a morgue. Deutsche Bank's representatives avoided casinos, for fear of giving investors the wrong impression. One of the consultants working on WaMu's bonds sat in a mostly empty bar at Caesar's Palace, sipping a drink as he watched the national news on TV. The segment described the mortgage largesse of the last several years. The camera panned to show the very bar where the WaMu consultant sat.

WaMu shareholders hadn't been told about the Bahamas soirée, but the unconscionable pay plan riled up the activists. They threatened to withhold votes from WaMu board members up for reelection at the annual meeting, including James Stever, the head of the human resources committee, who presided over executive compensation, and Mary Pugh, who chaired the finance committee. One Washington, D.C.–based activist representing several million WaMu shares flew to Seattle for a meeting with several directors and Killinger. He wanted to understand why the bank had expanded so heavily into risky mortgages and why it had approved the pay plan. He left unimpressed with the board's reasoning and reassurances and ultimately recommended a vote against Pugh and Stever. "I've never been at a meeting with a group of directors who seemed so afraid," he recalled.[5] WaMu would later announce that it had reversed its compensation plan criteria, but it then paid executives "retention bonuses."[6]

There was some reassuring news. WaMu had raised $7.2 billion in capital, a move that strengthened its financial position. The additional money would help the bank absorb losses from the bad loans. Even better, the money had been raised from TPG, a Texas-based private equity firm run by David Bonderman, a well-known and widely respected financier. Bonderman had sold American Savings Bank to WaMu in the 1990s and had sat on WaMu's board for six years until 2002. Now he would return, taking a director position. The TPG investment closed on the morning of WaMu's annual meeting, timed to appease angry investors. "It is a remarkable turnabout for Washington Mutual, whose once highflying stock has swooned along with home prices," *The New York Times* declared.[7] The news didn't calm shareholders, though. Their investment would be diluted because of the capital raise. *The Wall Street Journal* reported that WaMu turned down an $8 a share buyout offer from JPMorgan Chase,[8] and some shareholders would have preferred that the bank be acquired. They thought Killinger only wanted to keep his job. He was one of the longest-serving bank chief executives in the country.

At Benaroya Hall, shareholders streamed into the auditorium, the rows and rows of seats filling up. Soon, all 2,500 seats were full. Typically, the bank used only half the space. Members of the media, each with his or her own WaMu public relations "handler," were whisked to seats near the front of the room, just to the right of the stage. WaMu's board members filled the first two rows of seats. They faced forward, their expressions stony. Occasionally, one whispered something to another.

The lights dimmed and the room quieted. Kerry Killinger strode onto the stage and took his place behind the podium. To his right, the bank's executive team sat in folding chairs. Behind him, near a 4,500-piece organ, a screen had been set up to display slides. From the farthest reaches of the auditorium, Killinger looked about the same as he had at any of the shareholder meetings over the last eighteen years. He appeared confident, looking out at the crowd. But this confidence was a mirage. As anyone sitting close to him could tell, Killinger had lost weight. His face was gaunt. His suit hung loosely on his body. His hair, swept to the side, had further grayed. His hands shook slightly as he grasped his prepared script.

The capital raise had been particularly hard on Killinger. In a meeting at WaMu's headquarters, several dozen people had crammed into the boardroom to run through the presentation that executives would deliver to potential private equity investors. The room was full of investment bankers and WaMu executives. Perfecting the pitch was crucial. It would determine the bank's immediate survival. Killinger read from the script haltingly, stumbling on his words and speaking softly. He stopped and started. He slouched in his chair. "You would have just cringed to see it," said one of the people in attendance. The investment bankers realized that Killinger couldn't perform this way. They whittled his speaking time down.

The other executives wondered if Killinger was sick. One of them had heard he was taking sleeping pills, and another had observed him clutching his stomach. While Killinger would never discuss anything personal, he confessed to another executive: "I wish things could go back to the way they used to be."

But, of course, they couldn't. As he took the podium at the annual shareholder meeting, Killinger, for the first time in his life, looked out at a large group of people ferociously mad at him. All the executives and directors expected to face criticism at the meeting and had even endured some media training to prepare for it. Nothing, however, readied them for what came next.

"Well, good afternoon everyone and welcome," said Killinger, launching into the presentation.[9] "I am Kerry Killinger and I want to thank you all for joining us this afternoon for WaMu's twenty-fifth annual meeting of shareholders. I am glad to have this chance to spend some time with you today as we take a look at our 2007 results and what 2008 holds for WaMu. First off, I have been informed we have a quorum so I will officially call the meeting to order.

"Clearly, 2007 was an extraordinarily difficult year for WaMu but, you know, today I believe that we are at the beginning of the road back, back on a path of profitability and to creating the shareholder value that we all desire. Now, I expect that when we look back a year from now we are going to view April 2008 as a turning point in this company's history.

"And let me tell you why I think this is the case. What has happened the last couple of years in the mortgage and credit markets has never happened before in my lifetime. In fact, nothing of this scale has occurred since the Great Depression. It has had a crippling effect on the housing sector and on a large part of the financial services industry.

"You know, we did see a slowing housing market coming. In fact, the board and management took major actions to prepare for that slowdown, and we raised new capital on several occasions." Here Killinger referenced preferred stock the bank sold in late 2007. His voice betrayed no anxiety. He spoke as if he were describing a company that had made $1 billion in the quarter, not lost it. The audience listened.

"But the actual magnitude of the housing downturn and the unprecedented disruptions in the capital markets have simply overcome much of our preparation. However, we are fortunate that we have a great core business within our complex, especially our retail banking franchise. We have customers who really like to do business with us. We have a great team of people, we have liquidity, we have cash flow and we have just about everything we need to succeed."

He added: "Of course, I'm very unhappy with these results and I take responsibility for the business decisions we made along the way. But I'm also responsible for and completely committed to turning things around."

Killinger went on to speak about WaMu's recent capital raise. He described it as "a vote of confidence in our future from some of the smartest and most sophisticated investors around.

"Now I would like to thank everyone who is here today for your interest in and commitment to WaMu and its future success. You know, annual meetings are sometimes fairly routine, but that's obviously not the case today. Today we can expect both shareholders and other stakeholders will be expressing their opinions. We certainly have better attendance. I expect our question-and-answer session will bring some pointed questions."

Then came the first sign of instability. A murmur rippled through the crowd. "I also want to inform you," Killinger said, "that prior to our board meeting this morning, Mary Pugh submitted her resignation and it was accepted during the board meeting. Therefore, Mary is not standing for reelection."

Pugh had long supported Killinger, but as the subprime market fell apart, she had become increasingly worried about how the bank was managed. The reports the board received from executives were sometimes rosy, as if they weren't taking into account the full extent of a calamitous situation. In the fall of 2007, chief financial officer Tom Casey presented a table of projected loan loss forecasts to the board. There were three loss scenarios, the lowest of which WaMu had surpassed, even though the table represented a projection. The bank had nearly hit Casey's midrange figure. As a result, one of the board members questioned whether WaMu's forecast of its bad loans was *too high*, and wondered if the bank shouldn't be setting aside so much money to cover the losses. In fact, just the opposite was true. One of WaMu's examiners at the Office of Thrift Supervision worried that "the board is not getting sufficient, consistent or understandable information/reports from management."[10]

As in a game of telephone, David Schneider reported to Steve Rotella that the Home Loans Group was tightening underwriting standards, and Rotella then reported this to Killinger. Killinger, who generally trusted his direct reports, relayed this information to the board. "I think Kerry sincerely believed it," said one manager who worked closely with him. But sometimes Killinger would circumvent Schneider and ask WaMu's market research department for information on certain mortgage products.

Directors were told, "We're managing the risk," and they asked few questions. On top of everything else, WaMu had just gotten into serious trouble with the OTS for violating the Bank Secrecy Act, the federal law requiring banks to detect money laundering. In normal times, the public disgrace of receiving a cease-and-desist order from the government would have been a big problem all on its own. But now the board was preoccupied, trying to comply with the strict ultimatum from regulators and making sure the bank returned to compliance.

Pugh had always been skeptical about high-risk loans, particularly interest-only mortgages. She began to show up at WaMu's headquarters, asking more questions of the executives. She finally sent an e-mail to Steve Frank, the chair of the board's audit committee, suggesting directors meet with WaMu's federal regulators to get an outside opinion. Frank forwarded the e-mail to Killinger, who recommended against it. Killinger preferred that a smaller, informal group of directors meet with regulators. He wanted to be present. The discussion about WaMu's problems that Pugh hoped would take place never did.

Meanwhile, because she was chair of the board's finance committee, Pugh turned into a lightning rod for shareholder criticism. She wouldn't have been reelected by investors. Under pressure that morning, she resigned. Later, in her only public interview, with the *Puget Sound Business Journal,* she said, "Despite my willingness to offer views, in the end I can only control a single vote, and that is my own."[11]

On stage at the shareholder meeting, Killinger followed up the news of Pugh's departure with words of praise.

"Speaking on behalf of the board, those who have worked with Mary want to thank her for many, many years of service to WaMu and as a valued board member. We're very grateful for her tireless dedication and steadfast belief in this company."

He turned the presentation over to Casey, who ran through the bank's recent performance: "It's important to note that while credit costs are impacting our business, this will not last forever." Next it was Steve Rotella's turn.

"Big crowd!" said Rotella, at the podium. He didn't appear nervous. "Well, I think we know that credit costs and unacceptable financial results are likely to be the headlines most of you will take away from today's meetings. And, frankly, it's a headline that we understand is frustrating for our shareholders. And believe me, it's frustrating to management."

Rotella shifted the focus away from all the disturbing mortgage-related news and onto a bright spot: WaMu's retail bank. In spite of the overexpansion, WaMu's branch network had long been considered the best part of the company.

But the shareholders had grown restless as the executives carried on. Rotella's presentation seemed like a badly executed magic trick, a distraction to draw attention away from the real problems. The room echoed with whispers and the occasional snarky comment. "Whoo-hoo!" yelled one WaMu employee, a dig at the bank's current and badly timed ad campaign. The audience rumbled with laughter.

Killinger returned to the podium. He implored shareholders to trust management and the board. He pointed out WaMu's "very solid foundation for success.

"I also want you to know that, just from a personal standpoint, there is an absolute, total commitment that I'm bringing to it," said Killinger. "It's deep, it's personal, and the only reason I'm here is to help this remarkable company complete that turnaround and get back on the track that it deserves."

Then he opened up the meeting to the public. Right away lines formed behind two microphones, placed on either side of the main aisles of the wood-paneled auditorium.

One of the shareholder activists stood in front of the stage. The union he represented had two million members, and all of them held retirement plans invested in WaMu stock. "I would also like to state personally," said the activist, "that myself and my fifteen-year-old son are longtime customers of Washington Mutual, and to say that there was much love about this company. And what I have to say is somewhat difficult.

"To our great regret and alarm, Washington Mutual has become a poster child of board failure to protect the interests of shareholders. Specifically, from 2005 through 2007, the finance committee knew the housing bubble would burst, would collapse, yet allowed Washington Mutual to expand its Option ARM and subprime exposure, leading to a devastating 75 percent decline in shareholder value. Our board of directors, chaired by yourself, CEO, Mr. Killinger, joined Ms. Pugh's committee and ignored the risks to shareholders. Ms. Pugh's committee and the board failed to protect shareholders."

The anger poured out of shareholders, one after the other. Said another activist: "Sadly, here at WaMu, we really feel we have a board that has lost its way. It's no longer a WaMu board; it's more like a 'WaMe' board, short for 'What's in it for me?' The 'mutual' is gone. The company, as recently as last week, stood by its board. Quote: 'The directors that have been targeted have a demonstrable record of skill, diligence, and independent thinking. We cannot conceive of a more inopportune time to urge the needless disruption and distraction of a change in board composition.' We beg to differ."

On stage, Killinger and the other executives kept their composure, although the shareholder statements soon surpassed the negative reaction they had anticipated. Killinger, behind the podium, wore a frozen half-smile. In response to each burst of anger, he responded with a terse "Thank you." To this last comment, he replied, "Thank you. We appreciate your comments. As I said in my prepared remarks, I believe that this is a very engaged, very dedicated, and very hardworking board trying to do the absolute best things that they can do. And I disagree in a very significant way with the allegations that you made here."

One shareholder, who had recently filed a lawsuit against the company, stepped up to the microphone. He demanded Killinger's resignation, telling him, "Your greed is to keep the board in place and hold on to your job.

"I have listened to all of this, and I'm amazed at how gullible people can be. You've said what you've done. You haven't said what you haven't done. You haven't put forth your problems. Because that's what we're dealing with—problems. Problems which you, sir, have created. I've gotten letters from people, I've got letters from shareholders that basically say, 'Withhold this board member vote, withhold this one, withhold votes.' I don't understand it. We're the owners, not them. They're employees. Take the damn company back!"

He added: "What you've got to do is do what some real men do—real men. When you face a situation like this, you stand down."

Only one person stepped up to defend WaMu, sparking immediate audience speculation that the employee was a plant by the bank.*

"I have had the pleasure of working with Kerry and Steve one on one on projects, and there are a few things I'd also like to offer as a PhD holder in international economics," the employee said. "It is difficult to blame any single person, any single board, for the kind of transactional and fiscal things that we're seeing going on in the world. These problems are more pronounced in other countries right now than they are in the U.S. Pardon the quiver in my voice; this is very nerve-racking for me.

"I have seen Kerry fiercely protect the independence of Washington Mutual from gobbler-up banks like Chase. Having dealt with Jamie Dimon in the past, I'm very pleased that's happened."

---

*There is no evidence of this.

She went on: "And I'm probably going to get booed for this, but I think, Kerry and Steve, you're doing a wonderful job. Thank you for the diversity focus. Thanks for the community focus, and thanks for keeping WaMu independent."

"Thank you very much," Killinger replied.

From his seat in a balcony, overlooking the stage, Tom Golon listened through the length of the presentations. Golon was a WaMu home loan consultant in Seattle. He had been perplexed and annoyed by the bank's push to make riskier mortgages. That sort of lending might make sense in California, but not in the Northwest, he thought. "Our whole orientation was now going to be toward making Option ARMs," he said later. "It was pathetic. It kind of ignored reality." He brushed off the meetings and e-mails and conferences set up to convince him and his coworkers to push Option ARMs. One e-mail flash sent out by the Home Loans Group in 2006, announcing a training initiative to help people sell Option ARMS, read, in part: "This is a fantastic product for almost any borrower. To help our sales force feel more comfortable with selling the Option ARM to a wide variety of borrowers, we are rolling out a comprehensive skills assessment and training initiative."[12] The Home Loans Group staged a "Fall Kickoff Contest," awarding loan consultants with points for the number of loans they sold. An Option ARM was considered a "touchdown" and earned the highest amount—7 points. At the end of the quarter, the highest point earners received a $1,000 gift card.

Several weeks earlier Golon had received a layoff notice, one of the thousands the bank had doled out to its salespeople nationwide. Still, Golon hadn't planned to say anything at the annual meeting. Then Killinger, in his opening remarks, thanked his wife. "And speaking of supportive families," Killinger had said, "special thanks to my wife, Linda, for her patience, support, and love. Please join me in giving a round of applause to all of our employees and their families." Golon thought this remark was ludicrous. He stewed. "All these retired people are sitting here, losing their life savings, and he's thanking his wife for all that she's endured?" he thought.

At the microphone, he stood in front of Killinger and the other executives.

"I'm an employee and a shareholder, and want to give you the inside scoop on how this has all come down with Washington Mutual," he said. "And the man most responsible for the demise of Washington Mutual is sitting there with a glass of water, Steve Rotella, who was kicked out of Chase four years ago and came over to Washington Mutual to do his damage."

On stage, Rotella's expression didn't change, despite the unexpected rebuke. Until now all the shareholder anger had fallen on Killinger and the board.

"In the last three years, or however long Steve Rotella has been here, he has been emphasizing risky loans—paid the loan consultants more for subprime loans and for 1 percent start-rate Option ARMs than for the good loans, for fixed rates that couldn't harm anybody.

"So now we've got this huge portfolio down in California of people underwater because they went on 1 percent start-rate Option ARMs that were pioneered by Countrywide, and then we did the same thing. We have a lot more losses in the future with this company. This man has driven the company to the edge of bankruptcy. And he should be fired, and his bonuses should be taken back from him."

Once he got started, Golon had trouble stopping.

"Kerry Killinger is like the Ken Lay of this company," he said, comparing Killinger to the longtime chief executive of Enron. "Now he can go on and say, 'Oh, things are good!' And Steve Rotella can come out here and say, 'Oh, our new model is great!' You don't realize how bad this company is—the shape of this company."*

It was bad enough that an employee of WaMu, albeit one about to get laid off, had criticized the bank and its executives. But now Lee Lannoye stood up to the microphone. Lannoye had sat on WaMu's executive team in the 1990s, and he had been the strongest opponent of the purchase of Long Beach Mortgage. He feared that subprime mortgages

---

*After the meeting, Rotella called Golon to discuss his comments. They spoke for an hour and a half. In particular, Rotella took issue with Golon's characterization of his departure from JPMorgan Chase. According to Golon, Rotella also told him that the reason WaMu had pushed Option ARMs and subprime mortgages was that selling them to Wall Street fetched four times the price of a fixed-rate loan. Golon told Rotella that it was nice of him to call. "People have a right to get up and say what's on their minds," Rotella later told *The Seattle Times*.

would turn WaMu into a predatory lender, forcing borrowers who could have qualified for a prime loan into one with a higher rate. Lannoye's fear had come to pass, although he had no idea how bad the problems at the division had become.

As Killinger was speaking, Lannoye's frustration grew. In particular, he couldn't believe how much the executives attributed WaMu's problems to the economy and other lenders. Lannoye began scribbling rough notes about the presentation on a pad of paper resting in his lap. "Putting blame on WM losses on the capital markets, housing downturn—not decisions made by execs/directors!!" and "You are using the Herd Mentality as an excuse for WM's disastrous financial condition" and "Sophisticated, pretty slides do not answer why execs/directors are *not* being held accountable for strategic decisions" and "*Very* high risk home loans that analysts predict will result in as much as $14 billion in losses." (After the meeting, WaMu would in fact announce that it was expecting between $12 billion and $19 billion in loan losses over the next several years, a higher amount than even some analysts had predicted.)[13] In the margins of his notes, Lannoye had written again, "NO ONE is being held accountable."

The notes, however, did nothing to ease his annoyance. When the microphones came out, Lannoye got in line. "I couldn't help it," he said later.

Lannoye introduced himself to the crowd. "My name is Lee Lannoye. I still own a thousand shares of the bank. And I can tell you this is not easy for me to stand here. For twenty years, I have been attending the shareholder meeting. And ten of those, I was up at the front of the stage as a member of Kerry's executive committee.

"All the sophistry and pretty slides that you have been showing us really don't get to the heart of the question. The people sitting in the front of the room made conscious decisions to lower the credit and underwriting standards of the bank. The result is that they have got over a hundred billion dollars' worth of lousy subprime loans on the books that analysts estimate are going to lose fourteen billion. That's why you need seven billion dollars worth of credit. You have destroyed the bank. Why are you not being held accountable?"

Killinger, caught off guard, replied haltingly to his former executive team member.

"Well, as I said in my comments, we take responsibility for what we are doing, and we're in the process of turning it around," Killinger said.

"Why should we expect that the people sitting here, who have made some damn stupid decisions over the past four or five years, can make any better decisions going forward?" Lannoye demanded. "Why wouldn't we be better off with the stock of JPMorgan, which is a well-run organization, than stock in a company being managed by people who obviously don't know how to run a lending operation?"

"Thank you," Killinger said.

"You are not being held accountable," Lannoye said, ignoring his cue. "You haven't answered that question."

"Well, thanks. I understand the question. I'm telling you, we do take accountability, and we're working hard on turning this around."

Lannoye sat down. Killinger was shaken. He hated confrontation. Now shareholders, employees, and even former executives were berating him, one after another, in a public forum. His hands began to tremble again. Another shareholder threw him an easy question, asking Killinger to explain WaMu's current problems compared with the Savings and Loan Crisis. "Are we going to get out of it like we got out of that one?" the shareholder asked. This question gave Killinger the chance to flip the meeting back in his favor. He could have reminded the audience that, yes, WaMu had emerged mightily from that earlier crisis, just as it would emerge from this one. Instead, he gave a convoluted response, ending with what seemed a scolding of shareholders.

"I just want people to calm down," Killinger said, agitated. "Have a little faith. I know it's tough. I know nobody likes a one-cent dividend. Nobody likes the stock price where it is. Nobody likes dilution. Nobody likes to have to raise capital now. I've never had to do any of that, except we have to, because we've got to do it now. And if we do it correctly now and manage ourselves through . . . again, it was because this is the worst housing market since the Great Depression. And we've had to deal with it.

"And if we just stay with this for a few more quarters, I think . . . again, I said in my remarks earlier, this is a turning point. I expect us to stand here next year and look back and say, April of 2008 was the turning point. Yes, we can see why it was a tough time. But I think we will have seen a better time by then."

The shareholder who had asked the question didn't immediately respond. Killinger's answer had stunned the audience. Many of WaMu's employees, and even the bank's senior managers, had never seen Killinger lose his composure.

"Excuse me—I was wondering," the shareholder said, "could you just kind of answer? Is this similar to that situation? You're kind of rambling on now."

"I am, but it's similar in terms of the difficulties—caused by different things, but it was a very tough period. This is a very tough period."

Killinger soon called the tense question-and-answer session to an end. "I appreciate all the lively questions," he said. He announced preliminary voting results. All of WaMu's directors had received a majority of the shareholder vote. They had been reelected. The shareholders had also supported a resolution calling for Killinger to give up his role as chairman of the board. That didn't mean Killinger had to do it. It was like a suggestion for the company to take into consideration. Typically, however, companies listen to their shareholders. When an employee asked Killinger about it privately, he replied, quietly, "I'm still going to be the chairman of the board."

Over the years, WaMu had developed an unhealthy habit of churning through employees whose jobs involved monitoring risk or complying with federal regulations. In just two years, the bank had been through five credit officers—those most in charge of bad loans. Other employees moved in and out in similar short spurts of time. No one was providing a singular clear vision of how to fix all the loan issues, and there wouldn't have even been enough employees to carry out such a vision.

The latest to leave was Ron Cathcart, WaMu's chief risk officer. Over the preceding months, Cathcart had been marginalized. When other executives wanted information, they asked his direct reports instead of him, and they excluded him from important meetings. When the rest of the executive team members flew to New York to present to investors, they left him behind, much to his frustration. He stopped receiving invitations to board meetings, an oversight that he complained about to Killinger. Cathcart was allowed to return, but Killinger told him during one meeting related to the capital raise: "You can come to the board meeting, but you have to leave before the investment bankers come in." Cathcart believed he was being pushed aside because he had pointed out the company's poor controls and mismanagement, particularly in the Home Loans Group. Other members of the executive team, meanwhile, thought Cathcart's approach to risk management was misguided and weak. They instead invited John McMurray, the chief credit officer from Countrywide, who they believed had deeper, more technical experience with mortgages. Cathcart told one of WaMu's directors that he was being prevented from fulfilling his responsibilities, a move that he knew could cost him his job. Indeed, Killinger fired him.

The bank moved McMurray into Cathcart's position, although McMurray remained chief credit officer as well. McMurray spent some time investigating the way WaMu handled risk, then fired off a twenty-page missive to Killinger, outlining the many, many problems he saw at the bank. His e-mail was in part a response to an internal newsletter sent out by Killinger called *Moving Forward*. Killinger had failed to list "risk management" as one of the top priorities for the company in 2008. McMurray observed that no matter what happened, WaMu always lapsed right back into risky behavior. McMurray called his e-mail an "exposé." He labeled WaMu's perspective on risk "dysfunctional" and "anathematic."

McMurray's e-mail criticized nearly every aspect of WaMu's operations. Sometimes it bordered on patronizing: "Before we can forecast a variable, we need to have well-developed models that show we understand what has already happened." At other times, it was just disturbing: "WaMu did not measure, track and report home prices in a robust, consistent manner." And it called out a far greater problem: "WaMu has been managed at a tactical level, and has lacked a coherent, consistently communicated business strategy."

McMurray showed the letter to other WaMu executives, but he wasn't telling any of them anything they didn't already know. The frustratingly slow pace of change at the company, they believed, was caused partly by Killinger's inability to deal with the problems. Rotella and several of the other executives banded together. Sometimes they met up for drinks and dinner at a nearby restaurant in downtown Seattle, debating the fate of the company without having Killinger around. In turn, Killinger was increasingly isolated and became even more aloof and withdrawn. During the capital raise, when executives flew to New York for investor presentations, Killinger didn't join them for meals.

No one was more frustrated about the lack of action than Rotella. He began pushing Killinger even harder about his role at the company. He held more one-on-one meetings, asking Killinger more directly whether he was in line for the chief executive position. He wanted more authority—with more authority, he could make changes. "Steve was trying to get things done as much as he could get things done in the envelope Kerry gave him," observed one of the other executives. Killinger, always vague, said that he and the board liked Rotella, but he never gave a direct response. He said he would think about giving Rotella a board seat. Other executives warned Rotella that it wasn't a good idea to push Killinger too hard. He was the chief executive, after all. "You're in dangerous territory," they told him. Rotella finally sent an e-mail to director Steve Frank, offering to quit. Nothing changed.

At a board meeting in the spring of 2008, Rotella lost his temper. The directors and executives were discussing the bank's compliance with the Bank Secrecy Act. In the meeting, Killinger tried to spread blame about who had been responsible for the problems, implying that Rotella was at fault. Rotella, his anger growing, reminded Killinger that the manager in charge didn't report to him—the bank's Risk Management Group actually reported to Killinger—and that it had been Killinger's decision to hire that person in the first place. "I'm sorry," Rotella said, "but I'm not accepting responsibility for that. I had no oversight of it." As the problems at WaMu grew worse, the board of directors meetings weren't so tightly run, and more open discussions took place. Still, Frank went to see Rotella after his outburst and told him he was being disruptive. The message implied: Get back in line, or you're out of here. Rotella apologized.

• • •

On a morning in May 2008, a month after the shareholder meeting, a group of five emissaries arrived at WaMu's headquarters. They were Liane Wilson, the former head of WaMu's technology department; Lee Lannoye, who had spoken at the shareholder meeting; Al Doman, the leader of WaMu's A-team during the 1990s merger frenzy; Mike Towers, once in charge of the retail bank; and Lynn Ryder, the former head of human resources. All had retired before 2003 after long careers at the bank. Ryder and Doman had started working at WaMu in the 1970s, under the chief executive who had preceded Pepper. All five were part of a group of retired executives and managers who kept in touch after leaving WaMu.* Members of the group traveled together or met up over coffee or a meal. Invariably, the conversation would turn to the bank. All of them still spoke with ongoing employees from their respective departments. In recent months, they had heard snippets of troubling news, about the bank's culture change and the push to sell, above everything else. Rotella's leadership style often came up; some employees considered him and his direct reports cold and abrasive. The retirees believed that the rank-and-file workers no longer trusted senior management—either Rotella or Killinger. "It was not just one of us that was hearing these things," Wilson said later. "It was all of us—and we all had different tentacles in the bank."

With the exception of Craig Tall, Killinger didn't keep in close touch with WaMu's retirees. But out of the blue, two weeks before the disastrous shareholder meeting, Killinger sent an e-mail to Ryder. He had heard that she and other former employees had concerns about the company.

Killinger invited Ryder and several of the other "WaMulians" to meet with him to discuss the issues in person, and that is why the five WaMu retirees now stood in the bank's marble lobby. They had met for breakfast beforehand and driven into the city together in a minivan. Several of them had never been inside the bank's new skyscraper. The row of security guards that greeted them when they walked through the

---

*Many of the retirees, including Lou Pepper, didn't like the name "WaMu" and refused to accept it, even after it was officially changed in 2006. They continued calling the bank "Washington Mutual."

glass doors surprised them. One of the guards directed them through card-operated turnstiles, into the elevator bank and up to the thirty-second floor. The retirees took in the restrained decor of the executive floor. The walls in hallways and offices featured paintings and sculptures by well-known artists known as the Northwest School: Kenneth Callahan, Mark Tobey, and Morris Graves among them. WaMu had commissioned a curator to compile the collection, encompassing more than 500 pieces. To several of the former executives, the new building felt cold. The muted color choices, coupled with the art, made everything look modern and new.

Killinger greeted the executives and led them to a conference room. Some of them hadn't seen him face-to-face in years, although all of them had attended the shareholder meeting. Lannoye hadn't spoken to Killinger since then, but Killinger seemed to have forgiven, or was at least ignoring, Lannoye's public attack. There was an inherent strangeness about this meeting, and not just because of its subject matter. Around the table sat a group of people who had devoted their careers to a bank that no longer existed. The company they had worked for was much smaller and simpler and had encouraged an unusual sense of devotion that carried on years after they left. That bank had disappeared, a relic of another era. But here Killinger still sat. It was not the WaMu they once knew; nor was Killinger the same executive they had once worked with.

Killinger, thin and graying, looked more relaxed than he had at the shareholder meeting. As the former executives talked, he wrote copious notes on his legal pad. For a long time, the group discussed the mortgage problems. Killinger reiterated much of what he had told investors at the shareholder meeting and in his recent e-mails to Ryder. He outlined the scope of the problem and reassured the retirees that the bank was dealing with it. "It's a perfect storm," he remarked. And then later: "Why did this have to happen on my watch? In a normal world, things would have been just fine."

The group talked specifically about the failings of the volume-based commission structure of the Home Loans Group and the division in general. The division had long had a volume-based pay structure, but it was no longer in check. "There doesn't seem to be any accountability for lending," they told Killinger. The retirees tried to offer him comfort as well as a dose of reality. They offered two blunt suggestions, which they had tossed around and agreed on at breakfast before the meeting. The retirees believed that Killinger should cut his compensation to the bone, accepting just a dollar a year, as a show of faith to shareholders. Killinger reminded them that he had already refused his bonus for the year.

The retirees' second suggestion was even more controversial. They thought Killinger or Rotella should resign. Since they believed Killinger better understood WaMu's culture, the executives recommended that he ask Rotella to step down. None of the retirees had worked with Rotella; most had not met him. They based their recommendation on information they heard from the employees they kept in touch with. "He's out to get you," the retirees warned Killinger, as Fay Chapman had done months earlier.

During the discussion about Rotella, Killinger looked uncomfortable. The WaMu retirees had no way of knowing about the power struggles between the two men, or the extent to which the executive team had fractured. During the capital raising process, when the executives had flown to New York for investor presentations, the bank had used two private jets. Killinger flew in one plane, Rotella in another. The other executives argued quietly over who would have to sit in Killinger's jet, with Linda and Como the dog.

The retirees came from an era at the bank when personalities clashed but everyone respected the executive team's cohesiveness. Several had sat through the long-ago meeting when Pepper had appointed Killinger and Bill Longbrake dual presidents. "If any of you starts playing favorites, you'll be out of here, forthwith," Pepper had warned. "This is a cooperative effort, not a competition." The closeness of the executive team had endured long after Pepper stepped down, even as the bank grew larger. "I knew there were strong opinions and disagreement at the executive level, but to people outside, it was never evident," said Doman, the only retiree in the meeting with Killinger who hadn't served on the executive committee. "They gave a united front."

The hour-and-a-half meeting ended amicably, with hand shaking and smiles all around. Killinger had filled pages of his pad with notes. The retirees left the executive floor and took the elevator back down to the parking garage. As they rode along in the minivan on the way back home, they talked about the meeting. None of them felt reassured. "We didn't leave it with a great sense of 'Everything's going to be just fine,'" Wilson said later. When the van pulled up to the breakfast restaurant, where the other executives had left their cars, they continued their discussion as the van idled. "We all felt it was unlikely Kerry would take any action," Ryder said. "I don't think anyone felt there was much promise."

Neither did WaMu shareholders, who had not been placated by the annual meeting. WaMu's stock, trading at about $10, continued to fall. In the investor relations department, Iris Glaze's phone rang all day. She answered it in a voice as cheerful as she could muster. On the line, investors yelled at her or offered criticism. Sometimes they swore. In between calls, she could hear her coworker offering shareholders the same flat message, like a recording on repeat, "Yes, things are bad, but give us until 2009 or 2010. It will get better."

Glaze's boss, Doug Wisdorf, the deputy of the investor relations department, fielded many of the calls from WaMu's largest shareholders, the institutional investors. This job was arguably the hardest, since much bigger sums of money were involved. Glaze listened to Wisdorf speak calmly and confidently to anyone who called, her faith in WaMu restored by listening to him. Wisdorf, like Glaze, was a longtime WaMu employee. He had worked at the bank for more than two decades and had even met his wife at WaMu.

The small investor relations team absorbed all the hatred leveled at the bank. In her cube, Glaze kept a large cardboard cutout of Lorraine, one of the "Rodeo Grandmas" from a popular series of quirky ads WaMu had run in the 1990s. Lorraine, her face comically stern, her arms cradling a small pig, reminded Glaze of those much easier times. "If yer being saddled with a minimum balance, leave yer bank in the dust," the ads instructed.

With each call she answered, Glaze could feel her good spirits flagging. Each day she arrived at work deflated. She started eating more. Finally she stopped taking calls from shareholders. "I knew if I talked to these people," Glaze said, "I would blow up at them." She e-mailed them instead.

•   •   •

On Friday, June 27, 2008, a letter arrived at the Office of Thrift Supervision in Washington, D.C. A block away, the Federal Deposit Insurance Corp. received a copy, as did the Federal Home Loan Bank of San Francisco across the country in California. The first two agencies regulated WaMu, but they also watched over IndyMac Bank in Southern California. The Home Loan Bank provided large lines of credit to both banks.

The letter was signed by Senator Chuck Schumer (D-N.Y.), who headed the Senate subcommittee that oversees economic policy. The letter concerned IndyMac,[14] which, Schumer wrote, might have "serious problems" with its mortgages and could "face a failure if prescriptive measures are not taken quickly.

"I am concerned that IndyMac's financial deterioration poses significant risks to both taxpayers and borrowers," Schumer wrote, "and that the regulatory community may not be prepared to take measures that would help prevent the collapse of IndyMac or minimize the damage should a failure occur."

After mailing the letter to the various regulatory agencies, Schumer's office made it public. Thirteen days later IndyMac failed.

Like WaMu, IndyMac had been suffering as a result of the housing downturn and the subprime market collapse. The Pasadena-based bank, the ninth-largest lender nationwide, mostly made Alt A loans. IndyMac's chief executive, Michael Perry, didn't believe Alt A loans should be confused with subprime mortgages. "That's like saying that our headquarters in Pasadena is 'in between' Los Angeles and Las Vegas," he once tried to explain. "True enough, but there's the question of degree: Pasadena is 11 miles northeast of Los Angeles and Las Vegas is 262 miles northeast of Pasadena."[15] Whatever the mileage difference between subprime and Alt A borrowers, IndyMac's Alt A borrowers had mostly taken out Option ARMs. Just like many of the nation's subprime borrowers, they hadn't had to prove their income. And just like the subprime borrowers, they defaulted on their loans en masse in 2007. By the time Senator Schumer released his letter, IndyMac had reported three straight quarters of losses totaling almost $1 billion. Its stock price had plummeted to $1.08, from $31 a year earlier.[16] The bank ceased making Alt A loans as Perry and his staff scrambled to raise capital.

Schumer's letter about IndyMac made the national news. It was quoted in newspapers, on radio stations, and on television. IndyMac's customers began closing their accounts at the bank's 30 branches across Southern California. Within three days, the bank lost $100 million in deposits.

This situation was highly unusual—regulators normally never discuss publicly the health of a bank. The agencies that received the letter lashed out at Schumer. "Dissemination of incomplete or erroneous information can erode public confidence, mislead depositors and investors, and cause unintended consequences, including depositor runs and panic stock trades," John Reich, the director of the Office of Thrift Supervision, furiously told a reporter.[17] A former regulator was even less forgiving in his criticism, calling Schumer's action "incredibly stupid conduct" and warning other regulatory officials that "you'd be crazy" to share information with him. "If Schumer continues to go public with letters raising questions about the condition of individual institutions, he will cause havoc in the banking system. Leaking his IndyMac letter to the press was reckless and grossly irresponsible." Senator Schumer's office defended his action, saying, "We have found the only way to get the Home Loan Bank system to act appropriately and positively is to make public the concerns we've already expressed privately."

The damage was irreversible. A bank run is like a contagious virus. The panic it creates feeds off itself. The media carried the admonishment from regulators, but that only reminded the public of Schumer's reckless comments. IndyMac's reassurances did little to halt the run. "We are hopeful that this issue appropriately abates soon," the bank said in a statement that it quickly posted on its website, "so that we can focus, with our regulators' involvement, on the important issue of continuing to keep IndyMac Bank safe and sound through this unprecedented crisis period."[18] The bank reminded its customers that their money was insured up to $100,000 by the FDIC. Even if IndyMac failed, they would still be protected. The customers, however, didn't care—or often even know—whether they had insurance. They pulled out their money. By the time the OTS closed the lender, it had lost $1.3 billion, about 7 percent of its total deposits.[19]

Customers' fear didn't subside after the government moved in.

IndyMac was the first large bank failure in more than two years. No one could remember a time when a bank had been closed because of an actual run on deposits. That sort of event played out only in *It's a Wonderful Life*. "I didn't think this could happen," said one of IndyMac's customers, incredulously, summarizing the feelings of an entire country.[20]

People drove from all over Southern California to IndyMac's headquarters in Pasadena, waiting in the July desert heat to pull out their money from the institution, now run by the government. A line stretched around the sandy-colored headquarters building and down the palm-tree-lined block. Older customers, fanning themselves, sat on government-provided folding chairs. Young mothers stood anxiously by baby carriages. "This is my life savings here," said one customer, who had more than $100,000 in the bank. "What do you resort to now, putting money back in the mattress?"[21] By the second day, customers grew even more agitated. Some booked hotels in advance to ensure their place in line first thing in the morning. Others arrived at the bank as early as 1:30 a.m. Some set up tents while they waited. Nerves frayed and fights broke out. Security had to be called. "Once I get in the door," one customer told a reporter, "I'm going to get every penny I can out of there. I'm going to bury it in the backyard."[22]

The media descended on the spectacle. Unnerving photos of the lines, and the anxious customers, and the government officials in suits led the news across the country for days. Banks had suffered runs since the Great Depression, but none had been as well documented. In these photos, Americans saw fear, but they also saw something much worse. They saw that the banking system, a stable, little-considered cornerstone of the American economy, could fail them.

At WaMu, executives were plenty worried. At 10:30 p.m. on the Friday of IndyMac's failure, Ken Kido, in charge of WaMu's 2,200 branches, sent an e-mail to one of the managers of the bank's deposit team. "Given the IndyMac situation," wrote Kido, "we are going to want to watch the outflows. How often can we get this report? Is weekly the most frequent?" Kido, who was referring to the bank's regular deposit report, wanted to make sure the bank was monitoring its own customers. In Pasadena, ground zero of IndyMac's bank run, WaMu occupied a large, columned branch perched on the corner of a busy intersection. The branch was located just blocks from IndyMac headquarters. Kido wasn't concerned just about this branch, however. He was worried about the effect of the photos and news stories on all WaMu's locations, all across the country.

During a deposit run, the most important gauge of a bank's immediate health is its liquidity. While capital consists of shareholders' equity and a company's long-term reserves, liquidity is the money a bank has on hand, right away. It is the money used to pay back customers who want to close their accounts. To keep liquidity high, many banks rely on credit lines from the Federal Home Loan Bank system and sometimes, in times of financial stress, on the Federal Reserve Bank's discount window. Banks pledge collateral—usually mortgages—to secure the loans, and the collateral required is higher than the actual loan amount. Banks can also sell off assets like real estate or securities to generate more money. The job of a bank's treasury department is to juggle the inflow and outflow of all this money, making sure the bank has enough to pay its creditors on a daily basis.

Ironically, WaMu's treasury department had just spent the better part of two years overhauling the way it tracked WaMu's liquidity. Before, WaMu had operated with a backward-looking modeling system reminiscent of a much smaller bank. Now it had state-of-the-art projection capabilities, allowing it to predict the money moving into and out of the bank with more accuracy. The overhaul was completed mere weeks before the subprime market collapsed. Since then WaMu's treasury department had been stockpiling cash—borrowing more money than it needed in case of a crisis.

When IndyMac failed, WaMu had just boosted its liquidity to about $50 billion. While that was much lower than it had been in prior years, federal regulators considered the level healthy. "If we see some customers get jumpy, in other words, we're ready: the till is full to bursting," wrote Peter Freilinger, WaMu's deputy treasurer, in reply to Kido's e-mail on the night of IndyMac's failure.

Freilinger continued with a warning to WaMu managers: "It's important to remember that we can inadvertently create a negative dynamic by suddenly showing elevated concerns or asking aggressive, fast turnaround deposit requests to the field.

"Clearly, the risks remain elevated, and the external environment has taken another turn down, but we've been preparing for this for years now, and we've got the response mechanics in place to react now without placing additional strains—or unnecessarily highlighting risks that really are the same as we've seen for a year now—to our broader constituencies."

And finally: "Should be a fun week. This is what separates good bankers from the posers."

The e-mail exchange grew heated.

A manager in charge of WaMu's deposits responded defensively: "No one is panicking, so long emails that sound preachy don't help. We are not dumb, let us prepare."

Freilinger replied, "If you fire people up over weekends, you're fanning flames, not 'getting ready.' 'Getting ready' takes place months, not hours before a firestorm, by increasing branch awareness through clear pricing signals and encouragement of building deposit excess balances while no obvious sparks around. I never called anyone dumb—but I'll continue to dial back unnecessarily panicked executives wherever and whenever I find them."

Despite the bickering, the WaMu executives' concern was right on the mark. In just three days, customers pulled out a collective $1.5 *billion*, surpassing IndyMac's giant deposit loss. "We had never seen anything like it," said one of the deposit team managers later. WaMu's own bank run was now, officially, under way. On the fourth day, a Tuesday, customers withdrew $1.8 billion. Together those two numbers represented about 2 percent of WaMu's retail deposit base of $148.2 billion.*

The last time WaMu had suffered through a bank run of this magnitude was in midst of the Great Depression.[23] On a cold February morning in the winter of 1931, Seattle residents woke up to a banner headline in the local paper: the troubled Puget Sound Savings and Loan Association would not open the next day. WaMu customers read about the failed bank and worried about WaMu's health. They panicked. They flooded WaMu's downtown Seattle branch, crowding around the teller

---

*This number does not include about $30 billion in commercial and brokered deposits, which were not counted by WaMu's deposit tracking team in measuring the bank's run. WaMu's total deposit base was about $182 billion.

cages. The bank's then-chief executive, Raymond Frazier, strolled amid the mayhem, greeting people by name.

The tellers were polite. They had been instructed to allow customers to withdraw as much money as they wanted. Still, deposits flew out of the bank at a startling rate. Customers withdrew a collective $5 million, about 8 percent of the bank's total deposits at the time. WaMu was forced to ask Chase National Bank in New York, a predecessor to JPMorgan Chase, for help. Chase agreed and purchased $10 million of WaMu's securities, boosting its liquidity. Stacks of cash were rushed to WaMu's downtown Seattle branch.

After three days, customers calmed down. WaMu survived. Frazier received letters of praise. "I certainly want to congratulate you and your institution on the nice manner in which you handled the situation these last few trying days," wrote one man. "I am enclosing a check for $5,000. Please open a savings account."

At WaMu circa 2008, seventy-seven years later, the bank run had all the elements of the earlier crisis, but with a modern flair. Money changed hands furiously—but with less face-to-face interaction. Customers didn't line up by the hundreds at branches—they pulled out their money from ATMs and transferred it online. There were no media, no photos, no disclosures from the bank. There were only hints and speculations from analysts and whispers in the press. "We won't use the phrase 'run on the bank,' but we would be remiss if we did not observe that many creditors have quietly been pulling funds from the bank," wrote one banking analyst about WaMu.[24] A small newspaper in Southern California interviewed a customer who had just withdrawn some of his money. "I was watching CNBC and they mentioned that of the 10 banks that were in danger, they were right on the border," the customer explained.[25]

Inside WaMu, the person most closely watching the daily drain of customers' accounts was twenty-seven-year-old Brian Mueller, a financial analyst on the bank's small deposit tracking team. Mueller had had no previous banking experience, but now he found himself at the nation's largest savings and loan, right in the middle of the biggest run any U.S. bank had seen in decades. Before WaMu hired him in 2005, Mueller had spent eight years working at a bowling alley. "Interacted with customers, cashiered, answered phone, cleaned, assisted bar staff," Mueller's résumé read. And: "Reorganized candy machine to increase visual appeal. Ordered/stocked candy." In a major coup during that time, Mueller had boosted locker rental revenues by 30 percent by enforcing collections of delinquent accounts—"throwing down justice when appropriate," he noted in a later e-mail.

But by the time WaMu's customers started pulling out their money by the billions, Mueller had become a master at tracking bank deposits. Through the alchemy of Microsoft Excel, he devised programs to monitor customer activity. He figured out how to automate the reports, so they would be e-mailed off to executives without any effort on his part. The report went out each morning, including weekends. "It was just amazing what you can program Excel to do," said Mueller, who had barely used the program before arriving at WaMu. "People actually thought I was working Sunday mornings."

Mueller didn't stop there, though. He created a program that would text the members of the deposit team each morning with the change in account balance totals. At roughly 5:15 a.m., if their cell phones were on, the team members would awaken to the early news of the day's activities in the branches. Because the morning reports charted customer activity from the East Coast, the text was like an early warning sign. If there was a big deposit outflow first thing in the morning, it was an omen for the rest of the day. Killinger and Rotella, as well as WaMu's federal regulators, received the daily reports, though not by text message.

If WaMu's customers were frantic, the mood inside the bank was not. Aside from the first heated e-mail exchange, there was very little yelling or hand wringing or running down the hallways. Everyone remained calm, from Rotella down to Mueller, who sat at his desk, eyes focused on his Excel spreadsheet. Mueller had little sympathy for the customers. Didn't they understand about deposit insurance? "It kind of didn't make any sense," Mueller said. "But sometimes people's emotions don't make sense." Like many WaMu employees, Mueller had no clear picture of what was happening, or what had happened, in the Home Loans Group. "There were all these stories about these crappy loans," he said. "That's all I knew."

Inside hundreds of WaMu branches, tellers delivered talking points, battling customers' fears. They now knew much more about the bank's financial health than they ever had. "WaMu is a well-capitalized institution, with plenty of liquidity," they would tell customers. WaMu had trained them in how to answer the endless customer questions. One teller training pamphlet read: "If you are asked, 'Is my money safe with WaMu?' you might respond with the following: 'I understand your concern. There's been a lot of negative news in the press lately. WaMu is FDIC-insured, which means your deposits are covered up to FDIC insurance limits, which are no less than $100,000 per depositor." And then "REMINDER: Be careful to exercise good judgment when crafting responses; do not make broad statements or promises like, 'Yes, our stock will hit $50 soon.'" If the customers had further questions, the teller was supposed to hand them a brochure about FDIC insurance. "I don't know that I understood the whole thing," said one branch manager. "And if I don't understand it, how do I explain it to my employees or my customers?"

Branch employees were also schooled in how to deal with the press: "When you see a media truck or someone asks for a quote, you say, 'No comment,' and refer them to headquarters." A teller countered, "Well, can we offer them water or lemonade or cookies?" To which WaMu headquarters responded: "Yeah, do anything you want, but don't give them any information."

Other banks appeared to be spreading rumors about WaMu's health, telling their own customers that WaMu was closing or headed for bankruptcy. In Brooklyn, a Chase bank branch manager told customers to "remove funds from Washington Mutual because their failure is imminent." That statement sparked a frustrated letter from one of WaMu's lawyers to JPMorgan Chase's general counsel. "This is probably nothing more than a misunderstanding by the staff which can be addressed by training or additional information," WaMu's attorney wrote. "I will appreciate any help you can provide in snuffing out this ember." To keep from further spooking customers, WaMu held off on closing about a hundred branches across the country that hadn't been making money, and that had been scheduled to close before the run started. No one wanted to give the public any reason to think WaMu was shutting down.

On the Tuesday when WaMu customers withdrew $1.8 billion, the bank run peaked. Then it began to subside. Bank runs, while they are sparked by unknown events, generally play out like a bubble, with a run-up, a climax, and a fall. WaMu's run was no different. Soon deposit outflows fell back into the range of hundreds of millions of dollars. Two weeks after IndyMac's failure, the WaMu panic ended.

WaMu had lost a stunning $9.4 billion in deposits—nine times the amount of the much-publicized IndyMac run. Yet no one had heard about it. The media hadn't discovered it. Even inside the bank, few employees knew what had happened. "We did a good job of keeping the bad news quiet," said the deposit team manager.

The damage to WaMu had not been severe. It had lost about 6 percent of its total retail deposits. It still had about $138.4 billion in retail deposits remaining, and its liquidity levels remained healthy by government standards. Regulators will close a bank if its liquidity ratio dips below 5 percent of total assets; WaMu's ratio was well above that threshold. It still had a collective borrowing capacity of $35 billion at the San Francisco and Seattle Federal Home Loan Banks. WaMu offered a CD with a 5 percent interest rate, an unbelievable deal at the time. Customers brought their money back.

WaMu's treasury department began building a new liquidity model, the worst doomsday scenario it could imagine. The department contemplated what would happen if $23 billion evaporated in a one-day bank run. The group came up with that number because it represented the remainder of WaMu's deposits not insured by the FDIC. The scenario also imagined that all of WaMu's sources of funding had dried up. The bank could access its lines of credit with the Federal Home Loan Banks and the Fed, but neither lender would provide more money beyond what was already available. If the scenario happened, the treasury department predicted WaMu would run out of money in about three months. Someone suggested calling the model Gorditas, after the indigestion-inducing Mexican dish mainstreamed by Taco Bell. Instead, it was named Break the Bank.

Chapter Eight

PROJECT WEST

Things could get a lot more difficult for you.
—Treasury Secretary Henry "Hank" Paulson, Jr.

There is a line in Robert Frost's poem "The Black Cottage" that Sheila Bair once quoted in a speech in 2007. The poem is both grim and nostalgic. It tells about two men out for a walk, one a minister, who happen upon a house that has remained untouched long after the woman who owned it died. Bair, in her job as chairman of the Federal Deposit Insurance Corp. for about a year, quoted to her audience, "Most of the change we think we see in life / Is due to truths being in and out of favour."[1] Bair is fond of quoting Frost. She would later, in an acceptance speech for a prestigious Profile in Courage award, borrow another of his famous observations: "A bank is a place where they lend you an umbrella in fair weather, and ask for it back when it begins to rain."[2]

Bair was trying to explain the recent actions of her agency. The FDIC was spending time and money preparing for the failure of a giant U.S. bank, even though it had been a record two and a half years since any bank in the country had failed. "But who's counting?" Bair joked at the time. She had spent much of her first year at the helm of an agency that oversaw some 8,500 banks dealing not with banks at all but with a big-box store that wanted to become a bank. Wal-Mart had filed what's known as an "industrial loan company" application, which would allow it to offer limited bank services. The application was controversial.[3] Wal-Mart claimed it was just trying to cut the costs of processing customers' checks, but banks and credit unions were sure the company was trying to find a way to run its own commercial bank.[4] Bair solved this problem in an unusual fashion—by doing nothing at all. The FDIC's board of directors put a moratorium on industrial loan applications for six months, then extended it by another year. Frustrated by the delay, Wal-Mart eventually withdrew its application.

Now Bair was telling her team to focus on what was seemed like an unrealistic scenario: the fall of a financial institution with tens of billions of dollars in assets. The FDIC had formed a new unit to study more than 100 banks with $10 billion in assets or more, observing their strengths and weaknesses.[5] This strategy was another departure for the agency: historically, it had worried more about the thousands of small community banks across the country. The new FDIC unit ran through role-playing scenarios, each person in the group pretending to be a banker, or someone at the U.S. Department of the Treasury, or someone at the Federal Reserve Bank. What would happen if a big investment bank failed? What would happen if a big investment bank failed with operations in other countries? The FDIC studied how the different government agencies would work together, and how they would handle the failing bank. The exercise drew skepticism. "You can interpret the string of good luck we've had in two ways," Bair said at the time. "You might say we're in a new age and banks will never fail. Or you can say we're due; we're due for a big one. We have to prepare for all contingencies."

Bair, who wears her short brown hair coiffed and sports a wardrobe reminiscent of the university professor she once was, had gained a reputation as a thoughtful, intelligent thinker. "If she didn't understand something, she did not rest until she did," said one former FDIC official who worked with her. Raised in the small town of Independence, Kansas, she had worked as a bank teller before studying philosophy at the University of Kansas and also getting a law degree. "Everybody had a thirty-year fixed-rate mortgage back then," Bair later recalled with a tinge of nostalgia in an interview with *The New Yorker*. "It was a ritual to come in and make your mortgage payment personally. There was a kind of pride in living up to your obligations and, on the lender side, in making loans that people could understand and afford."[6] A Republican, she made a brief, failed attempt at running for an open House seat in Kansas in 1990 (she was the only woman in the primary, and the only candidate supporting abortion rights), then headed up the financial institutions group at the Treasury Department.

It was at Treasury that Bair embarked on a crusade of sorts against high-risk loans and in particular subprime mortgages.[7] She tried to require that outside "monitors" look in on subprime lenders.[8] Many of the lenders refused to accept the monitors. None of them really thought much of Bair's idea to adopt a "best practices" code for lending, either. "She had forums where various players from the whole securitization chain were together in the same room to discuss what was going on," the former coworker said. "No one else was doing that. She even had other regulators in the room so they could attend."

If Bair's position on careful lending or wise moneymaking decisions was at all unclear, all anyone had to do was read her children's books, dedicated to her young son and daughter. The first, *Isabel's Car Wa$h*, relays the story of young Isabel Dinero, who earns $20 dollars by scrubbing down her neighbors' vehicles.[9] She funds the business with investment money from her friends, which she doubles through her ventures. She has enough left over to buy a coveted doll. In *Rock, Brock and the Savings Shock*, Bair tells the story of two brothers, Rock and Brock, who choose to invest money from their grandfather in different ways.[10] Brock saves his money, each week doubling his investment, while Rock goes crazy, buying every toy he's ever wanted. Bair describes the bounty: a polka-dot snail, a fruit hat, and a big mustache! (The last purchase nicely rhymes with "cash.") Brock, as you might guess, saves hundreds of dollars, while Rock ends up with no money at all.

Other regulators, bankers, and industry watchers, however, viewed Bair as out of her league. Some saw the whole big-box-store-trying-to-become-a-bank episode as her first major "gaffe." "I thought the job of banking regulators was to regulate," quipped Tom Brown, the Bankstocks.com hedge fund manager. Said one of her harshest critics, bank consultant Burt Ely, "Quite frankly, I wish she would spend more time doing her job of running the FDIC. That's an agency that needs some adult supervision, which unfortunately she is not providing."[11] Bair could be antagonistic and stubborn if someone didn't agree with her policy. She sometimes got into what one observer politely called "strongly worded discussions" with other regulators, including John Dugan, the head of the Office of the Comptroller of the Currency. His agency watched over the largest investment banks. Tim Geithner, then the president of the Federal Reserve Bank of New York, and Treasury Secretary Hank Paulson thought she was more of a showboater than a team player.[12]

Paulson, in his book detailing the financial crisis, would describe his relationship with Bair as "constructive," often a euphemism for *strained*. "We usually agreed on policy," he wrote about Bair, "but she tended to view the world through the prism of the FDIC—an understandable but at times narrow focus."[13] Paulson would, at least on one occasion, leave Bair out of crucial discussions about regulatory policy. For example, he forgot to tell her that the government planned to guarantee money market funds during the financial crisis, a change on which he should have consulted her. She called him up angrily, admonishing him for the misstep.[14] Said one of her critics: "She has quite an ego and she loves praise," and "there's almost a certain insecurity on her part."

As the head of the FDIC, Bair ran an independent government agency with a grand, long-standing mission: to protect the money of bank customers across the country. The agency had been founded during the Great Depression, as part of a sweeping legislative overhaul aimed at quieting financial panic. While each bank in the country has its own main regulator, the FDIC has its hands in all banks, large and small, through its mission of insuring deposits. It guards the deposit insurance fund, a pot of money into which all banks pay a percentage of their deposits. In 2007, that amount stood at about $50 billion. If a bank fails, the pooled money covers losses.

But while its role in the grand scheme of bank regulation may seem large, the FDIC is far less august than some of the other agencies. Its power ebbs and flows with financial crises. When a crisis hits, the agency balloons with new workers who march across the country closing banks, earning the agency a reputation as a harbinger of gloom and doom. When the crisis abates, no one seems to remember what the FDIC does. Its headquarters in Washington, just around the corner from the White House, is a stark example of its place in the world. The building is dull gray, both inside and out, with a faded black "FDIC" mat blanketing the front entryway. The lobby, and the offices on the floors above, look like those of any government building: cold, with uncomfortable pieces of furniture scattered around. On the wall next to the elevator hang three rectangular portraits: the president of the United States, the vice president, and the chairman of the FDIC. A few blocks away, the Department of the Treasury is long, ivory-columned, and stately. Tourists snap pictures outside.

By the time WaMu began reporting huge losses on its bad loans in the winter of 2008, three important developments had occurred: (1) the FDIC was gaining power as a new crisis formed; (2) Bair, after years of warning about risky mortgages, had been proven correct; and (3) the FDIC was already fed up with WaMu and, increasingly, with its main regulator, the federal Office of Thrift Supervision.

Bank regulators like to say that there's a "healthy tension" between the different agencies that oversee banks. That's true to some extent. But the relationship between the FDIC and the OTS hadn't always been "healthy." The OTS's mission was to make sure that savings and loan banks remained healthy and viable. It was a policeman, theoretically writing tickets ("enforcement orders") when a bank stepped out of line. At its root, the OTS's main goal was to promote housing. Thrifts, by law, are required to hold over 65 percent of their assets in mortgages or other consumer loans. The OTS's mission wasn't opposed to that of the FDIC, but it also wasn't aligned with it. "The OTS did things to promote housing that, if you were at the FDIC, you might not like to see because it was creating more safety and soundness risk," said one former regulator.

While the FDIC suffered from feelings of inadequacy in comparison with other agencies, the OTS's ranking was even more diminutive. The agency was relatively new, formed as a result of the Savings and Loan Crisis in 1989. Before the crisis, a three-person Federal Home Loan Bank Board oversaw savings and loan banks and the country's home loan bank system. "That was a very powerful agency when it was set up that way," said the former regulator. New financial reform, passed as a result of the Savings and Loan Crisis, created the OTS. It was the smallest of the four regulatory agencies, overseeing about 850 banks, and was always considered the weaker of the banking regulators. Some claimed this disequilibrium was because the OTS regulators themselves were weaker. Others pointed out that thrift banks like WaMu, because they held so many mortgages, were more exposed to the rise and fall of the housing market. They were more susceptible to downturns and, therefore, losses. The OTS fought to be taken seriously.

At the OTS, Sheila Bair's counterpart was director John Reich (pro-nounced "rich"). As a child in small Mattoon, Illinois, Reich had known exactly what he wanted to be when he grew up—an FBI agent.[15] But after he graduated with an accounting degree from the University of Illinois at age twenty-one, he was still too young to enroll in FBI train-ing. Instead, he took a job as an auditor at a small community bank and eventually took the helm of another bank in Sarasota, Florida, which he ran for twelve years. (The FBI actually did later solicit him for a job, but by that time Reich and his wife were expecting their first child and the timing didn't seem great.) Because of this background, Reich considered himself a champion of small community banks. He described himself as a "community banker in regulatory cloth."

But Reich was also a politician. He followed Senator Connie Mack to Washington, working by his side for almost a decade. Then he jumped to the FDIC, serving on that agency's board of directors. He was ap-pointed director of the OTS in 2005. Reich, described as both stub-born and determined, boastful and proud, sympathetic and naive, once claimed that he would rather be right than popular. His critics disagree with that statement. "He's one of these guys who loves to be loved by the people," said a regulator who worked with him. "He's all sizzle and no steak." Said a community banker: "He is, in my opinion, the best regulator in my twenty years as a CEO."[16]

Reich arrived at the helm of the OTS with an ambitious goal: to make the agency the best of all the bank regulators. He hired dozens more bank examiners and directed the agency to build a trade show booth. He started advertising the OTS's charter to banks across the country, hoping that they would switch from their own regulators and move into the OTS's purview. "We're going to be all over the country this year," he declared at the time.[17] A bank regulatory agency is only as good—and as big—as the banks it regulates. The more assets it watches over, the more power it has. WaMu made up the largest chunk of assets under OTS's management and about 15 percent of the agency's funding.[18] WaMu paid the OTS about $30 million in annual fees. In the biggest boost to the OTS's power, Reich approved a thrift charter for Countrywide in early 2007, a move the lender had pushed for years— the OTS under its former head had twice turned Countrywide down. Countrywide's desire for OTS regulation was criticized as "regulator shopping," since upon its approval Countrywide moved from the Office of the Comptroller of the Currency, a much tougher agency, to the OTS. A year later Countrywide had to be purchased by Bank of America to avoid failure.*

Bair and Reich had always held philosophical differences about how to regulate the nation's banks. Reich opposed too much regulation. In 2006, he had led a successful nationwide effort to scale back regulation, saying, "We expect so much from institutions. It never stops."[19] He told *American Banker*: "Some people would interpret my views as resulting in a lower level of regulation than the other agencies. That could not be further from the truth. I want to be a tough but fair regulator." Just after Reich arrived at the OTS in 2005, the federal bank regulatory agencies decided to take a stand on "nontraditional mortgages" like Option ARM loans. They came out with more than 40 pages of "guidance," which they wanted all banks across the country to adopt. They asked banks to be conservative in deciding whether a borrower could afford these kinds of mortgages. They urged the banks to do a better job explaining the risks of the loans. Many of the guidelines, however, were just strongly worded suggestions. A bank "should" do something, rather than "must" do something.[20] It was a bit like an unarmed cop asking a robber to put down his weapon.

While Reich warned about the risk of Option ARMs in 2005, he

---

*On the other hand, much of the mortgage growth at Countrywide occurred in the years before it switched regulators.

defended them. "We want to make certain that institutions that have been offering nontraditional mortgage products, some on the West Coast for twenty-five to thirty years, that their business plans do not come to a screeching halt because of unintended consequences," he said.[21] He cushioned this remark by saying not everyone should get an Option ARM, just "a professional person with a high income."

WaMu figured out that if it listened to the regulators' suggestions, it would have to qualify borrowers at the higher rate that the loan would eventually carry, rather than the teaser rate. That would wipe out more than 30 percent of its home loan volume.[22] The OTS allowed WaMu, and other thrifts under its supervision, to delay adopting the new guidelines.[23]

In the spring of 2007, just a few months before the subprime market collapsed, Bair pitched the idea of a federal law that would protect the country's subprime borrowers. She believed—and she told the House Financial Services panel as much—that loan underwriting should take into account whether the borrower could pay over the entire life span of the mortgage, not just the low, teaser rate. Reich disagreed. He argued that the legislation Bair supported would push customers to take out subprime loans at less-regulated companies. He pointed out that, of the 8,700 lenders across the country, fewer than 2 percent faced what he called "significant" problems with subprime lending. "The vast majority of the institutions we regulate are operating in a safe and sound manner," he said at the time. (But he did argue for more regulation of mortgage brokers.)[24]

Over the years, even before Reich took over the agency, the OTS pointed out problems in WaMu's Home Loans Group and Long Beach Mortgage. Each time the OTS delivered a negative review of the bank's lending practices, WaMu would promise a solution, but it would never come to fruition. The OTS had, for example, pointed out that WaMu had only fourteen people watching over 34,000 brokers selling loans to the bank nationwide. OTS examiners wrote to WaMu: "Given the increase in fraud, early payment defaults, first payment defaults, subprime delinquencies, etc., management should reassess the adequacy of staffing."[25] WaMu agreed but offered up no solution. The problem was never fixed. Brokers kept making bad loans, and WaMu kept buying them.

After the bank embarked on its "higher-risk lending strategy" in 2004, the OTS, in a later exam review, said it was concerned about the quality of mortgages in WaMu's portfolio. "We believe the level of delinquencies, if left unchecked, could erode the credit quality of the portfolio. Our concerns are increased when the risk profile of the portfolio is considered, including concentrations in Option ARMs to higher-risk borrowers, in low and limited documentation loans, and loans with subprime or higher-risk characteristics."[26] But it didn't restrict the bank from making any of the loans. It could have slapped WaMu with a cease-and-desist order, as it had done as a result of the Bank Secrecy Act problems, forcing WaMu to switch strategies. It did not.

On and on it went—the OTS like a frustrated parent shouting at a closed door, WaMu like an out-of-control teenager with the upper hand. In five years, between 2003 and 2008, the OTS noted more than 500 problems at WaMu.[27] The agency was constantly "concerned," but the concern sparked little action at the bank. When WaMu moved out nine different chief compliance officers in just seven years, OTS compliance specialist Susie Clark wrote in a 2007 e-mail: "The OTS is very concerned that this lack of consistent, stable leadership leaves the program vulnerable. This amount of turnover is very unusual for an institution of this size and is a cause for concern. The board of directors should commission an evaluation of why smart, successful, effective managers can't succeed in this position. If you would like my opinion, just ask. (Hint: It has to do with top management not buying into the importance of compliance and turf warfare and Kerry not liking bad news.)"[28]

Part of the problem was that WaMu kept making money, so it was a challenge for the regulatory agency to object to what it was doing. The housing market was going up, and nearly every lender was making these kinds of loans. "It has been hard for us to justify doing much more than constantly nagging (okay, 'chastising')," another OTS examiner wrote in an e-mail.[29]

In mid-2006, as WaMu posted quarterly profits, the FDIC made its first serious attempts to intervene in WaMu's regulation. It asked the

OTS for permission to participate in WaMu's annual exam. Every bank across the country endures a yearly checkup, generally the most thorough review that government examiners conduct on a financial institution. The FDIC had to be careful when it got involved with WaMu's supervision. The agency wasn't WaMu's *primary* regulator, and that was an important political distinction. By law, the oversight of any financial institution was supposed to be left to the primary regulator, with the FDIC providing backup help. In general, the FDIC wasn't allowed to get involved in the daily details of banks unless they were in trouble.

The OTS objected to the FDIC's horning in on WaMu's exam. When the FDIC repeated its request several months later, the OTS objected again.[30] The OTS didn't want FDIC officials infiltrating WaMu and creating a perception of problems at the country's largest savings and loan bank. Meanwhile the FDIC wanted to make sure it understood what was going on; it also wanted to position itself as a tough regulator. Federal regulations concerning the division of regulatory power were on the side of the OTS. After the OTS refused for a second time to allow the FDIC to join in WaMu's exam, one of the FDIC's regional directors wrote a letter to the OTS, the first salvo in a battle that would last for years.

"As you are aware," the FDIC regional director wrote, "the FDIC and the OTS have a long, cooperative and productive working relationship with respect to the examination of Washington Mutual Bank, which we hope to continue."[31] This was not entirely true. In the past the OTS had stonewalled the FDIC, refusing to provide the agency with information about a fast-growing subprime lender in the suburbs of Chicago. When Superior Bank failed abruptly in 2001, one of the largest bank collapses in a decade, the Office of the Inspector General for the Department of the Treasury criticized the OTS for allowing it to happen. Under the agency's supervision, Superior had increased its subprime auto loans ninefold in just four years, from $38 million to $350 million, the report concluded. Borrowers defaulted on their loans, until eventually Superior lost $100 million. The FDIC—and the inspector general—had trouble getting information about Superior from the OTS. "They were sending in staff to the bank's facilities in Chicago, only to find out that the real area of risk were operations in New York," said one regulator familiar with Superior's failure.

The bank regulatory agencies signed an "interagency agreement," promising that they would work together in the future. It was a make-up pact. The FDIC director cited this agreement as a chief reason the OTS should now cooperate. "Washington Mutual Bank is a very large insured financial institution, and, in our view, participation on the up-coming targeted reviews is necessary to fulfill our responsibilities to protect the deposit insurance fund, a key objective of the 2002 agree-ment," he wrote.

The OTS caved in a bit but threw up additional resistance. "As we discussed, OTS does not seek to have FDIC staff actively participate in our examination activities and conclusions at Washington Mutual. We do understand your need for access to examination information and your need to meet with OTS staff to discuss our supervisory activities at Washington Mutual." The agency would allow WaMu's examiner from the FDIC, Steve Funaro, to join the OTS examiners as they reviewed the bank's financial information. "All FDIC requests for information should continue to be funneled through our examiner-in-charge," the OTS instructed.[32]

This solution seemed adequate, except that WaMu had just moved into its new skyscraper in downtown Seattle. When Funaro, the FDIC examiner, showed up at WaMu headquarters, he found that the OTS had failed to set aside any space for him to work. There wasn't an office, or even a desk. Worse, he didn't have access to the electronic library that WaMu compiled for its regulators. The desk issue wouldn't get worked out for several months. Funaro e-mailed his supervisors claim-ing that the OTS had misled him. The agency had promised him space and information, and he had received neither.

That spat was worked out, but the politically tempered letters con-tinued. The FDIC asked for information about WaMu, and the OTS eventually agreed—sort of. In early 2007, Funaro floated the idea of hiring an outside expert on market risk to help his agency sort through WaMu's home loan portfolio. He expected the OTS might think the FDIC had devised this tactic to check up on whether WaMu had ad-opted new mortgage rules, which the bank had so far avoided doing. "I'm just not relishing another round of 'No,'" Funaro's supervisor wrote in response to his suggestion.[33] "Well, let them make fools of themselves again!" Next, the OTS told the FDIC that it couldn't review WaMu's single-family home loan files, citing an obscure regulation that restricted the FDIC. Reviewing mortgage paperwork was "examination work, which is distinct from risk assessment activities," the OTS official wrote. Whatever that meant, the FDIC was furious. "This is unnecessary hair splitting by OTS Seattle," wrote one FDIC director, pointedly.[34]

By early 2008, the bickering between the two agencies had bubbled up to the level of Bair and Reich in Washington. Normally neither would get involved in the gritty details of bank supervision. There were simply too many banks under their jurisdiction for them to play a close role in each. But the stakes were high: WaMu was the largest savings and loan in the country, and its health was deteriorating. As it faltered, the bank became even more of a political threat to Bair, Reich, and their respective agencies. If WaMu failed, it had the potential to wipe out the FDIC's $45 billion insurance fund, a scenario that not only would place the country's financial system in a precarious position but would mar Bair's tenure at the agency's helm. Reich, meanwhile, faced the threat that if WaMu went under, the OTS might not survive as an agency at all. Reich had tried for years to grow the OTS, but his agency was shrinking. After Countrywide's fire sale, if WaMu also disappeared, the OTS would garner even less respect and would dwindle. Neither agency wanted WaMu to fail. But politically speaking, Reich would be better served if WaMu survived, while Bair would be better served by a solution that prevented a hit to the deposit insurance fund, even if WaMu no longer existed as an independent company.

Their philosophical divide on WaMu's health stretched wider than the block separating the two agencies' headquarters in Washington, D.C. Reich believed that WaMu should be able to work its way out of its problems, on its own. He had said as much to Killinger, who had come to visit him at the end of February 2008. Killinger wanted to know from Reich how much trouble WaMu was in. While Reich hadn't received a full report on WaMu from his staff, he told Killinger that the OTS would give the bank time to make improvements. The agency wouldn't "place unrealistic expectations or demands" on WaMu, Reich wrote to his direct reports in an e-mail summarizing the meeting.[35]

Recently, the OTS had sent WaMu the official notice that its CAMELS health rating had been downgraded from 2 to 3. In its letter, the agency noted the doubling of WaMu's bad loans and its fourth-quarter loss of $1.8 billion. A rating of 3 means a bank is borderline troubled, but it is rare for any bank with that grade to fail. Even so, the OTS had been pressuring WaMu to raise more money through private equity or to find a merger partner. The agency had no reason to believe that WaMu wouldn't be able to do one or the other.

Down 17th Street, the FDIC wasn't so sure. It was initiating the early steps in planning for WaMu's possible failure—the FDIC division that handles bank closures was put on alert. It characterized WaMu as "a slow burn," according to a regulator familiar with the agency's actions.

If a bank fails, its primary regulator must close it, but the FDIC has to clean up the mess: find a buyer for the failed bank, and take care of its customers. The FDIC is required by law to do this at the least cost to the deposit insurance fund. In an ideal (and typical) situation, the FDIC begins looking for a buyer a week or several days before the government moves in to close a bank. This government-run auction is secretive. If word leaks out that the bank is about to be closed, it could cause a run on deposits. Other banks bid on the failed bank's assets, so that when the government seizes the company, the FDIC can transfer power to the new owner.

With a bank as large as WaMu, finding a buyer would be hard, but Bair thought a sale would be the best outcome. If WaMu was purchased, that would save her agency the trouble of planning for its potential failure. The FDIC's Resolution and Receivership Division created scenarios examining how the FDIC could sell the bank. Bair put in a call to Reich, telling him her preference: How receptive would WaMu be to selling itself? she wondered.[36]

Killinger and his executive team were largely oblivious to all this back-and-forth in Washington as they tried to shore up WaMu's health. Along with investment banking advisers Goldman Sachs and Lehman Brothers, they came up with a plan to gather all the bank's Option ARM mortgages and subprime and home equity loans into a pile and sell them off in what was known as a good bank/bad bank scenario. But accounting rules got in the way, and the plan fell apart.

In March 2008, just before WaMu's ill-fated shareholder meeting, they launched two tracks under pressure from the OTS: raise private equity, and try to sell the company. Almost everyone preferred the first solution. Killinger was adamant about keeping WaMu independent, and most of the executive team agreed with him.

In not much time at all, dozens of private equity firms from across the country were scouring WaMu's online data room. WaMu executives made presentations to six of them. The bank wanted to raise about $4 billion in capital, based on about $19 billion in loan losses, at the high end. Soon, however, the OTS pushed that amount higher, instructing WaMu to raise a minimum of $5 billion.[37] Nobody knew just how much capital WaMu needed. It depended on the economy and on whether homeowners nationwide would pay back their loans.

On the sale track, WaMu talked with JPMorgan, Santander, Wells Fargo, and Barclays. But almost right away, WaMu executives could tell that only one company was really in the running: JPMorgan. Jamie Dimon, JPMorgan's chief executive, had long coveted WaMu. The reason was readily apparent to anyone who has ever put together a puzzle: JPMorgan's branches blanketed the East Coast, and WaMu's blanketed the West (and Florida). If JPMorgan bought WaMu, the New York company would own one of the largest retail banks in the country, second only to Bank of America. "It wasn't exactly rocket science," said one person close to JPMorgan. "You shade in where Chase is, and you shade in where they aren't and you look at what's possible." Much like WaMu, JPMorgan had been patched together through different bank mergers over the previous decades and was already a megabank. It had operations around the world and more than $2 trillion in assets. What it was missing, however, was a large-scale presence in the shopping centers and downtown streets of middle-class America. On at least two previous occasions, when the two chief executives had attended various events together, Dimon brought up with Killinger the possibility of a merger. Both times Killinger had brushed him off.

The two executives' leadership styles—and personalities—could not have been more different. Dimon runs JPMorgan like an efficient financial boot camp. There is nothing touchy-feely about it—no baseball cards printed with corporate values, no dressing up for Halloween.

"Every day was a fire drill," said one executive who worked for him. "Every day I felt like I was getting my PhD." Dimon and his team are driven and ruthless in a way that WaMu executives had never been, even after the shift in WaMu's culture. "Thirty or forty years ago, banks were very cushy places," said one former JPMorgan executive. "They didn't have to be tough or mean to compete. These days it's highly competitive, and you've got to keep pushing and pushing. Jamie is totally bloodless in doing that kind of thing." Said another investment banker who worked closely with him: "I think he would sell his mother if it was good for business."

As a manager, Dimon has his hands in everything. He possesses the uncanny ability to recall details that should not come easily to someone overseeing a company as large as his. He doesn't shy away from problems. On the contrary, he demands that every piece of bad news, every risk the company faces, be exposed and examined thoroughly. "Don't be a sheep," he repeatedly warned employees at Bank One. "I want you guys to be your fiercest critics. I want you to slice each other to shreds." Dimon's blunt, impassioned outbursts on any number of subjects are infamous—shouting at a U.S. congresswoman to make a point, telling JPMorgan internal auditors that a colleague "knows as much about accounting in her baby finger as all of you combined"[38]—and he does not hesitate to shout or swear when making a point. "That's the dumbest thing I've ever heard," or some form of this statement, is a constant refrain. But his gruff manner is often overlooked, because he possesses a charisma that acts like a salve on his rough edges.

Dimon grew up in Queens and went to Harvard, ascending through the banking ranks by following his mentor, the famed financier Sanford Weill. Dimon helped Weill build Citigroup, until Weill fired him in 1998. His relationship with Weill was dramatically severed after a series of disagreements involving Weill's daughter, who worked for Dimon at the time.[39] Then, during a dance floor brawl, Dimon grabbed a rival banker—tearing a button on his jacket—in defense of another executive's wife. Dimon clawed his way back into the inner banking circle, making his way into the top position at Bank One. He merged Bank One into JPMorgan. In 2006, recognizing that the subprime market might, indeed, collapse, he called up the JPMorgan executive in charge of securitized products, then vacationing in Rwanda. "We need to sell a lot of our positions!" Dimon exclaimed on the phone. "I've seen it before. This stuff could go up in smoke!"[40]

One particular difference between Dimon and Killinger would soon become apparent and important. Dimon, a Democrat, is shrewdly political, going so far as to call government relations JPMorgan's "seventh line of business."[41] Not only did he and his executives spend a lot of time getting to know various politicians and financial decision makers, but those politicians called on JPMorgan as well. In 2008, Treasury Secretary Henry "Hank" Paulson, Jr., would speak with Dimon more than twenty-five times for a total of almost six hours, and those are just the calls recorded in Paulson's log. The tally is likely much higher. Killinger, by comparison, spoke to Paulson just twice during that time. Both times Killinger made the call.[42]

While WaMu, like every large bank, employed a government relations team, Killinger had never placed a premium on Washington. The distance didn't help—Seattle, for all its industry, is hardly a financial power center. In 2006, Dimon and Killinger both attended the annual meeting of the Financial Services Roundtable in Washington, a trade organization made up of the country's hundred largest banks. After a day of long meetings with various regulatory agencies, all the bankers gathered in the upscale lounge of the Ritz-Carlton Hotel. Dimon brought an entourage of JPMorgan executives, as did Ken Lewis, the chief executive of Bank of America. Killinger brought only one other WaMu executive. While Dimon and the other bankers mingled, Killinger was nowhere to be found. He was sightseeing with Linda, taking in the nighttime lights of the nation's capital. "Kerry would go to these things because on his checklist it said, 'Spend time with community groups and regulators in DC,'" said one WaMu executive. "He only did it because he felt like he had to."

When Killinger called Dimon in March 2008 to let him know WaMu was up for sale, Dimon was interested. JPMorgan pulled together nearly 100 people to work on the potential acquisition, which the company nicknamed "Project West." (JPMorgan was "Park" after its Park Avenue headquarters in Midtown.)[43] Dimon put Charlie Scharf, then the head of JPMorgan's retail bank, in charge of the Project West group. Scharf and Dimon had worked together since the 1980s. Scharf flew out to Seattle to lead JPMorgan's due diligence at the Red Lion Hotel, a process that started the day after Dimon negotiated the $2-a-share purchase of failed investment bank Bear Stearns.

Scharf presented JPMorgan's planned acquisition of "West" to his bank's board of directors. The 30-page presentation, marked "confidential," noted the pros and cons of the deal. On one slide, JPMorgan showed a graph of WaMu's still-plummeting stock price, which had fallen to $11.50 from $40 three years earlier. On another, JPMorgan listed WaMu's assets—all the mortgages. WaMu held $60 billion in home equity loans and $58 billion in Option ARMs, which made up the bulk of its loan portfolio. At the back of the presentation, another graph illustrated how a large chunk of Option ARM borrowers would see their loans recast to a higher rate and would not be able to pay them back. One bar graph showed bad loans rising dramatically, while another table was a comparison: WaMu's projections of how much money it would lose from bad loans versus how much money JPMorgan thought it would lose. WaMu predicted losses of $19 billion. JPMorgan projected $27 billion. "No real history of Option ARMs," Scharf noted under a slide outlining potential problems JPMorgan might face if it bought the bank. "Extent of housing decline—ability to predict." Still, WaMu's branch network enticed Dimon and Scharf. JPMorgan planned to submit an offer letter. It would announce the merger on April 7.[44]

With the same presentation in hand, minus some slides containing JPMorgan statistics, Scharf and Michael Cavanagh, JPMorgan's chief financial officer, flew to Washington to meet with Bair and four of her deputies. They brought along H. Rodgin Cohen, the prominent Wall Street attorney, to advise them. The JPMorgan executives had ostensibly called the meeting to run through the bank's potential purchase of WaMu. While the Office of the Comptroller of the Currency was JPMorgan's primary regulator, the FDIC provided backup oversight, just as it did with WaMu.

The meeting under way, Scharf and Cavanagh told Bair and her team that they didn't think a capital raise would be enough to solve WaMu's problems. They complained that WaMu wasn't taking their overtures seriously.[45] Scharf had recently met Steve Rotella and Tom Casey for dinner in New York to talk over the potential acquisition. While Rotella and Casey thought the meeting had gone well, Scharf had walked away remembering what Rotella had told his former boss: "Look, no one wants to do this with you guys."[46] The FDIC would later characterize the meeting with JPMorgan as a "beef session," with JPMorgan pushing for the agency to pressure WaMu into a sale.[47]

That same day the JPMorgan group also met with the Office of the Comptroller of the Currency and with Bob Steel, Paulson's second in command at the Treasury Department. While the Treasury Department oversaw the OTS, it doesn't usually have a hand in bank regulation. Steel, like Bair, seemed to believe WaMu should try for an acquisition.[48]

In no time at all, news of those meetings reached the OTS, seemingly the only agency in Washington not invited to talk with JPMorgan that day. Reich was angry. Lobbying regulators about a potential acquisition was not only unusual but also dangerous. If JPMorgan was spreading negative information about WaMu, particularly in Washington, that would only hurt the bank more.* Even worse, now it wasn't just the FDIC infringing on the OTS's oversight of WaMu—Treasury was involved as well. Reich deployed his deputies to find out what JPMorgan had been saying.

By 7:00 that night, Reich's chief general counsel, John Bowman, fired off an e-mail update. "Gentlemen," he wrote to Reich and two other OTS officials, under the subject line "WAMU."[49] "I have now received the material that JPM provided various parties in DC this date." The JPMorgan presentations were distributed throughout the OTS's offices. "Mr. Cohen again indicated the willingness of JPM to discuss the material either over the phone or in person at our request should we have any questions," Bowman wrote. "In addition, he did confirm (when I asked him directly) that, in fact, JPM had met with Steel at Treasury to discuss the proposed transaction."

Minutes later Reich responded: "Most interesting to learn that they

---

*In later depositions as part of WaMu's bankruptcy, JPMorgan executives described the meeting with regulators as "routine," part of the normal course of planning for a potential merger. This discrepancy doesn't, however, explain why JPMorgan was talking to Treasury. One OTS official maintained that it was unusual.

met with Steel to discuss the transaction. And extremely surprising to me that Steel hasn't returned my call yet (and also an e-mail message this morning). I predict I will be summoned by Treasury on Monday."

Another deputy replied, with a set of instructions. "John B., could you, first thing in the a.m., have someone on your staff put together a position paper on the need for Treasury to stay removed from the supervision of WaMu, including any attempt to influence our supervision of WaMu's capital raising process. I suspect that such a position paper will come in handy soon."

"Already started," Bowman replied.

In Seattle, Killinger sat in a conference room on the executive floor of WaMu's headquarters, flanked by his investment bankers and several other members of the executive team. They were poring over financial documents related to the capital raise when an assistant walked in and whispered in Killinger's ear. Reich was on the phone. Killinger walked out of the room to take the call. Two minutes later he returned, looking disturbed. Reich had called to tell him about JPMorgan's meetings in Washington that day. He told him that the bank had been making "disparaging remarks" about WaMu. "You better take this seriously," Reich warned.[50] The news angered Killinger and the other executives, but they weren't surprised by the underhanded tactic. Around the office, the WaMu executives referred to JPMorgan as "the New York boys." "What do you expect?" they liked to say. "It's just the culture back there. We are here, in polite Seattle."

Killinger left the meeting again and shut the door of his office. He called Dimon directly. Why was his bank saying bad things about WaMu? he asked. Dimon denied doing anything improper, although he wouldn't tell Killinger what was said in any of the meetings with regulators.[51] (Dimon hadn't been there, but he would have received a full report from Scharf and Cavanagh. Every important decision ran through him.) Dimon also offered Killinger a piece of advice: if Killinger got a good private equity offer, it would be smart to take it. JPMorgan would be likely to bid low. This statement was odd, considering that JPMorgan had just been complaining to the FDIC that WaMu wasn't taking its overtures seriously.

The government lobbying wasn't over. JPMorgan called the OTS

under the guise of updating the agency on the status of its due diligence. The OTS believed the bank was just trying to sweeten its pitch
for WaMu. The FDIC also complained to the OTS that WaMu wasn't
cooperating with JPMorgan, prompting Reich to put in another call to
Killinger. Play nice with potential acquirers, Reich reminded the WaMu
chief executive in not so many words.[52]

The private equity proposals began to roll in. Oak Hill Capital Partners and Blackstone Management Associates sent in a joint, nonbinding
bid for $2.5 billion in capital, at $8 a share. The consortium pointed out
that it would need to be paired with another private equity firm to make
the investment large enough to help the bank.[53] Cerberus also wrote,
saying it had "significant interest in a partnership with WaMu" and that
it could "move quickly." But Cerberus proposed a complicated deal that
had WaMu buying its troubled auto loan company, Chrysler Financial.[54]
The best offer came from TPG, the Texas-based private equity group
led by billionaire David Bonderman. Bonderman had a history with
WaMu; he had sat on the bank's board for six years. The group would
lead a $7.2 billion investment at $8.75 a share.

Then Scharf wrote to Killinger—"Dear Kerry"—with JPMorgan's
own merger proposal, although it was also nonbinding. JPMorgan
planned to offer $5 a share, with a contingency for $3 more depending
on how WaMu mortgages fared. Scharf suggested placing the contingency on WaMu's large home equity portfolio. If the home equity loans
performed as well as WaMu expected, the bank's shareholders would
receive the full $8 a share. JPMorgan knew this scenario was unlikely.
"These are uncertain times," Scharf wrote. "It is difficult to estimate the
future loss experience in any consumer loan portfolio, especially real
estate related. Our base case estimate of the potential losses in Washington Mutual's loan portfolio substantially exceeds your high estimate."
Scharf added another contingency to the deal. JPMorgan wanted to
keep researching WaMu's financial information, even as it put together
the merger. "We are prepared to move forward provided that you agree
to do so on an exclusive basis with us," Scharf wrote.

The WaMu team hadn't been impressed by JPMorgan's backroom
dealings in Washington. WaMu was even less enamored of its merger
proposal. The executive team believed WaMu was worth far more than $5

a share. The bank's stock, while low, still traded at around $11. JPMorgan, meanwhile, thought its offer was already on the high end, considering that WaMu's losses on its mortgages were likely to be much higher.

Scharf sent another letter to Killinger, this time detailing the additional information JPMorgan wanted from WaMu. The Project West team had put together a list of more than thirty items it required, including comparing WaMu's mortgage information with management presentations, and a more detailed discussion on how the bank valued its Option ARMs. Killinger didn't think WaMu should provide some of it (and neither did the OTS), as it was competitive information.[55] Instead of responding to Scharf, Killinger waited a day, then wrote a letter to Dimon instead. It was now Saturday, April 5, two days before JPMorgan planned to announce the acquisition, and about two weeks before WaMu's annual shareholder meeting.

"Dear Jamie," Killinger wrote, tersely.[56] "I received a letter Friday evening from Charlie Scharf. While we believe that several statements in the letter were either misleading or inaccurate, rather than address them individually, I wanted to focus on the broader state of discussions between our firms.

"I continue to be disappointed with the inability (despite several attempts by the bankers) to make progress by improving price and terms of a proposal that would allow us to move forward. This impacts diligence, because we are reluctant to provide you with our most sensitive, confidential and competitive information until we get a better view from you on enhancing your initial pricing and terms. We continue to look for a way to break this logjam.

"My team, over this weekend, is doing its best to comply with your extensive due diligence request of Friday. However, to fully comply with your Friday request, I need something from you: your commitment to work to reach agreement on improved pricing and terms. In the meantime, our process to address capital needs continues to move forward. I look forward to discussing this with you."

JPMorgan didn't receive the letter until a day later, on Sunday night. Scharf typed out a reply to Killinger on his BlackBerry. "In response to your letter dated April 5, which we received only a few minutes ago, we had indicated, and I reiterate, a commitment to working toward an improvement in pricing and terms. As you can appreciate, however, any final agreement on improvement requires completion of the due diligence we have sought from the outset. We look forward to hearing from you as promptly as possible."

At 7:30 the next morning, Eastern Time, Dimon also sent an e-mail to Killinger: "Kerry—As I assume you are aware, we did not receive your letter until almost 10:00 last night and responded immediately and positively to your request. Please let us know promptly if you are truly interested in pursuing a transaction with us."[57]

By the time Dimon's e-mail reached Killinger's inbox, it was too late. That day Killinger presented the $7.2 billion private equity offer led by TPG to the bank's board of directors. The board weighed the lower offer (which still wasn't a formal offer) from JPMorgan and its need to spend more time researching WaMu, which would make it hard to announce anything quickly.[58] The board approved the TPG offer. In return for the $7.2 billion in private equity money, including TPG's lead investment of $2 billion, the group received 176 million WaMu shares for $8.75 per share, more than a 30 percent discount to WaMu's closing price on the day of the announcement. Still, the rating agency Moody's improved its outlook on the bank. The $7 billion was also $2 billion more than WaMu had been told by the OTS to bring in.

It was a big win for Killinger. Not only had he raised money, he had raised money from David Bonderman, whose investment decisions were respected in the financial world. This capital, Killinger said in announcing the deal, "will position us for a return to profitability as these elevated credit costs subside. With the support of these investors, we have every confidence in our ability to deal with today's market conditions and restore shareholder value."[59] The money had placated the OTS, which believed WaMu was in stable condition. But the private equity infusion had not been Bair's preference, and the FDIC was now still left with the possibility that WaMu might fail, affecting the deposit insurance fund. The agency would be stuck with cleaning up its mess. While that possibility was dimmer now, it still existed.

The Wall Street Journal, citing unnamed sources, soon broke the news that JPMorgan had made a play for WaMu—and had been uncharacteristically spurned. The New York bank offered "as much as $8 a share in JPMorgan stock" but WaMu passed it up because the offer was worth "far less than that," the *Journal* reported.[60] It was a rare loss for JPMorgan. Its executives were furious. "WaMu, in the world's worst way, did not want to do a deal with Chase and tried very, very hard to avoid engaging with Chase," said one person on JPMorgan's team. Inside WaMu, executives assumed the story was another trick from "the New York boys," one of whom they figured had leaked the news to the *Journal* and had conveniently forgotten to mention the $3-a-share contingency that JPMorgan had placed on the "$8 a share" offer. By the time the news spread across the country, most media simply reported that JPMorgan had offered $8 a share, without noting that the offer was actually "far less than that."

On the day WaMu made the TPG offer public, one of JPMorgan's executives sent out an e-mail to everyone who had worked on Project West. The subject: "West Document Destruction."

"Given the capital raise transaction announced today by West, we are asking that you promptly destroy any confidential information that you may have in your possession. This includes any information you may have in electronic form. Further, as I indicated in my note to you yesterday, we remind you of our ongoing confidentiality obligations with regard to all information related to this transaction, including the fact that we considered a transaction."[61] JPMorgan, along with all the parties that looked through WaMu's financial data, had signed strict confidentiality agreements with the bank.

One of the Project West team members at JPMorgan wrote back with a question: "Does that include our internal models we built?"

The response: "The numbers in the model, but not the model itself."

WaMu turned down JPMorgan, but JPMorgan wasn't giving up trying.*

On a cloudy June afternoon in 2008, 400 people packed into a ballroom at the Sheraton Hotel in downtown Seattle, some sitting on folding

---

*Another perspective, offered in a later book about Dimon, describes the JPMorgan executives taking their loss of WaMu "in stride," with Dimon speculating that there was a 50/50 chance JPMorgan would have another opportunity to purchase the bank.

chairs at the back of the room, others leaning against the wall. It was a meeting of the local Rotary Club. Killinger was the guest speaker. He arrived with a protective entourage of public relations employees, who sat around him at a luncheon table. It would be the first time Killinger had said anything publicly since the shareholder meeting two months earlier. WaMu was in a state of lockdown. No one was giving interviews. That morning, however, WaMu made the unusual move of responding to one of the dozens of rumors circulating about it. This rumor in particular charged that WaMu was about to be slapped with an enforcement order by its federal regulators. "Neither our primary federal regulator, the OTS, nor any other bank regulatory agency has taken any enforcement action against WaMu that we have not previously disclosed," WaMu wrote. "Further, the company is not currently in such discussions with any regulatory agency."[62]

At the same time, a UBS analyst issued a note saying that WaMu would lose much more money on its loans than it was projecting.[63] The analyst thought the bank would lose nearly $22 billion through 2011, rather than the $19 billion that WaMu had said. (UBS's thoughts were more in line with JPMorgan's projections, although those were not public.) On the news, WaMu's stock plunged to $5.75.

Only days earlier WaMu's board had stripped Killinger of the chairman title that he had held for seventeen years. Internally, WaMu's board was now trying to figure out what to do about Killinger. His continued reign at the head of WaMu had become a serious public relations issue. One of the board members told a WaMu executive not to listen to Killinger, that he was too much of a Pollyanna. Rotella was still pushing for Killinger's job but had also begun to lobby select board members to hire someone else—anyone who might take control of the problems. Steve Frank floated an unusual idea, not unlike Lou Pepper's idea of more than two decades earlier: why not create an "Office of the Chairman" and put both Killinger and Rotella there, at the helm of the company? Rotella was skeptical and declined. Frank, on the other hand, viewed it as a first step in stripping Killinger of power. The board took away Killinger's chairmanship instead.

At the Rotary Club meeting at the Sheraton Hotel, Killinger stepped up to the podium, just as he had at the shareholder meeting. This audience was much more forgiving—it was mostly business leaders. No shareholder activists appeared to be in attendance.

"I'm having a strange experience these days," Killinger told the crowd. "I consistently have friends, colleagues, and even family members come up to me and say, 'Kerry, how *are* you?'" He would reassure them that he was doing fine.[64]

"They'll say, 'You know, you look better than I thought you would.'"

With that Killinger launched into a half-hour speech that was half joking and half serious, certainly not the kind of presentation you would expect from an embattled chief executive. He told the audience that WaMu had "a very strategic plan in place," although he did not elaborate on the details.[65] (The plan was to focus on WaMu's retail bank, a decision recently announced with much fanfare at a company meeting.)

He joked about Wall Street's insatiable appetite for mortgages during the housing boom: "I think you guys could have gone out and securitized your coats and pants and shirts—somebody might have bought it."

He went through the reasons for the country's current peril, blaming just about everything but WaMu: the Federal Reserve for pushing interest rates down to 1 percent and fueling a rush for mortgages, the dramatic increase in housing speculators, the "irrational money flooding housing from Wall Street," and "there were some irresponsible brokers, out marketing products to people that may not have been appropriate."

Killinger continued: "What has been particularly challenging for a bank like WaMu is that the high lending standards that we've maintained for decades still resulted in unexpectedly high loan losses. When housing prices decline by up to 35 percent, even conservatively underwritten loans can perform poorly." He acknowledged that "of course it's a tough time, but it's also a time of true excitement and of being energized by all the initiatives that we have going on."

When he finished, the audience applauded. There were no angry questions or shareholder demands. A crowd of people swarmed him, many patting his back and shaking his hand. Amid all this well-wishing, a reporter asked him what the loss of his chairman's title meant to his future at the company.

Killinger faltered before he responded, "It was really that we chose to review all of our governance practices. This was one thing the share-holders wanted."

Several days later, in his annual memo about WaMu's strategic direction to the board of directors, Killinger told a slightly different but more frank story. He acknowledged that the bank "overinvested in mortgage lending," including Option ARMs, subprime mortgages, and home equity loans. "In hindsight, these products were expanded with too much dependence on appreciating home values and underwriting that followed secondary market guidelines," Killinger wrote.[66] This was a polite way of conceding that WaMu did, in fact, make terrible loans, because Wall Street had dictated it. That was a far different story from the "conservatively underwritten loans" that Killinger praised during his Rotary Club speech.

For all his assurances, Killinger was not doing fine. As he rode the elevator to his office on the executive floor of WaMu's headquarters, a longtime employee standing next to him asked what everyone had been asking: "Kerry, how are you doing?" This employee had worked with him though the 1990s, when Killinger had arrived at WaMu first thing in the morning, leaving at 10:00 or 11:00 p.m. Back then he had been building a bank. In the elevator, Killinger turned to the employee and said gravely, "I've never had so many sleepless nights in my career."

Predictably, the board hired a consultant, the McKinsey Group, to try to sort out WaMu's many problems and figure out what to do about the management of the bank. Most of the WaMu executives viewed this development as almost laughable—instead of making changes, the bank hired an overpriced consultant to spend a long time analyzing problems whose existence had long been established. "You would have thought that we would have made decisions based on economics," said one executive. "But there were all sorts of things that seemed to trump that."

The McKinsey consultants interviewed each of WaMu's executive team members and were particularly interested in Killinger. What were his strengths and weaknesses? How did executive team members interact? How did he and Steve Rotella get along? No one held back. The executives told the consultants about Killinger's deep conflict avoidance and his unrelenting optimism. "The board should have realized that Kerry ran out of gas one or two years ago," said another executive later.

They described the tension between Killinger and Rotella, who no one believed were getting along.

Soon the McKinsey consultants delivered their high-priced report. The results were damning for Killinger in particular. The majority of the executives and managers interviewed believed there should be a change at the top.

The abrupt failure of IndyMac in July 2008 exposed to the world the fragility of America's consumer banks and launched a silent deposit run at WaMu, but it also had another, quiet consequence: it further widened the rift between the FDIC and the OTS over the fate of WaMu. The closure of IndyMac did not make Bair, or the FDIC, look good. For all her advance planning for the failure of a giant bank, the agency had not been ready for the bank run at IndyMac. The FDIC had planned to close the bank in August, not July, and it hadn't had time to find a buyer. When customers lined up to take out their money—fighting in line, sleeping in tents through the night, fainting in the heat—most of them did so after the FDIC had taken over the institution, a stark illustration that few trusted the government.

That much was apparent from the dozens of media reports broadcast from Pasadena during those summer days, as dry heat rose in waves off the pavement. CBS captured a telling exchange between arguing customers who had been waiting in a line in front of IndyMac's headquarters since early in the morning.[67] An IndyMac employee stationed outside attempted to calm everyone, saying, "Your money is safe in an FDIC-insured institution. You don't have to wait in a long line to get your money." But a frustrated customer interrupted, "Believe me, if it were safe, all these people wouldn't be here." He pointed to the IndyMac employee. "That gentleman doesn't know what he's talking about." The CBS anchor concluded: "The federal government says most of the 275,000 depositors, 98 percent of them, can trust that their money is safe. It's just that people don't seem to be in a trusting mood."

Wrote a blogger for the *Los Angeles Times*, "On Day 3 of the financial hostage drama otherwise known as IndyMac Federal, someone needs to say it: The government's takeover of IndyMac has been a stunning display of cluelessness and incompetence and has given bank customers every reason to feel anxious and angry." While only 10,000 of IndyMac's customers, representing about $1 billion in deposits, were uninsured, that was enough to frighten customers further. After IndyMac was liquidated, those customers were expected to receive only half of that amount.

Bair defended her agency, in part, by blaming the media for stoking customers' fears. "There was virtually uninterrupted access to deposit insurance for insured depositors over the weekend, and Monday it was business as usual," she said testily.[68] "The only snafu we ran into were these long lines, and I'm sorry, but I think part of that was driven by some of the irresponsible reporting about this having some type of crisis proportions that it did not have. It was a disservice to depositors. They did not need to be there. Their money was quite safe." A senior fellow at the Milken Institute, an economics think tank, disagreed with her, saying, "It's a total lack of coordination and information that's being provided to people."

Bair tried to educate bank customers about FDIC insurance. She stood on stage at the Chicago Mercantile Exchange, next to TV personality Suze Orman, under a banner that read "CONFIDENCE AND STABILITY." As attendees picked at their lunch, Bair reminded the crowd that "the overwhelming majority of banks in this country continue to be well-capitalized." A reporter in attendance observed: "After several years on the D-list, deposit insurance is hot. The FDIC's Web site last Monday tallied a record 9 million hits, with nary a mention of Brangelina's twins."[69] Before a speech in San Francisco, Bair said that she "would be very surprised" to see another bank failure the size of IndyMac, or larger. "Based on what I'm seeing now, I really don't see we will have institutions of that significant size having serious problems."[70]

Of course, the FDIC thought WaMu had serious problems. The agency was now even more concerned about that bank's future. Indy-Mac's failure had cost the deposit insurance fund roughly $11 billion, the first time the pot of money had been used to that extent for years. If WaMu failed, the fund would likely be wiped clean. The agency did not want another IndyMac on its hands. The FDIC began to take an even tougher stance on WaMu.

The OTS, meanwhile, had regulated IndyMac and had allowed it to reach a very precarious position. When IndyMac failed, the agency lost yet another of the banks under its purview. The OTS's power shrank further. Politically for the OTS, it became even more important to keep WaMu alive.

The letters and e-mail exchanges between the two agencies became more heated. The lower-level staff of both agencies faced increasing pressure from their superiors in Washington. Toward the end of July, as WaMu's bank run was under way, the FDIC regional director in San Francisco wrote to the OTS regional director in Seattle, suggesting that WaMu raise an additional $5 billion in capital, on top of the $7 billion it had just brought in several months earlier. The FDIC thought WaMu's losses on its mortgages would be higher than the bank thought. The OTS disagreed. The regional director promptly wrote back, accusing the FDIC of conducting "a very rough capital analysis" that was outdated and slamming the agency, in a backhanded way, for getting involved.[71] "I value the constructive working relationship that we have had," wrote Darrel Dochow, the OTS regional director. "I would hope that we can continue to have ongoing discussion and not unexpected letter exchanges." Reich's deputy in Washington called the letter from the FDIC "inappropriate and disingenuous," noting that the agency had once again forgotten that the OTS held the role of WaMu's primary regulator.

Not long after this exchange, Killinger and several members of WaMu's executive team flew to Washington for a joint meeting with Reich, Bair, and their respective deputies. WaMu had called the meeting as a way to update the regulators on the bank's financial condition following the bank run. They had no idea that their bank had fueled such a battle between the two agencies. In Reich's conference room at the OTS's frayed headquarters, Killinger and WaMu's treasurer, Robert Williams, ran through WaMu's capital and liquidity positions. WaMu was considered well capitalized, even though it had just posted a stunning $3.3 billion loss in the second quarter because of its bad loans—its highest quarterly loss ever. As a result of the bank run, the bank's liquidity had drained to about $50 billion. The government agencies still deemed that amount healthy. Customers were bringing money back thanks to the 5 percent CD special.

Killinger and Williams finished talking and sat back down. Reich agreed with the two executives and their analysis of WaMu's financial position. Bair also agreed, despite her agency's recent plea for the bank to raise another $5 billion. She complimented the WaMu executives on their ability to pull out of the bank run. Just as it seemed the meeting was turning out well, Bair surprised everyone.[72]

"Washington Mutual is a big concern to the FDIC," she declared.

One of her deputies ordered: "You need to find a strategic partner." Any other plan would not be in the best interest of the deposit insurance fund.

The OTS officials were shocked. With that bold suggestion, the FDIC had overstepped its bounds—and while the bank in question was in the room.

Reich erupted. "This is not the time to discuss this in front of WaMu or any other bank," he said, nearly shouting.

The meeting ended. The stunned WaMu executives walked silently back out through the lobby and onto the busy street. Suddenly, it seemed, WaMu was the child of a divorce, pulled between two warring parents. One of those parents was not as supportive as the other. Reich e-mailed Killinger later, telling him the meeting was "totally inappropriate" and assuring the chief executive that the OTS believed in WaMu's financial condition.[73]

In New York, JPMorgan had not forgotten about WaMu. In June 2008, two months after it lost the bid to TPG, JPMorgan considered what sounded a lot like a hostile takeover of the Seattle company.[74] Plenty of WaMu shareholders were angry about the TPG capital infusion diluting their stock. Those shareholders still had to approve the private equity money before WaMu could take it. JPMorgan thought about offering shareholders a "sweetheart deal" above what TPG paid for the bank, right before the June 24 shareholder vote. TPG held an $8.75-a-share option on WaMu in case it wanted to make a further investment. To get rid of TPG, JPMorgan would simply have to pay it more than that $8.75 a share. Compared with other possible acquisitions, JPMorgan believed "that West is most financially compelling," wrote one executive to two other bankers on JPMorgan's team.

JPMorgan never made the attempt, and WaMu shareholders approved the TPG money. But after IndyMac failed, the Project West team started thinking that WaMu might fail as well. JPMorgan began considering a purchase of WaMu from the government, along with its other plan to buy WaMu on the open market.[75] It investigated whether the government might help it out with the purchase, as in its takeover of Bear Stearns. This sort of "government assistance" transaction would come to be known as a "Jamie Deal" by other bankers who admired Dimon's ability to get the government to kick in some money.[76] At this point, JPMorgan was one of the few financially viable investment banks around. In WaMu's case, the Project West team considered whether the FDIC might agree to share in losses on WaMu's Option ARM mortgages for a couple of years. "We are thinking through how to make up the assisted scenario," one JPMorgan executive wrote in an e-mail to Charlie Scharf. "We may get more color tomorrow with the regulators. If not, will make something up." The following day in Washington JPMorgan had regularly scheduled meetings with its primary regulator, the OCC, and the FDIC. The periodic meetings were held to discuss general banking issues.[77]

Next, the Project West team at JPMorgan mapped out two merger models under the assumption that WaMu failed and was taken over by the FDIC.* The Project West team e-mailed Dimon and Scharf a 35-page document ("strictly private and confidential") outlining the different scenarios.[78] JPMorgan was now assuming it would lose a total of $34 billion on WaMu because of WaMu's bad mortgage loans, $8 billion more than when the company looked at the bank in March. JPMorgan noted "uncertainty around loss estimates." In each of the scenarios in the report, JPMorgan assumed a purchase price of zero—on a bank with $310 billion in assets.

In Seattle, WaMu's own quiet bank run was under way, although it appeared to be slowing. Now another problem surfaced. Killinger had

---

*JPMorgan would later explain this away, saying several of its own clients were, at the time, asking for similar models of troubled institutions they were thinking of buying. JPMorgan said it received no advance information from regulators.

heard that Jim Cramer, the outspoken host of the popular television show *Mad Money*, planned to stage a segment about WaMu.[79] It was among the worst publicity events imaginable. Earlier in the year, Cramer had called Killinger "one of the worst CEOs in the world" and placed the entire WaMu board on his "Wall of Shame."[80] If Cramer made another such proclamation, the viewers would grow more panicked about the bank's financial condition. The bank run might reignite. Negative perceptions about WaMu weren't affecting only customers, though. The bank had been set to sell about forty-five of its Chicago branches to U.S. Bank when the Minnesota company made the unusual move of demanding a letter of credit to back the deal.[81] It had heard that WaMu was on a list of banks pegged for a possible takeover. The deal fell apart.

Killinger shut himself in his office and picked up the phone. It was a beautiful summer day. Ferries shuttled tourists across Puget Sound, and the Space Needle glimmered from a mile away. Killinger first called John Reich in Washington. Reich echoed his concern about the possible TV show and promised to see what he could do. Killinger then called Bair. She also said she would look into it. Next Killinger put in a rare call to Treasury Secretary Paulson. Banks, no matter how large, don't usually elevate concerns to that level. Killinger didn't want to talk to Paulson just about Cramer's *Mad Money*—he also wanted to see if Paulson would help protect WaMu from naked short sellers. Short selling is essentially betting that a company will do badly: investors sell shares of borrowed stock (from a broker, for example) and then buy new shares to replace the old ones. If the new shares were bought for less than the original borrowed stock, the investor makes money. Naked short selling means that original shares aren't borrowed. Either way, both forms of trading were driving down WaMu's stock, which was now hovering around $3.

Killinger thought Paulson could use his influence at the Securities and Exchange Commission (SEC) to help WaMu get on a list of 19 financial institutions temporarily protected from naked short selling. The SEC had given JPMorgan, Bank of America, and Citigroup this privilege. "What's interesting about that list," noted the *Seattle Post-Intelligencer* at the time, "is one name conspicuous by its absence—Seattle-based Washington Mutual Inc., whose stock has been of more than passing interest to short-sellers."

Once Paulson came to the phone, Killinger asked him if he would help WaMu get on the list. Paulson refused. On the East Coast, he was in the middle of lining up a bailout for Fannie Mae and Freddie Mac.

"You should have sold to JPMorgan in the spring, and you should do so now," Paulson told Killinger sharply. "Things could get a lot more difficult for you."[82]

The unusual and unexpected rebuke from the Treasury secretary startled Killinger. He stammered a response, and then hung up.

As the summer wore on, the argument between the FDIC and the OTS over WaMu grew more serious and the exchanges between Bair and Reich even more heated. This rift was no longer just about turf—the agencies were now battling over WaMu's survival. This angst emerged in one new disagreement in particular: WaMu's new CAMELS rating. Earlier in the year, the OTS had lowered WaMu's grade to 3, and it stuck by that rating. But in light of WaMu's bank run, the FDIC wanted to lower the grade further. The FDIC thought WaMu ranked as 4, the second-worst mark.

This was dangerous territory. A 4-rating, whether or not WaMu deserved it, could become a self-fulfilling prophecy. Downgrading a suffering bank to a 4 can launch a chain of events that will push the bank toward failure. A 4-rated institution has a much harder time getting crucial loans from the Federal Home Loan Banks and the Federal Reserve. The bank lands on the FDIC's problem bank list, publicly distributed nationwide each quarter and closely watched by analysts. The list doesn't name a bank, but it notes banks' assets. WaMu was so large that everyone would recognize its addition.

That, in turn, could spark further uncertainty about WaMu's health. It could trigger another deposit run, possibly even activating WaMu's dreaded Break the Bank scenario. Indeed, an institution with a 4-rating receives this description from regulators: "Failure is a distinct possibility if the problems and weaknesses are not satisfactorily addressed and resolved." While only a small fraction of the banks on the FDIC's problem list fail, almost all the banks that collapsed during the Savings and Loan Crisis had been on the list first.[83] WaMu itself had made an appearance on the list in the early 1980s before Pepper rescued it.

A 4-rating, however, would give the FDIC a much stronger position in WaMu's oversight and also give Bair and her agency some measure of political protection. IndyMac had been downgraded to 4 just before its failure, and this was another aspect of its collapse that caused the FDIC to be criticized. "If a bank is rated a 3 and all of a sudden it fails, the agency looks stupid and they're going to get hauled up in front of Congress and be berated for not being tough enough," explained one former regulator. "Regulators don't like to get hauled up in front of Congress." With a 4-rating, the FDIC could push for a stronger enforcement order against WaMu, forcing the bank to make sweeping changes to its operations. For the FDIC, changing a bank rating can be a frustrating, circular battle. "When an institution gets downgraded, that's when they can do their more intensive work," said one regulator. "But that rating is determined by the primary regulator." And in WaMu's case, as the FDIC had long been reminded, the primary regulator was the OTS.

Reich didn't know there was a problem between the two agencies about WaMu's rating until Bair announced it on a joint conference call. The agencies' dual regional directors in San Francisco and Seattle, who were more intimately involved in WaMu's oversight, had talked about the rating and seemed to agree on 3. Nerves were already frayed in Washington; Reich had recently e-mailed one of his deputies that "the headbutting is currently going on in DC between myself and Sheila Bair."[84] Upon learning of the rating disagreement, Reich shot off an e-mail to Bair. "In my view," he wrote, "rating WaMu a 4 would be a big error in judging the facts in this situation. It would appear to be a rating resulting from fear and not a rating based on the condition of the institution. WaMu has both the capital and the liquidity to justify a 3 rating.

"It seems based on e-mail exchanges which have taken place that the FDIC supervisory staff in San Francisco is under pressure by the fear in Washington to downgrade this institution. If, in fact, the FDIC intends to rate this institution as a 4-rated troubled institution, then prior to such action I would request a Board meeting to consider the proper rating on this institution." In the rare case of a strong rating disagreement between two agencies, regulators had to take a number of steps, among them making a presentation arguing their position to the FDIC's board of directors.

Bair e-mailed back, "We will follow the appropriate procedures if the staff cannot agree. You asked me to hear out WaMu. I hope that you would also hear out our examination staff if it comes to that."

The argument on hold, Reich went on vacation with his family. Bair, meanwhile, asked one of her deputies if he would ask Scott Polakoff, who was the OTS's deputy director and Reich's second in command, to make some discreet inquiries into whether any banks were interested in buying WaMu—bad loans and all.[85] This request was unusual, for two reasons. One, the agency in charge of shopping around a bank on the verge of failure is the FDIC, not the OTS; and two, despite all its problems and the bank run, WaMu was not on the verge of failure. Polakoff told Bair's deputy that it wasn't his job to look at potential acquirers.

Meanwhile Bair called Donald Kohn—the vice chairman of the Federal Reserve and Fed chairman Ben Bernanke's deputy—to give him a heads-up on the brewing conflict. While Kohn didn't follow the details of WaMu's oversight, he, like Bair, worried about WaMu's liquidity following the bank run.

Next, Bair wrote an e-mail to Reich.[86]

"I'd like to further discuss contingency planning for W during the call on Friday," she wrote. "Art talked with Scott about making some discrete [sic] inquiries to determine whether there are institutions which would be willing to acquire it on a whole bank basis if we had to do an emergency closing, and on what terms.

"I understand you have strong objections to our doing so, so I'd like to talk this through. My interest is in assuring that IF we have to market it on an emergency basis, there is multiple bidder interest. In any event, both the FDIC and the FRB agree that there needs to be a contingency plan in place, so let's talk this through on Friday. I'd really like to develop a plan everyone is comfortable with."

Several hours later Reich responded, furiously.

"You really know to stir up a colleague's vacation," he wrote. "I do not, under any circumstances, want to discuss this on Friday's conference call, in which I may or may not be able to participate, depending on cell phone service availability on the cruise ship location.

"Instead, I want to have a one on one meeting with Ben Bernanke prior to any such discussion—as early next week as possible following my return to the office. Also, I may or may not choose to have a similar meeting with Secretary Paulson."

Here Reich reminded Bair that the FDIC, as federal regulations dictate, couldn't get involved in trying to sell a bank unless that bank's primary regulator had declared the bank insolvent. The OTS had not declared WaMu insolvent.

"You personally, and the FDIC as an agency, would likely create added instability if you pursue what I strongly believe would be a precipitous and unprecedented action," Reich continued. "And if it occurs without my consent, I will not sit quietly by and observe—there would be a public reaction. Put yourself in the [primary federal regulator's] shoes in this situation. We have responsibilities, including the right of primary supervisory determination of this institution's condition, and until Congress changes the statutes under which we operate, our responsibilities as the [primary federal regulator] are not to be simply tendered to the FDIC in a down economic cycle. It seems as if the FDIC is behaving as some sort of super-regulator—which you, and it, are not.

"I also believe there could be a high potential for FDIC actions of the type you are contemplating to cause irreparable harm to WaMu if, at any point in the near future, WaMu wishes to actually seek a buyer. The potential harm could stem from the fact that any such potential buyer may allready [sic] have been contacted by the FDIC.*

"If, in fact, any meetings or discussions have already taken place by the FDIC with either JPMC, Wells Fargo, or any other entity, in any capacity in which WaMu was even mentioned, I would like to see a copy of the signed confidentiality agreement signed by the bank—required in any resolution scenario before an institution is told the name of the failing bank.

*Later, this would prove to be another point of contention between the two agencies. The FDIC would say that shopping around a bank that is about to fail and be sold on the cheap would not dissuade interested buyers from bidding on it on the open market. One FDIC official described this statement as "an urban legend." The OTS would argue, in effect, that there's no way companies would buy something more expensive now when they knew they could get it cheaper later.

"This is an OTS regulated institution, not an FDIC regulated institution. We make any decision on solvency, not the FDIC, and I have staff equally as competent as staff at the FDIC, whom I know well.

"The FDIC can do whatever internal contingency planning it wishes, but should in no way go outside the FDIC. This is a 3-rated institution. Are you also trying to find buyers for Citi, Wachovia, Nat City and others?

"Finally, if WaMu were to learn of the FDIC's actions, there may well be a question as to whether these actions may constitute a disclosable event. That, in and of itself, is a reason not to proceed with this approach for a publicly traded institution. The government should not be in the business of arranging mergers—particularly before they are necessary, and we are not at that point in WaMu's situation.

"I will attempt to be on Friday's conference call, and I am going to assume this notion is not going to be raised."

Bair forwarded Reich's e-mail to Kohn at the Fed, with a note: "This is pretty over the top."

"I'll say," Kohn replied after reading it. "Bernanke would be glad to talk to him, but John won't like the message. Ben has several times pushed on us contingency planning and volunteered to meet with Reich if we think it would be helpful."

The disagreement was left unsettled as the summer waned.

On the first Thursday in September, during the lunch hour, two of WaMu's board members strode onto WaMu's executive floor: Steve Frank, the chairman of WaMu's board, and Orin Smith, the former chief executive of Starbucks. Both men's presence was unusual. There was no meeting scheduled for that day. They were polite, greeting the executive assistants who worked on the floor as they passed. The two walked into Killinger's office—his own assistant happened to be at a rare out-of-office lunch—and shut the door.

Soon they emerged, walked back across the floor, and took the secure elevator down to the lobby. When Killinger's assistant returned from lunch, he summoned her into his office. She came carrying his calendar, as she had done every day for the last decade. She took a seat across from him at his desk, her pen poised to start taking notes.

Killinger hardly waited until she sat down.

"Well," he told her frankly, "I just got canned."

He didn't look upset or surprised or even angry. His face betrayed no emotion at all.

His longtime assistant, meanwhile, was shocked. "Are you kidding me?" she exclaimed. "Are you okay?"

Across the desk, Killinger looked at her in his usual reserved way.

"It's just so embarrassing."

Chapter Nine

THE FINAL HOURS

The stakes are very high.

> —WaMu chief executive Alan Fishman and
> board chairman Steve Frank to federal regulators

Sunday, September 7, 2008

From the local TV news: *"Major shake-up for WaMu.* The Wall Street Journal *says CEO Kerry Killinger has been forced out. He's been in charge of the bank since 1990, and built it into one of the nation's largest mortgage lenders. But stock prices are down 88 percent since last year . . . The government is now in charge of mortgage giants Fannie Mae and Freddie Mac. Treasury Secretary Henry Paulson announced the takeover of the companies this morning."*

Alan Fishman was in London, on his way to Israel, when he got a call from an attorney back in New York. "I have this crazy, crazy idea," said the lawyer, an old friend of Fishman's. Would Fishman consider talking to WaMu's board of directors about stepping in as chief executive of the troubled bank? The request surprised Fishman. He and a partner were in the process of starting a national commercial real estate lender, Ladder Capital, and they had raised money from investors. Fishman would be chairman, while his partner ran the company. Fishman's mind was hardly on anything else.

"That's nice," he told the attorney. "I'll be back in a few days, and I'll see you then."

"You should expect a call from the chairman," the attorney said. As it turned out, WaMu's board wanted to meet with Fishman immediately. He flew from London to New York, had dinner with several of the bank's board members, flew back to London, and still made it to Israel. It was nearing the end of August 2008. WaMu's board had discreetly been looking for a new chief executive for the better part of the month.

Steve Rotella, who had long lobbied for the job, had never been considered a serious candidate. His appointment would have been too controversial and likely wouldn't have been approved by WaMu's regulators. Not only had company politics marred his reputation in the eyes of directors, but he had direct supervision of the Home Loans Group.

The board hadn't been able to find anyone to take the position. It was now under heavy pressure from the OTS to replace Killinger. The board had come close to hiring Liam McGee, Bank of America's president for global consumer and small business banking.[1] Steve Frank, the chairman of WaMu's board, met with McGee and thought the meeting went well. McGee seemed interested, and Frank expected to start negotiating a contract. But it hadn't worked out.

The board soon found Fishman, whose ties to the financial industry were long and deep—almost as long and deep as his ties to New York. He had held top positions at Chemical Bank, where he had worked for almost twenty years, before moving on to AIG. More recently, he had convinced the chief executive of Independence Community Bank in Brooklyn to retire and hire him for the job. Fishman spent several years improving the company before he sold it to Sovereign Bancorp for $42 a share, a deal that proved a coup for Independence's shareholders and an expensive mistake for Sovereign.[2] Fishman stayed on briefly as Sovereign's president and chief operating officer before taking the chairman position at Meridian Capital Group.

These were his credentials, but Fishman was known, more than anything else, as a turnaround artist for troubled companies, with deep contacts in the banking industry. "If WaMu can be fixed, he can fix it," Charles Hamm, Independence's former chairman and CEO, later told *The Seattle Times*. Fishman has a lot of white hair, a Cheshire cat grin, and even more bluntness than is usual in New York.

He got the job. Like Steve Rotella, he had never been to Seattle before. Fishman did know WaMu, though. Fishman and Killinger both belonged to a similar national banking organization and were friendly in an I-see-you-once-a-year kind of way. (When Killinger found out that Fishman would replace him, he was surprised because Fishman hadn't run a bank as large as WaMu. Said Fishman of Killinger: "He had a fabulous notion of scale.")

Fishman had also done some research on WaMu in 2004, when he was looking to sell Independence Community Bank. "I'd always been intrigued by what they'd done in the earliest days," Fishman said later. But after studying WaMu more closely, Fishman arrived at a different conclusion. "There were things about the bank I thought were illogical," he said. "I didn't like the business model so much. Quite frankly, I thought it was too big for the management team." In the end, Killinger wouldn't meet Fishman's price and Fishman didn't want to do a stock deal. He didn't want WaMu stock. "The real estate market had lost its mind, in my view," said Fishman.

After he returned from Israel at the end of August, Fishman and his wife, Judy, took a long walk around their home in upstate New York. While they live primarily in Brooklyn—Fishman was born and raised there—they also own property in Columbia County, an agricultural community of rolling foothills and farmhouses, three hours from the city. Not only was Fishman starting a new business, but his children and his five grandchildren were all on the East Coast.

"We're going to move our roots from New York, and I'm going to work around the clock for the next three years," Fishman said, as they walked.

His wife thought about it. "It's very important," she replied. "It's a big bank and this is very important. It will be a nice adventure."

The couple would simply fly the family back and forth. "I actually thought it was important for the country's financial system," Fishman said later. "I thought, if we could create this perfect consumer bank where people get a fair deal and it made sense and we didn't lend to people that couldn't pay it back, or to dead people—the whole thing was just madness. I thought, 'This needs an intervention. So here I am.'"

Fishman flew to Seattle on Saturday, September 6, and took a room at the upscale Fairmont Olympic Hotel. He planned to stay there until he found a house in the city. The next night, as the government put Fannie Mae and Freddie Mac into receivership, WaMu's executive team and its board members arrived at the hotel to have dinner with Fishman. Steve Frank had earlier held a private meeting in a conference room at the hotel, without Fishman, to let the executive team know about Killinger's departure. At dinner that night, Fishman stood up to say a few words as everyone ate.

"I'm not here to sell the company," he told the group. "I'm here to turn it around. It's salvageable."

Fishman isn't humble, but he also isn't naive. He believed WaMu was a solvable problem. The bank had terrible assets—the bad mortgages—and he had to figure out the extent of the problem. But he was confident he could turn it around and start expanding into lines of business beyond mortgage lending. He had done it as chief executive of Independence Bank, bulking up the company's commercial real estate and business-banking divisions while reducing its concentration in multifamily mortgages. At WaMu, Fishman also had the backing of TPG, one of the most well-respected private equity firms in the country.

"I knew exactly what to do, because I had done it before," he said. "The hard part was rebranding the thing and knocking out some of that really weird stuff—like those branches. I was thinking two or three years, and then I would hire a replacement, I'd become chairman, and we're done.

"It all changed the day I walked in there."

Monday, September 8

NET CHANGE IN WAMU'S DEPOSIT BALANCE: +$200 MILLION*

From the local news: *"This morning, confirmation came that the new CEO of Washington Mutual has been announced and the people who work at the WaMu branches throughout our region will soon have a new boss. Alan H. Fishman said he would hit the ground running in Seattle and get the company back to profitability as soon as possible."*

Everyone at WaMu's headquarters was on edge. Employees had received an e-mail that morning, telling them that Killinger had left "to pursue other opportunities." He would receive a severance package worth as much as $22 million, depending on how the bank calculated his stock. The news of Killinger's departure had not surprised anyone. For the better part of a year and a half, the stable company that they had known for so long had turned into a flimsy plastic raft, lurching among waves that only kept getting bigger. "Everybody was angry," one employee said. "We didn't know this Fishman guy." That morning, at the same time as the news of Fishman's arrival, WaMu announced that the OTS had served the bank with an enforcement order, known as a "Memorandum of Understanding."[3] The order instructed WaMu to come up with a new business plan within 30 days and deliver it to the OTS. It forced WaMu to figure out its problems with underwriting mortgages and repair its ability to manage risk. More significantly, the order warned that WaMu's capital should not fall below a level considered by regulators to be "well-capitalized." The bank needed a contingency plan to raise more money. That plan would be expected within three months.

Before Fishman arrived, WaMu had lobbied against the MOU.[4] No bank ever wants an enforcement order. Such an order sounds scary and makes it obvious to the public that the bank is having trouble. John Reich at the OTS debated whether to go forward with the order. After

---

*These numbers don't include non-interest-bearing accounts of $18.6 billion, or about 12 percent of WaMu's retail deposits in September. Those accounts were typically volatile, so they were not used by WaMu as an accurate measure of money flowing into and out of the bank. The numbers are also rounded.

the agency director made a decision over the summer, he sent Killinger an apologetic e-mail. "I've been wrestling with the issue of an MOU versus a board resolution," Reich wrote.[5] A board resolution would have been the lighter, less public punishment. "We almost always do an MOU for 3-rated institutions, and if someone were looking over our shoulder, they would probably be surprised we don't already have one in place." He added: "So as much as I would like to be able to say a board resolution is the appropriate response, I don't really believe it is."

Still, it took the OTS two months since that e-mail to deliver the MOU. WaMu's stock promptly fell in morning trading.

Fishman sequestered himself in a conference room with a speaker-phone and his new executive team. He held a call with WaMu senior managers across the country. "The place was comatose," Fishman said later. "They were all in shock." Before he said anything about WaMu, he asked the bank's managers in Texas how they were faring after Hurricane Gustav, which had swept through the state several days earlier. The mood in the room changed to relief. At that moment, the WaMu managers glimpsed what the bank used to be—an institution that cared about its employees and customers. "That reality had been lost at WaMu over a very long, long period of time," Fishman said later. "I don't know how it was lost, or who lost it; I don't know about the old WaMu. I do know that you had a group of people who were working under enormous pressure."

Fishman was decisive and honest. He had a plan. He told the executives over dinner the previous night: "Work together, or leave tonight." Said one executive: "There was a sense of relief that finally, something had happened." Said another: "We thought the board should have brought him in a year or two ago." Rotella had become so used to carrying out many of Killinger's duties that he found it a bit startling when Fishman reclaimed the role of chief executive. "If I'm not your guy," Rotella told Fishman, "I'll leave. Otherwise, you have my full support." Fishman, largely oblivious to the internal politics that had preceded him, responded, "We'll make that decision another time."

After the conference call, Fishman settled into Killinger's empty office, which the new chief executive found to be palatial. ("Somewhere in that office I found a place to sit down because I was getting tired of walking around it.") "We're going to have some fun here," he told one of the executive assistants. The first thing he did was call Sheila Bair. Fishman had been briefed on the divide between the FDIC and the OTS—at least so far as WaMu knew about it. He had heard about the now-infamous shouting match between the two agencies in front of WaMu executives. He didn't, however, know how deep the problems ran. But Fishman also had a good relationship with the FDIC. He and one of Bair's deputies once worked together on a community service venture, volunteering to provide tax services to the poor.

When Fishman got Bair on the phone, he introduced himself.

"I've checked you out," Bair told him. "You're fine. You're not the problem. You've got a good reputation."

But she added: "I hate this thing. You've got to sell it."

"Let me get my hands on it," Fishman assured her. "We're not fooling around here. Let me give it a little bit of time."

The mood in Washington had already turned against the bank. A week earlier Senator Chuck Schumer, the New York Democrat who had sent the letter about IndyMac earlier in the summer, made the unusual move of returning a $2,000 donation from WaMu's political action committee. The donation had been made only several days earlier. Schumer's staff offered no explanation.[6]

That afternoon, as the stock of Lehman Brothers plunged 20 percent amid fears about its ability to survive, Fishman met with WaMu's chief credit officer, John McMurray. McMurray was the Countrywide expat who had arrived at WaMu in late 2007 and had soon written Killinger a long e-mail outlining all the problems at the bank. McMurray was in charge of sorting out WaMu's bad loans. He had prepared a thick binder outlining all the mortgage problems, and the steps WaMu was taking to fix them. That day WaMu's internal auditor produced another report on all the loan problems. WaMu's losses from mortgage fraud had jumped to $121 million, up $80 million over the previous year, with the greatest increase among home equity loans. The internal review also found that of more than two dozen loans sampled, nearly half had been sold after the fraud was found—proof that WaMu was knowingly selling bad loans to other investors.[7] Those investors typically included investment banks.

"You have one shot to be honest," Fishman told McMurray. "How bad is it?"

Fishman's bluntness refreshed McMurray.

"No, I think we've got it," McMurray replied. He believed that the bank, although it still had many problems, had figured out how to handle its many loan issues. McMurray was in the process of walking Fishman through the details when Tom Casey, WaMu's chief financial officer, burst into the room.

"Because of the actions on Fannie and Freddie, Moody's is considering a downgrade," Casey told the two executives. This was terrible news. If any of the three rating agencies, including Moody's, downgraded WaMu's debt, the move would again spark fears about the bank's health.

"What do you think we should do?" Casey asked.

"I think we should get in front of it," Fishman replied.

Fishman's assistant had already booked him flights over the next several days to Jacksonville, Florida, to check on WaMu's loan servicing center ("In my experience, that's where you get the truth," Fishman said later. "Everything else is just guys with reports") and to California to visit its credit card operations. He canceled these trips. Instead, Fishman would spend two more days in Seattle, then fly to New York to meet with Moody's.

Jamie Dimon also called on Fishman's first day at WaMu. The JPMorgan chief executive wanted to introduce himself and offer any assistance, if Fishman needed it. "I wish you well," Dimon said.

Tuesday, September 9

Net change in WaMu's deposit balance: 0

From the local news, a commercial: *"Signing up for WaMu's free checking online takes less than seven minutes. Pretty fast, huh? Whoo-hoo!"*

That morning Dow Jones broke the news that talks between Lehman Brothers and Korea Development Bank (KDB) had fallen apart. For the last few weeks, it had looked as if the state-run KDB might buy a stake in the suffering investment bank, propping it up and allowing it to survive. Lehman's future now seemed much more uncertain. Its stock plunged 45 percent to its lowest level in more than 10 years.[8] The next day analysts expected the firm to announce quarterly losses in the billions of dollars.

In Washington, the FDIC was on high alert about WaMu. The agency had written what it called a "problem bank memo," a devastating report that detailed the numerous problems at the bank, leaving the impression that WaMu had no chance for survival. The agency ripped apart WaMu's projections on earnings—in October 2007, the bank had said it would make $2 billion in 2008, but now the FDIC was projecting it would lose $6 billion. The FDIC called WaMu's capital reserves "optimistic," even with the $7 billion in private equity raised earlier in the year. That money would be drained to pay off losses from bad loans, the FDIC noted. The agency pointed out that nearly *80 percent* of the mortgages in WaMu's $53 billion Option ARM portfolio had been made to borrowers who provided low documentation.

The FDIC shredded WaMu's management (Fishman notwithstanding, since he had just arrived as the report was written), saying: "While unprecedented housing and banking conditions have contributed to the bank's unsatisfactory financial condition, management and the board are responsible for WMB's liberal loan underwriting and concentrated exposure to declining real estate markets and higher risk loan products. The board has continued to support top leaders, who may not have the capabilities to deal with the problems now facing the bank."[9] Even with Fishman on board, the FDIC didn't think WaMu's management could change the course of the bank, especially as the problems with the financial system grew worse by the day.

Bair called Fishman in Seattle. She revealed that the FDIC and the OTS couldn't agree on how to rate WaMu. The FDIC was pushing for a CAMELS rating of 4, while the OTS wanted to maintain 3. Fishman already knew this news, but Bair's call made it formal.

"We have a problem," she told him. "If we rate the bank like we think we should rate the bank, everyone will know it's on the problem list."

To avoid all the bad publicity, Bair instructed Fishman to sell the bank or raise more capital by September 30, the end of the third quarter. The problem bank list would be made public two or three weeks after that.

Fishman thought Bair was using her agency's leverage in the situation. Despite the ultimatum, he believed he could convince her that selling WaMu wasn't necessary.

He had only just arrived at WaMu. There was time.

Wednesday, September 10

NET CHANGE IN WAMU'S DEPOSIT BALANCE: –$200 MILLION

From the local news: *"Washington Mutual stock took a dive for the third straight day as investors are increasingly pessimistic about the company's future. Shares in WaMu dropped 98 cents to close at $2. On Sunday, the company fired CEO Kerry Killinger."*

At 5:15 a.m., all across Seattle, the cell phones of WaMu's deposit tracking team reverberated with Brian Mueller's automated text message. The message compared WaMu customers' account balances from the previous day with that morning's activity on the East Coast. For the first time since late July, the tally was lower than it had been the day before. Customers were pulling out their money again. Mueller didn't wake up when the text message came in. He had set his RAZR phone to silent.

In New York, Lehman announced a staggering $3.9 billion quarterly loss, the worst since the 158-year-old company went public.[10] The investment bank tried to cushion this announcement with news of the steps it was taking to revive the firm, including spinning off part of its commercial real estate assets and selling a majority stake in its investment management division. None of these plans quelled fears. WaMu customers had heard the news about Lehman like everyone else, and it caused them to worry about their money all over again.

Shortly after Lehman's earnings call ended, Bair e-mailed Reich from across 17th Street in Washington. "I called Allan [*sic*] Fishman yesterday to make sure he was aware of our likely rating disagreement and the time sensitivity of the matter," she wrote.[11]

Within two minutes, Reich responded: "As his [primary federal regulator], I would have appreciated advance notice of your intent to do this. We would have preferred to be the first bearer of that news."

Then Reich forwarded Bair's e-mail to his deputy director, Scott Polakoff, with an outraged note. "I cannot believe the continuing audacity of this woman. I don't know if I can wait much longer to announce my intentions."

"What a lousy way to start your day," Polakoff sympathized.

Back in Seattle, WaMu's deposit team assembled at the bank's headquarters. They had received the text message, and everyone understood the implications of those numbers.

"Here we go again," said one of the deposit managers, wearily.

Thursday, September 11

NET CHANGE IN WAMU'S DEPOSIT BALANCE: -$600 MILLION

From the local news: *"Washington Mutual says it will take another multibillion-dollar write-down for bad debts on mortgage securities, but the savings and loan insists it has enough capital to keep operations going. Today WaMu's stock dipped below $2."*

Tom Casey and John McMurray arrived in New York in the early hours of the morning, after taking a red-eye flight from Seattle. The two executives had slept for only a couple of hours, and now they sat at breakfast at their hotel, eyes glazed, talking over the presentation for the upcoming meeting with Moody's.* David Bonderman, already on business in New York, soon joined them, as did Fishman, who had stayed the night at his own house. Together the executives made their way toward Moody's headquarters, located in the new 52-story 7 World Trade Center building. Thousands of people crowded the streets on their way to nearby Zuccotti Park, where New York City mayor Michael Bloomberg would commemorate the seventh anniversary of September 11. The somber melody of taps could be heard. Senators Barack Obama and John McCain, vying for the U.S. presidency, were both in town to visit Ground Zero, promising to put aside politics for the day.[12] In Washington, President George W. Bush stood on a makeshift stage at a newly unveiled Pentagon memorial. "A day will come when Americans have no memory of the events of September 11," he said. "When they visit this memorial, they will learn that the twenty-first century began with a great struggle."[13]

Fishman and his team faced a monumental task: trying to convince

---

*At least one record refers to this as a meeting with rating agency Standard & Poor's. However, numerous people in attendance or executives who were later briefed recall it as a meeting with Moody's.

the rating agency that WaMu did not deserve a downgrade of its debt. The situation did not look promising. Over the summer, before Fishman came on board, WaMu executives had met with the rating agency. The meeting had not gone well. Moody's greeted Steve Rotella and Treasurer Robert Williams with a team of people rather than the senior credit officer who handled the bank. For a tense hour and a half, the analysts fired off pointed questions: How was WaMu dealing with its bad mortgages and home equity lines of credit? Did it have any further strategy to bring in more deposits? Were those 5 percent CDs really working?

Rotella, calmly and persuasively, had tried to tell the analysts that WaMu had enough capital and enough liquidity, despite the bank run several weeks earlier. The argument did not go over well. The analysts listened to Rotella grimly, their arms crossed. Rotella and Williams had left thinking they hadn't convinced the rating agency of anything.[14]

Earlier in the week Fishman called Dick Fuld, Lehman's chief executive, and Bob Steel, who had recently left Treasury to take the helm of Wachovia. Fishman wanted advice on how to deal with the rating agencies. Both executives took Fishman's calls, despite the enormous pressure they were under at their own companies. Wachovia had bought Golden West Financial, the large Option ARM lender, and was facing many of the same mortgage problems as WaMu. "I was trying to get clever," said Fishman about the outreach.

To meet with WaMu this time, Moody's brought out its entire higher-level staff rather than the bank's normal "caseworker." Fishman viewed this as a sign of goodwill. The executives ran through their presentation, pointing out that WaMu was still considered "well capitalized" and that its liquidity position stood at $50 billion. That day WaMu released an update on its condition, an unusual move. It said it would set aside $4.5 billion for bad loans, less than it had the previous quarter.[15]

"We talk to you guys all the time," said Casey, convincingly, at the Moody's meeting. "Nothing has changed."

The Moody's team wanted to know about a provision in the terms of TPG's capital infusion that could make it hard for WaMu to raise more money if it needed to. If WaMu raised more capital at less than $8.75

a share, the price TPG paid to invest, the bank would have to make up the difference.

"Would TPG be cooperative in removing that provision if necessary?" Moody's asked.

"We want to see the bank be successful," Bonderman responded. "If the change is needed, we will consider it."

The Moody's officials said they would meet after the WaMu executives left and make a decision. "We really connected there," Fishman thought, as the group left the building.

But later Fishman, enjoying a rare meal with his wife, fielded a call from Casey. Casey and McMurray were at the airport, waiting for their flight back to Seattle. "I just got off the phone with Moody's," Casey said. "They're considering a downgrade anyway."

Across Manhattan in Midtown, JPMorgan's Project West team continued planning a purchase of WaMu. Two days earlier Charlie Scharf and Michael Cavanagh had met with Bair in Washington. Now the group focused on one of the government-assisted-deal scenarios it had come up with over the summer. The team still planned to buy both WaMu's assets and its liabilities from the FDIC, but it would leave behind $15 billion of the bank's debt with the government agency.[16]

In Washington, the OTS had put together its own view of WaMu and sent it over to the FDIC.[17] The two agencies did not disagree on WaMu's ailing health. Indeed, the OTS wrote in its letter: "We share a common perspective about the company's deteriorated financial condition." The disagreement was over how much, and how fast, the bank was deteriorating and whether the company would be allowed to work its own way out of the problems. The Option ARM loans were like a time bomb—most of them wouldn't adjust for another year or two, so no one could accurately predict WaMu's future financial condition. Would all those borrowers default? Would half of them? How would the general economy be faring? The FDIC thought WaMu's capital base would be eroded by 2010; the OTS disagreed. Reich's agency pointed out that WaMu had started a loan modification program, allowing Option ARM borrowers to refinance into a better loan. The OTS reminded the FDIC that it had, as part of the recent

"Memorandum of Understanding," told the bank to raise more capital within three months, in case the bank's worst-case recession planning came true. The OTS stood by its 3 rating of the bank. The disagreement having reached the highest levels, in less than a week the two agencies would argue their respective positions in front of the FDIC's board of directors.

That evening Moody's issued its release.[18] It downgraded WaMu's debt to junk status and issued a negative outlook on the company, citing the bank's "reduced financial flexibility," "deteriorating asset quality," and "expected franchise erosion." It graded WaMu's financial strength D+. Like the FDIC, Moody's left little room for interpretation: the bank was headed toward failure. The difference was that Moody's assessment was public.

Friday, September 12

NET CHANGE IN WAMU'S DEPOSIT BALANCE: −$500 MILLION

From the local news: *"There are reports this morning that Seattle-based Washington Mutual is in advanced talks with JPMorgan Chase about a possible buyout deal. However, a source close to the bank's chief executive says it's not true."*

In downtown Seattle, news vans parked along the stretch of Second Avenue in front of WaMu's headquarters. In some places, just one van claimed a spot in front of the skyscraper; elsewhere many vans lined the street. Often "CNN" or "CNBC" was painted across the side of a van.

WaMu's employees walked past the vans as they entered the building, often skirting around a reporter or two relaying the latest headlines about the bank. Employees were under strict instructions not to speak to the media. "If they corner you, don't acknowledge them," the bank's headquarters warned them. "Just don't speak to them. Nothing good will come out of it."

Upstairs on the twenty-first floor, the members of WaMu's communications team spent most of the day with their phones pressed to their ears, fielding call after call from the local and national press. The negative rating from Moody's had roared across the country, causing doubt, once again, about WaMu's health. A story in *American Banker* claimed that JPMorgan was in advanced discussions to buy WaMu, possibly as soon as the weekend. The story was later discounted, but that didn't matter. Speculation continued. "It was absolute insanity," said an employee handling the media.

No matter what question the journalists asked, the communications team told them that WaMu didn't comment on rumors and speculation, but that it had plenty of capital and liquidity. It didn't matter if the story was about WaMu, either—any new development on Lehman, for example, triggered a round of media calls.

The information flow had become a giant whirlpool from which no one at WaMu could swim to the surface. "I would get off the phone and go, 'What are they talking about!? I don't even know about this,'" said one communications team member. "The rules of engagement had changed with PR. Prior to that, it was more of a measured, let's-develop-messaging-that's-consistent approach. When we got into September, the rules were off. You responded to the media as immediately as possible, and you shot down rumors as quickly as you could."

The communications team members knew only as much as their managers told them, and that wasn't much. They had no idea, for example, that a bank run was under way, just as they had had no idea about the panicked customers over the summer.

The same was true in the investor relations department—Iris Glaze had no idea that three floors above her, another team of WaMu employees was working frantically to monitor the growing bank run. For her part, Glaze had stuck to her policy of not answering shareholder calls, as a measure of self-preservation. She e-mailed, telling them, "You know we're having some difficult times. We're going to work it out, and give us until 2010." It was much easier to relay this message over the computer. "I couldn't say it," she said later. "I don't have that much of a poker face."

To avoid leaks, Mueller's deposit group cut the number of people receiving the daily reports down to the bare minimum. Meetings were held in conference rooms with the door closed, rather than in the shared areas that WaMu had created when it built the skyscraper.

Everyone avoided the bank's cubes, the tall, echoing "shower stalls" that could transmit noise across the room.

At the FDIC in Washington, a representative in the agency's call center e-mailed one of Bair's deputies with an update at the end of the day.

"The FDIC call center received 233 inquiries from WaMu customers concerned about the safety of their deposits. Call center staff indicated the volume was steady and the callers appeared to be very concerned."

That evening the three men most responsible for the country's financial system—Treasury secretary Hank Paulson, New York Fed chairman Tim Geithner, and Fed chairman Ben Bernanke—delivered an ultimatum to a group of Wall Street bankers who had been instructed to gather at the Fed's offices in lower Manhattan. There would be no government bailout of Lehman Brothers. The bankers would have to figure out another way to help Lehman, or risk the investment bank's epic collapse.[19] A headline in *The New York Sun* read: "City Bracing for Lehman's Demise."

Saturday and Sunday, September 13 and 14

NET CHANGE IN WaMu's DEPOSIT BALANCE:

−$1.8 BILLION (INCLUDING MONDAY, SEPTEMBER 15)

From the local news: *"There are questions about Washington Mutual's ability to stay afloat."*

A large windowed conference room in the law offices of Simpson, Thacher & Bartlett in Midtown Manhattan had turned into a satellite office of WaMu. Fishman and his investment banking advisers from Morgan Stanley and Goldman Sachs sat around a conference table covered with stacks of paper and cell phones and speakerphones and laptops; the remains of a catered lunch of deli sandwiches were strewn across the table. Tom Casey and John McMurray had arrived from Seattle—they had gone home after the Moody's meeting, only to return to New York immediately. Steve Frank, chairman of WaMu's board, and David Bonderman also arrived to help. For the next ten days, the people in the WaMu camp would rarely leave the room. They were now trying to sell the bank. Even though WaMu was still considered well capitalized, the team began pulling together a plan to raise more money faster than the three months demanded by the OTS's enforcement order.

Fishman called Bair regularly, even if he really had nothing in particular to update her about. The group wanted to keep WaMu on the FDIC's radar and remind it that they were making progress. "His approach with her was very different than Kerry," said one WaMu executive. "He tried to actively engage her, and Kerry would look for reasons to avoid it." Said Fishman later: "I knew exactly what my job was. I knew that the OTS was going to favor WaMu and I knew Sheila was going to argue against it. So I said, 'Sheila, John's a really good guy,' and I said, 'John, she's a really bad person, go get her.'" The group tried to reach Bair, but she had gone camping with her family.

On Sunday, McMurray stumbled out of the Simpson Thacher skyscraper into daylight for the first time in three days to buy a couple of shirts at the nearby Banana Republic. The executives were staying at the St. Regis Hotel in Midtown, not far from the law offices, but the trip had been thrown together so quickly that no one had brought enough clothes.

The rush of New York City, which tapered off somewhat on Sunday, nonetheless continued as if nothing important were under way. Cabbies still honked, and tourists still wandered into and out of stores on Fifth Avenue. As darkness fell, a steady stream of employees left Lehman's headquarters, carrying boxes filled with their belongings.[20] The newspapers were reporting that the Wall Street bankers, holed up at the Fed, hadn't yet figured out a way to save Lehman. It seemed possible that the investment bank might file for bankruptcy protection later that night.

Monday, September 15

NET CHANGE IN WaMu's DEPOSIT BALANCE:

-$1.8 BILLION (INCLUDING SATURDAY, SEPTEMBER 13)

From the local news: *"We're keeping an eye on Washington Mutual. They survived today, but their stock plummeted after a horrible day on Wall Street. After the bankruptcy collapse of investment giant Lehman Brothers, after the last-minute purchase by Bank of America to save Merrill Lynch, after the announcement that the world's largest insurer, AIG, is now fighting for survival . . . All of it, experts say, can be blamed on rotten mortgage loans made over the years. And there may be more fallout to come."*

In San Francisco and in Seattle, the Federal Home Loan Banks watched WaMu closely. They provided about half of WaMu's liquidity through credit lines. While customers borrowed money from banks like WaMu, WaMu and other banks borrowed money from the Federal Home Loan Bank system. Throughout its rapid growth, WaMu had been split between two bank charters—one in Nevada, and one in Utah. The Nevada charter held most of WaMu's assets and fell under the jurisdiction of the Federal Home Loan Bank of San Francisco. WaMu borrowed money at the Federal Home Loan Bank of Seattle on the basis of the smaller Utah charter. To take out loans from both banks, WaMu pledged mortgages as collateral.

Because the San Francisco Home Loan Bank held the larger loan to WaMu, it was getting skittish. If WaMu failed, it would be left with a pile of mortgages and no one to pay back its loan. While the Seattle Bank was less concerned, both banks had switched how they administered WaMu's lines of credit. Usually, WaMu negotiated a new loan every several months, receiving a different rate each time. Now the Home Loan Banks were meeting with WaMu's treasury team every day to decide how much money to lend WaMu the following day; the amount was based on the value of its collateral—the mortgages. This was a much more uncertain way of doing things, because WaMu never knew what loan terms it would receive. An FDIC deputy in San Francisco called both Home Loan Banks to make sure they wouldn't pull WaMu's crucial loans.

For the first time since the spring, WaMu's online data room, chockfull of the bank's financial information, opened for suitors to peruse. In New York, Fishman and the investment bankers talked with Citigroup, TD Bank, Wells Fargo, Banco Santander, and JPMorgan, letting them know that WaMu was for sale. John Mahoney, WaMu's investment banking adviser from Goldman Sachs, spoke to Charlie Scharf at JPMorgan. We're interested, Scharf told him.

But six hours later Scharf called back. JPMorgan wouldn't make a bid after all. It would keep exploring the data room, however, and WaMu agreed to leave the data room open to placate the regulators. Scharf didn't offer an explanation as to his company's sudden lack of interest in WaMu. Later Michael Cavanagh, JPMorgan's chief financial officer, said that after spending some time in WaMu's data room, he concluded that the bank's numbers were too rosy. He expressed surprise that WaMu still thought it had equity value.[21] Its stock price had withered, wiping out its market capitalization, and its billions of dollars in mortgage assets were losing value rapidly. JPMorgan didn't think WaMu was worth nearly as much as it believed.

The WaMu camp had another suspicion: JPMorgan was waiting for a better deal.

Tuesday, September 16

NET CHANGE IN WAMU'S DEPOSIT BALANCE: –$2.4 BILLION

From the local news: *"I'm in front of WaMu's headquarters in Seattle . . . Lehman Brothers filed for bankruptcy yesterday, causing a huge slide for the Dow. What company will be next? Will that list include WaMu? WaMu has the same problem Lehman Brothers had—billions of dollars in bad mortgage debt."*

At the FDIC's headquarters in Washington, Fishman and John Robinson, WaMu's head of regulatory relations, sat across a conference table from Bair and one of her deputies. This was the first time Fishman had met Bair, and he had scheduled this time with her as a meet-and-greet. He was, after all, the new chief executive of WaMu. But the situation had moved far beyond simple introductions. That morning WaMu customers had awoken to news that the government would bail out giant insurer AIG with an $85 billion loan. Nothing made sense anymore. Only two days before, the government had allowed Lehman to fail, and now it was bailing out a company? Even those in the financial industry didn't understand what was going on. "It was like walking around a maze in the dark—you kept bumping into corners you didn't know were there," said one banking veteran later. Nor could the average person— WaMu's customer base—figure it out.

When Fishman had come on board just eight days earlier, he had viewed WaMu's condition as resembling that of a cancer patient. Now, just eight days later, WaMu was a cancer patient who had been hit by a bus on the way to chemotherapy. "The Lehman bankruptcy changed everything," Fishman said later. "Things began to unravel." Today WaMu's customers would pull a stunning $2.4 billion from the bank.

That morning Fishman arrived in Washington after taking an early flight from New York. Robinson had flown in the night before from Seattle. The two men walked over to the FDIC. They wanted to know from Bair what consequences WaMu might face if it missed the September 30 deadline that she had imposed the week before.

"What happens if we don't sell the bank or raise capital by then?" Fishman asked, after updating Bair and her deputy on the sale process. Bair reiterated that WaMu would be placed on the problem bank list.

She also told the two executives that more than one bank had called the FDIC and asked whether there would be an opportunity to buy WaMu as a distressed asset. The banks were wondering: Would the FDIC be closing WaMu? Because if the FDIC *did* close the bank, then WaMu, already on sale at a steep discount, would be even cheaper. It was the equivalent of a customer calling a department store to ask if a particular item was about to be marked down. Bair did not reveal the names of the parties that had called. She had instructed them to contact Fishman.

"That's appropriate," Fishman responded politely. "I'm happy to talk to whoever wants to talk about buying Washington Mutual. We appreciate you taking that position."

Fishman and Robinson walked out of the FDIC with greater clarity. Bair had imposed a strict deadline but also seemed to be helping them find a buyer. Still, Fishman wasn't reassured. He called the investment bankers in New York and told them to speed up the sale process.[22]

Fishman and Robinson next walked over to the OTS for a meeting with Reich and his deputy, Scott Polakoff. Fishman gave the two regulators the same update he had just provided Bair, telling them that WaMu had lined up meetings with potential buyers, and that the bank was also working on raising capital. Reich and Polakoff were firm but supportive.

They wanted Fishman to find a buyer or more capital by October 22, the day before WaMu's third-quarter earnings announcement.[23] Those earnings would almost certainly be awful. "Keep going," they encouraged Fishman. Reich and Polakoff recommended that Fishman meet with the board of governors of the Federal Reserve System. Fishman agreed. A meeting was scheduled for later that afternoon.

Meanwhile, a block away, the FDIC and the OTS met to settle their rating disagreement. WaMu's OTS examiners, Darrel Dochow and Ben Franklin, presented their view that WaMu deserved a rating of 3, not 4. WaMu could take action to save itself before a closure was considered. "Let our enforcement run its course," the examiners argued.[24]

The FDIC presented its much more dire view, a case that was becoming stronger by the day. Before, the main problem with WaMu had been its rotten mortgages. Now WaMu still had rotten mortgages, but it was also in the middle of a massive bank run. Also helping the FDIC's point of view was the OTS's reputation as a weak regulator, which IndyMac's failure had only reinforced. The OTS was losing bargaining power. Still, the agencies could not agree. "The knock-down, drag-out fight between them just kept going," said one close observer later. The FDIC told the OTS examiners that WaMu would be given a week to raise capital or sell itself, a deadline that one OTS regulator later described as "arbitrary." After that WaMu would land on the problem bank list. This deadline was tighter than the one Bair had earlier communicated to Fishman and Robinson.

One of Bair's deputies spent the day calling WaMu's suitors, asking them whether they would bid on WaMu as part of Fishman's private sale.[25] On the phone with buyers, the FDIC relayed yet another deadline: it wanted something worked out by Friday, September 26. It preferred, however, that WaMu be sold on the open market. When Bair's deputy reached Scharf at JPMorgan, Scharf told him that JPMorgan would look into it but didn't think it was possible. He didn't want the FDIC to think that JPMorgan would necessarily step in as the government's savior.[26]

Bair also called Jamie Dimon himself. She asked him if he would be interested in buying WaMu if the bank failed, in a way that wouldn't cost the FDIC's deposit insurance fund anything.* She needed a backup plan.

Maybe, Dimon told her. "Sheila Bair wanted JPMC to fix her problem," he later recalled.[27]

That afternoon Fishman and Robinson trooped over to the Fed for the previously scheduled meeting with Donald Kohn, the vice-chairman of the board of governors, and Randy Kroszner, a Fed governor who chaired the committee on supervision and regulation of banking institutions. The meeting was unusual. Although the Fed was in charge of regulating WaMu's holding company, it almost never got involved in the bank's day-to-day details. However, Kohn, a balding, bespectacled man, had fallen into the role of go-between in the battle between Bair and Reich. He had spent—and would spend—a lot of time on the phone and on e-mail playing the middleman between the two regulators. Fishman didn't know that Kohn played this role; all he knew was that Kohn could affect policy, and he needed politicians on his side. Washington State's two senators, Maria Cantwell and Patty Murray, both Democrats, had so far been absent from the fray.

As he had with the OTS and the FDIC, Fishman outlined his plans to sell WaMu or raise capital. He did so calmly and reasonably, never raising his voice or growing agitated. He knew he couldn't become emotional. He had to convince the Fed officials that he was a good steward of WaMu, since few in the government trusted anyone at the bank anymore. If he could do that, regulators might give him a chance to sell WaMu.

Kohn was skeptical of Fishman's plans. "Your stock's worth nothing," he pointed out. "Why do you think you're going to be able to sell the bank? The market has spoken."

Fishman explained that he believed in WaMu's intrinsic value, and that he just needed time to clean up the mortgage mess. The more

---

*In later interviews with WaMu's bankruptcy examiner, the FDIC disagreed with JPMorgan's recollection of the call, saying Bair encouraged JPMorgan to buy WaMu on the open market, not after a failure.

immediate crisis was the bank run. "Guys," Fishman said. "This is a simple problem. Change the FDIC insurance limit, and this problem goes away. The crisis goes away. When you do that, you'll stop the run here. Then I'll go back and do my work and deliver a terrific bank."

Fishman and other WaMu executives believed that if the government raised the deposit insurance limit by $100,000 to $200,000 or so, it would calm down customers who were pulling out their money. The move would send a message that the government did not tolerate bank runs. It would be symbolic more than anything else. This would not be the only time that WaMu executives pleaded with government officials and bank industry lobbyists to raise the insurance limit. Each time they did, they were told, in different words, that it was impossible.

At the Fed, Kohn interrupted Fishman's pitch. "I'm not sure that this is a company that deserves to survive," he said.

"Don't miss the big picture," Fishman responded emphatically. "The big picture is, we are Main Street. WaMu is the symbolic problem on Main Street."

"You are persuasive," Kohn replied. He thought for a moment. "Here's what I promise you," he said. "I will be on the phone whenever you call, and we will be in the process moving forward." Then he added: "You're thinking about it right."

Fishman left the meeting encouraged. "I have someone who will listen to me," he thought to himself.

Wednesday, September 17

NET CHANGE IN WAMU'S DEPOSIT BALANCE: –$2 BILLION

From the local news: *"It is clear that Washington Mutual is a company on life support . . . The bank that was founded to help rebuild Seattle after the great fire, well, it may be sold at fire-sale prices."*

In the early hours of the morning, Brian Mueller lay awake in bed, staring up at the ceiling. He couldn't sleep. Thoughts of the last few days, spent watching money fly out of WaMu, tumbled through his head. He turned over and grabbed his cell phone from the nightstand. In the dark, he flipped open the phone, and the small frame of light revealed the deposit text message that had just come through. "Oh, no," he thought. Hundreds of millions of dollars had already left WaMu that morning. The run was getting worse.

All across the country, customers streamed into hundreds of WaMu branches, on edge, brimming with questions. This run was nothing like July's, which had been tame by comparison. Now people were frenzied, acting purely out of fear. "We just didn't have any control," said one branch manager. The tellers' talking points no longer placated the customers—even the tellers didn't understand them. "They kept telling us to say that we have $44 billion, whatever that meant," said one employee, likely referencing WaMu's liquidity position. The customers demanded to talk to whoever was in charge. At one Seattle location, they lined up and waited all day to speak to the branch manager. "Should I take my money out?" they asked her when they reached her, over and over again. "Is WaMu going under?" And they asked the inevitable question: "What would *you* do?"

The branch manager, who knew most of the people's names and their kids, would say, "I don't know any more than you do. But if you're uncomfortable, do what makes you sleep at night." She wasn't sleeping, either. "You went to work and you got hammered," the branch manager said later. "By the end of the day, you were exhausted. And you didn't know if you had a job, or what was going on." WaMu headquarters told the branches repeatedly that everything was fine, but the news reports and the blogs and the stories posted on Facebook all said otherwise. "You told the customers something, and then they watched the news, and then they would come back," the branch manager said. Many took their money out anyway. On the other side of her branch, the manager could see another line forming. Those customers were waiting to see a financial adviser to liquidate their investments. The Dow had plunged 449 points that morning, its second-worst trading day of the year.

Many customers were perplexed to receive a cashier's check from the teller, rather than an actual stack of money. They didn't know that banks didn't keep that much cash on hand, and they didn't trust a piece of paper. "What makes you think that piece of paper is okay?" they would ask. The tellers would point out that a third-party vendor—not WaMu—had approved the funds. The bank again offered its certificate of deposit with a 5 percent rate. But few customers paid attention. Every day Brinks Security trucks pulled up to all of WaMu's thousands of ATMs across the country with a replenishment of cash. The trucks would typically deliver about $30 million nationwide each day. Now they dropped off as much as $250 million.[28]

At least half of the customers who pulled out their money were covered up to $100,000; this defied the Break the Bank scenario that WaMu's treasury department had put together over the summer. "We thought, by then, that people knew about deposit insurance," said one of Mueller's coworkers. "It turns out they still didn't." Or they did know but didn't care. Mueller was bowling after work when a member of his league confessed, guiltily, to closing his family's WaMu accounts, even though they had far less than $100,000 in the bank. "Your money is insured," Mueller said, trying to reason with him. "We just don't want to deal with it," his friend replied. They had seen what happened at IndyMac. Another of Mueller's friends gave a different reason for pulling his money from WaMu. "He told me he thought the stock price was related to how much money the bank had," Mueller said later, incredulously. (The day before, Suze Orman had told viewers on her popular television show that the leading indicator of a bank failure is its stock price declining.) But before long, even Mueller was tempted to pull his money out, even though his checking account balance was insured. He wasn't the only WaMu employee thinking that way. Some lined up for their money right along with the customers.

Some customers were apologetic; they had banked with WaMu for years or even decades. One woman brought in a homemade cake to her tellers at a branch in Orange County, with "We love you, WaMu" spelled out in the frosting.[29] She then withdrew $20,000. Another customer at a branch in Southern California closed her accounts and returned the next day with a freshly baked peach cobbler for the branch's staff. She didn't bring her money back, though.

The WaMu deposit team started each day at a sprint and maintained that pace until late in the evening. Executives demanded deposit reports by 7:00 a.m. instead of 9:00 a.m., requiring team managers to arrive at work by 6:00 a.m. The deposit tracking team played a morbid game, each morning writing numbers on a giant whiteboard. The numbers represented each team member's guess of how much money WaMu would lose that day. "Even the people with all the data sometimes couldn't come up with a guess that was any more accurate than someone's gut feeling," said one of the team members.

One of the managers in charge of WaMu's liquidity sent out an e-mail to his staff with the subject line "Think Happy Thoughts."[30]

"It's going to be ugly out there today and over the next several weeks, but when in doubt, repeat after me: '$50 billion dollars!'" The manager wanted to remind his group about the bank's still-strong liquidity position. "WaMu is going to come out the other end of this craziness in great shape," he wrote.

That e-mail, which was leaked to the local papers, rallied employees briefly, but it was hard to think happy thoughts after *The New York Times* reported that WaMu was up for sale and looking for bids from other banks.[31] TPG announced that it was lifting the provision, tied to its private equity infusion, that would have made it hard for WaMu to sell itself. Only Fishman, his executive team, and the WaMu board knew the details of the planned sale, but now it was clear to employees as well. "At that point, you ultimately know you're going to get sold to Chase or someone else," said one employee. "What's the point?"

At the end of the day, Bair called Fishman and told him of a new deadline: "You have to find a buyer by this weekend."[32]

She didn't have to say what might happen if Fishman wasn't able to find one.

Thursday, September 18

NET CHANGE IN WAMU'S DEPOSIT BALANCE: –$2.8 BILLION

From the local news: *"Today, in an exclusive interview, a Washington Mutual executive told us there is no sale or bailout planned. He says customers shouldn't worry about their money."*

In New York, Fishman and his team spent every waking minute on the phone with bank chief executives, or their executives in charge of mergers and acquisitions, or those banks' advisers, or anyone related to a possible sale of WaMu. They hardly slept and barely ate. These circumstances weren't at all unusual—most of Wall Street, at that moment, wasn't sleeping or eating. Someone had to stay and run the actual bank. That task had fallen to Rotella. He regretted being left behind.

Rotella received daily updates from Fishman and Casey, but mostly he was trying to manage the largest bank run any thrift had suffered since the 1930s. Each day Rotella updated an internal blog he had started a year earlier, as a way of reaching employees across the country. The blog got a lot of traffic, and it sometimes grew heated. At one point, the comment section devolved into bickering over gay rights, fueled by outrageous comments from WaMu's southern employees.

On the blog today, however, Rotella posted a pointed plea to employees. "This is an incredibly difficult time for everyone here at WaMu," he wrote.[33] "Beyond that, what is occurring in our industry and the broad global economy is unprecedented.

"Hard as it is, it seems to me that we all have a choice—join the rumor cycle, speculate and buy into a cycle that is just creating more concerns, or get back to work and focus on doing all we can for our customers, which is all we can do for the company, ourselves, and our colleagues.

"My request is, let's take the latter path and control what we can control and don't succumb to the former."

No one on the deposit-tracking team thought it could possibly get worse when WaMu lost $2.4 billion in one day. But today it would lose nearly $3 billion in deposits, three times the size of the entire IndyMac run. *In just one day.* The bank released a letter, signed by Fishman, who had not made a single public statement since arriving on board a week and a half earlier. The letter would be handed out to customers in WaMu's 2,200 branches around the country.

"When I was recently approached about the opportunity to lead this great company," Fishman's letter read, "I did my homework to satisfy myself that WaMu has the capital, the liquidity, and the business plan to serve your needs and protect your money through these challenging times.

"I came to WaMu because I think it is a great bank with a strong franchise and a solid financial position. We take very seriously our role as the stewards of your hard-earned money."[34]

The communications team had been begging management to produce someone, anyone, to speak to the ravenous members of the press. An information lockdown had initially seemed like a good idea, but now the communications team felt it was only fueling rumors. The bank delivered Ken Kido, the head of WaMu's retail bank. The plan was to station Kido inside a WaMu branch in downtown Seattle and invite a small, select group of local reporters to interview him. National media wouldn't be invited, since those reporters tended to be more unpredictable and less likely to follow the rules. Journalists would not be allowed to ask Kido whether his bank was up for sale.

At first, the decision seemed a good one. Kido, in a suit, stood confidently in the middle of the warmly lit WaMu branch lobby. The first television news team trained a camera on him. He got going, speaking in clipped sentences, sticking to the message. WaMu was hoping this broadcast would help calm customers. A reporter asked Kido, "What do you say to the customers who wake up and read these headlines? *The Seattle Times* reads, 'WaMu Scrambles to Stay Alive.' The *PI* boldly proclaims, 'WaMu for Sale.'"

"Thanks for asking," Kido replied with a half-smile. "We welcome our customers to come in, and they are coming in, and we're taking care of them . . ."

The interview continued until a commotion near the doorway interrupted it. The communications team members, who had been hovering around the journalists waiting to interview Kido, broke the protective barrier, surrounded Kido, whisked him away from the TV cameras, and shuttled him toward the branch door. Someone mumbled something about his need to get back to a meeting. Within seconds, he was gone. The journalists looked at each other, perplexed. After Kido left, WaMu's communications team revealed what had happened: a national TV station had tried to crash the interview. The team had staged the episode in order to project a bank that had matters under control. Instead, everyone left more convinced that, actually, things weren't under control at all. The team just couldn't rein in the story.

The bank run finally bridged the divide between the OTS and the FDIC. After so many weeks, and under pressure from the FDIC, the OTS agreed to downgrade WaMu to 4. It was now, officially, a troubled bank. It would become much more difficult for WaMu to borrow money from its own lenders, and this would put it in an even more precarious situation. One OTS official recalled thinking, for the first time, that WaMu might fail.[35]

Friday, September 19

NET CHANGE IN WAMU'S DEPOSIT BALANCE: –$1.3 BILLION

From the local news: *"It could be the largest bailout ever, potentially leaving taxpayers on the hook for more than a trillion dollars."*

John Reich and Scott Polakoff flew from Washington to New York for back-to-back meetings with the banks interested in acquiring WaMu.[36] The OTS officials wanted to hear for themselves whether any of these banks actually planned to make an offer. Afterward they walked away from the meetings with an assessment similar to that of Fishman and his team, who by this time had met with all the banks as well.

The WaMu executives thought they had the best chance of selling WaMu to either Citigroup or Santander, Spain's largest bank.* (When the *Financial Times* broke the news that WaMu was talking to Santander,[37] customers showed up at WaMu branches even more concerned. "People thought these Mexican banks were going to buy us—it was in the paper," recalled one branch manager.) Fishman favored Santander. He had dealt with its executives as part of the sale of Independence Community Bank several years earlier. Santander had bought a 20 percent stake in

---

*There is speculation as to whether JPMorgan and Santander agreed not to compete with each other when bidding on U.S. banks during the financial crisis. The speculation arises largely from a June 2008 e-mail sent by a JPMorgan executive, summarizing a meeting between Dimon and Santander's chairman. WaMu, Wachovia, Suntrust, and PNC were among the possible acquisitions discussed by the two executives. "We covered them in detail and Jamie reckoned that these are opportunities in which JPMorgan would also be interested," the e-mail read. "It is important to have an open dialogue with them as Santander would not pursue any one of these opportunities if JPMorgan were to do the same (can't compete on price with JPMorgan for an acquisition in the USA). But Santander would probably hire JPMorgan as an advisor if we are not going after them." A later report by the independent examiner hired in the bankruptcy of WaMu's holding company dismissed claims of bid-rigging between the two companies.

Sovereign, helping fund the purchase of Independence.[38] Fishman spent all hours of the night on the phone with Santander in Spain, trying to hash something out. The discussions seemed promising. Santander was healthier than Citigroup, and the Spanish bank didn't have a large presence in the United States. If it bought WaMu, it would be likely to keep the bank's operations intact. Not as many WaMu employees—particularly at headquarters—would lose their jobs.

Citigroup was also interested in WaMu (or "Project Dolphin" as the company had nicknamed it), calling the bank "very attractive" in a presentation circulated just that morning. But Citigroup was planning a WaMu purchase assuming that it would be seized by the government and placed into receivership. In that case, Citigroup was hoping the government would pitch in money to cover some of WaMu's mortgage losses. Even so, Citigroup would have to raise $15 billion to buy the bank.[39]

TD Bank from Canada and Wells Fargo seemed less interested than the others. But Goldman, WaMu's investment banking adviser, thought the FDIC's demand wasn't unreasonable—a deal could be put together by the weekend.[40] Goldman wasn't sure how much Fishman and his team would get for WaMu. Goldman was hoping for several dollars a share, a shockingly low amount for a bank with $310 billion in assets. The shareholders, at least, would not be wiped out completely.

Reich and Polakoff also met with JPMorgan at the bank's Park Avenue headquarters, but at the end of the hour-long discussion, the two government officials were fairly certain the bank would not be making Fishman an offer.[41] They were right. Later that afternoon Charlie Scharf called the FDIC. He had just made a presentation, by teleconference, to JPMorgan's board of directors on the two Project West acquisition scenarios. One was the private sale; the other was the purchase of WaMu from the FDIC, after the agency closed the bank. Scharf noted the pros and cons of each purchase. JPMorgan couldn't, for example, predict the amount of deposits WaMu would lose in its bank run, and the company wasn't sure how flexible the FDIC might be in negotiating a deal.[42] The benefits of buying WaMu after it failed far outweighed the benefits of buying it before. Among them, listed in Scharf's board report, were: "No shareholder approval" and "Close immediately" and

"Significantly less capital required."[43] Scharf called Jim Wigand, Bair's deputy in charge of the FDIC's Resolutions and Receiverships Division. Scharf told Wigand that JPMorgan was not interested in buying WaMu on the open market.

"We don't know if Washington Mutual will fail," Wigand responded carefully. "However, they're in liquidity distress, so there is a possibility. If it does, we want to get your reaction to the way we would do this. We want to have a discussion with you."

Wigand had a list of all the banks that Fishman had contacted and that were combing through WaMu's data room. As each of those banks called the FDIC to say it wasn't interested in buying WaMu, Wigand told it about the possibility of WaMu's failure and a purchase from the FDIC.

Neither Fishman nor the OTS knew for sure that the FDIC had begun to shop WaMu around, although Fishman and his advisers suspected it. While the secretive process is normal, as the FDIC prepares for a potential bank failure, the move put Fishman at a disadvantage. In New York, he and his team were trying to sell WaMu in a normal fashion, at a cheap price that would at least fetch shareholders something. In Washington, the FDIC was telling those same bidders that WaMu might fail, opening the potential for buying it at an even bigger discount. Theoretically, the FDIC's process should not influence a bank's efforts to sell itself or raise capital. But in a high-level situation, in which the country's largest thrift is at stake, the risk of that influence is much higher.

In Washington, Scott Gaspard, the WaMu executive in charge of government and industry relations, got a call from one of Reich's deputies. Gaspard had recently met with congressional staffers of the Senate Banking Committee to update them on WaMu's condition. The reception had been chilly.

"The FDIC said it doesn't want you on the Hill anymore," the OTS deputy told Gaspard. "You're frozen, Scott."

At the Treasury Department, Secretary Paulson strode on stage for an early press conference, cameras flashing, the room packed with journalists. At the podium, he looked out briefly across the room and attempted a joke. "Good morning everyone," he said. "Hope you got a lot of sleep last night." There was little laughter, and Paulson launched directly into his speech. He told the room that the government needed to spend "hundreds of billions of dollars" to buy up bad mortgages and other distressed debt from financial institutions across the country.[44]

"The financial security of all Americans—their retirement savings, their home values, their ability to borrow for college, and the opportunities for more and higher-paying jobs—depends on our ability to restore our financial institutions to a sound footing," Paulson said.[45]

Paulson would need the backing of Congress to make the Troubled Asset Relief Program a reality.

Saturday, September 20

NET CHANGE IN WAMU'S DEPOSIT BALANCE:
-$1.2 BILLION (INCLUDING MONDAY, SEPTEMBER 22)

From the local news: *"Another restless weekend for the Treasury Department and members of Congress as they try to come up with a comprehensive plan to put an end to the country's worst financial crisis since the Great Depression . . . Washington Mutual says it's encouraged by the direction of the plan."*

Around the world, banks large and small were borrowing from the Federal Reserve's discount window, a sign of the panic spreading in financial institutions everywhere, not just at WaMu. Usually banks tap the Fed only in an emergency. But during the first week in September, banks borrowed a collective $19 *billion*, compared with an average of less than $50 *million* a week in prior years.[46] The borrowing volume continued to grow after the collapse of Lehman Brothers and the government bailout of AIG. Some of the largest borrowers were companies that weren't in the headlines at all. Right after the government forced Fannie Mae and Freddie Mac into conservatorship, U.S. Bancorp, another large consumer bank like WaMu, took out a $3.4 billion overnight loan. It was the largest amount of money borrowed from the Fed during that time.[47]

The Fed was encouraging banks to get over the stigma associated with borrowing, and to access money if they needed it. WaMu had been borrowing through a new Fed program called the Term Auction Facility (TAF), which allowed banks to bid on available credit.

Now WaMu tapped the Fed's discount window for the first time, borrowing $2 billion, an amount it would roll over for the next several days.* The bank had $9.2 billion left on its credit line, wrote WaMu's deputy treasurer, Peter Freilinger, in an e-mail updating the OTS on the bank's liquidity.[48] But the negative grades from the rating agencies and now the downgrade by the federal regulators made the bank an unpopular candidate for any loan. "We do not believe fresher window advances will be forthcoming until a deal is signed," Freilinger wrote in his e-mail.

Meanwhile, the Federal Home Loan Bank of San Francisco had grown increasingly antsy. It was considering slashing the value of the mortgages backing WaMu's line of credit. That meant WaMu would get less, and perhaps a lot less—30 cents on the dollar, for example—for its collateral. The Home Loan Bank was evaluating the mortgages, to determine the extent of the cut. WaMu still had $7 billion available at the San Francisco bank, including $1 billion that WaMu planned to tap on Monday. "Beyond that," Freilinger wrote, "we are concerned that FHLB SF may not extend further advances." The Home Loan Bank of Seattle was decidedly less nervous. WaMu still had a $4 billion credit line available there. WaMu's total liquidity stood at $28 billion, or about 9 percent of its assets.

WaMu's survival depended on the severity of the bank run. If customers kept pulling out as much as $2.8 billion a day, WaMu might make it only another week. If deposit outflows slowed, that would give the bank more time. If not, "we'd probably tip on Monday, September 29," Freilinger wrote, citing the worst-case scenario.

Rotella, who was copied on the e-mail from Freilinger, forwarded it to Freilinger's boss with a note. "Uh, did we need to use the tip language with the OTS?"

The tenor of the FDIC's calls to the Federal Home Loan Banks in Seattle and San Francisco changed. Before, the FDIC had been pleading with the banks to keep their lines of credit open to WaMu. Now the

---

*At least one later report showed WaMu borrowing a total of $6 billion, but the bank was repaying the Fed loan each night and taking it out again the next day. Its Fed borrowings were relatively small compared with those of some other institutions.

FDIC told the banks that they wouldn't have to hold on much longer. The situation would soon be resolved.

In Washington, Reich and Bair both watched WaMu's liquidity, but now Bair had a different concern. Morgan Stanley was facing its own set of problems, and Bair had heard that JPMorgan might step in to buy the company. If that happened, JPMorgan almost certainly wouldn't bid for WaMu. And that might leave Bair in a situation reminiscent of IndyMac.

She e-mailed Dimon at JPMorgan. "Just cking in," she wrote. "Hear others may be seeking your help."[49] But Dimon and his team weren't really interested in Morgan Stanley. They wanted to reserve their buying power for WaMu.[50]

Bair also typed out a conciliatory e-mail to Reich, noting the end of the long feud between the two regulators and their agencies.

"Glad we are all working toward the same end," she wrote. "Many thanks for your efforts."[51] (Reich had once said about Bair, after she complimented the OTS on a presentation about WaMu: "I would like to think she meant it, but I'm always a bit skeptical of her compliments.")[52]

That evening in Seattle, Rotella, dressed for the occasion, sat with his wife and several other WaMu managers at the opening season preview performance of the Pacific Northwest Ballet. The Rotellas were sponsors of the black-tie event, held at a hall adjacent to the Space Needle. They had long supported the arts. Rotella's phone rang just as the performance was about to begin. A relieved Tom Casey was on the line from New York.

"We have a verbal offer from Santander," Casey said. The Spanish bank would be bringing the formal offer to its board for approval that day, he told Rotella. "They're going to pay $10 billion for the company."

The amount stung, even if it was about what the executives had been expecting. But at least WaMu wouldn't fail—that was the important thing.

Rotella hung up, cautiously relieved. Fishman, in just a few days, had found a buyer for WaMu.

In New York, Fishman sat at the conference table in the offices of

Simpson Thacher, glancing out the window at the nighttime skyline. That day Paulson and his team had released the details of the country's largest-ever financial bailout. The U.S. Treasury was asking for a stunning $700 billion to halt the crisis. The government's outline of the plan totaled just three pages. "This is a big package, because it was a big problem," President Bush had said at the White House.[53]

In the last several days, a thought had kept running through Fishman's head: "The world is losing its mind." It was late, and probably time to call it a night. He didn't expect to hear anything else from Santander until the next day. He looked around the table and noticed something strange. Casey and McMurray were still there, huddled over paperwork, but Fishman's advisers from Goldman Sachs and Morgan Stanley were nowhere to be found. For the last week, the two bankers had hardly left the room. Fishman realized that both men were off dealing with their own firms' massive problems. The next day both Goldman and Morgan Stanley would make the extraordinary move of filing to become bank holding companies to bolster their financial positions. The newspapers would proclaim the end of modern Wall Street.[54]

At this moment, Fishman felt a strong sense of his place in the unfolding crisis. He sat in a quiet, dark room with few people around.

Sunday, September 21

From the local news: *"Washington Mutual is keeping up talks with potential buyers in hopes of striking a deal in the next few days."*

Alberto Sanchez, the head of Santander's Consumer Finance Group in the United States, called Fishman with some bad news. Santander's board had met and decided not to approve an acquisition of WaMu. It was too rushed, particularly in light of everything going on, he told Fishman. Santander also wanted government assistance in the form of a $26 billion cap on mortgage losses.[55]

The deal that Fishman and the WaMu camp considered the most likely had disappeared. Later one European financial investor observed: "European banks were reluctant to get involved in any U.S. bank—they had sort of a theoretical appetite, but somehow didn't have the guts."

At close to 11:00 p.m., Jim Wigand, the FDIC official in charge of WaMu's sale process, got a call at home. Edward "Ned" Kelly, the head of global banking for Citigroup, was on the phone. Over the weekend, Citigroup executives had debated whether to bid on WaMu in Fishman's private auction. They kept coming up with reasons not to do so. The biggest impediment was WaMu's portfolio of bad loans. "Bad economic deal no matter how you cut it," the co-head of Citigroup's mergers and acquisitions team wrote in an e-mail.[56]

Once Kelly had Wigand on the phone, the Citigroup executive explained, "We can't make a transaction work. I was told I should contact you."

Wigand launched into the speech that he had, by this time, delivered to JPMorgan, Wells Fargo, Santander, and TD Bank. *If* WaMu failed, would Citigroup be interested in buying the bank from the government? Kelly agreed to meet with Wigand the next day to hear the FDIC's pitch.

Citigroup was the last of the banks Wigand had been waiting to hear from. The sale process for WaMu had now shifted. Although Fishman didn't yet know it, his auction had ended, and the FDIC's had begun in earnest.

Monday, September 22

Net change in WaMu's deposit balance:
-$1.2 billion (including Saturday, September 20)

From the local news: *"The government hasn't yet released details on whether Washington Mutual is on its bailout list. But tonight the list of companies bidding for WaMu continues to grow."*

The next morning Wigand and two other FDIC officials stood in front of a full conference room of JPMorgan executives at the bank's headquarters in New York. The attendance was larger than the FDIC had been expecting. Scharf was there, as were other members of the Project West team. Dimon dropped by for part of the meeting.[57]

"Thanks for coming on such short notice," Wigand began. "We're doing some contingency planning, and as everyone knows,

Washington Mutual is in a state of distress. We don't know if it's going to fail, but in the event that the FDIC does move in, we want to talk to you about it."

For the next hour, the FDIC walked the JPMorgan executives through the bid process, explaining the type of offer the agency would seek. The FDIC had come up with five possible bid structures, all of which assumed the buyer would take on all of WaMu's bad loans. The FDIC would not provide any money to help absorb the losses. In each scenario, WaMu's shareholders and TPG would be wiped out completely.

"Is Washington Mutual going to be resolved by the weekend?" one of the JPMorgan executives called out.

"I don't know," Wigand said.*

"Well, we need to be doing our own resource planning. Should we be thinking about this sooner or later?"

"Well, given its liquidity stress, you may want to think about that sooner [rather] than later."

The explanations continued throughout the day. Wigand and the other FDIC officials went from back-to-back meetings with Citigroup, Wells Fargo, and Santander, explaining the FDIC's bidding process.[58]

As Wigand traveled back and forth across Midtown, Moody's issued a press release. The agency had decided to downgrade WaMu's financial strength to its lowest possible grade, a move that S&P would soon follow. When Moody's made its decision, it considered that WaMu might fail. The rating agency had learned of this possibility the previous week at a meeting with JPMorgan. In the normal course of events, JPMorgan had had to let the rating agencies know that it might be buying another company. The bank told Moody's that it was considering a purchase of WaMu from the FDIC. After hearing that, Moody's became even more worried.[59]

---

*In a later interview with WaMu's bankruptcy examiner, Scharf disagreed with this recollection of the meeting. He recalled that Wigand was much more definitive, telling executives that the agency planned to close WaMu on Friday, September 26, and bids would be due September 24. Scharf's board presentation from September 19, in which he discussed a purchase of WaMu from the FDIC, also reflects a September 26 closure date.

"Although Moody's believes that the U.S. Treasury's $700 billion asset purchase program has the potential to restore confidence in U.S. banks, benefits of the program to WaMu are uncertain in the short-term," Moody's wrote in its release.[60] "WaMu's troubled asset portfolios are sizeable in relation to its capital base." In other words, WaMu might lose so much money on its bad loans that the bailout might not even help. Moody's also worried that the government money would come too late. Paulson was trying to win over Congress, but it was unclear whether he could convince lawmakers to accept his plan.

All day JPMorgan executives tried to get more financial information from WaMu, but they could no longer log into the online data room. They kept getting an error message: "Your rights have changed. This item or action is no longer available to you. Please click 'close' to continue working."[61]

"I have checked and other Intralinks data rooms to which I have access are working," wrote one JPMorgan executive to Scharf and three other executives on the Project West team, "so it does not appear to be an Intralinks issue. Could be for a number of reasons, most of which are harmless."

"This is no accident," one executive replied.

By that night, the JPMorgan executives had learned from WaMu's investment bankers that no more information would be forthcoming unless Scharf called Fishman personally and explained why it was necessary. The JPMorgan executives became frustrated enough about the data room problem that one of them e-mailed Wigand at the FDIC.

"We will try to get the information," Wigand replied. "Let me know if you have any more access problems."

Fishman was indeed stonewalling JPMorgan. The New York bank wanted to gather financial information about WaMu even though executives had already said they wouldn't bid in Fishman's auction. If that were the case, why did the company still need WaMu's financial data? "I was trying to torture them—to smoke them out," Fishman said later. "They're torturing me, I'm torturing them. Everyone thinks we're kind of muttonheads. You're playing a weak hand, the world's coming to an end, and you're trying to run an auction on a bank when no one knows where the bottom is. So you torture people."

Tuesday, September 23

NET CHANGE IN WAMU'S DEPOSIT BALANCE: –$600 MILLION

From the local news: *"The end may be near for Seattle-based Washington Mutual as we know it."*

At WaMu's headquarters, Brian Mueller's Excel programs provided a welcome measure of relief. The bank run had slowed. The first signs that customers weren't quite as frantic appeared over the weekend and continued into Monday, despite Moody's dash of horrible WaMu news. Now it looked as if WaMu was coming out of the run, just as it had done in July, after IndyMac. The bubble had peaked four days earlier, on Thursday, when customers pulled out $2.8 billion.

At about 1:00 p.m. Eastern Time, the FDIC sent out its official e-mail to potential bidders for WaMu, inviting them to make an offer on the bank. "The FDIC is offering select financial institutions, such as yours, the opportunity to bid on a financial institution." To find out more, potential bidders clicked into the FDIC's own data room on WaMu. There they could access a lengthy explanation of the process. "Potential acquirers are permitted and encouraged to submit multiple bids. The Corporation will select the most cost-effective bids for the FDIC." By law, the FDIC had to choose the offer that represented the least cost to the deposit insurance fund. Bids on WaMu were due the following evening, September 24, by 6:00 p.m. Eastern Time.[62]

The JPMorgan Project West team began speculating about the competition. The bank had to start thinking how much it would pay for WaMu from the government, and that would depend in large part on who else might be interested.

"TD still in West process," e-mailed one executive, referencing TD Bank. "Any of you think they post?"[63]

"Yes."

"How aggressive do you think they'd be? Wld be huge capital raise. 10–20bn common."

"This would be the 'low risk' deal to catapult them ahead of RBC to be Canada's largest company + plays to their retail power alley. I don't [*sic*] 10 is a problem, 20 starts to get big."

At the OTS, one of Reich's deputies instructed Darrel Dochow, WaMu's main regulator in Seattle, to prepare a Supervisory Report on WaMu, known as the "S" report.[64] The report details the reasons a federal agency has chosen to close a bank. The deputy told Dochow that a deal was being negotiated with JPMorgan.*

On Capitol Hill, Senator Maria Cantwell (D-Wash.) cornered Paulson before a congressional hearing to ask about WaMu. Cantwell had twice tried to reach the treasury secretary. He hadn't returned her calls. Now, as rumors swirled about WaMu's fate, she reminded him that the bank had adequate capital and liquidity. "I know all this," Paulson answered hurriedly.[65]

Paulson's pitch to lawmakers to approve his $700 billion bailout plan was not going well. His hours-long testimony to the Senate Banking Committee had been met with skepticism. "After reading this proposal, I can only conclude that it is not only our economy that is at risk, Mr. Secretary, but our Constitution, as well," said Senator Chris Dodd, the Democratic chair of the committee. Senator Jim Bunning, a Republican from Kentucky, said the plan would "take Wall Street's pain and spread it to the taxpayers." He added, "It's financial socialism and it's un-American."[66]

Cantwell also tracked down Bair and told the FDIC chairman that she didn't understand why regulators would take action against WaMu when the government anticipated legislation that would help all the banks. "Whatever you do better be clear and transparent," Cantwell told Bair.†

In New York, the WaMu conference room in the law offices of Simpson Thacher had grown quiet. No more bidders were tramping through, listening to Fishman's pitch for a WaMu purchase. None of the bankers called anymore, and Fishman and his team couldn't get anyone on the phone. The WaMu team suspected that the FDIC had initiated its own secretive sales process for WaMu, and that this was why bankers who had shown such interest only days earlier were now

---

*This conversation might have occurred the previous day.
†Cantwell's conversation with Bair may have happened on another day during the week of September 21.

ignoring them. If that was the case, the FDIC could be planning to seize the bank as early as the coming Friday. The agency always planned takeovers on Fridays, as it could then spend the weekend transferring the failed bank to the new company's systems, minimizing disruptions to customers.

In between the frenzied talks of the last week, Fishman and his team had come up with a detailed capital-raising plan—the "Go It Alone" proposal, as the WaMu camp called it—in case, for some reason, the bank couldn't find a buyer. Regulators still considered WaMu well capitalized.

On a conference call with Bair at the FDIC, Reich at the OTS, and Kohn at the Fed, Fishman and the investment bankers went over a plan that would raise about $19 billion. The cornerstone of the plan involved converting some of WaMu's debt to equity, a move that would increase the bank's capital by $13 billion. WaMu also planned to move $4 billion of cash from WaMu's holding company into the bank, boosting the bank's liquidity in the face of the bank run.[67]

Fishman and the investment bankers believed the first two actions alone would help stabilize WaMu, but they also floated some other ideas. They could sell WaMu's branches in New York and New Jersey, and about $30 billion in deposits, to TD Bank. The Canadian financial institution wanted to expand its presence on the East Coast. TD Bank would also give WaMu access to a $5 billion line of credit for the next year and a half. WaMu proposed asking the Treasury to provide a $20 billion loan, in return for a 79.9 percent ownership stake. WaMu would also sell the government a bulk of its bad loans under the proposed bailout.

The regulators asked several detailed questions about WaMu's proposal but didn't seem entirely enthusiastic. The FDIC believed WaMu's projections were optimistic.

Kohn at the Fed asked, "Do you expect us to do all of this to overwhelm the economic destruction that the board and management created?"

Fishman didn't miss a beat. "Yes. You should do that. For the good of the country, these guys ought to be saved."

The speakerphone fell silent.

"We'll think about it," Kohn replied.

Wednesday, September 24

Net change in WaMu's deposit balance: –$400 million

From the local news: *"The proposed $700 billion bailout could help Seattle-based Washington Mutual."*

At 11:30 a.m. Eastern Time, Charlie Scharf, by teleconference, presented to JPMorgan's board of directors the proposal to buy WaMu from the FDIC.[68] Scharf's slide show noted that a WaMu/JPMorgan combination would create a company with about 5,400 bank branches nationwide and $900 billion in deposits.[69] JPMorgan would hold the most deposits of any bank in the country. Scharf's presentation pointed out JPMorgan's extensive research into WaMu, including during the spring. The bank estimated that over the life of the WaMu purchase, it would lose $36 billion on WaMu's mortgages. The JPMorgan board approved the purchase.

From Simpson Thacher's offices in New York, Fishman and board chairman Steve Frank composed a letter to Reich, Bair, and Kohn. A follow-up to the conversation of the previous evening, it was also the executives' last, desperate attempt to save WaMu. By now, Fishman and his team were almost certain that the regulators planned to move in on Friday. Their phones remained silent.

"The stakes are very high," Fishman and Frank wrote to the regulators.[70] "Washington Mutual is the sixth-largest depository institution in the United States, with $310 billion in assets and 25 million households in every part of the country. WaMu serves the needs of ordinary Americans. Its assets consist almost entirely of mortgages, home equity loans, and credit card advances to U.S. homeowners and consumers. It has no CDOs, complex derivatives, or other esoteric financial instruments.* WaMu employs more than 43,000 employees in over 2,300 branches spread throughout the country. Over 6,500 of those employees are located in Seattle, where WaMu is one of the major employers and a major supporter of the community.

"As shown in the presentation we sent you, WaMu's deposit levels

---

*This was true, although WaMu had contemplated establishing a CDO business, as detailed earlier in this book. It's unclear if Fishman was aware of that attempt.

have fluctuated in response to two 'headline' events of the last several months—the IndyMac failure in mid-July and the Lehman bankruptcy/AIG collapse last week. Deposit outflows later stabilized and reversed after IndyMac, and we believe the same stabilization trend is occurring again now."

Fishman and Frank outlined the details of the recapitalization plan they had presented the night before.

"We urge you to let us implement this plan," they wrote. "Its completion will produce a well-capitalized competitor able to serve the needs of ordinary Americans across the country. WaMu will also be well-positioned to take further steps, including sales of higher-risk assets to private investors and branch sales, to provide even greater strength. We have already had discussions with private investors on the former and at least one international bank on the latter. Finally, WaMu will be well-positioned to raise additional capital or find a merger partner once market conditions stabilize.

"In contrast, the seizure of WaMu would represent a further destabilizing event in the financial markets, adversely affecting the deposit bases and share prices of many other financial institutions—as has already happened so often this year. With an institution as large and complex as WaMu—having nearly 3,000 domestic locations, 5,300 ATMs, 5 million online customers and $600 billion in mortgages serviced—the risk of major disruptions to operations and customer service [is] extremely high. The impact on depositors and markets everywhere will be especially dramatic because WaMu's capital ratios exceed, by billions of dollars, the requirements for well-capitalized banks. The seizure by the FDIC of a large, well-capitalized U.S. banking organization is without precedent in U.S. history and will send a stark message to bank customers and investors.

"We think there is no reason to take such a drastic step when our proposal would, quickly and simply, create $19 billion more capital for WaMu and reposition it to easily withstand the current market turmoil—all without a penny of government assistance."

Fishman and Frank concluded the letter with "Very truly yours" and their signatures.

They never received a reply.

• • •

In New York, Alan Magleby, the head of WaMu's investor relations department, fielded a call from the lead analyst at Toscafund Asset Management, a London-based hedge fund and one of WaMu's largest shareholders. Over the summer, the British company had acquired a 6 percent stake in the bank.[71]

"What's the matter?" Magleby asked.

The analyst sounded distraught. He told Magleby about recent conversations with several European banks and their investors, including Santander and Banco Bilbao Vizcaya Argentaria (BBVA), Spain's second-largest bank. BBVA had briefly been interested in bidding on WaMu through Fishman's private auction. The Toscafund analyst didn't think the U.S. government would favor any European banks. One of the Spanish banks had considered making a bid on WaMu, but the U.S. government had told the Spaniards that "there was a U.S. solution to the problem," the analyst told Magleby, although he didn't specify the bank in question. "I don't think you're going to be allowed to sell," the analyst said.

At the FDIC, the 6:00 p.m. deadline for bids approached. Richard Kovacevich, the chairman of Wells Fargo, wrote to Bair from San Francisco that Wells Fargo would not be making a bid.[72] In his letter, Kovacevich listed the reasons: "the limited due diligence afforded us, the severe time constraints, the extreme uncertainty associated with potential losses to Washington Mutual's loan portfolio, interest rate sensitivity, and the pressures created by the process on market values that could result in a fire sale disposition of Washington Mutual's troubled assets." Kovacevich felt it would be "extremely imprudent" of Wells Fargo and "detrimental to its stockholders" to bid for WaMu.

But the Wells Fargo chairman then pitched another idea. The FDIC could hold WaMu's assets and liabilities, excluding deposits, for 60 days, giving Wells Fargo a chance to conduct a detailed financial review. During that time, the bank would pick and choose which parts of WaMu it wanted to keep. Not only was this plan a bad idea in the eyes of the FDIC (since the agency would have to share in WaMu's potential mortgage losses), but it also didn't meet the agency's criteria. So Wells Fargo was out.

Ned Kelly at Citigroup sent in a letter. Citigroup also worried about WaMu's mortgages. No matter the price, the company felt taking on the loans would represent a big risk. "We believe there is very substantial negative value in the institution running to the tens of billions of dollars under the terms the FDIC has offered," Kelly wrote.

Therefore, Kelly continued, Citigroup (much like Wells Fargo) thought the FDIC should share in WaMu's losses. Citigroup would sequester WaMu's mortgages for 18 months while it worked with homeowners (retaining the bulk of WaMu's employees in the process), and when it figured out how much it might lose, it would split that loss with the FDIC. Waiting that long might allow the economy to recover, and the FDIC might then be able to afford it. Kelly also thought the FDIC should cap loan losses to anyone buying WaMu.

But Citigroup's bid was "nonbinding," which meant it wasn't formal. It also didn't meet the FDIC's criteria. It too was disqualified.

At 6:52 p.m., after the government auction was scheduled to end, JPMorgan faxed in its own offer for WaMu.

"We are very pleased to have the opportunity to work with you and your colleagues on this matter," JPMorgan wrote to the FDIC.

The purchase price scrawled on the bid sheet: $1.888 billion.

The Project West team had arrived at a range between $1.7 billion and $2 billion, and had determined the more precise bid amount after someone noted that 8 is a lucky number in both the Chinese and the Japanese cultures.[73]

An hour and a half later, just before President Bush made an unprecedented prime-time address, imploring the nation to support the financial bailout, Sheila Bair e-mailed Jamie Dimon. At the FDIC, JPMorgan's offer both surprised and pleased Bair's deputies.[74]

"Congrats," Bair wrote in the subject line. "You are the high bid."[75]

Thursday, September 25

NET CHANGE IN WAMU'S DEPOSIT BALANCE: –$600 MILLION

From the local news, 6:30 a.m. Pacific Time: *"Two major newspapers are reporting different scenarios for Washington Mutual this morning. The* New York Times *says Federal regulators have stepped in to help push a sale to another bank.* The Wall Street Journal *says that WaMu is talking to a number of private equity firms."*

An odd stillness gripped WaMu's headquarters. "Like a hush," one employee recalled. For the last two weeks, employees had felt as though they were trapped in a runaway train, hurtling out of control toward . . . something. The news trucks, the headlines, the bank run—all that was still there. But there were even fewer answers than before. "There was a sense that a shoe was about to fall," said the employee. The bank run had slowed, and this encouraged the people who knew about it, but a decision about the fate of WaMu had not been forthcoming. Everyone at the bank believed, having read it online or in the newspapers, that WaMu's fate should have been announced by now—a purchase deal, a bailout, another round of private equity. But there was only silence.

At 9:00 a.m. Pacific Time, WaMu's treasury department held its regular morning meeting with representatives from the OTS and the FDIC. The Fed listened in by speakerphone from San Francisco. The treasury team brought a new liquidity projection, showing that WaMu could pay off creditors and depositors through the next month, while the bank worked to arrange a sale or raise more money. The projection assumed a deposit run of roughly $2 billion a day and the continued cooperation of the Federal Home Loan Banks. Rather than ask detailed questions or offer the usual scrutiny, the government officials sat stone-faced. "That's weird," the treasury team members thought as they trooped out of the room.

The board of directors of the FDIC had already gathered that morning at agency headquarters in Washington. Reich, as director of the OTS, approved the closure of Washington Mutual Bank. Darrel Dochow, WaMu's examiner from the OTS, prepared the "S" report, outlining the reasons for the bank's failure.[76] In the 10-page document, Dochow presented a dire view of WaMu's liquidity position. WaMu had just $13.4 billion to support its operations, he wrote: $3.8 billion in cash and investments, $2.9 billion available from the Seattle and San Francisco Home Loan Banks, and $6.7 billion from the Fed's discount window. Dochow noted the uncertainty of all these funding sources. The San Francisco Home Loan Bank kept reducing its loans to WaMu, and the Fed had lowered WaMu's credit status that day, effectively cutting $1 billion of its borrowing capacity.

The "S" report, while based on bank projections, contradicted WaMu's own daily tally of its liquidity, which the bank's treasury department had been tracking and reporting each day to the FDIC and the OTS. WaMu had $20.8 billion* in available liquidity, including $5.3 billion in cash and investments, $8.6 billion from the Home Loan Banks, and $6.4 billion from the Fed discount window. The remaining $500 million came from other short-term borrowing facilities. While WaMu knew that the San Francisco Home Loan Bank was considering an additional haircut on its collateral, WaMu hadn't heard definitively whether it had made that decision, or to what extent the collateral would be devalued. The bank's credit line at the Seattle Home Loan Bank, while lower than its line at the San Francisco bank, was unaffected, and WaMu hadn't accessed it for a couple of days. The Federal Reserve Bank, meanwhile, told WaMu that it could no longer participate in the Reserve Bank's Term Auction Facility lending program because of its CAMELS downgrade, but the Fed hadn't said anything about WaMu's discount window line being in jeopardy.

The FDIC board, which Reich sat on, had to bless the decision to close WaMu before the government could seize the bank. The FDIC board also had to approve JPMorgan's bid. The two agencies had planned to move in on Friday. But the night before, in her congratulatory note to Dimon, Bair relayed some unfortunate news: both *The Wall Street Journal* and *The New York Times* were working on stories about the FDIC's sale of WaMu. "We may have to accelerate the announcement," Bair wrote. "Our lawyers are trying to head them off but may not be able to."[77] If the papers broke the news, it could be a disaster for the

---

*WaMu's liquidity figure on the day of its failure is unresolved, as is the difference between these assessments. The numbers here are based on documents from the OTS and WaMu, respectively, and represent the clearest picture of WaMu's liquidity. Additionally, two WaMu executives involved in tracking the bank's liquidity recall the number as $29 billion, but that figure may have represented a three-month projection. Typically, regulators close a bank if its liquidity dips below 5 percent of total assets; both $20.8 billion and $29 billion were above this threshold. The OTS's $13.4 billion figure put WaMu's liquidity levels at 4.4 percent of total assets.

regulators. Customers that hadn't already pulled out their money might rush the bank, overwhelming the branches. JPMorgan had also lobbied for a Thursday closure. If WaMu closed on a Thursday, JPMorgan would have a business day on Friday to raise money from investors to fund the purchase.[78]

In half an hour, the FDIC board approved both items. Bair left the meeting and called Treasury Secretary Paulson, who was still working to get the $700 billion bailout passed. She told him that the FDIC would seize WaMu and sell its assets to JPMorgan. WaMu would become the largest bank failure in U.S. history—eight times the size of Continental Illinois's failure in the 1980s.

Later, Paulson spoke with Senator John McCain (R-Ariz.), an opponent of Paulson's plan. "John, our system is on edge," Paulson told him. "WaMu barely got bailed out today. Several other institutions are on the brink. If we don't get something done soon, this economy is going to collapse."[79]

In New York, Alan Fishman, Tom Casey, Fishman's special consultant Frank Baier (who had been hired to help out with the capital raise), and John McMurray boarded the private jet back to Seattle. They had no further reason to stay on the East Coast. The private auction had failed, and they had received no word from the regulators about WaMu's capital-raising plan. As they left, investment bankers in New York continued to camp out at the offices of Simpson Thacher, trying to find other ways to save the company.

The WaMu executives debated for a long time whether to fly Net-Jets, which was already paid for, or commercial, which would look better publicly. In the end, they decided it was more important to return quickly and took the private plane. As they sat on the tarmac, waiting to take off, someone got an e-mail: JPMorgan was planning to hold an investor conference call at 9:00 p.m. Eastern Time.

In Seattle, at about a quarter to 4:00 p.m. Pacific Time, several members of WaMu's communications team stood in the bank's lobby chatting after a coffee break. Upstairs on the executive floor, Steve Rotella had just received a call back from John Robinson in San Francisco.

"Steve, it's over," Robinson told him. "They're coming in to close us this afternoon."

"Is there anything we can do to put it off?" Rotella replied.

"No. There's not any time left."

The members of the communications team took the elevator back up to the twenty-first floor, where their cubes were clustered. As they returned to their desks, their phones, at the same moment, all lit up ("like a Christmas tree" one recalled later) and began ringing. They looked at each other, perplexed, until one of them answered. "Hi, this is ABC News," said the caller. "I hear this rumor that the FDIC is going to seize the bank and Chase is going to buy you guys." Stunned, the communications team member replied, haltingly, "Let me look into it."

Several floors above, an employee stood up in his cube and called out to everyone around him, "Holy shit. *The Wall Street Journal* is reporting we got sold to JPMorgan Chase!"[80] Within minutes, the news had traveled up and down the skyscraper's 42 floors. WaMu employees streamed out of their cubicles and gathered around television sets and computers, waiting to hear more details. Others got on to Rotella's internal blog, posting dozens of questions in the comment section. What's going on? What happened? Have we been sold? No answers came.

All across the country, employees received telephone calls and text messages from worried relatives and friends. "Oh my gosh, what does this mean for you?!" texted one longtime employee's niece. The immediate response: "I think it means I've lost my job."

There had been no time to gather anyone ahead of time. The initial news reports said nothing about a government seizure, so most employees thought WaMu had been sold to JPMorgan in Fishman's private auction. In that case, this news was somewhat good—at least the shareholders would get something.

Along with the surprise came a refreshing sense of relief. The waiting was over. "Now we know," thought one employee. The deposit tracking team decamped to a nearby Mexican restaurant for margaritas. After their three intense weeks of monitoring panicky customers, that job was now someone else's. The team toasted their long weeks of effort. In New York, WaMu's exhausted investment bankers heard the news inside Simpson Thacher. One of them took the elevator downstairs to the bar.

In Henderson, Nevada, an FDIC official strode into a WaMu branch in a shopping center on the outskirts of the city. Because the bank held a large charter in Nevada, the FDIC was required to deliver a notice of its failure to this obscure location. The branch was WaMu's official headquarters. Since there were no WaMu executives in Henderson, the FDIC official delivered the paperwork to a distraught and confused young employee. Shaking, she signed her name to the document indicating the government's monumental decision to take over her company. Later, the FDIC sent her an apologetic bouquet of flowers.

At about 5:45 p.m. Pacific Time, a group of FDIC and OTS officials strode into the marble lobby of WaMu's Seattle headquarters, passing a poster in the window bearing the bank's new ad campaign: "Whoo-hoo!" The FDIC sent just nine people to handle the largest bank failure in U.S. history, a sign of how smoothly the takeover had come together. In comparison, months later it would pull together more than 100 people to close a bank in Pittsburgh a sliver of the size. A larger agency attendance would become routine for community bank failures across the country. Outside, a group of news trucks buzzed with heightened activity, and anxious reporters tried to ascertain what was happening inside.

The government officials took the elevator up to WaMu's executive floor, walking past the collection of Northwest art hanging on the putty-colored walls. They walked into the bank's boardroom, where Rotella, Frank, and other members of the board waited. Not everyone could be pulled together on such short notice. Rotella and Frank tried to reach Fishman and Casey on the plane, calling their cell phones again and again. Fishman's executive assistant called NetJets and asked the company to place an emergency call to the pilot, instructing Fishman to call her. He did, and she passed him through to Rotella, who delivered the news.

Among the government officials standing in the boardroom was Dochow, from the OTS. He looked ashen as he read off an official letter to the board. "This is to notify you," he said, "that the director, Office of Thrift Supervision, by Order Number 2008–36, dated September 25, 2008, appointed the Federal Deposit Insurance Corporation receiver for Washington Mutual Bank . . . The receiver is now taking possession of the bank." Frank, as chairman of the board, scribbled his name on the document, turning control over to the government. It was WaMu's 119th birthday. On this day in 1889, when Seattle was a fledgling city ravaged by fire, two industrious men had signed their names to a document incorporating the Washington Building Loan and Investment Association.[81]

By this time, employees knew the government had seized WaMu. One manager instructed his staff to go buy beer and popcorn at a nearby minimart, but the government security guards confiscated the goodies when the staffers were on the way back in.[82] Just after 6:00 p.m. Pacific Time, employees received an e-mail from Jamie Dimon, welcoming them to JPMorgan. JPMorgan had worked with WaMu's auditors to secretly retrieve employees' e-mail addresses, without alerting WaMu management to the upcoming news. Dimon and Scharf had spent the day calling around to investors, trying to raise money for the deal. They had been successful, raising $7 billion in pledges from nine investors,* even though they couldn't yet relay the details of the purchase.[83] At 6:15 p.m. Pacific Time, JPMorgan held an investor conference call to announce the purchase. "Hello. It's Jamie Dimon here, and I'd like to thank you all for coming on the phone this late at night. I know it's 9:15, and we do appreciate it. If you're from Washington Mutual—I gather some of the employees are listening—welcome to JPMorgan Chase. We do think we're going to help build a great company together."[84]

Bair held another call from Washington announcing the news. For the first time, the public heard of WaMu's bank run. The bank had lost $16.7 billion in the weeks before its closure. Its deteriorating condition had pushed regulators to move in on Thursday, instead of Friday, Bair said. JPMorgan's purchase meant that WaMu's failure didn't cost the deposit insurance a dime. The company planned to write down WaMu's loan portfolio by $31 billion.

"This institution was a big question mark about the health of the deposit fund," Bair said in the conference call.[85] "It was unique in its size and exposure to higher risk mortgages and the distressed housing market. This is the big one that everybody was worried about." She continued, "I was worried about it."[86]

The OTS issued its own press release.[87] "With insufficient liquidity to meet its obligations, WaMu was in an unsafe and unsound condition

---

*JPMorgan eventually raised $11.5 billion to fund the purchase.

to transact business," the agency wrote. Over the preceding three quarters, WaMu had lost $6.1 billion in bad loans, it noted, although the loans were not a chief cause of the bank's failure. WaMu was still considered well capitalized at the time of its closure.

WaMu employees kept posting desperate questions on Rotella's blog until right after the conference calls started. Soon afterward WaMu executives shut down the website.

The last comment came right before the site went dark.

"Goodbye, WaMu," it read.

"BARELY A BLIP"

The sun was shining on a clear autumn afternoon in late September 2009, but inside a restaurant in Seattle's South Lake Union neighborhood, the drapes over the windows were partially closed. A buffet of appetizers lined one side of the room, and in a corner a bartender poured glasses of wine. Tables were scattered across the space, arranged to make it look as if it this were any other busy lunchtime, the business crowd lingering over cups of coffee. But on this Sunday, the restaurant was closed for a private event.

In the half-light, WaMu employees and executives gathered in small groups. Several of them sat at tables, while others stood, holding drinks. Many of the people who had worked together to build WaMu in its earlier years were in the room. Fay Chapman, the former chief legal officer, was there, as was Liane Wilson, former head of technology. Al Doman of the A-Team and Lynn Ryder of the human resources department were there, as was Iris Glaze from investor relations. Others who had influenced pieces of the bank stood in groups around the room. While many had kept in touch, even years after their respective departures from WaMu, this reunion was unsettling.

A year and two days had passed since WaMu failed. Shortly before the momentous anniversary of the bank's collapse, WaMu employees had suffered a terrible loss. Doug Wisdorf, the deputy in charge of WaMu's investor relations department, had committed suicide—he hanged himself in the basement of his Seattle house.[1] Wisdorf had a history of depression, although this suffering was never apparent to many of those who worked with him. In a police report following his death, deputies noted that Wisdorf had lost his job, and that this had created "significant increasing financial pressures" over the last several months.[2]

Wisdorf epitomized WaMu. He worked at the bank since the mid-1970s, never straying to another company. He bounced around in senior management positions, serving as deputy chief financial officer and then, eventually, as second in command in the investor relations department. He labored with good humor from behind the scenes, always part of monumental events at the bank, but never at the forefront. When the executive team traveled to New York to ring the opening bell at the New York Stock Exchange in the 1990s, Wisdorf had gone along for the trip. He joined the others in a raucous group cheer, celebrating in the middle of the trading floor. Over the years, he had mentored dozens of other WaMu employees, played on the bank's sports teams, and earned the nickname "Mr. Wizard" for his analytical skills. Against the barrage of angry shareholder calls in the last few months of WaMu's existence, he had positioned himself as a steady rock, serving as a measured support system for his staff. He had been scheduled to start a new job as the chief financial officer at a community bank in Washington State the week following his suicide.

Many WaMu employees had already gathered, mingling with the dozens of other guests, when Kerry Killinger arrived at the restaurant with his wife, Linda. Few in the room had seen Killinger since the summer of 2008, when he had been ousted as chief executive. For many of the WaMu employees who had retired in earlier years, it had been much longer than that. He kept in touch with few people. According to a friend, the Killingers, particularly Linda, had not been handling the fallout from the bank's collapse well. The newspapers still published critical profiles of Killinger and WaMu, the lawsuits stretched on, and it was all like "death by a thousand cuts" to the couple, as one acquaintance said. Killinger had halfheartedly filed paperwork to start a consulting firm but was otherwise out of work. Wisdorf's death saddened him. The two men had worked together a long time. On the evening after WaMu's board of directors appointed Killinger as president in 1988, several WaMu executives had gathered after work at a favorite bar, near the bank's small headquarters. It was December, and it had begun to snow in downtown Seattle as the coworkers sat around a table, drinks in hand, celebrating Killinger's achievement. Everyone left soon, worried about getting home as the storm worsened. Only Wisdorf and Killinger had remained, sitting across from each other, oblivious to the snow falling outside.

Now when Killinger and Linda walked into the restaurant, several WaMu employees moved to the other side of the room. Others turned their backs. Soon afterward Lou Pepper arrived with his wife, Mollie. Pepper was eighty-four now and had a bad hip. He sometimes used a cane or a wheelchair to get around. He sat more than he liked. Pepper did not want to see Killinger, and he and other WaMu employees had been under the impression that Killinger would not be invited to the memorial. The two WaMu chief executives had not seen each other in a long time, even though they both spent part of the year in Palm Desert.

The growing problems at WaMu before its collapse had weighed on Pepper. He had lost confidence in Killinger not long after sending him the e-mail in 2005, warning him about the high-risk housing market. After Fay Chapman, Pepper's other protégé, resigned, Pepper became despondent with worry about the bank and its employees. The day after WaMu failed, when a reporter from *The Seattle Times* called, asking for a quote, he unleashed his anger.[3] "That it comes to a demise like this is absolutely pathetic," he said. "It was a great institution for 110 years or more, and to see it so mishandled that it would be the largest bank failure in the country is abominable, to put it mildly." While the debate over whether banks had grown too large ("too big to fail") had entered popular consciousness, Pepper didn't think that was the problem at WaMu. "Big institutions can succeed," he told the newspaper, "but they have to be run like little institutions. You have to give autonomy to the branches, and have people being nice to each other. You can't have this monolith."

As Wisdorf's memorial began, a group of WaMu employees surrounded Pepper, moving him and Mollie to a seat at the back of the restaurant, away from Killinger.

After WaMu failed, Fay Chapman had called Pepper at his home north of Seattle. She had suffered the same kind of devastation that beset Pepper, and she didn't think she could just sit around and stew about it. On the phone, the two devised a plan to raise money for the hundreds of workers who they knew would soon lose their jobs. Specifically, they wanted to help the people working in WaMu's call centers or its branches across the country—the ones working for less than $25 an hour. It would be known as the WaMu Alumni Fund. Other former WaMu executives joined the effort.

Pepper wrote a long e-mail to the bank's employees, explaining the group's plans. Over the years, he had written many letters about the bank. This last one was almost a eulogy, the only kind of closure that the employees would ever receive. Several cried. Others kept it and read it occasionally over the following years. "It was like the WaMu we used to work for," said one employee. "That whole feeling came through again."

"We have all been dealing with our feelings of anger and sadness over the ignominious demise of what not long ago was the premier consumer bank in the country," Pepper wrote. "And remember, you made it that; so take pride in what you wrought even though others took it down.

"But in the midst of that, many people have asked me if there is anything we can do for the many hard-working people who are suffering because much of their savings was invested in the bank's stock, and their jobs are now in jeopardy. We were all family and friends and it is hard to see anyone in the family suffer hardship."

Pepper noted that many employees had invested their 401(k)s in WaMu stock and had likely lost even more money through the bank's Employee Stock Purchase Plan. Indeed, WaMu historically didn't place a limit on the amount of stock employees could own in their 401(k)s. It had capped the amount at 20 percent only a month before its failure.

Pepper outlined the former WaMu executives' plans to solicit funds only from former employees and executives "who were lucky enough to have sold their stock before the big mess." The group would not be asking the general public to donate. "We think of this as a family matter," Pepper wrote. "We just might make a small dent in the huge hardship caused by the bank's failure. . . .

"What happened in the last few years was an aberration in the long history of a great institution," Pepper concluded. "It should have been able to weather this financial turmoil and come out the other end. That it got so bad that all was lost is not your fault and should not reduce the pride you always took in your work and the bank you served."

The WaMu Alumni Fund group raised nearly $1 million, hardly enough to cover the many people who lost their jobs. Although they were asked, none of the executives who most recently worked at the bank contributed. The money was awarded each year at a potluck dinner that evolved into an annual WaMu reunion. Only employees and managers with deep roots in the company attended. Killinger was never invited, but his ex-wife Debbie stopped by. She was twelve years sober and had become a major donor to the arts community in Seattle. She also ran a scholarship program for students at her former high school in Des Moines, "North."

At the FDIC, the reverberations of the country's largest bank failure came fast and furious. At 9:41 a.m. Eastern Time on September 26, 2008, the morning after WaMu's collapse, Sheila Bair's chief of staff sent her an urgent e-mail. "They are calling the office demanding that the chairman intervene," he wrote.[4] Shareholders were angry and confused. The holding company of WaMu—Washington Mutual, Inc.—had filed for bankruptcy, a move that wiped out $7 billion in shareholder wealth, $2 billion in preferred shares, and more than $20 billion for bondholders.[5] It was the first time the government had allowed a bank's debt to evaporate in a bank failure. Hundreds of WaMu's investors called the government agency that day.

The shareholders and bondholders also wrote pleading letters, addressed to Bair or the FDIC or the trustee in charge of the bankruptcy. The letters would continue for months.

From Washington: *"Your agency took over Washington Mutual and left countless investors in both the common and preferred stock out to dry. I knew going into the stock there was going to be risk. But I would rather that the market itself dictated that risk and hope that government intervention would not change that process for me."*[6]

From Florida: *"This savings & loan institution was the largest S&L in the US and was founded in the 19th century. I am 84 years old, am blessed with good health, but the FDIC has caused me considerable pain. I invested in Washington Mutual because of the dividends paid year after year. As a common stock holder, I stand to lose $121,616.50 because of the FDIC, the government agency that I thought was there to protect everyone. Those members of the FDIC who are responsible for taking over Washington Mutual and selling it to JPMorgan Chase for a fraction of its value should be held accountable."*[7]

From North Carolina: *"We don't feel that the FDIC handled this properly and leaving [sic] the shareholders with nothing while JPMorgan made a steal. We thought, when banks first start up, shareholders are what gets them up and running. What respect do shareholders get? The government seems to be helping banks, but what are they doing for the working class? The working class is the majority which supports this country. Even when the Feds knew they were going to seize and close WaMu, they continued to let the public invest money in WaMu stocks. Where were they when the bank made risky loans?"*[8]

From Illinois: *"The FDIC action and the matters surrounding the WaMu seizure wiped out my retirement account as well as other shareholders of this company. It looks that the action was taken prematurely at the expense of investors for the benefit of the FDIC and subsequent buyer JPMorgan Chase. The selective FDIC seizure of WaMu was unprecedented as it was not applied to any other institution before or after that."*[9]

From Puerto Rico: *"I am writing to beg for your assistance. The seizure of Washington Mutual Bank has been devastating to me. I have lost my life savings from this event and I believe the FDIC committed a thoughtless error by seizing a solvent bank prematurely. I sincerely feel that Washington Mutual* *was a 'sacrificial lamb' in order to put the pressure on Congress to pass the bailout."*[10]

From North Carolina: *"My wife and I are now retired and living off our life savings. While being very conservative investors all our lives, we saw (at least in our eyes) an opportunity to invest in Washington Mutual when its stock went below $5.00 per share. All our research showed other companies being very interested in buying WM and all stock commentators that we watched were saying what a buying opportunity this could be. NEVER in our wildest dreams did we think a seizure of WM was even an option! Until this wrongdoing is righted, we will never invest in anything again."*[11]

The Osorios in Thousand Oaks, California, also wrote. In the weeks after WaMu's failure, they had watched the news, searching for some sign that their $202,000 investment, the bulk of their life savings, might be restored. But the news they hoped for never came.

"I am Luis A. Osorio. I have worked for many years as a banker and just retired at the end of 2007. I invested about $200,000 of my retirement money in over 5,000 shares of Washington Mutual. I invested my money in good faith, planning for my retirement, counting on an income from dividends to help me pay for my health insurance and all of my medicines.

"As a small investor and citizen of this country I ask you: Are you going to do anything to help me recuperate some of my retirement money? I am sure that there are many other retired investors that find themselves in the same situation. I need help! I need at least to recuperate some of the money I invested."[12]

Even after her husband wrote, Ada Osorio sometimes composed letters to Sheila Bair in her head. "Don't forget us," she thought about writing. "Don't forget the situation we're in." Or "Is there anything you can do to help us? Can you recognize our losses and do something about it?" She would never write anything, though. What good would it do? "WaMu," said Ada Osorio later, "is the pain in my heart."

Bair didn't respond to the voluminous letters and e-mails sent to the FDIC—at least not all of them. She forwarded a page-long message from one irate shareholder to her chief of staff. "Getting a lot of these," she wrote. "Is there a form we can send them?" Later, in testimony to the Financial Crisis Commission, Bair characterized WaMu's failure as "practically a nonevent": "If you go back and look at the press reports, it was below the fold, if it was even on the front page. It was the largest bank failure in history, but it was barely a blip given everything else that was going on."[13]

The day after WaMu's failure, corporate and institutional customers of Wachovia began pulling their money out of their accounts at the struggling North Carolina–based bank. By the end of the day, Wachovia had lost $5 billion—double the amount of any day during WaMu's run—and its stock plummeted 27 percent. "The collapse of WaMu was awful," Treasury Secretary Hank Paulson later wrote in his book detailing the crisis, "but Wachovia was another order of magnitude altogether."[14] The government decided that Wachovia, as the fourth-largest bank nationwide, was precariously connected to the rest of the financial system. For the first time in history, the government invoked what's known as a "systemic risk" exception. Usually the FDIC must liquidate a bank at the least cost to the deposit insurance fund. By deeming Wachovia a "systemic risk," the FDIC could step in and provide money to save the bank. The government brokered a purchase of Wachovia by Wells Fargo, saving it.

The panic only continued. In the first week of October 2008, borrowing from the Fed's discount window soared to $100 billion, from $19 billion only a month earlier.[15] As the global crisis spread, banks across the world used the Fed as a crutch. Citigroup, with more than $2 trillion in assets, nearly failed, but a patchwork of help from the government propped it up.* Six days after WaMu collapsed, Paulson won enough votes in Congress to support his bailout plan. President George W. Bush signed the Emergency Economic Stabilization Act of 2008, unprecedented legislation that created the $700 billion Troubled Asset Relief Program. Rather than using the money to buy up the bad mortgages from banks, the program morphed into a way for the government

---

*Bair initially lobbied against government support for Citigroup, believing it should go through the FDIC's receivership process like other failed banks.

to inject capital into companies by buying up preferred stock. Paulson called the chief executives of all the largest banks—JPMorgan, Citigroup, and Bank of America among them—and implored them to take the money. They did. As part of the new legislation, the government increased the deposit insurance limit from $100,000 to $250,000, a move that various politicians and decision makers repeatedly told WaMu executives would never happen. The insurance limit remains at the higher level today.

In the FDIC's view, WaMu's closure was a success. Not a dime of the deposit insurance fund had been used in connection with the largest bank failure in U.S. history. The government agency isn't charged with protecting bank shareholders or employees. Its job is to protect bank customers. In this respect, the agency fulfilled its mission. "The FDIC would always like to see troubled institutions return to health," Bair said in later congressional testimony. "However, as was the case with WaMu, when the institution is no longer viable, a resolution represents the best course. Further delay by the government would have further increased the cost to the FDIC insurance fund. Most of WaMu was saved; the institution was not bailed out, but completely bidded [*sic*] out."[16] She later repeated this view to the Financial Crisis Commission, saying that she was proud of the way the failure was handled. By this time, she had received a Profile in Courage award from the John F. Kennedy Library Foundation for sounding early warnings about the financial crisis.

In his book, Paulson seems to disagree with Bair, saying, "The solution wasn't perfect . . . Crushing the owners of preferred and subordinated debt and clipping senior debt holders only served to unsettle the debt holders in other institutions, adding to the market's uncertainty. Banks were even less willing to lend to one another." Neel Kashkari, one of Paulson's deputies, who later presided over TARP, offered a stronger opinion in his deposition to the Financial Crisis Commission, calling WaMu's seizure a "mistake." "At that time, the economy was in such a perilous state, it was like playing with fire," he said. "In my view, we should have found a way to allow somebody to acquire WaMu prebankruptcy."

Some details of WaMu's last days, and particularly the role of the

FDIC and the OTS in the closure of the bank, remain a mystery even years after its collapse. Hundreds of public records—e-mails that flew back and forth in the two months before the bank collapsed, in particular—obtained through the federal Freedom of Information Act from both agencies, have been almost entirely redacted, their contents blacked out by a thick marker. Thousands of other records, released through the subpoena power of various government agencies and through lawsuits, fill in some of the gaps but not all of them. Bair, in particular, has been reticent about her agency's role in WaMu's closure, and she has delivered little public testimony about it since September 2008. The federal court handling the bankruptcy of WaMu's holding company ordered an independent examiner to look into WaMu's failure. The FDIC declined to make Bair available and wouldn't allow the examiner to interview any of her top deputies.[17] The FDIC released some records, withholding some of the documents the examiner requested. The agency made it clear that it would throw up obstacles ("including time-consuming, multi-step regulatory procedures," the examiner wrote) if the examiner attempted to access its records. "In sum, the FDIC, has refused to make fully transparent some of its dealings with [JPMorgan] and others," the examiner concluded in the final report.

The OTS and JPMorgan cooperated fully. JPMorgan executives, however, could not recall certain meetings they had attended related to the bank. Michael Cavanagh, JPMorgan's chief financial officer, for example, remembered riding in a cab to Bair's office on September 9 for a meeting about WaMu, but he cannot recall what they spoke about. Charlie Scharf also attended the meeting but had no recollection whatsoever. Of course, as Bair herself later pointed out in her Financial Crisis Commission testimony, these events occurred in "the fog of war." Many executives and government officials involved in the financial crisis have trouble recalling key events.

After researching for three months, WaMu's bankruptcy examiner found that WaMu's failure had been handled properly all around—by the FDIC, the OTS, and JPMorgan. The examiner described the bidding process as "reasonably fair" and noted that there was no evidence that JPMorgan had access to any information not available to all potential bidders.[18] "In the end, [JPMorgan] was the only potential bidder willing to absorb all of [WaMu's] toxic loan pools without government guarantees," the examiner wrote in hundreds of pages of analysis about the bank's failure and bankruptcy. The report would be the most in-depth review of WaMu's final days.

It found that the OTS reached "reasonable conclusions" about WaMu's withered financial condition as a result of the bank run, and it noted that it would be hard for anyone to sue the OTS for shutting down the institution. The report also found that the FDIC acted reasonably to protect its deposit insurance fund. "Moreover," the examiner wrote, "even assuming the government made a bad decision in seizing [WaMu], there is no practical way to undo what has been done."

WaMu shareholders, unhappy with the outcome of the report, moved successfully to have it thrown out of federal bankruptcy court. Its contents wouldn't be used in settlement deliberations.

A separate review, conducted by the Offices of Inspector General for the FDIC and the U.S. Treasury Department, looked more closely at the FDIC and OTS's role in regulating WaMu in prior years. That report concluded that WaMu failed because of its high-risk loan strategy, a strategy made worse by the bank's liberal mortgage underwriting and poor oversight of its operations.[19] The reviewers asked the OTS why it allowed WaMu to make bad loans for so many years. While the agency acknowledged there were problems, OTS examiners pointed out, "WaMu was making money and loans were performing."

In the end, the OTS lost the battle over its existence. Congress passed the Dodd-Frank financial regulatory reform, a sweeping set of changes to financial institution oversight. The hundreds of pages of new rules obliterated the OTS. The agency was merged into the Office of the Comptroller of the Currency, a process that took place in the summer of 2011. OTS officials fought this change and defended their oversight of WaMu and other troubled banks. "Institutions much larger than Washington Mutual, for example, Citigroup and Bank of America, had collapsed, but the federal government prevented their failure by providing open bank assistance," said John Bowman, the acting director of the agency, who had stepped in after John Reich retired, in testimony on Capitol Hill.[20] "The OTS did not regulate the largest banks that failed; the OTS regulated the largest banks that were *allowed to fail*."*

Reich also later made this point at a congressional hearing into WaMu's bad mortgage practices. "It's important to point out that although WaMu has been referred to as the largest failure in American history, Citi was actually bigger," he said. "WaMu wasn't deemed to be a systemic risk and was not bailed out." Reich's defense, however, fell flat. The U.S. Senate's Permanent Subcommittee on Investigations, chaired by Senator Carl Levin, had no interest in a philosophical debate when it called Reich and other regulators to testify in the spring of 2010. The group wanted only to know why—and how it was possible—that the OTS had missed so many warning signs about WaMu.

The OTS was receiving little public sympathy at this point, and its demise went largely unnoticed. In the financial crisis, "it was the sacrificial lamb," one banking attorney observed. *The New York Times* wrote an obituary of sorts, pointing out that Congress almost never gets rid of a regulator, and in that sense, the OTS's own failure was "remarkable."[21] "The decision is all the more remarkable because it cuts against the grain of a bill devoted to expanding federal regulation, and because it has had virtually no opposition, save for the obligatory protests of the agency's senior management," the *Times* noted. The failure of the OTS meant more than the death of an agency, however. It marked the end of an era for a certain group of financial institutions. The savings and loan bank, the kind that Pepper and Killinger had built, and the one that Alan Fishman later fought to save, has disappeared. As Bill Longbrake told the *Times*, "It's going to be increasingly difficult to say there's any true thrift industry any longer."

Fishman believed that WaMu could have been saved—if the government wanted to save it. "People were running for cover, but if Paulson or someone else said, 'Let's settle this thing now,' it would have been solved," he said later. "The financial position [of WaMu], under any

---

*The government's definition of a bank failure changed during the financial crisis. For example, Continental Illinois was widely known as the largest bank failure in U.S. history before WaMu's collapse, but it was propped up by the government and was allowed to continue operating.

standard of care, was dire. It was serious, it was imprudent—but it was solvable, if you wanted to solve it."

Fishman worked at WaMu for only three weeks, but the bank's collapse is never far from his mind. He and other members of his team often replay events, wondering what they could have done to change the outcome.

"I tried to argue as forcefully and intelligently and legitimately as I could that stopping the crisis at WaMu was stopping the Main Street crisis," Fishman said later about his conversations with various government officials. "All of this other crap was really a financial crisis. We were the Main Street crisis. And I could never get, because of the lack of attention, because of the anger at Kerry and the bank, I could never get enough traction around that argument. They were done with WaMu."

The banking crisis on Main Street continued strongly for the next two years. More than 280 community banks in all corners of the country closed, to be sold by the FDIC, a flood of failures soon overlooked as the normal course of business. The community bank for which Doug Wisdorf had been scheduled to start work the week after he died later failed. When the housing market was growing, the smaller banks made billions of dollars of loans to real estate developers. When the market crashed, those houses and condos and lots were left empty, leaving the community banks on the hook. The struggle that Fishman faced in WaMu's last weeks played out in a similar fashion at other banks, as turnaround chief executives fought to save longtime institutions. Often their struggles proved fruitless. The banks tried to raise private equity, but TPG's massive loss in WaMu's failure chilled potential investors across the country. Many community banks were passed over for TARP because they were deemed too troubled: TARP was supposed to be used for banks that had a chance of surviving. The number of community banks had withered since Lou Pepper's time at WaMu; their ranks were nearly half of what they once were, while the larger banks only kept growing.[22]

The regulation pendulum swung in the other direction, and the FDIC was criticized for closing smaller banks without giving them a chance to save themselves. After the FDIC and the OTS shut down a small bank in Idaho, the state's congressmen wrote a public letter, claiming the federal agencies had "intentionally destroyed" a pillar of

the community through "inappropriate use of their powers." The bank
had been about to raise $10 million to save itself.[23] In Oregon, the chief
executive of a three-decades-old bank, a stalwart business in a small
agricultural community, wrote a desperate letter to the FDIC and its
state regulators.[24] As Fishman had done, the turnaround chief executive pleaded for leniency rather than closure and outlined plans to raise
capital. The bank, considered "critically undercapitalized," was about
to turn a quarterly profit and was "viable and solvent by dictionary and
business definitions," the chief executive wrote. He didn't hear back
from regulators. The bank was shut down. Across the Columbia River
Valley in Oregon, cherry farmers who invested in the bank decades earlier lost a collective $20 million.

The night that WaMu failed, Brian Mueller had a terrible dream.
He dreamed that Jamie Dimon fired him. In real life, there is no way
Dimon would have personally fired Mueller—Mueller was many levels
removed from JPMorgan's chief executive. But dreams distort reality,
and in Mueller's, it was Dimon himself who pointed his finger at Mueller and told him, "You're fired." Mueller had never met Dimon. He had
only seen him on TV and heard his voice on the investor conference
call that evening. "He seems like a diabolical leader," Mueller said later.
"Like Mr. Burns."

The next day JPMorgan executives swept through WaMu's headquarters. They wore tailored suits and clutched BlackBerries into which
they typed constantly, or which they kept pressed to their ears. "New
York is on the floor, New York is on the floor," the WaMu employees
whispered to each other jokingly. "You could see them coming a mile
away," one employee said. The JPMorgan executives moved purpose-
fully, ordered expensive lunches, and spoke loudly. They swore much
more frequently than anyone was used to. "They were exactly what
we were trying not to be," Mueller said. "The classic stodgy banker."
Charlie Scharf flew into Seattle the night of WaMu's seizure and held
an early morning meeting with the bank's executive team. He reassured
them: "We know this is a difficult situation for you," and "We view
this as a merger, not an acquisition," and "We've always respected and,
frankly, coveted Washington Mutual. We're happy to have you as part

of the family." Right away Scharf got rid of his former direct report, Steve Rotella, as well as Tom Casey and Alan Fishman. Fishman, who had worked at WaMu just 18 days, turned down the millions of dollars in severance that he might have received, but he kept his $7.5 million signing bonus and the roughly $60,000 he had earned from his annual base salary of $1 million. David Schneider, the head of the Home Loans Group, kept his job.

At first WaMu employees waited. As JPMorgan sorted out their fates, they had nothing to do. They played computer games or worked on their résumés in full view of the rest of the office. Often they didn't come in to work at all. Sometimes they showed up at 9:00 a.m. and left at 3:00 p.m., with a two-hour lunch in between. There was relief that the hard work of the last year and a half had come to an end, and many slept well, and long, for the first time in many months. Much of the general public believed WaMu deserved to fail, but many employees felt a strong sense of loss. "You just went through the five stages of grief," said one employee. "At some point, you were just angry at everybody."

Two months later, in December 2008, JPMorgan announced it would lay off 12,000 WaMu employees across the country, including thousands at the bank's headquarters in Seattle. It would cut WaMu workers in stages. Some would stay on as part of the transition, for a duration that could last months or even years. Others would leave immediately. Dimon told a Seattle reporter, "I could say we saved 30,000 jobs as opposed to 12,000 layoffs. When you do a big deal like this, you have to get it to the right size so you can be vibrant and healthy and grow in the future, and so it's highly unfortunate, we hate doing it, but it is the right thing to do so you can build the company from there."[25] JPMorgan handsomely paid the employees who stayed on as part of the transition, awarding them money for the time they had worked, a hefty prorated bonus, and a severance package.[26] But those who remained carried the additional burden of feeling like outsiders in a new company. JPMorgan reminded them, in ways big and small, that it had won, while WaMu had lost.

The WaMu employees, meanwhile, harbored suspicion that JPMorgan's fire-sale purchase had not been kosher. One night, several weeks after WaMu's failure, three of JPMorgan's communication executives invited their counterparts at WaMu out to dinner at a downtown Seattle wine bar.[27] Several of the WaMu employees complained about the challenges of getting ahead of all the bad news that had beset WaMu in its final weeks. The JPMorgan executives listened sympathetically. Then one of the JPMorgan executives relayed that they had been watching money "fly out of the bank" from a "war room" at JPMorgan headquarters. The remark startled the WaMu employees, who hadn't thought JPMorgan executives had had access to that kind of detailed deposit information. Even if they did, they shouldn't have been bragging about it. (JPMorgan did have access, as did all of WaMu's potential acquirers browsing through the data room in September.) "There were several of us that looked at each other and thought, 'Did he just say that?'" said one of the WaMu employees who attended.

After four months, the first large group of WaMu employees left the company, representing the start of rolling layoffs that would continue for almost two years. Iris Glaze, as was her way, threw a party: the WaMu Last Hurrah Party. Several hundred rowdy WaMu employees gathered at an events center in Seattle to memorialize the bank. Glaze auctioned off historical artifacts—the WaMu teller dolls; a signed, limited edition Kerry Killinger bobble-head doll (this item fetched $175);[28] stacks of annual reports; and the medallion reflecting WaMu's move to the New York Stock exchange in the 1990s. The "WaMurabilia," as the employees called it, raised $2,500, which was turned over to the newly created Alumni Fund. "I danced, I sang; I never worked an audience like that before," said Glaze, who would end up unemployed for more than two years before finally finding another job. As WaMu's employees left, they found a job market decimated by a deep recession. They also carried an albatross: they had worked for a bank that had become the largest failure in U.S. history. "Do you feel tainted?" one potential employer asked a WaMu employee in a job interview.

At the party, Glaze cried only after two employees presented a goodbye song.

Sometimes, we made us some good loans;
Sometimes, them loans weren't so hot.
We got so big and successful,

Then things fell in, now we're not.
Friend of the Family's departed,
But not the folks of WaMu:
Fair, caring, hardworking, honest, and fun—
This farewell song is for you!

Brian Mueller, who had tracked WaMu's bank runs, now used Excel to discreetly monitor the ongoing layoffs at the bank's headquarters. Each month his bar charts tallying remaining employees decreased in height as more people left. Each month the remaining group of employees gathered to celebrate the ones leaving. "It became like this ghost town," one employee said. Mueller worked on his computer in a space once built to promote interaction. It now had very few people in it. Each time he entered a figure into his spreadsheet, another cluster of desks would empty out, until some floors shut down entirely. The WaMu employees whom JPMorgan planned to keep were moved to higher levels, while the transition workers were moved to lower floors. As a transition employee, Mueller no longer had access to the whole building. Sections of the skyscraper had been barricaded with Sheetrock. JPMorgan took over the top floor of the building, and WaMu's holding company, embroiled in a bitter bankruptcy that would last years, moved into another.

Mueller's fiancée met him for lunch in WaMu's once-crowded cafeteria. Finding a place to sit had once been a challenge; now they were the only two diners. Sometimes, on a break, Mueller would walk around the empty space. Piles of electrical equipment and computers were piled into the center of each empty floor. Employees heard that JPMorgan had hired someone just to go around and pick up the abandoned office accessories. Eventually the bank invited local nonprofits to visit WaMu's headquarters with a pallet and cart off the extra goods. In the evening, Mueller looked up at the skyscraper. It had once glowed brightly at all hours of the day and night. Now it was largely dark.

Mueller was part of the last group of transition employees to leave, more than a year after WaMu failed. His Excel chart showed a jagged, decreasing line. Roughly 4,000 WaMu employees had left headquarters before him. Mueller had been working on a long good-bye letter to his colleagues and, as usual, had programmed it to go out at a specific time. That time was 3:33 on the morning of his departure, a time chosen so that his coworkers would know that, once again, he had automated his work. "I think what makes most jobs great or unbearable are the people you work with," Mueller wrote, under the subject line "Rambling, Obligatory Departure Email." "I've definitely had the privilege of working with, learning from, helping out, and occasionally having a few drinks with a very talented and awesome group of people. One of the reasons I stayed at the bowling alley so long was the strong sense of community I found there. At WaMu, I felt that there was a similar camaraderie, and I definitely miss it already, with so many of my friends already moved on. I want to thank you for the friendship, support, and mentoring you gave me throughout my time at WaMu, especially in this last crazy year."

He left WaMu with a clear memory of the bank's last day in existence, down to the weather report, a lump sum of pay from his 13 months of transition work for JPMorgan, a handsome bonus, 208 hours of vacation pay (it would have been more, except for a week-long bowling tournament in Las Vegas), and a bin full of WaMu mementos.

Within a year of its failure, little trace of Washington Mutual remained. JPMorgan spent tens of millions of dollars in Washington State alone to convert the bank, pulling down signs and sandblasting the word *WaMu* from the sides of bank branches and from the marble lobby of the headquarters building. JPMorgan pulled out of its leases in large office buildings across Seattle, leaving behind hundreds of thousands of square feet of vacant space, a move that helped push the city into a commercial real estate downturn. (All purchasers of failed banks are allowed to cancel leases during a set time frame after their acquisition.) One of those leases included the floors rented from the Seattle Art Museum, which years earlier had struck what seemed to be a banner deal with WaMu, allowing it to expand. While JPMorgan gave a $10 million, five-year grant to the museum, it wasn't nearly enough to make up for the lost annual rent.[29] The museum lost $25 million in revenue during that time and eventually borrowed from its endowment. For two years the museum struggled to find new tenants, until it filled the building.

JPMorgan got rid of WaMu's Occasio branches, replacing them with normal rows of tellers and ATM machines. Traditional branches "are superior in every way," Scharf told *The Wall Street Journal* about the decision. "They might be boring, but they're practical."[30] JPMorgan stopped offering free checking, a cornerstone of WaMu's retail bank strategy. Newly passed financial reform made it harder for banks to charge overdraft and debit card fees, so free accounts do not make as much money. In the branches, everything has returned to normal, except that now customers complain about dealing with big, out-of-town banks. "You can never please them," observed one branch manager.

In July 2009 at the Hilton Hotel in Seattle, local business leaders packed into a banquet hall to hear Jamie Dimon speak publicly in their city for the first time since WaMu's failure. Dimon had visited WaMu shortly after its purchase, but he spoke only to a select group of local company executives. He had emerged from the financial crisis like a god. He had seen the crisis coming and steered JPMorgan in the other direction. He had saved Bear Stearns and WaMu. He has been the subject of long, glowing articles and even a book. The book, incidentally, is called *Last Man Standing*. In 2011, *Time* named him one of the most influential people in the world, along with President Obama and Oprah Winfrey.

But while JPMorgan avoided some of the higher-risk loans like Option ARMs, its own losses on subprime mortgages ballooned right along with the rest of the industry's in 2007, increasing from $47 million the year before to $157 million. In his annual letter to shareholders, Dimon—sounding not unlike Killinger or any of the other bank executives suffering losses from mortgages—admitted that early attempts to fix problems with JPMorgan's subprime loans hadn't worked. He wrote: "We still found ourselves having to tighten our underwriting of subprime mortgage loans six times through the end of 2007. (Yes, this means our standards were not tough enough the first five times.)" JPMorgan also held a large portfolio of home equity loans. "The losses in this portfolio are increasing rapidly and rising at a higher rate than we ever could have expected, even in a severe recession," Dimon wrote to shareholders.

Before he arrived at the Hilton to address Seattle, Dimon met with a handful of reporters and television news stations. One reporter asked if he had anything to say to WaMu's shareholders.

"You know, I don't know what to say to them," said Dimon, who was wearing a tie decorated with tiny dinosaurs.[31] "You know, as it turns out, you all know that when the FDIC put the company up for sale and we paid a billion eight for what they were selling, including the branch network, there was one bidder. So, you know, when there's one bidder, that means there were hundreds of companies around the world that chose not to. Remember, it was a very scary time.

"It was a risk to do what we did, and you know, look at it the other way around. We salvaged a lot of jobs, we saved a lot of people, we're still doing business, we'll be a great citizen here and in California and Oregon. So investors take risks. Always remember when you buy stocks, you're taking a risk." He added: "I feel bad for them, but I don't know what I'm supposed to do about that."

A reporter asked how Dimon felt about a recently filed lawsuit against the company, which essentially accused JPMorgan of driving down WaMu's stock in the weeks before the failure so it could acquire the bank on the cheap.

Dimon laughed. "That is a pathetic and ridiculous statement," he said. "If you want to have conspiracy theories, that doesn't fly. Remember, we are going to lose that $30 billion we wrote off—that's a tremendous sum of money. We are going to lose that money. That would have wiped out the net worth of WaMu all by itself. I don't comprehend how people would make statements like that, particularly in the environment in which we acquired WaMu."

He thundered, "There are tons of lawsuits and we're going to defeat them all!"

At this point one of the local television reporters asked Dimon about the city's canceled fireworks show. JPMorgan, as part of its acquisition, had evaluated WaMu's philanthropic efforts, deciding which causes it would or wouldn't support. The bank had opted to keep giving the same amount as WaMu—$2.6 million—but it chose not to sponsor Seattle's much-loved annual fireworks show.[32] The event takes place each year over Lake Union (not far from the houseboat where Tom Hanks lived in *Sleepless in Seattle*) at the cost of several hundred thousand dollars. WaMu had covered the amount each year. News that JPMorgan would drop that commitment broke just before Dimon flew into Seattle. The city was in an uproar over the canceled fireworks.

Dimon either ignored or didn't hear the TV reporter's first question as he answered another one. The reporter interjected once more: "I'm going to ask you about the fireworks again."

Again, Dimon continued speaking about something else. The reporter tried again.

"So, Jamie, just to ask you again, to belabor this subject a little more about the fireworks—big, big deal to this community, big deal. And you've come in saying you want to be a member of this community, that you want to be welcomed in. People are saying, 'Well, gee, this is what Seattle is, this is what's been happening for years.' So it's not a money-economy thing to not do this sponsorship? Any more about that you can enlighten us on?"

Dimon was clearly annoyed. "Yeah, you know, I'm surprised you guys focus on stuff like that," he said, as the other reporters around the table watched the exchange in amusement.

"Well, it's just me, I'm focusing on it—" ventured the reporter, before Dimon interrupted her.

"Well, yeah, I know everyone wants to focus on their one little pet peeve," he said. "When I first got to Bank One and JPMorgan Chase—we give away a lot of money. I was shocked how badly some of that money was given away. I feel as much of an obligation to make sure that money is given away wisely as anything else. We help inner city kids get jobs, we help the disabled, we help schools, we help hospitals, we help the needy . . . there are a lot of great things we do. If you want to focus on fireworks, go ahead."

Dimon's tirade stunned the room. The local press wasn't familiar with his infamous outbursts. The reporters sat silently for a moment, unsure how to proceed. Eventually, JPMorgan's newly hired "chairwoman of the Pacific Northwest" interjected, glazing over the silence with reassurances that JPMorgan would be giving "in many other areas of the community."

(Dimon also apparently wasn't a fan of supporting the Seattle Art

Museum, at least initially. When one of his lieutenants suggested that he continue to donate to the museum because Kerry and Linda Killinger had a named wing, and Bill Gates, Jr.'s mom was involved, Dimon exclaimed: "Are you fucking stupid? Why the fuck would I do that? I will honor whatever we legally have to honor. Are you going to tell me that Bill Gates doesn't have enough money to support the museum?" He added: "Those are charities for the rich. If this were something for the Seattle schools, or housing, I would support it to the nth degree." JPMorgan did, however, later help sponsor the museum's popular Picasso exhibit.)

For the Hilton event, Dimon took his place on the podium in front of several hundred Seattle business leaders. It was standing room only. Within moments, he had the audience enthralled, regaling them with stories about the financial crisis. He told them how Hank Paulson had called him and his fellow bankers into a meeting in October 2008, explaining that they all must accept TARP money so that no other bank that really needed it would be afraid of doing so. "I actually think they did the right thing and it stabilized the system," said Dimon. "But then TARP morphed and I learned a great lesson in life."[33] He told the audience how he wrote a letter to Paulson after JPMorgan paid back the $25 billion, saying, "We hope you enjoyed the experience as much as we did." The audience laughed.

He reminded everyone, as he had earlier reminded the media, that JPMorgan had taken a big risk when it bought WaMu and overpaid for it. "One of the dark, dirty secrets is there were no other bidders on the bank," he said. "So we could have gotten it for $1."

As the hour-long presentation came to an end, Dimon looked out across the room and asked into the microphone, "Is Lou Pepper here?" No one responded. Pepper was not in the audience. He was at his home, north of Seattle.

"We are going to make him really proud of the company that he built," Dimon proclaimed. As he stepped down from the podium, the crowd cheered and gave him a standing ovation.

By 2010, JPMorgan was making about $3 billion a year on the WaMu purchase. Dimon and his team thought losses on WaMu's mortgages and credit cards could be $10 billion worse than the $30 billion the bank initially wrote down; only half of that additional amount had so far materialized. WaMu's mortgage business performed better than JPMorgan expected, although its retail bank performed worse. JPMorgan gave few details on either operation. In 2010, JPMorgan posted record earnings of $17 billion, up nearly 50 percent from the previous year. Dimon got a $17 million bonus, among the highest for bank executives on Wall Street. The purchase of WaMu—and Bear Stearns—catapulted JPMorgan to an astonishing *Forbes* ranking: the largest company in the world.

In the spring of 2010, WaMu executives testified on Capitol Hill as part of an extensive investigation into the bank's lending practices. The Permanent Subcommittee on Investigations had chosen WaMu to illustrate the rise of high-risk lending during the housing boom. WaMu, the committee concluded, had polluted the financial system by churning out bad loans and securities. "To rebuild our defenses, it is critical to understand that the recent financial crisis was not a natural disaster," Levin said in his opening testimony. "It was a man-made economic assault. People did it. Extreme greed was the driving force, and it will happen again unless we change the rules."[34]

He continued: "Washington Mutual was not, of course, the only one running a conveyor belt, dumping high-risk, poor-quality mortgages into the financial system. Far from it. Some of the perpetrators like Countrywide and New Century have already been hit with Federal enforcement actions and shareholder lawsuits. Others may never be held accountable. But all of us are still paying the price."

Kerry Killinger and Steve Rotella were forced to speak publicly for the first time since the bank's collapse. Neither had offered so much as a quote in a newspaper article since then. They also hadn't seen each other since Killinger left the bank. Killinger lived part of the time in Palm Desert, and Rotella moved his family back to New York. Rotella's house in Seattle languished on the market for about six months before he sold it for $1.5 million less than the original asking price.

Because they were forced to sit on the same panel (testifying with Killinger was considered a public relations disaster, but on the other hand, anyone who did it was likely to appear more sympathetic by

comparison), they approached their seats at the front of the congressional hearing room at the same time. Rotella offered his hand, and
Killinger shook it, but Killinger looked away while he did so.

"As CEO," Killinger told the panel of senators, reading from his prepared testimony, "I accept responsibility for our performance and am
deeply saddened by and sorry for what happened."[35]

He told the congressional committee that WaMu had been left out of
an exclusive group of financial institutions favored by the government
during the financial crisis. He pointed out that WaMu wasn't allowed on
a list of banks protected from short sellers, and it hadn't been invited to
hundreds of meetings and telephone calls in which high-level decisions
were made about the future of the country's banking system.

"For those that were part of the inner circle and were 'too clubby to
fail,' the benefits were obvious. For those outside the club, the penalty
was severe," he said. Asked to elaborate, Killinger said WaMu was seized
"in an unnecessary manner."

The committee seemed thoroughly unimpressed by Killinger's testimony. He seemed to blame policy makers for his mistakes at the helm
of WaMu. Senators questioned him on WaMu's mortgage practices
and its securitizations of loans sold to the secondary market. Killinger
repeatedly professed that he didn't know or didn't recall. "I was simply
just not involved in any of those," he said, when asked about the stated-
income loans WaMu sold on the secondary market.

At home in Seattle, former executives and managers of WaMu
watched the congressional grilling, thinking nothing unusual of Killinger's responses. It was entirely possible, they believed, that Killinger
didn't know what was happening because he didn't want to know what
was happening. He had continued to believe that the risks the bank took
could be managed. He didn't see how his strategy decisions, made at the
highest level of the company, had created a poisonous lending culture at
the bottom.

SENATOR TED KAUFMAN (D-DEL.): "Do you think people were actually
lying about their income on these stated income loans?"[36]
KILLINGER: "Well, clearly, it is speculation because I just don't know. I
am certainly very disappointed to think about my customers lying to me

because that is fraud and it shouldn't happen. But I think an objective look at things is that there must have been situations where people did not tell the truth on their applications."

And later:

SENATOR LEVIN: "Did you know that during the first quarter of 2007, that WaMu was securitizing Option ARM loans because of their greater likelihood to fail? Did you know that?"

KILLINGER: "I don't have a recollection of that."

SENATOR LEVIN, referencing e-mails in which Killinger encouraged the sale of Option ARMs during that time: "What did you think when you heard these e-mails today? Did that surprise you? Did that trouble you, that suddenly delinquencies hit very hard, and now you have got your staff that is saying, 'We better get rid of these quick.' Did that trouble you when you heard it today?"

KILLINGER: "Well, I don't recall having seen something like that before, so it was—it is just something that was new to me."

Rotella, meanwhile, claimed that the decision to expand into high-risk loans happened before he arrived at WaMu in 2005. "Total high-risk lending was not expanded and did not accelerate after 2005, as some have reported," Rotella said. "The facts show the opposite." But the congressional committee, in its report chronicling its investigation, disagreed with Rotella, pointing out that his own e-mails show his eagerness to expand into subprime and home equity lending, at least initially.[37]

Killinger had also said in his testimony that WaMu tried to curtail its high-risk lending. The committee refuted this testimony as well.

In California, as WaMu executives fought to defend themselves and as Wall Street bonuses returned as if the financial crisis had never happened, Ramona Jiminez put her house up for sale. For more than two years, she and her family had struggled to hold on to their property in El Monte, California, financed with a subprime loan from WaMu.

Jiminez had tried to renegotiate her loan terms with JPMorgan, the new owner of the mortgage, but she had been confused about what the bank offered. She thought if she made four lump-sum payments, she would receive a loan modification. That wasn't the case. Meanwhile, a moratorium on foreclosures caused a nationwide backlog, leaving many homeowners in limbo. Then banks couldn't find all the paperwork associated with homeowners' mortgages. This problem had emerged long ago at Long Beach Mortgage. Now it was happening on a nationwide scale. Ramirez put the property in El Monte on the market as a short sale. It was listed for almost $300,000 less than she had bought it for five years earlier, a 40 percent drop in value.

In her house—where a small table was pushed against a streaked window, and a metal Jesus on a cross was the only decoration on one living room wall—Jiminez considered her situation. Her children were sprawled across the cramped living room; two played a game of Operation, the board faded and cracked, while another checked her Facebook on a years-old desktop PC. Jiminez pointed to her oldest daughter, sitting on the couch. She was almost eighteen. If Jiminez saw her credit destroyed by foreclosure, her daughter's might qualify the family for another mortgage.

All across Southern California, many of the same home loan consultants who helped fuel WaMu's mortgage machine, including Tom Ramirez, have found new jobs at other banks and mortgage companies.

The U.S. Department of Justice, along with six other federal agencies, launched a criminal investigation into WaMu and its executives.[38] But in the summer of 2011, nearly three years after the bank's failure, the agencies dropped all criminal charges. The U.S. Attorney's Office in Seattle released a brief statement of explanation. After it had conducted hundreds of interviews and reviewed millions of files, the evidence did not meet "exacting standards for criminal charges," the agency said. No executives whose companies played major roles in the financial crisis have been indicted. Earlier in 2011, a long criminal investigation into Countrywide's Angelo Mozilo was dropped after no wrongdoing was found.[39] So far, only a mortgage trader from Goldman Sachs has been criminally charged. As Fay Chapman would later observe about the financial crisis in general, "There is no law against stupidity."

The FDIC filed a federal lawsuit against Killinger, Rotella, and David Schneider, alleging that the bank lost billions of dollars on bad mortgage loans because of their negligence. The FDIC asked for $900 million from the three executives, a startling sum of money,[40] particularly because the FDIC's deposit insurance fund wasn't used when WaMu failed. The FDIC also named Linda Killinger and Rotella's wife of thirty years, Esther, in the suit, claiming the wives aided their husbands in defrauding creditors. The Killingers had moved their homes in Seattle and Palm Desert into irrevocable trusts in August 2008, less than two months before the bank failed. The Rotellas did the same with their house in New York, although earlier in 2008, at about the time that WaMu had raised capital and appeared in better condition.

Rotella wrote a long letter to his family and friends decrying the FDIC's suit. "My parents, God bless them both, now at or near 90 years old, brought me up in a humble, but honorable environment," he wrote. "My father, a blue collar worker, and my mother, a homemaker, taught me to work hard and play by the rules. I have always done my best to do just that and have said many times that what I have achieved in life was an example of what can only happen in America. They also instilled in me a fierce sense of fairness and right and wrong. This action by the FDIC betrays any sense of common decency or fairness." He described himself as an "effective, hardworking bank manager who performed well under extraordinary conditions in an effort to save an important financial institution."

Killinger, who by this time had hired a high-priced Washington lawyer, the same lawyer who defended Lt. Col. Oliver North, released a statement. He called the FDIC's allegations "political theater."[41] "Trial in a courtroom that honors the rule of law—and not the will of Washington, D.C.—will confirm that Kerry Killinger's management, diligence, and commitment to Washington Mutual responsibly and consistently served the interests of its depositors, customers and shareholders." The statement continued: "Washington Mutual's management structure was a model of corporate governance."

In December 2011, Killinger, Rotella, and Schneider settled with the FDIC for $64 million, a small fraction of what the government agency initially sought. The payout would come not from the executives themselves, but rather from their insurance policies through WaMu. The settlement amount, as *The Wall Street Journal* pointed out, was still among the largest since the financial crisis.

Even before the settlement, Senator Levin's committee disagreed with the executives' conclusions. WaMu and other lenders were not victims of the financial crisis, the committee wrote in its final report.

Rather, their loans became the fuel that ignited it all.

ACKNOWLEDGMENTS

Two days before Christmas in December 2009, I logged onto my Facebook account and posted a jubilant message: "I'M DONE."

I had just finished the third installment of an investigative series of stories on Washington Mutual's September 25, 2008, failure for the *Puget Sound Business Journal* in Seattle, and I was feeling that strange mix of elation and nostalgia that besets every writer at the conclusion of a large project. Since the beginning of 2007, I had done little else but cover WaMu or the financial crisis, and the last year researching the bank's controversial downfall had taken an enormous amount of time, effort, and personal sacrifice. Because of the scope of the financial crisis, the details of WaMu's final days had gone largely unreported. In short order, I received hundreds of e-mails and phone calls from across the world—several readers professed to have cried over the stories; one asked if he could adopt me. (I'm assuming that he wasn't serious.) Soon the articles would receive national awards and a Pulitzer finalist citation. I thought that the story was over. My time covering WaMu had ended. What more could I possibly write?

Then came this book project, and I realized I had barely even begun.

There are many people to thank here. I'll start with those who made this book possible: my sources and, in particular, the numerous WaMu employees, executives, and consultants who contributed to this story.

Throughout the book research, it was my privilege to spend time with them. Many recounted their stories for the first time and trusted me with personal information that has never before been made public. They endured hours-long interviews and phone calls, never minding when I showed up at their house for a fourth time or called repeatedly to fact-check the most obscure detail—"Where was the washroom on the executive floor in 2003?" or "What color was your shirt on that day?" I will forever be grateful to them for their patience.

Some went above and beyond the call of duty: one executive provided three thick binders of historical information and photos, and one consultant spontaneously acted out part of a WaMu brand rally in the middle of a Starbucks outside Seattle, just for example. I owe a special debt to those who risked the ire of their current and former employers, or who risked a lawsuit, to speak with me. While I found documents from a number of different places, I am especially thankful for Senator Carl Levin's Permanent Subcommittee on Investigations and its helpful staff. The committee's investigation of WaMu forced the public release of thousands of documents that would otherwise have remained secret. I found the committee's final report on WaMu to be invaluable.

My editor at Simon & Schuster, Ben Loehnen, has been a godsend. His wise, deft edits and suggestions have made this book so much better than it otherwise would have been. He has been enthusiastic about this project from the start and entirely supportive throughout, always responding to questions right away and with thoughtful insight. That we have had a shared vision for how this story should be told has made the process all the more rewarding. Others at Simon & Schuster who deserve thanks: Jonathan Karp, Sammy Perlmutter, Richard Rhorer, Michael Accordino, Jessica Abell, Kelly Welsh, and Nancy Inglis.

Not long after I wrote about WaMu's failure in the *Puget Sound Business Journal*, Elizabeth Wales heard me speaking about the articles on KUOW, Seattle's NPR affiliate. I am forever grateful that she turned on her radio that day. I'm not exaggerating when I say that Elizabeth is the best literary agent an author could hope for. It was she who realized right away that the WaMu story should unfold in book form, and her e-mail to me suggesting as much launched this project. She has shepherded me patiently and kindly through this process, sending notes of encouragement and explanation about the mysteries of book publishing, even weeding through drafts of the manuscript to offer up improvements. Assistant agent Neal Swain at Wales Literary Agency has also been a terrific help.

I would never have been able to write this book without the support of my former employer, the *Puget Sound Business Journal,* and its parent company, American City Business Journals. My editors at the *Puget Sound Business Journal* and their managers at ACBJ cleared the way for me to spend nearly a year investigating WaMu's failure for the newspaper and then graciously provided an extended leave for me to write the book. Emory Thomas, Jr., former publisher of the *Puget Sound Business Journal,* led the charge on my WaMu stories at the newspaper. He cleared all obstacles to coverage and provided terrific guidance throughout. Executive editor George Erb's strong and steady leadership of the newsroom, and his belief in the WaMu story, made my articles possible. He (and his lovely wife Mavis) have been big supporters of this book, always asking all the right questions. Alwyn Scott, former managing editor of the newspaper and my direct editor, was my partner and adviser on all the WaMu coverage (as well as my other work at the paper) and is one of the most talented journalists I have ever worked with. He has improved my writing by leaps and bounds. He continued to be a crutch for me on this book project, lifting my spirits and offering ideas at all the right moments. I am lucky to have his support. I worked with reporter Jeanne Lang Jones on other projects at the newspaper, and I blatantly copied her dogged reporting techniques and document-diving skills many times in my research. At a small newspaper in particular, it is hard to sacrifice a reporter for a long project or leave, and for that reason, I am grateful to all my former coworkers and managers who covered for me in my absence, with no complaint.

I have been very blessed to have an amazing group of family and friends who lifted me up throughout this time, all of whom I can't possibly name here. They patiently allowed me to talk about WaMu incessantly for three straight years, skip plans at the last minute, and ignore all important occasions. My biggest support is my husband, Steve Grind, whom I can never thank enough. He read through numerous book drafts and offered suggestions, all while finishing his MBA.

He let me lapse into writer's tendencies (hand-wringing, complaining, despondency) whenever I needed to. It is challenging to be married to a journalist, and Steve does it with grace, humor, and love. My parents, Pat Orsini and Klaus Meinhard, have always encouraged me to do anything I wanted, and I would not be anywhere near where I am without them. They continue to be as supportive and enthusiastic as I could ever hope. My sister Sonja, a gifted high school Spanish teacher, read through my manuscript and offered great suggestions—her initial positive reaction to the first half of the book gave me inspiration to write the second. My other siblings have also lent a great deal of support and the occasional much-needed trip to Las Vegas or the beach: Iman, Vanessa, and Nick. Also, my other fantastic parents: Ursula, Don, Ginny, and Pat. My friend and former editor, Pat Ferrier, sped through a book draft in only two and a half weeks when I dropped it into her lap, on top of her demanding day job. My good friend and fellow writer Heidi Dietrich walked countless laps around Seattle's Green Lake with me and listened patiently to all things WaMu; Kelly Coakley, my childhood friend, made sure I got out of the house. Others I would be remiss not to mention are Kim Torch, Auna Moser (and Jake!), Clay Holtzman, the Ks (Karen, Karen, and Katie), and Zachary Schisgal, for his initial work on this project.

Other authors lent their encouragement and offered general advice, for which I am grateful. Among them: Craig Welch, Andrew Ross Sorkin, Bill Dietrich, Jerry Brewer, Diana Hendriques, Duff McDonald, William Cohan, and Michael Hudson. Journalists whose stellar work covering WaMu I repeatedly cite within this book include: Drew DeSilver, David Heath, Bill Virgin, Dan Fitzpatrick, Peter Goodman, and Gretchen Morgenson.

To all who contributed in some way to this project—thank you.

NOTES ON SOURCING

A note about the research and the story

This book is the accumulation of several hundred hours of interviews with more than 200 people related to Washington Mutual and its trajectory over the last 20 years—executives of the bank, directors, employees, customers, consultants, regulators, attorneys, industry experts, and other bankers. Because of the controversial nature of WaMu's recent history, and because of ongoing lawsuits and contractual agreements with JPMorgan Chase, the acquirer of WaMu, many people interviewed for this book spoke on condition of anonymity. Others spoke on the record for the first time, and still others—particularly those related to the events surrounding WaMu's last few weeks—refused to speak at all. Even many of those who did participate did so reluctantly, and only after a long period of relationship building. To all the many people who did participate, I owe an enormous amount of gratitude.

I relied heavily on public and internal documents to piece together this narrative, particularly those covering the last four years of the bank's existence. By my estimation, I have read more than 10,000 documents related to WaMu, its government regulators, and its potential acquirers—internal e-mails, board reports and minutes, Securities and Exchange Commission filings, independent investigative reports, management and employee presentations, letters, property records, lawsuits, interview transcripts, meeting notes, scripts, and newspaper and magazine articles. The documents came from a wide range of sources, but most notably from the U.S. Senate's Permanent Subcommittee on Investigations; from lawsuits and bankruptcy court proceedings; and from employees, executives, and others related to WaMu and other parties in this book.

In my work at the *Puget Sound Business Journal*, I filed numerous public records requests through the federal Freedom of Information Act, seeking information about WaMu's final months. I was largely unsuccessful. The Federal Deposit Insurance Corp. turned over hundreds of e-mails sent between Chairman Sheila Bair and her deputies that were redacted—blacked out with a marker—most frequently citing subsection (b)(4) of the FOIA, which "permits the withholding of commercial or financial information obtained from a person and considered privileged or confidential"; subsection (b)(5), which "permits the withholding of information contained in internal communications which relate to predecisional staff opinions, recommendations and discussions of policy alternatives"; subsection (b)(6), which "permits the withholding of information, the disclosure of which would constitute a clearly unwarranted invasion of personal privacy"; and finally subsection (b)(8), which "permits the withholding of information contained in, or related to, the examination, operating or condition reports prepared by, on behalf of, or for the use of the FDIC in its regulation or supervision of financial institutions." The Office of Thrift Supervision also was unhelpful. The Permanent Subcommittee on Investigations, through its power of subpoena, obtained the largest cache of public records related to WaMu, but even so, much of the internal communication between government regulators during WaMu's last weeks remains a mystery.

The dialogue at and descriptions of key meetings and events were pieced together through numerous people's recollections, newspaper articles, public records, meeting notes, and e-mails. It is important to note that people who figure prominently in the story, or who are quoted in conversation, aren't necessarily the same people who gave me the information. Meetings were often attended by numerous people, key conversations were frequently relayed to others directly after they occurred, and e-mails were often sent out summarizing the details of an event. I tried, as much as possible, to tell the story through the eyes of the people who witnessed the events.

As with any controversial story, there are frequently competing story lines, with people disagreeing on how, or why, key events unfolded. In WaMu's case, I encountered plenty of discrepancies, particularly surrounding its last two years. When accounts differed to such an extent— between two people or multiple parties—I attempted to present all sides in the narrative or, in some cases, to note the difference of opinion or view in a footnote. In each instance, I attempted to talk to as many people as possible to present the most balanced account. Another pitfall is that of fading memories or, as Sheila Bair would say later, "the fog of war." Here again I checked all information by as many as possible of the people involved, often melding together several people's recollections of a key event or meeting. In WaMu's later years, I witnessed some of the key events through my work at the *Puget Sound Business Journal*: among them were the infamous last annual shareholder meeting, Kerry Killinger's speech to the Rotary Club, and Jamie Dimon's fireworks outburst and speech in Seattle.

For the early chapters, I relied on Lou Pepper's book *When You Get a Moment, Would You Please . . .* to reconstruct events and to get a feel for the bank over the years. I was fortunate that Murray Morgan wrote a very thorough account of WaMu's early history, *The Friend of the Family: 100 Years with Washington Mutual*, published by WaMu in 1989. Other books that I refer to frequently deserve mention. On the roots of the financial crisis: *All the Devils Are Here: The Hidden History of the Financial Crisis* by Bethany McLean and Joe Nocera. On the early years at Long Beach Mortgage: *The Monster: How a Gang of Predatory Lenders and Wall Street Bankers Fleeced America—and Spawned a Global Crisis* by Michael W. Hudson. On the ticktock of the crucial months of the crisis in 2008: *Too Big to Fail* by Andrew Ross Sorkin. And on JPMorgan Chase: *Last Man Standing: The Ascent of Jamie Dimon and JPMorgan Chase* by Duff McDonald.

To research Long Beach Mortgage, I took a weeks-long road trip to Southern California, interviewing brokers and account executives at Long Beach and at other companies in the subprime industry. I waded through property records at a government office building in Los Angeles County to find subprime borrowers of WaMu and drove hundreds of miles around the county to talk to them. I spent a lot of time in New York City and Washington, D.C., interviewing others related to the bank, JPMorgan Chase, and the regulatory agencies. In Seattle, most of my time was spent in the dining rooms, living rooms, back patios, and neighborhood coffee shops of the numerous executives and employees who still live in the city. WaMu's reach stretched far, and its employees are scattered throughout the world, so I also conducted interviews, often via Skype, and at odd hours of the day and night, with sources in multiple other countries.

When I embarked on this project full-time in the summer of 2010, I discovered a large knowledge gap related to the financial crisis. On the one hand, many people I talked with—namely those in some way related to the banking, finance, mortgage, or real estate industries—had been bombarded with information about the inner workings of a subprime security and unusual mortgages. Already a flurry of books and long articles had come out that helped explain many of these concepts. Congressional committees convened; lengthy reports detailing the crisis followed. But on the other hand, I was astounded to find that many smart people still had no clear idea of how this crisis happened—or how all these pieces fit together—including some who played a role. I set about writing this book for the latter group of people, and I tried to do it in a way that was relatable to the average person. As a result, I'm sure I will have offended some with my simple explanation of some concepts, while others will find some descriptions repetitive after other, more definitive accounts of certain aspects of the crisis.

As I wrote this book, the story of WaMu continued to unfold, more than three years after its September 25, 2008, failure. Mere weeks before I turned in my first draft, the FDIC filed a massive lawsuit against several WaMu executives, another large shareholder suit was settled out of court, and the Permanent Subcommittee on Investigations released its final report dissecting WaMu's high-risk lending (and other aspects of the financial crisis), as well as hundreds of additional documents. The bitter bankruptcy of WaMu's holding company continued with no resolution and its own set of dramatic twists and turns. A criminal investigation into WaMu's executives, announced just after the bank's failure, was officially dropped in the summer of 2011. This book is based on the most current information available, but it's entirely possible that new documents or interviews or insights could emerge, helping to shed light on what happened at the bank.

PARTIAL
(b)(4)(b)(5)(b)(6)
(b)(8)

From: Bair, Sheila C.
Sent: Tuesday, September 16, 2008 8:41 PM
To: Spoth, Christopher J.; Ivie, Stan
Subject: Re: WAMU

1 Page

This is one of several hundred similarly redacted emails that journalist Kirsten Grind received from the Federal Deposit Insurance Corp. as part of a Freedom of Information Act Request filed while at the *Puget Sound Business Journal*. The request asked for former FDIC chairman Sheila Bair's emails with the subject of "Washington Mutual" in September 2008.

NOTES

PROLOGUE: OUT OF TIME

1. Justin Matlick, "Questions for Steve Rotella, WaMu President and COO," *Puget Sound Business Journal*, April 30, 2006.
2. Sheryl Gay Stolberg and David M. Herszenhorn, "Bush and Candidates to Meet on Bailout," *New York Times*, Sept. 24, 2008.
3. David Faber, "Is Your Money Safe: WaMu Update," *CNBC*, Sept. 25, 2008.

CHAPTER ONE: FRIEND OF THE FAMILY

1. *Washington Mutual Savings Bank and Subsidiaries: Annual Report, 1982*, Northwest Historical Annual Reports Collection, University of Washington.
2. Murray Morgan, *The Friend of the Family: 100 Years with Washington Mutual* (Washington Mutual Financial Group, 1989).
3. Ibid.
4. Federal Deposit Insurance Corp., *The Banking Crises of the 1980s and Early 1990s: Summary and Implications*, http://www.fdic.gov/bank/historical/history/, 6/5/2000.
5. *Washington Mutual Savings Bank and Subsidiaries: Annual Report, 1978*, Northwest Historical Annual Reports Collection, University of Washington.
6. Morgan, *Friend of the Family*.
7. Federal Deposit Insurance Corp., *Banking Crises*.
8. Murray, *Friend of the Family*.
9. Ibid.

10. *Washington Mutual Savings Bank and Subsidiaries: Annual Report, 1982.*

11. Lee J. Sahlin, *A History: The First 100 Years of Murphey Favre Incorporated* (Murphey Favre Inc., 1987).

12. Washington Mutual, *Performance: Washington Mutual Savings Bank, Annual Report 1986.*

13. Federal Deposit Insurance Corp., *Continental Illinois and "Too Big to Fail,"* www.fdic.gov, June 5, 2000.

14. Washington Mutual, *General Ledger: Washington Mutual Savings Bank, 1989 Annual Report.*

15. Louis H. Pepper, *If You Get a Moment Would You Please . . .* (Pullman: Washington State University Publishing, 2005).

CHAPTER TWO: REMOVE THE CORPORATE JETS

1. Kathleen Morris, "Washington Mutual's CEO: Energizer Banker," *BusinessWeek*, July 14, 1997.

2. "Obituary: Karl Killinger," *Des Moines Register*, Nov. 12, 2008.

3. Kerry Killinger, interview by Joe Carolus, *Kids and the American Dream* radio show, 2001.

4. U.S. Securities and Exchange Commission, *Washington Mutual: 1995 Annual Report and Form 10-K*, www.sec.gov.

5. U.S. Securities and Exchange Commission, *Washington Mutual: 1997 Annual Report and Form 10-K*, www.sec.gov.

6. Timothy Curry and Lynn Shibut, "The Cost of the Savings and Loan Crisis: Truth and Consequences," *FDIC Banking Review*, 1986.

7. Sam Zuckerman, "Thrifts Ads Expoit Merger Upheaval," *American Banker*, June 22, 1992.

8. Saul Hansell, "Ahmanson Sets a $5.8 Billion Hostile Bid for Great Western," *New York Times*, Feb. 18, 1997.

9. Christopher Rhoads, "Ahmanson Ad Campaign Urges Great Western to Enter Talks," *American Banker*, Feb. 28, 1997.

10. Hansell, "Ahmanson Sets a $5.8 Billion Hostile Bid."

11. Kenneth Gilpin, "Ahmanson Sweetens Its Bid in Duel for Great Western," *New York Times*, Mar. 18, 1997.

12. Ibid.

13. John Gorman, "Tallest Midget," *Forbes*, July 23, 2001.

14. Kenneth Gilpin, "Behind a Huge S&L Empire, a Low-Key Superstar," *New York Times*, Mar. 19, 1998.

15. Christopher Rhoads, "Ahmanson CEO's Pitch Fails to Jar the Market," *American Banker*, Mar. 11, 1997.

16. Peter Neurath, "All the Right Assets for Washington Mutual's Kerry Killinger," *Puget Sound Business Journal*, Dec. 26, 1997.

17. Saul Hansell, "Ahmanson Ends Hostile Bid for S&L," *New York Times*, June 5, 1997.

18. "Ahmanson Gives Up Bid for Great Western," United Press International, June 4, 1997.

19. Christopher Rhoads, "WaMu Nabs Great Western as Ahmanson Drops Bid," *American Banker*, June 5, 1997.

20. Securities and Exchange Commission, *Washington Mutual: 1997 Annual Report and Form 10-K*.

21. Michael Liedke, "Glitch Hobbles Direct Deposits at Wells Fargo & Co.," *Contra Costa Times*, July 25, 1996.

22. Thomas Hoffman, "Merger Glitches Hit Banks Bottom Line; Downsizing Leaves Few with Back-Office Smarts," *ComputerWorld*, July 28, 1997.

23. Steve Cocheo, "Kerry Killinger Builds His Dream Bank," *ABA Banking Journal*, Aug. 1, 2001.

24. Federal Deposit Insurance Corp., *Deposit Market Share Report*, June 30, 1998.

25. Paul Muolo, "WaMu Does Biggest Thrift Deal Ever," *National Mortgage News*, Mar. 23, 1998.

26. Louis H. Pepper, *If You Get a Moment Would You Please . . .* (Pullman: Washington State University, 2005).

27. Ibid.

28. Bill Virgin, "Seattle's 'Really Nice' Killer; CEO Has Turned Washington Mutual into a Behemoth," *Seattle Post-Intelligencer*, Oct. 1, 1998.

CHAPTER THREE: THE POWER OF YES

1. U.S. Senate, Permanent Subcommittee on Investigations, *Wall Street and the Financial Crisis: The Role of High Risk Home Loans*, April 13, 2010, Exhibit 8b, p. 150. (Hereafter cited as Senate Investigations Subcommittee.)

2. Brenda White, "A Short History of Subprime," *Mortgage Banking*, Mar. 1, 2006.

3. U.S. Securities and Exchange Commission, *Long Beach Financial: Form 10-K, Year Ended Dec. 31, 1998*, http://www.sec.gov/Archives/edgar/data/1034011/0000892569–99–000753.txt.

4. David Heath, "WaMu: Hometown Bank Turned Predatory Lender," *Seattle Times*, Oct. 2009.

5. Jeff Harrington, "CEO Named for Tampa At-Risk Lender Aristar," *St. Petersburg Times*, May 14, 1998.

6. "Washington Mutual Agrees to Purchase Long Beach Financial," *Puget Sound Business Journal*, May 19, 1999.

7. Michael W. Hudson, *The Monster: How a Gang of Predatory Lenders and Wall Street Bankers Fleeced America—and Spawned a Global Crisis* (New York: Times Books, 2010).

8. Dennis Hevesi, "Roland Arnall, 68, Mortgage Innovator," *New York Times*, Mar. 19, 2008.

9. Hudson, *The Monster*.

10. Kathleen Day, "Raising the Roof on Riskier Lending; 'Subprime' Mortgage Practices by Banks and Finance Firms Draw Federal, State Scrutiny," *Washington Post*, Feb. 6, 2000.

11. John Harris, "Clinton Pushes 'Homeownership Strategy'; in Era of Reduced Government, Administration Stresses Private Sector," *Washington Post*, June 6, 1995.

12. Steven Holmes, "Fannie Mae Eases Credit to Aid Mortgage Lending," *New York Times*, Sept. 30, 1999.

13. Hudson, *The Monster*.

14. U.S. Securities and Exchange Commission, *Long Beach Financial: Form 10-K, Year Ended Dec. 31, 1998*.

15. Edward Gramlich, *Subprime Mortgages: America's Latest Boom and Bust* (Washington, D.C.: Urban Institute Press, 2007).

16. Gretchen Morgenson and Peter Goodman, "The Reckoning: Saying Yes, WaMu Built Empire on Shaky Loans," *New York Times*, Dec. 27, 2008.

17. "Washington Mutual Builds on Power of Yes," *Brandweek*, Mar. 4, 2002.

18. Robert Stowe, "WaMu—The Power of Yes," *Mortgage Banking*, June 1, 2001.

19. Senate Investigations Subcommittee, *Wall Street and the Financial Crisis: The Role of High Risk Loans*, Memorandum, p. 11.

20. Ibid., Exhibit 59a, p. 463.

21. Gramlich, *Subprime Mortgages*.

22. "Subprime Wholesale Volume Leaders in 2003," *Origination News*, April 2004.

23. Mike Hudson and E. Scott Reckard, "Workers Say Lender Ran 'Boiler Rooms,'" *Los Angeles Times*, Feb. 4, 2005.

24. Senate Investigations Subcommittee, *Wall Street and the Financial Crisis: The Role of High Risk Home Loans*, James Vanasek interview.

25. Fannie Mae International Finance Services, *Mortgage-Backed Securities: The U.S. Approach*, 2003.

26. Senate Investigations Subcommittee, *Wall Street and the Financial Crisis: The Role of High Risk Home Loans*, Exhibit 8b, p. 151.

CHAPTER FOUR: ALEXANDER THE GREAT

1. *In the Superior Court of the State of Washington in and for the County of King in re the Marriage of Kerry K. Killinger and Deborah T. Killinger*, Seattle, May 1, 2000, Summons.

2. Ibid., Jan. 9, 2001, Property Settlement Agreement/Separation Contract.
3. "Miller, Cottington Are Granted Divorce," *Des Moines Register,* May 31, 2001.
4. U.S. Securities and Exchange Commission, *Washington Mutual: 2001 Annual Report on Form 10-K,* Mar. 19, 2003, www.sec.gov.
5. "Washington Mutual to Acquire Dime Bancorp," *ATM Marketplace.com,* Jan. 2, 2002.
6. "Thousands of Teachers Amass on Broadway for a Special Performance," *Business Wire,* Nov. 15, 2002.
7. "Homeboy—II Magazine Platinum," *Insititutional Investor,* Americas ed., Mar. 1, 2002.
8. Washington Mutual, *Washington Mutual's Branded Retail Store Concept a Winner,* June 28, 2000.
9. Laura Mandaro, "WaMu CEO Unveils 'Aggressive' Chicago, U.S. Growth Plans," *American Banker,* Oct. 17, 2002.
10. Bill Virgin, "WaMu Goes Over $1 Billion Mark; Loan Sales More Than Make Up for Drop in Non-Interest Income," *Seattle Post-Intelligencer,* April 16, 2003.
11. Kerry Killinger, *Lehman Bros. 2003 Financial Services Conference,* Sept. 9, 2003.
12. Laura Mandaro, "2001 Banker of the Year: Kerry Killinger," *American Banker,* Dec. 7, 2001.
13. Richard Buck, "Chief Is Spark Behind WaMu Growth," *Seattle Times,* Mar. 9, 1997.
14. Kenneth Gilpin, "Behind a Huge S&L Empire, a Low-Key Superstar," *New York Times,* Mar. 19, 1998.
15. Ibid.
16. Buck, "Chief Is Spark."
17. Bethany Mclean, "Washington Mutual's Remarkable Rise: The Alexander the Great of the Thrift Industry," *Fortune,* Dec. 8, 1997.
18. Virgin, "WaMu Goes over $1 Billion Mark."
19. John Gorman, "Tallest Midget," *Forbes,* July 23, 2001.
20. Steve Cocheo, "Kerry Killinger Builds His Dream Bank," *ABA Banking Journal,* Aug. 1, 2001.
21. Shawn Tully, "What Went Wrong at WaMu," *Fortune,* Aug. 9, 2004.
22. Jenny Mero, "People Are His Bottom Line," *Fortune,* April 16, 2007.
23. Kerry Killinger, interview by Joe Carolus, *Kids and the American Dream* radio show, 2001.
24. U.S. Securities and Exchange Commission, *Washington Mutual: Definitive Proxy Statement,* Mar. 17, 2004, http://www.sec.gov/Archives/edgar/data/933136/000089102004000330/v96013dedef14a.htm.

25. U.S. Senate, Permanent Subcommittee on Investigations, *Wall Street and the Financial Crisis: The Role of High Risk Home Loans*, April 13, 2010, Exhibit 1h, p. 26. (Hereafter cited as Senate Investigations Subcommittee.)

26. Kirsten Grind, "Insiders Detail Reasons for WaMu's Failure," *Puget Sound Business Journal*, Jan. 23, 2009.

27. Melissa Allison, "Less Office, More Space for WaMu," *Seattle Times*, Mar. 10, 2006.

28. Robert Slater, *Jack Welch and the GE Way* (New York: McGraw-Hill, 1999).

29. Shoshana Zuboff, "The New Adulthood," *Fast Company*, Aug. 1, 2004.

30. Senate Investigations Subcommittee, *Wall Street and the Financial Crisis: The Role of High Risk Loans*, Steve Rotella interview.

31. Stephanie Anderson Forest, "Is This Any Way to Run a Bank?" *Bloomberg BusinessWeek*, Oct. 13, 2003.

32. Bill Virgin, "Class-Action Bid in WaMu Lawsuit Will Be Argued at Court Hearing," *Seattle Post-Intelligencer*, May 9, 2002.

33. U.S. Securities and Exchange Commission, *Washington Mutual: Form 10-K, 2002*, http://www.sec.gov/Archives/edgar/data/933136/00010474690 3008846/a2105105z10-k.htm.

34. Tully, "What Went Wrong at WaMu."

35. E. Scott Reckard, "Washington Mutual's Growth Strategy Plagued by Missteps," *Los Angeles Times*, Aug. 25, 2004.

36. "Double WaMu; Mortgage Banks," *Economist*, Aug. 21, 2004.

37. Bill Virgin, "WaMu's Plan for Ailing Mortgage Unit: Close 100 Home Loan Centers," *Seattle Post-Intelligencer*, July 22, 2004.

38. Ibid.

39. U.S. Securities and Exchange Commission, *Washington Mutual: Form 10-K, 2003*, http://www.sec.gov/Archives/edgar/data/933136/000104746904007947/a2129328z10-k.htm.

40. "$58B Bank Deal Set," *CNNMoney*, Jan. 15, 2004.

41. Duff McDonald, *Last Man Standing: The Ascent of Jamie Dimon and JPMorgan Chase* (New York: Simon & Schuster, 2009).

42. Dalia Fahmy, "The 25 Most Powerful Women in Banking: #2 Deanna Oppenheimer," *US Banker*, Oct. 2010.

43. *In the District Court of Galveston County, Texas*, Mar. 25, 2009, Case No. 09CV0199, Lawsuit.

44. Kerry Killinger, "Washington Mutual Memorandum to Board of Directors, re Strategic Direction," 2004.

45. Federal Deposit Insurance Corp., *Deposit Market Share Report*, June 30, 2006.

46. Ann Carrns, "WaMu Whiplash: Fast Expansion Yields Problems," *Wall Street Journal*, Dec. 16, 2006.

47. Senate Investigations Subcommittee, *Wall Street and the Financial Crisis: The Role of High Risk Loans*, Exhibit 79, p. 554.

CHAPTER FIVE: THE DARK SIDE

1. U.S. Securities and Exchange Commission, *Washington Mutual: Form 10-K*, 2004, http://www.sec.gov/Archives/edgar/data/933136/000104746904007947/a2129328z10-k.htm.

2. U.S. Senate, Permanent Subcommittee on Investigations, *Wall Street and the Financial Crisis: The Role of High Risk Home Loans*, April 13, 2010, Exhibit 35, p. 338. (Hereafter cited as Senate Investigations Subcommittee.)

3. Ibid.

4. Ibid., Memorandum, p. 11.

5. "Remarks by President Bush on Homeownership," *PR Newswire*, Mar. 26, 2004.

6. Senate Investigations Subcommittee, *Wall Street and the Financial Crisis: The Role of High Risk Loans*, Exhibit 35, p. 338.

7. Ibid.

8. Ibid.

9. Ibid.

10. Ibid.

11. Ibid., p. 341.

12. Ibid., p. 349.

13. Ibid., p. 348.

14. Bill Sones and Rich Sones, "Mortgage Means 'Death Pledge,'" *Deseret News*, Mar. 2010.

15. U.S. Securities and Exchange Commission, *Washington Mutual: Form 10-K, 2005*, http://www.sec.gov/Archives/edgar/data/933136/000110465906016786/a06-2446_110k.htm.

16. David Heath, "WaMu: Hometown Bank Turned Predatory Lender," *Seattle Times*, Oct. 2009.

17. Senate Investigations Subcommittee, *Wall Street and the Financial Crisis: The Role of High Risk Loans*, Exhibit 1i, p. 27.

18. Ibid.

19. Greg Ip, "Fed Chief Questions Loan Choices," *Wall Street Journal*, Feb. 23, 2004.

20. U.S. Securities and Exchange Commission, *IndyMac Bancorp: Form 10-K, 2006*, http://www.sec.gov/Archives/edgar/data/773468/000095012906002125/a17844e10vk.htm.

21. U.S. Securities and Exchange Commission, *Golden West Financial Corp.: Form 10-K, 2006*, http://www.sec.gov/Archives/edgar/data/42293/000119312506048352/d10k.htm.

22. U.S. Securities and Exchange Commission, *Washington Mutual: Form 10-K*, 2006, http://www.sec.gov/Archives/edgar/data/933136/000110465906016786/a06-2446_110k.htm.

23. Senate Investigations Subcommittee, *Wall Street and the Financial Crisis: The Role of High Risk Loans*, Exhibit 3, p. 83.

24. Bethany McLean and Joe Nocera, *All the Devils Are Here* (New York: Penguin, 2010).

25. Senate Investigations Subcommittee, *Wall Street and the Financial Crisis: The Role of High Risk Loans*, Memorandum, p. 12.

26. U.S. Senate, Permanent Subcommittee on Investigations, *Wall Street and the Financial Crisis: The Role of Investment Banks*, 2010, Memorandum, p. 6.

27. U.S. Senate, Permanent Subcommittee on Investigations, *Wall Street and the Financial Crisis*, 2011, Report Footnote 154, p. 25.

28. Senate Investigations Subcommittee, *Wall Street and the Financial Crisis: The Role of High Risk Loans*, Exhibit 2b, p. 49.

29. Drew DeSilver, "Reckless Strategies Doomed WaMu," *Seattle Times*, Oct. 25, 2009.

30. Senate Investigations Subcommittee, *Wall Street and the Financial Crisis: The Role of High Risk Loans*, James Vanasek interview.

31. Ibid.

32. Ibid., Exhibit 2a, 30.

33. Tom Brown, "Ken Lewis Shafts His Shareholders—Again," *Bankstocks.com*, July 6, 2005.

34. Gretchen Morgenson and Peter Goodman, "The Reckoning: Saying Yes, WaMu Built Empire on Shaky Loans," *New York Times*, Dec. 27, 2008.

35. Senate Investigations Subcommittee, *Wall Street and the Financial Crisis: The Role of High Risk Loans*, James Vanasek interview.

36. Ibid.

37. Drew DeSilver, "Reckless Strategies Doomed WaMu."

38. Senate Investigations Subcommittee, *Wall Street and the Financial Crisis: The Role of High Risk Loans*, Exhibit 7, p. 144.

39. Connie Bruck, "Angelo's Ashes: The Man Who Became the Face of the Financial Crisis," *New Yorker*, June 29, 2009.

40. Senate Investigations Subcommittee, *Wall Street and the Financial Crisis: The Role of High Risk Loans*, Exhibit 79, p. 553.

41. McLean and Nocera, *All the Devils Are Here*.

42. Senate Investigations Subcommittee, *Wall Street and the Financial Crisis*, Report Footnote 275, p. 60.

43. Ibid., Report Footnote 197, p. 45.

44. Senate Investigations Subcommittee, *Wall Street and the Financial Crisis: The Role of High Risk Loans*, Exhibit 79, p. 553.

45. Ibid., Exhibit 49, p. 427.

46. DeSilver, "Reckless Strategies Doomed WaMu."

47. Gretchen Morgenson, "Fair Game—Was There a Loan It Didn't Like?" *New York Times*, Nov. 1, 2008.

48. U.S. Treasury Department, Offices of Inspector General, Federal Deposit Insurance Corp., *Evaluation of Federal Regulatory Oversight of Washington Mutual Bank*, 2010, p. 23.

49. Ibid., p. 24.

50. Mortgage Bankers Association, *Federal Assistance Needed to Keep Mortgage Capital Flowing Through Warehouse Lines of Credit*, 2009.

51. James Hagerty and Ann Carrns, "WaMu Leads in Risky Type of Lending—Analysis Shows Thrift Makes Frequent Loans for Investment Homes," *Wall Street Journal*, April 17, 2007.

52. Michael Corkery and Christine Haughney, "Investors Hold the Key to Housing Boom's Fate," *Wall Street Journal*, Aug. 17, 2005.

53. Murray Morgan, *The Friend of the Family: 100 Years with Washington Mutual* (Washington Mutual Financial Group, 1989).

54. Senate Investigations Subcommittee, *Wall Street and the Financial Crisis: The Role of High Risk Loans*, Exhibit 78, p. 551.

55. Ibid., James Vanasek interview.

56. Nell Henderson, "Bernanke: There's No Housing Bubble to Go Bust," *Washington Post*, Oct. 27, 2005.

57. National Association of Realtors, *Anti-Bubble Reports* (Washington, D.C., 2005).

58. David Lereah, interview by Gwen Ifill, "Housing Market Update," *News-Hour with Jim Lehrer*, Nov. 29, 2005.

59. David Lereah, *Are You Missing the Real Estate BOOM?* (New York: Crown Business, 2005).

60. "Are You Missing the Real Estate Boom? 2.0," *Big Picture*, Oct. 30, 2006.

61. Securities and Exchange Commission, *Washington Mutual: Form 10-K, 2006*.

62. Colin Robertson, "Subprime Lending Volume over the Years," *National Mortgage News*, Dec. 9, 2008.

63. Senate Investigations Subcommittee, *Wall Street and the Financial Crisis: The Role of High Risk Loans*, Exhibit 10, p. 169.

64. Senate Investigations Subcommittee, *Wall Street and the Financial Crisis*, Report Footnote 197, p. 45.

65. Ted Cornwell, "Killinger: Industry Shakeout?" *National Mortgage News*, Oct. 25, 2005.

66. Securities and Exchange Commission, *Washington Mutual: Form 10-K, 2006*.

67. Ibid.

68. Jesse Eisinger, "Investors Fret Mortgage Balloons Will Burst," *Wall Street Journal*, July 27, 2005.

69. Ibid.

70. Senate Investigations Subcommittee, *Wall Street and the Financial Crisis: The Role of High Risk Loans*, Exhibit 62, p. 488.

71. Ibid., Exhibit 61, p. 487.

72. Ibid., Exhibit 63a, p. 489.

73. Gretchen Morgenson and Peter Goodman, "The Reckoning: Saying Yes, WaMu Built Empire on Shaky Loans," *New York Times*, Dec. 27, 2008.

74. Amilda Dymi, "WaMu Exec Eyes Financial Literacy," *Origination News*, 2006.

75. Senate Investigations Subcommittee, *Wall Street and the Financial Crisis*, Report Footnote 333, p. 75.

76. Senate Investigations Subcommittee, *Wall Street and the Financial Crisis: The Role of High Risk Loans*, Exhibit 22a, p. 257.

77. Ibid., Exhibit 4, p. 92.

78. Ibid., Exhibit 22a, p. 257.

79. Ibid., Exhibit 22a, p. 264.

80. U.S. Senate, Permanent Subcommittee on Investigations, *Wall Street and the Financial Crisis: Anatomy of a Financial Collapse*, April 13, 2011, p. 106.

CHAPTER SIX: THE GROWING TROUBLE

1. Louis H. Pepper, *If You Get a Moment Would You Please . . .* (Pullman: Washington State University, 2005).

2. U.S. Senate, Permanent Subcommittee on Investigations, *Wall Street and the Financial Crisis: Anatomy of a Financial Collapse*, April 13, 2011, p. 89, note 393.

3. U.S. Senate, Permanent Subcommittee on Investigations, *Wall Street and the Financial Crisis: The Role of High Risk Home Loans*, April 13, 2010, Exhibit 4, p. 79. (Hereafter cited as Senate Investigations Subcommittee.)

4. Ibid., Exhibit 71, p. 527.

5. Ibid., Exhibit 64, p. 511.

6. Ibid., Exhibit 77, p. 548.

7. Ibid., Exhibit 73, p. 536.

8. Senate Permanent Subcommittee on Investigations, *Wall Street and the Financial Crisis: Anatomy of a Financial Collapse*, p. 112.

9. Michael Corkery, "Existing Homes' Median Price Falls," *Wall Street Journal*, Sept. 26, 2006.

10. Phil Izzo, "Existing-Homes Sales Data Show Welcome Correction or Burst Bubble?" *Wall Street Journal*, Sept. 25, 2006.

11. Senate Investigations Subcommittee, *Wall Street and the Financial Crisis: The Role of High Risk Loans*, Exhibit 15, p. 204.

12. Ruth Simon and James Hagerty, "More Borrowers with Risky Loans Are Falling Behind," *Wall Street Journal*, Dec. 5, 2006.

13. Lingling Wei, "Subprime Lenders Are Hard Sell," *Wall Street Journal*, Dec. 5, 2006.

14. Senate Investigations Subcommittee, *Wall Street and the Financial Crisis: The Role of High Risk Loans*, Exhibit 40a, p. 391.

15. Ibid., Exhibit 17, p. 212.

16. "Become a Mortgage Broker in California," *Mortgage News Daily*, http://www.mortgagenewsdaily.com/mortgage_license/California.asp.

17. U.S. Securities and Exchange Commission, "WaMu Asset-Backed Certificates, WaMu Series 2007-He4," http://www.sec.gov/Archives/edgar/data/1401898/000127727707000434/exh991to8kwamu07he4_abs.htm.

18. "Crime in Compton, California," *City-data.com*, http://www.city-data.com/crime/crime-Compton-California.html.

19. Senate Investigations Subcommittee, *Wall Street and the Financial Crisis: The Role of High Risk Loans*, Exhibit 50, p. 431.

20. Ibid., Exhibit 54a, p. 443.

21. Ibid., Exhibit 69b, p. 523.

22. Ibid., Exhibit 81, p. 572.

23. Ibid., Exhibit 40b, p. 393.

24. U.S. Senate, Permanent Subcommittee on Investigations, *Wall Street and the Financial Crisis: Anatomy of a Financial Collapse*, p. 144.

25. Bethany McLean and Joe Nocera, *All the Devils Are Here* (New York: Penguin, 2010).

26. Christopher Conkey, "End of Housing Slump Seems to Be Drawing Near," *Wall Street Journal*, Dec. 28, 2006.

27. U.S. Securities and Exchange Commission, *Washington Mutual Inc.: Form 10-K, 2007*, http://www.sec.gov/Archives/edgar/data/933136/000110465907015590/a07-3851_110k.htm.

28. Senate Investigations Subcommittee, *Wall Street and the Financial Crisis: The Role of High Risk Loans*, Exhibit 60a, p. 472.

29. *The Federal Deposit Insurance Corp., as Receiver for Washington Mutual Bank v. Kerry K. Killinger, Stephen J. Rotella, David C. Schneider, Linda C. Killinger, and Esther T. Rotella.* Case 2:11-cv-00459, U.S. District Court Western District of Washington at Seattle, Mar. 16, 2011.

30. Justin Matlick, "Questions for Kerry Killinger, Chairman and CEO, Washington Mutual," *Puget Sound Business Journal*, April 27, 2007.

31. Senate Investigations Subcommittee, *Wall Street and the Financial Crisis: The Role of High Risk Loans*, Exhibit 63c, p. 509.

32. Ibid., Exhibit 60a, p. 472.

33. Ibid., Exhibit 63c, p. 506.

34. U.S. Securities and Exchange Commission, *Washington Mutual: Form 10-Q, June 30, 2007,* http://www.sec.gov/Archives/edgar/data/933136/00011046590 7061031/a07–19022_110q.htm.

35. Senate Investigations Subcommittee, *Wall Street and the Financial Crisis: The Role of High Risk Loans,* Exhibit 6a, p. 133.

36. Ibid., Ron Cathcart interview.

37. Ibid., Exhibit 19, p. 223.

38. Ibid., Exhibit 24, p. 276.

39. Emily Kaiser, "Subprime Losses Could Hit $100 Billion: Bernanke," Reuters, July 23, 2007.

40. Gretchen Morgenson, "Bear Stearns Says Battered Hedge Funds Are Worth Little," *New York Times,* July 18, 2007.

41. Michael W. Hudson, *The Monster: How a Gang of Predatory Lenders and Wall Street Bankers Fleeced America—and Spawned a Global Crisis* (New York: Times Books, 2010).

42. U.S. Securities and Exchange Commission, *Washington Mutual Form 10-Q, Sept. 30, 2007,* http://www.sec.gov/Archives/edgar/data/933136/00010474690 7008929/a2180750z10-q.htm.

43. Bill Virgin, "WaMu Shares Fall an Additional 12 Percent," *Seattle Post-Intelligencer,* Dec. 11, 2007.

44. Senate Investigations Subcommittee, *Wall Street and the Financial Crisis: The Role of High Risk Loans,* Exhibit 1g, p. 25.

45. "Washington Mutual, Inc. Q3 2007 Earnings Call Transcript," *Seeking Alpha,* Oct. 18, 2007.

46. Drew DeSilver, "Despite Lending Crisis, WaMu Expands Loans," *Seattle Times,* Sept. 11, 2007.

47. Kirsten Grind, "Insiders Detail Reasons for WaMu's Failure," *Puget Sound Business Journal,* Jan. 25, 2009.

48. Senate Investigations Subcommittee, *Wall Street and the Financial Crisis: The Role of High Risk Loans,* Exhibit 1h, p. 26.

49. Ibid., Exhibit 58, p. 459.

50. Jad Mouawad, "Washington Mutual Cutting Dividend and Jobs," *New York Times,* Dec. 11, 2007.

51. *Washington Mutual Inc. Securities Litigation,* 2:08-md-1919 MJP, U.S. District Court Western District of Washington at Seattle, Oct. 21, 2008.

52. Drew DeSilver, "WaMu Accused of Pushing Appraisers to Inflate Home Values," *Seattle Times,* Nov. 2, 2007.

53. Drew DeSilver, "Reckless Strategies Doomed WaMu," *Seattle Times,* Oct. 25, 2009.

54. U.S. Senate, Permanent Subcommittee on Investigations. *Wall Street and the Financial Crisis: The Role of Bank Regulators*, 2010, Exhibit 40, p. 198.

CHAPTER SEVEN: SCENES FROM THE GREAT DEPRESSION

1. "The Benaroya Gift," Seattle Symphony, http://www.seattlesymphony .org/benaroya/about/gift.aspx.
2. U.S. Securities and Exchange Commission, *Washington Mutual: Form 10-K, 2007*, http://www.sec.gov/Archives/edgar/data/933136/000104746908002083/ a2182890z10-k.htm.
3. U.S. Senate, Permanent Subcommittee on Investigations. *Wall Street and the Financial Crisis: The Role of High Risk Home Loans*, April 13, 2010, Exhibit 75, p. 542.
4. Andrew Ross Sorkin, "JP Morgan Pays $2 a Share for Bear Stearns," *New York Times*, Mar. 17, 2008.
5. Kirsten Grind, "Experts Say WaMu's Meltdown Offers a Case Study of Board Oversight Problems," *Puget Sound Business Journal*, April 26, 2009.
6. U.S. Senate, Permanent Subcommittee on Investigations, *Wall Street and the Financial Crisis: Anatomy of a Financial Collapse*, April 13, 2011, p. 163.
7. "TPG Leads $7 Billion WaMu Investment," *New York Times*, April 9, 2008.
8. Robin Sidel, "WaMu's Hedge: CEO Called in Dimon & Co," *Wall Street Journal*, April 9, 2008.
9. "Washington Mutual Annual Meeting of Shareholders—Final," *Fairwire Disclosure.* April 15, 2008.
10. U.S. Senate, Permanent Subcommittee on Investigations, *Wall Street and the Financial Crisis: The Role of Bank Regulators*, 2010, Exhibit 46, p. 196.
11. Kirsten Grind, "WaMu Director Says Bank Could Have Done More," *Puget Sound Business Journal*, April 11, 2008.
12. U.S. Senate, Permanent Subcommittee on Investigations, *Wall Street and the Financial Crisis*, April 13, 2011, Report Footnote 372, p. 78.
13. "Washington Mutual, Inc. Q1 2008 Earnings Call Transcript," *Seeking Alpha*, April 16, 2008.
14. "Senator Asks Regulators to Probe the Financial Health of IndyMac," *Los Angeles Times*, June 27, 2008.
15. Vikas Bajaj, "Chronology of a U.S. Bank Failure," *New York Times*, July 29, 2008.
16. U.S. Securities and Exchange Commission, *IndyMac Bancorp: Form 10-Q*, http://www.sec.gov/Archives/edgar/data/773468/000104746908006343/ a2185707z10-q.htm.
17. "Regulators to Schumer on IndyMac: Please Shut Up," *Los Angeles Times*, July 2, 2008.

18. "After Some Depositors Pull Funds, IndyMac Responds to Latest Rumors About Its Health; Says It's Working with Regulators," *Los Angeles Times*, June 30, 2008.

19. Burt Ely, interview by Andrea Seabrook, National Public Radio, July 12, 2008.

20. "IndyMac Reopens Under Eyes of Government," Associated Press, July 14, 2008.

21. Ibid.

22. Jacob Adelman, "Scared IndyMac Bank Customers Demand Their Money," Associated Press, July 16, 2008.

23. Murray Morgan, *The Friend of the Family: 100 Years with Washington Mutual* (Washington Mutual Financial Group, 1989).

24. Ari Levy, "WaMu Slumps as Gimme Credit Cites Liquidity Concern," *Bloomberg*, July 24, 2008.

25. "Washington Mutual Shares Crash 35 Percent," *North County Times*, July 15, 2008.

CHAPTER EIGHT: PROJECT WEST

1. Steven Sloan, Joe Adler, and Stacy Kaper, "Washington People," *American Banker*, Mar. 26, 2007.

2. Sheila Bair, "Sheila Bair Acceptance Speech," John F. Kennedy Presidential Library and Museum, Jfklibrary.org.

3. Joe Adler, "How's She Doing? Bair at One Year," *American Banker*, June 29, 2007.

4. Parija B. Kavilanz, "Wal-Mart Withdraws Industrial Banking Push," *CNNMoney*, Mar. 16, 2007.

5. Joe Adler, "FDIC Unit to Explore Megafailure Scenario; New Team Not Geared Toward 'It's Going to Happen' but 'If It Did,'" *American Banker*, Jan. 7, 2007.

6. Ryan Lizza, "The Contrarian: Sheila Bair and the White House Financial Debate," *New Yorker*, July 6, 2009.

7. "Is Your Bank at Risk? A Q&A with FDIC Chairwoman Sheila Bair," *Newsweek*, July 17, 2008.

8. Edmond L. Andrews, "Fed and Regulators Shrugged as the Subprime Crisis Spread," *New York Times*, Dec. 18, 2007.

9. Sheila Bair, *Isabel's Car Wa$h* (Morton Grove, Ill.: Albert Whitman & Co., 2008).

10. Sheila Bair, *Rock, Brock and the Savings Shock* (Morton Grove, Ill.: Albert Whitman & Co., 2006).

11. Lizza, "The Contrarian: Sheila Bair."

12. Andrew Ross Sorkin, *Too Big to Fail* (New York: Penguin, 2009).

13. Henry M. Paulson, Jr., *On the Brink: Inside the Race to Stop the Collapse of the Global Financial System* (New York: Hachette, 2011).

14. Ibid.

15. Barbara Rehm, "OTS 'Sells' Thrift Charter in Pursuit of Start-Ups," *American Banker*, Dec. 15, 2006.

16. Ibid.

17. Ibid.

18. U.S. Senate, Permanent Subcommittee on Investigations, *Wall Street and the Financial Crisis: The Role of Bank Regulators*, 2010, Memorandum, p. 14.

19. Rehm, "OTS 'Sells' Thrift Charter."

20. Ethan Zindler, "Agencies Urge Tighter Exotic-Loan Standards," *American Banker*, Dec. 21, 2005.

21. Ethan Zindler, "From the OTS, a Benign View on Negative Amortization," *American Banker*, Dec. 15, 2005.

22. U.S. Senate, Permanent Subcommittee on Investigations, *Wall Street and the Financial Crisis: The Role of High Risk Home Loans*, April 13, 2010, Exhibit 77, p. 548.

23. U.S. Senate, Permanent Subcommittee on Investigations, *Wall Street and the Financial Crisis: The Role of Bank Regulators*, Memorandum, p. 21.

24. "FDIC Chairwoman Calls for Subprime Lending Standards," *BestWire*, Mar. 27, 2007.

25. U.S. Senate, Permanent Subcommittee on Investigations, *Wall Street and the Financial Crisis: The Role of Bank Regulators*, Memorandum, p. 17.

26. U.S. Department of the Treasury, Offices of Inspector General, Office of Thrift Supervision, *Evaluation of Regulatory Oversight of Washington Mutual Bank*, 2010.

27. Ibid.

28. U.S. Senate, Permanent Subcommittee on Investigations, *Wall Street the and Financial Crisis: The Role of Bank Regulators*, Exhibit 9, p. 55.

29. Ibid., Exhibit 6. p. 49.

30. Ibid., Exhibit 50, p. 216.

31. Ibid., Exhibit 52a, p. 234.

32. Ibid., Exhibit 52b, p. 235.

33. Ibid., Exhibit 54, p. 240.

34. Ibid., Exhibit 55, p. 241.

35. Ibid., Exhibit 43, p. 190.

36. Ibid., Exhibit 56, p. 242.

37. Joshua Hochberg, *Final Report of the Examiner: Washington Mutual Inc.*, 2010.

38. Shawn Tully, "In This Corner! The Contender," *Fortune*, Mar. 29, 2006.

39. Duff McDonald, *Last Man Standing: The Ascent of Jamie Dimon and JPMorgan Chase* (New York: Simon & Schuster, 2009).

40. Shawn Tully, "Jamie Dimon's Swat Team," *Fortune*, Sept. 2, 2008.

41. Jackie Calmes and Louise Story, "In Washington, One Bank Chief Still Holds Sway," *New York Times*, July 18, 2009.

42. Kirsten Grind, "The Washington Mutual Decision," *Puget Sound Business Journal*, Dec. 6, 2009.

43. Hochberg, *Final Report of the Examiner*.

44. JPMorgan Chase, "Project West, Presentation to Board," 2008.

45. Hochberg, *Final Report of the Examiner*.

46. McDonald, *Last Man Standing*.

47. Hochberg, *Final Report of the Examiner*.

48. U.S. Senate, Permanent Subcommittee on Investigations, *Wall Street and the Financial Crisis: The Role of Bank Regulators*, Exhibit 56, p. 242.

49. Ibid., Exhibit 58, p. 244.

50. Kirsten Grind, "Washington Mutual's Final Days—The Deal," *Puget Sound Business Journal*, Dec. 27, 2009.

51. Hochberg, *Final Report of the Examiner*.

52. Ibid.

53. Oak Hill Capital Management Partners III LP, Blackstone Capital Partners V LP, Blackstone Management Associates V LLC General Partner, "Letter re Washington Mutual."

54. Cerberus, *Discussion Materials: Project Olympic*, 2008.

55. Hochberg, *Final Report of the Examiner*.

56. Kerry Killinger to Jamie Dimon, April 5, 2008.

57. Dimon to Killinger, April 7, 2008.

58. Hochberg, *Final Report of the Examiner*.

59. Riley McDermid, "WaMu Spurned an Earlier J.P. Morgan Bid: Report," *MarketWatch*, April 9, 2008.

60. Robin Sidel, "WaMu's Hedge: CEO Called in Dimon & Co.," *Wall Street Journal*, April 9, 2008.

61. Brian Bessey, e-mail exchange re WaMu Document Destruction, April 8, 2008.

62. "WaMu Denies Action by Regulatory Agencies," *Seattle Post-Intelligencer*, June 11, 2008.

63. Lina Shen and Ari Levy, "Washington Mutual Falls on $22 Billion Loss Estimate," *Bloomberg*, June 9, 2008.

64. Rami Grunbaum, "Killinger Makes No Apologies for WaMu Record," *Seattle Times*, June 15, 2008.

65. Kirsten Grind, "WaMu's Killinger Says Bank Has 'Aggressive Strategic Plan,'" *Puget Sound Business Journal*, June 11, 2008.

66. *The Federal Deposit Insurance Corp., as Receiver for Washington Mutual Bank v. Kerry K. Killinger, Stephen J. Rotella, David C. Schneider, Linda C. Killinger, and Esther T. Rotella,* Case 2:11-cv-00459, U.S. District Court, Western District of Washington at Seattle, Mar. 16, 2011.

67. Bill Whitaker, "IndyMac Customers Line Up for Second Day to Get Their Money Out of Failing Bank, but Tempers Beginning to Flare," *CBS Evening News,* July 15, 2008.

68. Joe Adler, "FDIC Defends Handling of IndyMac Run," *American Banker,* July 18, 2008.

69. Daniel Gross, "A Chicken Little Tale for Adults; 'The Overwhelming Majority of Banks in This Country Continue to Be Well Capitalized,' Assures FDIC Chairman Sheila Bair," *Newsweek,* July 28, 2008.

70. Greg Morcroft, "FDIC Chief Doesn't See Bank Failure as Big as IndyMac: Report," *MarketWatch,* July 22, 2008.

71. U.S. Senate, Permanent Subcommittee on Investigations, *Wall Street and the Financial Crisis: The Role of Bank Regulators,* Exhibit 60, p. 251.

72. Grind, "The Washington Mutual Decision."

73. U.S. Senate, Permanent Subcommittee on Investigations, *Wall Street and the Financial Crisis: Anatomy of a Financial Collapse,* p. 200.

74. Gregg Gunselman, e-mail exchange re West, June 18, 2008.

75. Hochberg, *Final Report of the Examiner.*

76. Sorkin, *Too Big to Fail.*

77. Hochberg, *Final Report of the Examiner.*

78. JPMorgan Chase, Discussion Materials, 2008.

79. Grind, "Washington Mutual's Final Days."

80. "Jim Cramer's *Mad Money* In-Depth, 3/5/08: Killinger Makes a Killing," *Seeking Alpha,* Mar. 6, 2008.

81. U.S. Senate, Permanent Subcommittee on Investigations, *Wall Street and the Financial Crisis,* 2011, Report Footnote 633, p. 264.

82. Rami Grumbaum, "Treasury's Paulson Warned WaMu CEO to Sell Before It Failed," *Seattle Times,* Nov. 9, 2008.

83. Kathleen Pender, "Why Wasn't IndyMac on FDIC Problem List?" *SFGate.com,* July 2008, 2008.

84. U.S. Senate, Permanent Subcommittee on Investigations, *Wall Street and the Financial Crisis: The Role of Bank Regulators,* Exhibit 64, p. 260.

85. Ibid., Exhibit 66, p. 262.

86. Ibid.

CHAPTER NINE: THE FINAL HOURS

1. U.S. Senate, Permanent Subcommittee on Investigations, *Wall Street and the Financial Crisis: The Role of Bank Regulators,* 2010, Exhibit 65, p. 260.

2. Drew DeSilver, "New WaMu CEO Called a Savvy, Scrappy Exec," *Seattle Times*, Sept. 14, 2008.

3. Office of Thrift Supervision, "Memorandum of Understanding: WaMu," 2008.

4. U.S. Senate, Permanent Subcommittee on Investigations, *Wall Street and the Financial Crisis: The Role of Bank Regulators*, Exhibit 44, p. 192.

5. Ibid.

6. Washington Mutual Political Action Committee, *Report of Receipts and Disbursements*, FEC Form 3x, 2008.

7. U.S. Senate, Permanent Subcommittee on Investigations, *Wall Street and the Financial Crisis: The Role of High Risk Home Loans*, April 13, 2010, Exhibit 34, p. 325.

8. Colin Barr and Roddy Boyd, "Lehman: Running Out of Options," *CNN Money*, Sept. 9, 2008.

9. Federal Deposit Insurance Corp., "Confidential Problem Memorandum," 2008.

10. David Ellis, "Lehman Suffers Nearly $4 Billion Loss," *CNN Money*, Sept. 10, 2008.

11. U.S. Senate, Permanent Subcommittee on Investigations, *Wall Street and the Financial Crisis: The Role of Bank Regulators*, Exhibit 68, p. 266.

12. "New York Remembers Victims of 9/11 Terror Attacks," Sept. 11, 2008, http://www.zimbio.com/pictures/SzE3XSEoRFD/New+York+Remembers+Victims+9+11+Terror+Attacks/4nSYP4Fmcip/Michael+Bloomberg.

13. Richard Schapiro, "President Bush Honors 9/11 Victims at Newly Unveiled Pentagon Memorial," *New York Daily News*, Sept. 11, 2008.

14. Kirsten Grind, "The Downfall of Washington Mutual," *Puget Sound Business Journal*, Sept. 25, 2009.

15. Bill Virgin, "Ailing WaMu Pays Millions to Ousted, New CEOs," *Seattle Post-Intelligencer*, Sept. 11, 2008.

16. Brian Bessey, "West Case 2(b)," Sept. 11, 2008.

17. Office of Thrift Supervision, "OTS Letter to FDIC re WaMu Ratings," 2008.

18. Moody's Investors Service, "Moody's Downgrades WaMu Ratings, Outlook Negative," press release, 2008.

19. Deborah Solomon, Dennis K. Berman, Susanne Craig, and Carrick Mollenkamp, "Ultimatum by Paulson Sparked Frantic End," *Wall Street Journal*, Sept. 15, 2008.

20. Aline van Duyn, "Lehman Employees Prepare for Exit," *Financial Times*, Sept. 15, 2008.

21. Duff McDonald, *Last Man Standing: The Ascent of Jamie Dimon and JPMorgan Chase* (New York: Simon & Schuster, 2009).

22. Joshua Hochberg, *Final Report of the Examiner: Washington Mutual Inc.*, 2010.
23. Ibid.
24. Ibid.
25. Ibid.
26. Ibid.
27. Ibid.
28. Grind, "The Downfall of Washington Mutual."
29. Ibid.
30. "Investors Fret over WaMu's Survival Odds," *Seattle Times*, Sept. 16, 2008.
31. Geraldine Fabrikant, "Washington Mutual Is Said to Consider Sale," *New York Times*, Sept. 17, 2008.
32. Hochberg, *Final Report of the Examiner.*
33. Kirsten Grind, "WaMu President to Employees: 'Get Back to Work, Focus,'" *Puget Sound Business Journal*, Sept. 18, 2008.
34. Kirsten Grind, "WaMu Launches Effort to Reassure Anxious Customers," *Puget Sound Business Journal*, Sept. 18, 2008.
35. Hochberg, *Final Report of the Examiner.*
36. Ibid.
37. Saskia Scholtes, Julie MacIntosh, and Henny Sender, "WaMu Waits for Firm Offer," *Financial Times*, Sept. 19, 2008.
38. "Santander to Pay $2.4 Billion for Sovereign Stake," Associated Press, Oct. 25, 2005.
39. Citigroup, "Project Dolphin," Sept. 19, 2008.
40. Hochberg, *Final Report of the Examiner.*
41. Ibid.
42. JPMorgan Chase. "Board of Directors Meeting, Sept. 19, 2008," 2008.
43. JPMorgan Chase. "Board of Directors Presentation: Park Potential Acquisition of West," 2008.
44. David Stout, "Paulson Argues for Need to Buy Mortgages," *New York Times*, Sept. 19, 2008.
45. "Paulson's Rescue Plan Is Called 'TARP,'" *Politico*, Sept. 19, 2008.
46. Binyamin Appelbaum and Jo Craven McGinty, "The Fed's Crisis Lending: A Billion Here, a Thousand There," *New York Times*, Mar. 31, 2011.
47. Liz Moyer, David Benoit, and Matthias Rieker, "Fed Unveils Discount-Window Loans," *Wall Street Journal*, Mar. 31, 2011.
48. Peter Freilinger, e-mail re "Near Term Liquidity Sources," Sept. 20, 2008.
49. Sheila Bair, e-mail to Jamie Dimon, Sept. 20, 2008.
50. Henry M. Paulson, Jr., *On the Brink: Inside the Race to Stop the Collapse of the Global Financial System* (New York: Hachette, 2011).

51. Kirsten Grind, "The Washington Mutual Decision," *Puget Sound Business Journal*, Dec. 4, 2009.

52. U.S. Senate, Permanent Subcommittee on Investigations, *Wall Street and the Financial Crisis: The Role of Bank Regulators*, Exhibit 56, p. 242.

53. David M. Herszenhorn, "Administration Is Seeking $700 Billion for Wall Street," *New York Times*, Sept. 20, 2008.

54. Andrew Ross Sorkin and Vikas Bajaj, "Shift for Goldman and Morgan Marks the End of an Era," *New York Times*, Sept. 21, 2008.

55. Hochberg, *Final Report of the Examiner.*

56. Robert Beck, e-mail chain re WaMu, Sept. 20, 2008.

57. McDonald, *Last Man Standing.*

58. Hochberg, *Final Report of the Examiner.*

59. Ibid.

60. Sue Chang, "Moody's Cuts WaMu's Prefferred Stock to 'Most Speculative,'" *MarketWatch*, Sept. 22, 2008.

61. Brian Bessey, "Intralinks Access," Sept. 22, 2008.

62. Sheri Foster, e-mail, "FDIC Acquisition Opportunity," Sept. 23, 2008.

63. Fernando Rivas, e-mail "TD Still in West Process," Sept. 23, 2008.

64. Hochberg, *Final Report of the Examiner.*

65. Kirsten Grind, "Cantwell Reveals Another WaMu Inquiry," *Puget Sound Business Journal*, Feb. 5, 2010.

66. Mark Landler and Steven Lee Myers, "Buyout Plan for Wall Street Is Hard Sell on Capitol Hill," *New York Times*, Sept. 23, 2008.

67. Washington Mutual, "Discussion Materials," 2008.

68. JPMorgan Chase, "Board of Directors Meeting," Sept. 24, 2008.

69. JPMorgan Chase, "Presentation to Board of Directors: Potential Acquisition of West," Sept. 24, 2008.

70. Dan Fitzpatrick, "The Untold Story: How WaMu Execs Fought Government Seizure," *Wall Street Journal*, Sept. 28, 2010.

71. Carl Gutierrez, "Tosca Casts WaMu in Portfolio Role," *Forbes*, July 31, 2008.

72. Richard Kovacevich to Sheila Bair, "re WaMu," Sept. 24, 2008.

73. McDonald, *Last Man Standing.*

74. Hochberg, *Final Report of the Examiner.*

75. Sheila Bair, e-mail, "Congrats," Sept. 24, 2008.

76. Darrel Dochow, "S Memo for Washington Mutual Bank," *Report*, Sept. 25, 2008.

77. Bair, "Congrats."

78. McDonald, *Last Man Standing.*

79. Paulson, *On the Brink.*

80. Grind, "The Downfall of Washington Mutual."
81. Murray Morgan, *The Friend of the Family: 100 Years with Washington Mutual* (Washington Mutual Financial Group, 1989).
82. Grind, "The Downfall of Washington Mutual."
83. Ibid.
84. Heidi N. Moore, "Highlights of the J.P. Morgan–WaMu Analyst Conference Call," *Wall Street Journal*, Sept. 25, 2008.
85. Eric Dash and Andrew Ross Sorkin,. "Government Seizes WaMu and Sells Some Assets," *New York Times*, Sept. 25, 2008.
86. Drew DeSilver, "Feds Seize WaMu in Nation's Largest Bank Failure," *Seattle Times*, Sept. 25, 2008.
87. Office of Thrift Supervision. "OTS 08–046—Washington Mutual Acquired by JPMorgan Chase," press release, 2008.

EPILOGUE: "BARELY A BLIP"

1. King County Medical Examiner's Office, Case No. 09–01542, Medical Examiner's Record, 2009.
2. Seattle Police Department, GO 2009–329591, General Offense Hardcopy, 2009.
3. Melissa Allison, "WaMu's Former CEO: Bank's Demise 'Abominable, to Put It Mildly,'" *Seattle Times*, Sept. 26, 2008.
4. Kirsten Grind, "The Washington Mutual Decision," *Puget Sound Business Journal*, Dec. 4, 2009.
5. Saskia Scholtes, Joanna Chung, Henny Sender, and Deborah Brewster, "JPMorgan Swoops in Again," *Financial Times*, Sept. 27, 2008.
6. Kirsten Grind, "The Washington Mutual Decision," *Puget Sound Business Journal*, Sept. 25, 2009.
7. John VanderClock, letter to U.S. Bankruptcy Court, District of Delaware, Dec., 10 2008.
8. Willard Locklear, e-mail to U.S. Bankruptcy Court, District of Delaware, Oct. 10, 2008.
9. Peter Necklaws, letter to U.S. Bankruptcy Court, District of Delaware, Nov. 2, 2008.
10. Sydney Prevor, letter to U.S. Bankruptcy Court, District of Delaware, Oct. 28, 2008.
11. Ted Mitchell and Susan Mitchell, e-mail to U.S. Bankruptcy Court, District of Delaware, Oct. 29, 2008.
12. Luis Osorio, letter to U.S. Bankruptcy Court, District of Delaware, Jan. 1, 2009.
13. Sheila Bair, interview by Financial Crisis Commission, *Financial Crisis Commission Deposition*, 2010.

14. Henry M. Paulson, Jr., *On the Brink: Inside the Race to Stop the Collapse of the Global Financial System* (New York: Hachette, 2011).

15. Liz Moyer, David Benoit, and Matthias Rieker, "Fed Unveils Discount-Window Loans," *Wall Street Journal*, Mar. 31, 2011.

16. U.S. Senate, Permanent Subcommittee on Investigations, *Wall Street and the Financial Crisis: The Role of Bank Regulators*, April 16, 2010, Sheila Bair interview.

17. Joshua Hochberg, *Final Report of the Examiner: Washington Mutual Inc.*, 2010.

18. Ibid.

19. U.S. Department of the Treasury, Offices of Inspector General, Office of Thrift Supervision, *Evaluation of Regulatory Oversight of Washington Mutual Bank*, 2010.

20. John Bowman, *Administration's Financial Regulatory Reform Proposal Before the Committee on Financial Services United States House of Representatives*, Office of the Comptroller of the Currency, July 24, 2009.

21. Binyamin Appelbaum, "Financial Bill to Close Regulator of Fading Industry," *New York Times*, July 13, 2010.

22. U.S. Senate, Permanent Subcommittee on Investigations, *Wall Street and the Financial Crisis: Anatomy of a Financial Collapse*, April 13, 2011, p. 23.

23. Kirsten Grind, "The Washington Mutual Decision," *Puget Sound Business Journal*, Dec. 4, 2009.

24. Kirsten Grind,. "A Town's Crisis, Seized and Sold: Inside the Hidden World of Bank Failures," *Puget Sound Business Journal*, Dec. 10, 2010.

25. Kirsten Grind, "Chase CEO Dimon Q&A: 'WaMu Layoffs Nearly Done,'" *Puget Sound Business Journal*, Mar. 2, 2009.

26. Kirsten Grind, "WaMu Employees' Pensions Fate Unclear; Many to Lose Jobs," *Puget Sound Business Journal*, Oct. 2, 2008.

27. Kirsten Grind, "Washington Mutual's Final Days: The Deal," *Puget Sound Business Journal*, Dec. 27, 2009.

28. Eric Scigliano, "Boo Hoo WaMu," *Seattle Metropolitan Magazine*, Jan. 24, 2009.

29. Clay Holtzman and Kirsten Grind, "WaMu Breaks Lease; Seattle Art Museum Faces Revenue Shortfall," *Puget Sound Business Journal*, Jan. 22, 2009.

30. Robin Sidel, "WaMu's Branches Lose the Smiles," *Wall Street Journal*, April 7, 2009.

31. Kirsten Grind, "Testy Subject for Chase: Fireworks," *Puget Sound Business Journal*, July 15, 2009.

32. Sanjay Bhatt, "Chase Won't Pay for Seattle's Lake Union Fireworks Next Year," *Seattle Times*, July 10, 2009.

33. Kirsten Grind, "Chase Chief Dimon Talks About WaMu Acquisition," *Puget Sound Business Journal,* July 16, 2009.

34. U.S. Senate, Permanent Subcommittee on Investigations, *Wall Street and the Financial Crisis: The Role of High Risk Home Loans,* April 13, 2010, Carl Levin.

35. U.S. Senate, Permanent Subcommitee on Investigations, *Wall Street and the Financial Crisis,* April 13, 2010, testimony of Kerry Killinger.

36. Ibid.

37. U.S. Senate, Permanent Subcommittee on Investigations, *Wall Street and the Financial Crisis: Anatomy of a Financial Crisis,* April 13, 2011, p. 650.

38. Kirsten Grind, "FBI Investigating WaMu's Collapse," *Puget Sound Business Journal,* Oct. 15, 2008.

39. E. Scott Reckard, "U.S. Drops Criminal Probe of Former Countrywide Chief Angelo Mozilo," *Los Angeles Times,* Feb. 18, 2011.

40. Kirsten Grind, "FDIC Sues WaMu Execs and Their Wives," *Puget Sound Business Journal,* Mar. 17, 2011.

41. Kirsten Grind, "WaMu Execs: FDIC Suit Is Political Theater," *Puget Sound Business Journal,* Mar. 17, 2011.

INDEX

NOTE: JPM refers to JPMorgan Chase

A-Team, WaMu, 50, 51
Aames Financial, 59
account executives
  calls to default borrowers by, 167
  Chapman (Fay) review of loans and, 78
  compensation for, 69–70, 78
  fraud and, 72–74, 93
  underwriting guidelines and, 137
Action Teller Dolls, WaMu, 86
Ahmanson Savings and Loan Bank, 40–41,
    42–43, 46–47, 48, 51, 53, 58, 62
AIG, 166, 255, 270–71, 272, 285, 296
Alliance for Education, 83
Alt A mortgages, 137–38, 150, 207
Alumni Fund, WaMu, 310–11, 322
American Banker, 87, 222, 268
American Bankers Association, 22
"American Pie" (song): Perrin version of, 146,
    168–69
American Savings Bank, 42, 67, 112, 189
American Securitization Forum, 57, 188
American's Community Bankers, 83
Ameriquest Mortgage, 65, 71–72, 129, 153,
    154, 154n
analysts
  criticisms of Killinger by, 102
  FDIC problem bank list and, 248
  Killinger's leadership style and, 55
  losses at WaMu and, 198, 239
  pressures on WaMu from, 122
appraisals, 178–79, 180–81, 181n

Aristar, 61–62, 66, 96
ARMs (adjustable-rate mortgages)
  banks as overcharging for, 22
  compensation and, 128
  decline of housing prices and, 153
  defaults and delinquencies on, 186
  government review of, 22
  Greenspan views about, 119, 119n
  hybrid, 69
  increase in offerings of, 74
  interest rates and, 22, 121–22
  popularity of, 22
  See also Option ARMs
Arnall, Roland, 63, 64–65, 153
Arthur Anderson, 91
ATM machines, 14, 212, 278, 325

B paper loans. *See* subprime loans
"Baby Got Back" (song): WaMu version of,
    159–60
Baier, Frank, 301
Bair, Sheila
  appearance of, 217
  awards and honors for, 216, 315
  Cantwell meeting with, 293, 293n
  children's books by, 218
  Citigroup case and, 314n
  closure/seizure of WaMu and, 316
  congressional testimonies of, 314, 315, 316
  criticisms of, 218–19
  deadline for WaMu by, 262, 273, 274, 279

Bair, Sheila (*cont.*)
  defense of FDIC by, 243
  Dimon discussions with, 274–75, 275*n*, 287
  FDIC preparation for bank failures and,
    216–17
  Fishman and, 260, 262, 270, 272, 273, 279
  and Fishman-Frank letter to save WaMu,
    295–96
  Frost poem quote by, 216
  high-risk loan concerns of, 218, 220, 223
  IndyMac closure and, 242, 243, 287
  initial views about WaMu of, 227–28
  JPM acquisition of Morgan Stanley and, 287
  JPM acquisition of WaMu and, 298, 304
  JPM meetings with, 232–33, 266, 316
  Killinger discussions with, 247
  Killinger-OTS meeting with, 244–45
  liquidity of WaMu and, 287
  on Orman TV show, 243
  Paulson and, 219
  personal background of, 217–18
  personality and character of, 219
  Reich/OTS and, 222–23, 227–28, 248, 249,
    250–52, 263, 270, 275, 287
  reputation of, 217
  reverberations of WaMu failure and, 311–14
  sale of WaMu and, 228, 233, 245, 250–51,
    260, 262, 273, 274–75, 275*n*, 279, 287, 297,
    298, 304
  Wal-Mart bank application and, 217
  WaMu capital raise and, 237, 262, 294
  WaMu as political threat to, 227
  WaMu ratings and, 249, 250–52, 262, 263
  See also Federal Deposit Insurance Corp.
Baker, Todd, 97, 125, 152–53
Banaroya, Jack, 184
Banco Bilbao Vizcaya Argentaria (BBVA), 297
Bank of America, 29, 53, 54, 125, 187, 222,
  229, 231, 247, 270, 315, 317
Bank One, 104–5, 230, 327
bank runs
  as contagious, 208
  in Great Depression, 211–12
  on IndyMac, 207–9, 211, 215, 242
  liquidity and, 210
  media and, 2, 201, 207–8, 209, 211–12, 214,
    215, 243, 279, 282
  Schumer's letter and, 207–8
bank runs, WaMu
  ATM and online transfers and, 212
  beginning of, 211–15
  closure of WaMu and, 301
  concerns at WaMu about possible, 209–11
  dealing with customers during, 214

FDIC-OTS relations and, 281–82
FDIC-OTS-WaMu discussion about,
  244–45
Fishman-Frank letter to save WaMu and, 296
Fishman's capital raise plan and, 294
Fishman's letter to customers during,
  280–81
during Great Depression, 211–12
JPM direct purchase of WaMu and, 283
liquidity and, 209–15, 211*n*, 212, 214, 215
Mueller's tracking of, 212–13
OTS-FDIC relations and, 242
public knowledge about, 304
ratings of WaMu and, 248
reports about, 2, 213, 263, 264, 267, 268–69,
  270–71, 272, 273, 274, 276–79, 280–81,
  282, 283, 285, 289, 292, 295, 298
Rotella's management of, 2, 213, 280
rumors about health of WaMu and, 214
Schumer's IndyMac letter to media and, 208
secrecy about, 268–69
slowing of, 2, 5, 246, 292, 299
troubled banks list and, 3
WaMu survival dependent on, 286
Bank Secrecy Act, 192, 202, 224
Bank United, 84–85, 130
banking industry
  in 1980s, 11, 15, 25
  Continental failure and, 26
  expansion of, 15
  interstate banking and, 15, 39
  mergers in 1990s in, 39, 49–50
  risk in, 122*n*
  See also specific bank
Bankstocks.com, 125
Barclays Bank, 106, 229
Bear Stearns, 120, 167, 187, 232, 246, 325, 329
Beck, David, 157, 169
Benaroya Hall (Seattle): WaMu shareholders
  meeting (2008) at, 184–86, 189–91,
  193–200
Bernanke, Ben, 135–36, 167, 174, 251, 269
"The Black Cottage" (Frost poem), 216
Blackstone Management Associates, 235
Bloomberg, Michael, 264
board of directors, WaMu
  appraisal issues and, 180
  capital raise and, 237
  Cathcart's marginalization and, 201
  Cathcart's testimony about, 163
  Chapman (Fay) retirement and, 182
  compensation for, 164
  FDIC-OTS seizure of WaMu and, 303–4
  Fishman's appointment by, 254–55, 257

Fishman's attempts to sell WaMu and, 279
five-year/strategic plans and, 108, 241
fraud findings and, 164
Great Western acquisition and, 42
"higher-risk lending strategy" and, 124, 135, 150, 164, 166
JPM merger offer and, 237
Killinger-Rotella relationship and, 202
Killinger's appointment as president by, 30, 309
at Killinger's birthday party, 79
Killinger's chairmanship of, 200, 239, 240–41
Killinger's firing by, 252–53
Killinger's housing memo to, 161
Killinger's marital problems and, 82
Killinger's personal use of corporate jets and, 174
Killinger's relationship with, 164–65, 170, 186–87, 239
as lacking information, 165, 192
Long Beach Mortgage and, 63, 78
McKinsey Group review and, 241–42
McMurray's presentation to, 186–87
members of, 163–64
1981 problems at WaMu and, 9–10
organization and structure of WaMu and, 96
OTS-Bank Secrecy Act problem and, 192
OTS concerns about WaMu and, 192, 224
OTS pressures to replace Killinger and, 255
Pepper's temporary appointment as CEO by, 10, 11
reelection of, 188, 200
regulators meeting with, 192–93
Rotella and, 104, 202, 239
Rotella-Chapman (Craig) relationship and, 128
Schneider presentation to, 150
shareholder lawsuits against, 178
shareholders' concerns about, 188, 191, 194
WaMu acquisition of subprime lenders and, 59
warnings about housing decline and, 161–62, 163, 186–87
Bohemian Grove (California), 60
Bonderman, David, 189, 235, 237, 264, 266, 269
borrowers, WaMu/Long Beach Mortgage
complaints from, 99–100
decline in housing prices and, 151–54
fraud and, 73–75
as house flippers, 72
minorities as, 60, 64
software problems and, 99, 101, 165

talking about defaults to, 166–67
tracking of complex data and, 165
See also Community Fulfillment Centers; defaults; delinquencies; foreclosures; type of loan or mortgage
Bowman, John, 233, 234, 317–18
branches, WaMu
closing of, 109, 176, 214
expansion of, 30, 38, 39, 49, 54, 85–86
Fishman's views about, 257
JPM's conversion of WaMu and, 325
Killinger's acquisitions and, 38, 39, 49, 54
Killinger's five-year plan and, 108
Killinger's visits to, 43, 55
losses at, 108–9
in 1980s, 14, 30
number of, 88
Occasio, 85–86, 106, 325
Pepper and, 54
Rotella defense to shareholders about, 193
Rotella's tour of, 109
runs on, 2, 209–15, 277–78
selling off of, 247, 294, 296
"brand rallies," WaMu, 89–93
Break the Bank scenario, 215, 248, 278
Brown, Tom, 125, 218
Buffett, Warren, 33
Bunning, Jim, 293
Bush, George W., 2, 113, 155, 264, 288, 298

California
AIG complaint about WaMu to, 166
banking preferences in, 53
decline in home prices in, 157, 185, 187
impact of WaMu sale in, 331–32
Killinger brand rally in, 92–93
naming of WaMu in, 90n
Option ARMs in, 197
real estate market in, 47
subprime lending in, 58, 64, 71
tracking of complex data and customers in, 165
CAMELS ratings, 176, 228, 248, 262, 300
Cantwell, Maria, 275, 293, 293n
Capital Markets Group, WaMu, 158, 169
capital raise, WaMu
Bair-JPM representatives discussion about, 232
Cathcart and, 201
deadline for, 262
disagreements among regulators and, 234
FDIC/Bair and, 262, 275, 294
Fishman-Frank letter to save WaMu and, 296

capital raise, WaMu (*cont.*)
  Fishman's attempts at, 270, 294, 296
  "Go It Alone" proposal and, 294
  Killinger and, 188–90, 191, 199, 201, 202,
    205, 234, 237
  Moody's-WaMu meeting and, 265–66
  OTS enforcement order and, 258, 267, 270
  OTS-FDIC relations and, 244
  OTS-Fishman/WaMu meeting about,
    273–74
  OTS pressures on WaMu for, 228, 229, 234,
    237, 244
  potential sources for, 235
  sale of WaMu and, 279, 301
  shareholder relations and, 188–90, 191, 199,
    202, 205, 245–46
  TPG and, 189, 237, 238, 279
Casey, Tom
  attempts to sell WaMu and, 232–33, 269,
    280, 287, 288, 301
  board presentations of, 192, 193
  Chapman (Fay) disagreements with, 179–80
  concerns about decline in housing market
    of, 153
  definition of subprime loan of, 179
  FDIC seizure of WaMu and, 303
  JPM negotiations and, 232–33
  JPM severance of, 321
  Killinger's hiring of, 98
  loan loss forecast of, 192
  Moody's downgrade news and, 261, 264,
    265, 266
  off-loading of subprime and Option ARMs
    and, 154
  professional background of, 98–99, 107
  Rotella's relationship with, 107
  shareholder lawsuits against, 178
"category killers," 91, 92
Cathcart, Ron, 150–51, 151*n*, 153, 154, 163,
    164, 176, 178, 200–201
Cavanagh, Michael, 232, 234, 266, 272, 316
CBS: IndyMac story on, 242
Centrust Savings and Loan, 28
Cerberus, 235
Chapman, Craig, 61–62, 66, 78, 96, 97, 101,
    106, 123, 128
Chapman, Fay
  appraisal problems and, 178–79, 180–82,
    181*n*
  financial crisis comment of, 333
  hiring of, 19
  housing market concerns of, 179–80
  Killinger's "higher-risk lending strategy"
    and, 123

  Killinger's relationship with, 30, 97, 107,
    180, 181–82, 183, 205
  Long Beach Mortgage concerns of, 56–58,
    60–61, 62, 63, 72, 75–78
  NYSE bell ringing and, 54
  Pepper and, 19, 310
  on Pepper's leadership style, 20
  personal and professional background of,
    19, 61, 75
  personality and character of, 57, 75
  resignation/retirement of, 182–83, 309
  Rotella's relationship with, 180
  settlement for, 182
  WaMu acquisitions and, 49
  WaMu Alumni Fund and, 310
  WaMu responsibilities of, 49
  at WaMu reunion, 307
Chase Bank. *See* JPMorgan Chase
Chase Home Finance, 104
Chicago, Illinois
  Jenne's delinquent homeowner tour and,
    171–72
  WaMu branches in, 86, 108, 109
chief operating officer (COO), WaMu
  Pepper's advice to Killinger about, 103–4
  Rotella hired as first, 104–5, 106
Chrysler Financial, 235
Citigroup
  Dimon at, 230
  as largest U.S. bank, 104
  naked short selling protection for, 247
  near failure of, 314, 314*n*
  OTS defense of oversight and, 317, 318
  as potential buyer of WaMu, 3, 271, 282,
    283, 289, 290, 298
  TARP and, 315
Clark, Susie, 224
Clinton, Bill, 64, 113, 155
CNBC, 212, 267
CNN, 267
Coburn, Tom, 135
Cohen, H. Rodgin, 232, 233
Collateralized Debt Obligations (CDOs), 158,
    295, 295*n*
commercial real estate loans, 26–27
community banks: closure of, 319–20
Community Fulfillment Centers, WaMu,
    142–43, 144–45, 144*n*, 159, 166
Community Reinvestment Act, 59
compensation
  Countrywide-WaMu competition and, 160
  five emissaries–Killinger discussion about,
    204–5
  for fixed-rate loans/mortgages, 128, 129, 197

for Goldman Sachs board members, 164
for loan consultants, 117, 128–29, 188, 196, 197
at Long Beach Mortgage, 69–70, 78, 166–67
for Option ARMs sales, 117, 197
Pepper's advice to Killinger about, 103–4
for real estate agents, 143
for salespeople, 140, 166–67
shareholders concerns about WaMu, 187–88
for subprime loans, 197
for WaMu board members, 164
for WaMu senior executives, 131, 187–88
See also specific person
Congress, U.S.
Dodd-Frank legislation and, 317
FDIC and, 249
TARP and, 2, 285, 291, 293, 313, 314–15
See also congressional hearings, testimony at
congressional hearings, testimony at of Bair, 314, 315, 316
of Bernanke, 136
of Bowman, 317–18
of Cathcart, 163, 164
and Countrywide Financial, 329
of Kaufman, 126
of Killinger, 329–31
of Paulson, 293
of Reich, 318
of Rotella, 144*n*, 329–30, 331
of Vanasek, 124, 135
Continental Illinois National Bank and Trust Co., 25–26, 301, 318*n*
corporate jets, 44–45, 88–89, 97, 174, 205
See also NetJets
Correspondent Division, WaMu, 129–30, 154*n*, 170
Cost of Funds Index (COFI), 115*n*
Countrywide Financial
BoA acquisition of, 187, 222
congressional hearings and, 329
criminal investigation of, 332–33
delinquencies at, 152
Goldman Sachs and, 121
McMurray at, 186
Option ARMs and, 197
OTS and, 222, 222*n*, 227
SEC-Mozilo lawsuit and, 186*n*
subprime loans at, 152
tracking of complex data at, 165*n*
WaMu attempts to buy, 127
WaMu compared with, 102
WaMu competition with, 120, 126–28, 140, 160–61
WaMu mock funeral for, 160–61

See also Mozilo, Angelo
Cramer, Jim, 246–47
credit cards, 158, 161, 171, 329
credit lines
of Federal Home Loan Banks, 210, 215, 248, 271, 286–87, 299–300
for WaMu, 4, 271, 286–87, 286*n*, 294, 300
See also Federal Reserve Bank: discount window at
Credit Union National Association, 119
credit unions, 119, 217
criminal investigations, 332–33
Cuomo, Andrew, 178, 180, 181*n*

Davis, Craig, 67–68, 69, 75–76, 100, 101, 111, 112
deadline
Bair-Fishman, 262, 273, 274, 279
for FDIC sale of WaMu, 274
OTS-WaMu, 274
defaults
decline of housing prices and, 153
hedging and, 122
increase in number of, 137, 173
at IndyMac, 207
at Long Beach Mortgage, 137
mortgage-backed securities and, 173
off-loading of risky loans and, 158
salespeople compensation and, 166–67
at Superior Bank, 225
See also type of mortgage or loan
delinquencies
Goldman Sachs–Long Beach Mortgage relationship and, 157
increase in number of, 137, 170–73
Jenne's study of, 170–72
at Long Beach Mortgage, 137, 153, 157
off-loading of risky loans and, 157, 158
OTS review of WaMu and, 224
Pepper's concerns about, 134
See also type of mortgage or loan
deposit insurance limit, FDIC: raising of, 276, 315
DeSilver, Drew, 173–74
Deutsche Bank, 188
Dime Bancorp., 85
Dimon, Jaime
Bair discussions with, 274–75, 275*n*, 287
Bank One-JPM merger and, 105
as "Banker of the Year," 87
compensation for, 329
FDIC sale of WaMu and, 246, 274–75, 275*n*, 289–90, 298
Fishman and, 261

Dimon, Jaime (*cont.*)
   funding for WaMu acquisition and, 304
   investor conference call by, 304
   "Jamie Deals" of, 246
   JPM-WaMu direct sale negotiations and,
      229–30, 231–38, 238*n*
   Killinger compared with, 229–30
   Killinger discussions with, 195, 234, 236, 237
   leadership style of, 229–30
   letter to shareholders from, 325
   Morgan Stanley acquisition and, 287
   Mueller "firing" by, 320
   named president and COO of JPM, 105
   political connections of, 231
   professional background of, 230–31
   reputation of, 325
   Rotella at JPM and, 105
   Santander bids and, 282*n*
   Seattle speech of, 325, 326–28
   subprime mortgage market and, 230–31
   TARP money and, 328
   WaMu acquisition comments of, 328
   WaMu layoffs and, 321
   WaMu shareholder views about, 195
   welcoming e-mail to WaMu employees
      from, 304
Dochow, Darrel, 4, 5, 180, 244, 274, 293, 299,
   303
Dodd, Chris4, 293
Dodd-Frank legislation, 317
Doman, Al
   Killinger–five emissaries meeting and,
      203–6
   at WaMu reunion, 307
Downey, California
   Community Fulfillment Center in, 142–43,
      144–45, 144*n*, 166
   fraud at, 166
   Option ARMs in, 154
Dugan, John, 219
Dunnell, William, 124–25

eAppraiselT lawsuit, 178, 178*n*
Eisinger, Jesse, 138–39
Eldridge, Wally, 12
Ely, Burt, 219
Emergency Economic Stabilization Act (2008).
   See TARP
employees, WaMu
   concerns about JPM purchase of WaMu by,
      321–22
   Dimon welcoming e-mail to, 304
   and five emissaries–Killinger meeting,
      203–6

former, 203–6, 203*n*
   impact of WaMu failure on, 310–11
   JPM conversion of WaMu and, 321–24
   layoffs of, 102, 158, 176, 196, 321–24
   pension plans of, 310
   Pepper's e-mail to, 310–11
   reactions to sale of WaMu by, 302–3, 305
   and WaMu as name of bank, 203*n*
   See also specific person
Enron, 91, 138, 197

Faber, David, 6
Fannie Mae, 64, 120–21, 130, 187, 248, 254,
   257, 261, 285
Farkas, Lee, 130
Federal Deposit Insurance Corp. (FDIC)
   Bair defense of, 243
   bank runs and, 214
   banking crisis on Main Street and, 319–20
   Citigroup case and, 314*n*
   Congress and, 249
   criticisms of, 319–20
   deposit insurance fund of, 219, 227, 228,
      237, 243, 245, 275, 292, 304, 317, 333
   deposit insurance limit at, 276, 315
   founding of, 219
   headquarters of, 220
   IndyMac closure and, 207, 208, 242, 243,
      249
   JPM relationship with, 232, 246, 316
   mission of, 219, 315
   OTS relationship with, 220, 224–28, 233,
      242, 244–45, 248–52, 260, 262, 266–67,
      270, 274, 275, 281, 287
   power of, 219–20
   preparation for bank failures by, 216–17, 228
   reputation of, 220
   Superior Bank case and, 225
   "systemic risk" exceptions and, 314
   troubled bank list of, 3, 248–49, 262, 273
   Wachovia case and, 314
   Walmart bank application and, 217
   See also Bair, Sheila; Federal Deposit
      Insurance Corp. (FDIC), WaMu and
Federal Deposit Insurance Corp. (FDIC),
   WaMu and
   bank run and, 269, 281–82
   bid process for WaMu and, 290, 290*n*,
      292–93, 297
   capital raise and, 237, 294
   closure/seizure of WaMu and, 6, 294, 296,
      299–300, 301–5, 315–17
   contingency plans for WaMu and, 250
   credit lines and, 286–87

deadline for WaMu and, 262, 273
Fishman/WaMu–FDIC meeting and, 272–73
JPM access to WaMu data and, 291
JPM acquisition of WaMu and, 20, 246, 283–84, 295, 301, 304
JPM-WaMu direct negotiations and, 235
Killinger-OTS meeting and, 244–45
lawsuit against WaMu executives by FDIC and, 333–34
liquidity of WaMu and, 300n
OTS-FDIC relationship and, 220, 224–25, 226–28, 242, 243
oversight of WaMu and, 4
Pepper as WaMu general counsel and, 10, 12
ratings for WaMu and, 248–50, 262, 274, 281–82
relationship between, 220, 243
reverberations of WaMu failure and, 311–14
sale of WaMu and, 228, 250–52, 251n, 260, 262, 274–75, 275n, 279, 283, 284, 289–90, 290n, 292–94, 297, 300
WaMu daily reports to, 299, 300
WaMu plans and, 270
WaMu as problem bank and, 262
Federal Home Loan Bank of San Francisco, 4, 115n, 207, 215, 271, 286–87, 299–300
Federal Home Loan Bank of Seattle, 215, 271, 286–87, 299, 300
Federal Home Loan Banks
  credit lines of, 210, 215, 248, 271, 286–87, 299–300
  Savings and Loan Crisis and, 220–21
  WaMu reports to regulators and, 299
Federal Reserve Bank
  Bair's discussions with, 250
  discount window at, 210, 215, 248, 285–86, 299–300, 314
  FDIC study of bank failures and, 217
  Killinger's blame for WaMu problems and, 240
  predictions about decline in housing market of, 161
  WaMu capital raise efforts and, 294
  WaMu meeting with, 274, 275–76
  See also Bernanke, Ben; Kohn, Donald
Feltgen, Cheryl, 150–51, 157, 159, 180–81, 181n, 186
Financial Crisis Commission, 314, 315, 316
Financial Services Roundtable, 162, 231
Financial Times, 282
First American, 178
First Interstate Bank, 40, 50
First Magnus Financial Corp., 168

first-time homebuyers, 113–14
Fishman, Alan
  appointed CEO and president of WaMu, 254–55, 257, 258
  attempts to sell WaMu by, 2–5, 262, 269–73, 279–80, 282–83, 284, 287–88, 293–97, 301
  Bair and, 260, 262, 270, 272, 273, 279
  capital raise attempts by, 270, 294, 296
  compensation for, 321
  Dimon and, 261
  FDIC sale of WaMu and, 301
  FDIC seizure of WaMu and, 303
  Federal Reserve meeting with, 274, 275–76
  first day at WaMu of, 258–61
  fraud problems and, 260
  "Go It Alone" proposal and, 294
  at Independence Community Bank, 282
  JPM request for WaMu data and, 291
  Killinger and, 256, 319
  last attempt to save WaMu by, 295–96
  letter to customers from, 280–81
  Moody's meeting with, 264–66
  OTS-FDIC relations and, 260
  OTS meeting with, 273–74
  personal life of, 256
  plan/vision for WaMu of, 257, 259, 269–70, 273
  professional background of, 255
  ratings of WaMu and, 263
  regulators meeting with, 254
  reputation of, 256, 260
  research about WaMu by, 256
  Rotella and, 259, 280
  saving WaMu comments of, 318–19
  severance of, 321
Fishman, Judy, 256, 266
five emissaries meeting, Killinger's, 203–6
fixed-rate loans/mortgages, 11, 117, 119, 119n, 121, 122n, 128, 129, 150, 197
Fleet Mortgage Corp., 84
Flores, Jose, 72
Forbes magazine, 88, 329
foreclosures
  decline of housing prices and, 153
  increase in, 152, 170, 185
  Long Beach Mortgage reputation and, 176
  moratorium on, 332
  off-loading of risky loans and, 157, 158
  Pepper's concerns about, 134
  and problems associated with subprime mortgages, 77
  See also type of mortgage or loan
Fortune magazine, 44, 90, 91, 102
Foster Pepper & Riviera, 10, 10n, 16, 22, 182

Fragoso, Luis, 145, 146n
Frank, Steve, 163–64, 166, 192–93, 202, 239, 252, 254, 255, 257, 269, 295–96
Franklin, Ben, 274
fraud
  Cathcart and, 151
  at Community Fulfillment Centers, 144–45, 144n, 166
  decline in housing prices and, 154
  at Downey and Montebello offices, 166
  increase in, 260
  Killinger's congressional testimony about, 331
  Long Beach Mortgage and, 71–73, 76, 93, 154, 166
  Rotella's congressional testimony about, 144n
  subprime loans/mortgages and, 71–73, 76, 164
  underwriting guidelines and, 137
  WaMu board reactions to findings about, 164
  Warehouse Lending Division and, 130–31
Frazier, Raymond, 212
Freddie Mac, 64, 120–21, 130, 187, 248, 254, 257, 261, 285
free checking, 54, 85, 106, 325
Freedom of Information Act, 316
Freilinger, Peter, 210–11, 286
Friedlander, Lindy, 19, 38
"Friend of the Family," WaMu, 24–25, 25n, 60
Frontier Bank, 38
Frost, Robert, 216
Fuld, Dick, 174, 265
Funaro, Steve, 226–27

Gaspard, Scott, 284
Gates, Bill, 46, 328
Geithner, Tim, 219, 269
General Electric, 96
Glass-Steagall Act, 121
Glaze, Iris, 176–78, 187, 206, 268, 307, 322–23
"Go It Alone" proposal, 294
Golden West Financial, 119, 120n, 138, 139, 265
Goldman Sachs
  as advisor to WaMu, 3, 121, 228, 269, 271, 283, 288
  bank holding company filing of, 288
  bundling of mortgage-backed securities by, 120, 121, 157
  as buyer of WaMu securities and loans, 121, 157
  compensation for board members of, 164
  Countrywide Financial and, 121
  criminal investigation of trader at, 333
  Great Western acquisition and, 32, 33, 40, 42
  Killinger's views about, 121
  Long Beach Mortgage and, 121, 131, 157
Golon, Tom, 196–97, 197n
good bank/bad bank scenario, 228
Great Depression
  bank failures during, 13–14
  FDIC founding during, 219
  2008 events compared with, 185, 191, 199, 209, 211–12
  WaMu during, 134, 211–12
  WaMu as survivor of, 6
Great Western Savings and Loan Bank, 32, 33, 40–48, 49, 51, 58, 60, 61, 183
Greater Seattle Chamber of Commerce, 84
Greenspan, Alan, 119, 119n, 174

H&R Block, 153
Hamm, Charles, 255
Hawaii: WaMu promise to developers in, 12, 134
hedge funds, 167, 173
hedging, 17, 101–2, 104, 121–22
Henderson, Nevada: FDIC seizure of WaMu in, 302
high-margin products, 150, 151
  See also "higher-risk lending strategy," WaMu
"higher-risk lending strategy," WaMu, 122–24, 133, 135, 150, 151, 164, 166, 179, 180, 224, 262, 330–31
home equity loans
  compensation and, 128
  delinquencies and, 171
  fraud and, 260
  as high-margin product, 150
  at JPM, 325
  JPM-WaMu merger proposal and, 235
  Killinger's views about, 122, 137–38, 241
  lack of documentation for, 126
  Longbrake's warnings about housing and, 162
  McMurray's report about, 187
  off-loading of, 158
  plans to save WaMu and, 228
  Rotella and, 331
  underwriting guidelines and, 126
  WaMu assets and, 232
Home Loans Group, WaMu
  appraisal issue and, 180, 181n
  Cathcart and, 151, 201

Chapman (Craig) as head of, 101
Chapman-Killinger relationship and, 181
Chapman's (Fay) concerns about housing
   market and, 179, 179*n*
commitment to sale of high risk loans by,
   158–59
compensation for loan consultants and,
   128–29
Dark Side nickname of, 111
Davis as head of, 67–68, 69, 101, 111
Downey Community Fulfillment Center
   and, 143
expansion of, 93
Feltgren as risk officer with, 150–51
five emissaries–Killinger discussion about,
   204–5
goal of, 68
guidelines for, 125–26, 151, 167, 192
hidden problems in, 110
"higher-risk lending strategy" and, 122
increase in volume of home loans and, 111
influence on Killinger of, 67
Jenne's homeowner delinquency video and,
   172
Jenne's meeting with, 167–68
Jenne's Option ARMs assignment and,
   112–13
Killinger's apologies to stockholders
   concerning, 102
lack of leadership in, 101
Long Beach Mortgage and, 75–76, 167
naming of, 67*n*
off-loading of risky loans and, 158
Option ARMs and, 112–18, 186, 196
Optis software program and, 100–101
OTS concerns about, 223–24
power and influence of, 96, 97
"The Power of Yes" campaign and, 68–69,
   125
President's Club and, 68–69, 140
Rotella and, 109–10, 128, 137, 180, 192, 255
run on WaMu and, 213
shareholder relations and, 186
tracking of complex data by, 165
"2007 Product Strategy" report of, 158–59,
   160
Vanasek and, 123
volume of mortgages and, 100
Home Savings of America. *See* Ahmanson
   Savings and Loan Bank
HomeSide Lending, 97
House Financial Services Committee, U.S.,
   223
Household Finance Corp., 61

housing market
   Baker's concerns about, 152–53
   belief in invulnerability of, 135–36
   bubble in, 133–36, 151–52, 161, 163, 178,
      194
   Chapman's (Fay) concerns about, 179
   decline in, 125, 133–35, 138, 151–52,
      153–54, 166, 185–86, 191, 240, 262
   Killinger's concerns about, 133–35, 138, 161,
      163, 166, 179, 186–87, 199, 240
   Longbrake's concerns about, 161–63
   OTS promotion of, 220
   Pepper's concerns about, 133–35
   price of housing and, 151–52, 153–54, 166,
      185, 240
housing speculators/flippers, 72, 240
Housing and Urban Development, U.S.
   Department of, 168

"I Think I Did It Again" (WaMu-themed
   song), 91–92
Ifill, Gwen, 136
Independence Community Bank, 255, 256,
   257, 282, 283
indexing, 114–15, 115*n*
"industrial loan company" applications, 217
IndyMac Bank, 119, 171, 172, 207–9, 211, 215,
   242–44, 249, 274, 278, 280, 287, 296
interest rates
   hedging and, 17, 101–2, 121–22
   Killinger's dilemma and, 121–22
   Killinger's views about, 240
   in 1970s, 36
   in 980s, 11, 17, 22
   refinancing of mortgages and, 85
   See also type of mortgage or loan
investment banks/houses
   bundling of mortgage-backed securities by,
      120
   Great Western acquisitions and, 44
   losses of, 173
   Pepper's views about, 18–19
   Perrin's fish analogy and, 130
   regulator for, 219
   selling of mortgage-backed securities to,
      74–75
   WaMu knowingly selling bad loans to, 260
   See also specific firm
investment properties: Option ARMs and, 114
Investor Relations Department, WaMu,
   176–77, 268
   See also Glaze, Iris
investors. *See* secondary market; shareholders/
   investors, WaMu; *type of investor*

irrational money lenders, Killinger's comment about, 163, 170, 240

Jenne, Kevin, 112–18, 167–68, 170–72
Jiminez (Ramona and Gerardo) family: mortgage loan to, 154–57, 172–73, 331–32
Johnson, Earvin "Magic," 141–42
JPMorgan Chase
assets of, 229
Bair meetings with representatives from, 232–33, 266, 316
Bank One acquisition by, 104–5, 230
Bear Stearns acquisition by, 187, 232, 246, 325, 329
board of, 295
bundling of mortgage-backed securities by, 120
Dimon appointment as president and COO of, 105
FDIC-OTS relationship and, 251
FDIC relationship with, 232, 246, 316
Great Depression and, 212
high-risk mortgages at, 138
home equity loans at, 325
investor conference call at, 301, 304
as largest company in world, 329
lawsuits against, 326
losses at, 325
Morgan Stanley acquisition rumors and, 287, 293
OTS/Reich and, 233–35, 283
philanthropy of, 326–28
political connections of, 231
regulators' meetings with, 232–34
Rotella hiring of employees from, 107
SEC protection from naked short selling of, 247
shareholders at, 325
subprime mortgages and, 325
TARP and, 315, 328
See also JPMorgan Chase, WaMu and; specific person
JPMorgan Chase, WaMu and
acquisition of WaMu by, 3, 4, 6, 7, 300, 321–22
bidding for WaMu by, 300, 316–17
Chapman's (Fay) recommendation to sell WaMu to, 179
closure of WaMu and, 301, 316–17
conversion of WaMu by, 320–24
direct negotiations for JPM acquisition of WaMu and, 189, 195, 229–38, 238n
FDIC sale of WaMu and, 274–75, 289–90, 292–93, 298, 300, 316–17

and Fishman attempts to sell WaMu to JPM, 271–72
and funding for WaMu acquisition, 301, 304, 304n
hostile takeover of WaMu proposal by, 245–46
Moody's downgrade of WaMu and, 290
Paulson's views about WaMu offer from, 248
plans for acquisition of WaMu by, 266, 274–75, 275n, 283–84, 295
press conference of, 4
profits on WaMu purchase by, 328–29
renegotiation of WaMu borrowers with, 332
rumors about WaMu deal with, 267, 268
rumors about WaMu health and, 214
Santander-JPM bid-rigging allegations and, 282n
and WaMu as government-assisted deal, 266
WaMu online data room and, 291, 322
and WaMu sale as "government assistance" transaction, 246, 246n
WaMu stockholders and, 245–46
junk bonds, 28
Justice Department, U.S., 60, 332

Kashkari, Neel, 315
Kaufman, Ted, 126, 330
Kelly, Edward "Ned," 289, 298
Keystone Holdings, 42
Kido, Ken, 209–10, 281
Killinger, Brad, 29, 33, 37, 45, 81
Killinger, Bryan, 29, 33, 35, 36, 37, 45, 81
Killinger, Debbie, 29, 30, 33, 34–36, 37, 43, 45, 46, 79, 80–84, 88, 311
Killinger, Karl, 33–34, 35, 37
Killinger, Kerry
absence from Seattle office of, 93–94
as Alexander the Great, 88
appearance of, 88, 189
appointment as president and CEO of, 30, 309
Baker e-mail about housing to, 152
as "Banker of the Year," 87
blame for WaMu problems and, 241, 330
board memberships of, 83
board regulators meeting and, 192–93
caricatures of, 49, 322
compensation for, 45, 94, 104, 174, 205
congressional testimonies of, 329–31
corporate jets and, 88–89, 97, 174, 205
demands for resignation of, 195, 205
dilemma of, 121–22
employee views about, 93–94, 177, 180, 201–2, 241–42
FDIC lawsuit against, 333–34

firing of, 3, 252–53, 254, 263
five emissaries meeting with, 203–6
hiring by, 98–99
Linda thanked by, 196
management style of, 52, 55, 57, 62–63, 87, 96, 123, 174–76, 177
marginalization and isolation of, 201–2
marital problems of, 80–83
McKinsey review and, 241–42
McMurray's report and, 186–87, 201
media criticisms of, 102, 308
nickname for, 33
NYSE bell ringing and, 54
optimism of, 173–75
organization and structure of WaMu and, 67, 96, 101, 108
OTS pressures to replace, 255
Pepper's advice to, 102–4, 133–35, 133n
Pepper's CD gift to, 30–31
Pepper's hiring of, 18, 19
Pepper's relationship with, 149, 309
as Pepper's successor, 27–31, 205
Pepper's views about, 29–30, 87, 102–4
Pepper's visits to WaMu and, 148
personal life of, 33–38, 45–46, 52–53, 80–84, 94
personality and character of, 28–29, 36–37, 43, 44, 45–46, 47, 53, 87–88, 90–91, 102, 105, 132, 135, 173–75, 199–200
plans/vision for WaMu of, 67, 85, 86, 87, 88, 96, 108, 109, 122–23, 228–29, 240, 241
political connections of, 231
popularity of, 87, 93
potential successors to, 106, 107, 175, 202
professional background of, 18–19, 28, 29, 37, 38
reputation/image of, 43, 44, 88, 99
resignation thoughts of, 175
sale of WaMu and, 179, 330
Seattle office of, 32–33, 95
severance package for, 258
shareholder/investor relations and, 47, 55, 81–82, 102, 173, 188, 189–91, 193–200
shareholder lawsuits against, 102, 178
stress on, 190, 241
surprise birthday party for, 79–80
as WaMu board chairman, 30, 200, 239, 240–41, 309
WaMu board relationship with, 164–65, 170, 186–87, 239
WaMu as "category killer" and, 91
WaMu culture/values and, 94–95, 98, 107, 132–33
WaMu reunions and, 308–9, 311

wealth of, 37–38, 46, 82–83
work ethic of, 35
See also specific person, merger, acquisition, or topic
Killinger, Linda Cottington, 83–84, 89–90, 94, 174, 196, 205, 231, 308, 309, 328, 333
Kohn, Donald, 250, 252, 275, 294, 295–96
Korea Development Bank (KDB), 261
Korszner, Randy, 275
Kovacevich, Richard, 297

Ladder Capital, 254
Lannoye, Lee
  Killinger–five emissaries meeting and, 203–6
  Long Beach Mortgage acquisition and, 59–60, 62–63
  retirement of, 62
  at shareholders 2008 meeting, 197–99
Last Hurrah Party, WaMu, 322
Lehman Brothers
  as advisor to WaMu, 228
  bankruptcy of, 270, 272, 273, 296
  capital raise at, 187
  concerns about survival of, 260, 261
  decision not to bail out, 269
  decline in stock price of, 260, 261
  Financial Services Conference of, 87
  Great Western acquisition and, 41, 44
  impact on borrowing at Fed's discount window of, 285
  impact on WaMu of problems at, 268, 272, 273, 296
  KDB deal and, 261
  losses at, 261, 263
  mortgage-backed securities sales at, 120
Lehman Investors Conference, 153, 173
Leonard, Andrew, 128
Leppert, Tom, 163
Lereah, David, 136, 152, 152n
Levin, Carl: Senate Committee hearings and, 318, 329–31, 334
Lewis, Kenneth D., 125, 231
Lillis, Charles, 164
liquidity, WaMu
  Break the Bank model for, 215, 248, 278
  Cantwell-Paulson conversation about, 293
  closing of banks and ratio for, 215
  closure of WaMu and, 299–300, 300n, 304–5
  FDIC-OTS-WaMu discussion about, 244
  Fishman capital raise plan and, 294
  Fishman letter to customers about, 280
  Moody's-WaMu meeting about, 265
  OTS press release about, 304–5

liquidity, WaMu (*cont.*)
  OTS report and, 300
  regulators' concerns about, 250
  sale of WaMu and, 284, 290
  WaMu reports to regulators about, 286, 299
  See also bank runs, WaMu; credit lines
The Little Prince (children's book), 49
loan consultants/managers
  compensation for, 117, 128–29, 188, 196, 197
  Countrywide-WaMu competition and, 126–28
  fraud among, 145
  Jenne's Option ARMs focus groups and,
    116–18
  layoffs of, 188
  at President's Club meetings, 142–44
  pressures on, 129
  underwriting guidelines and, 125–26
  See also Ramirez, Tom
Long Beach Mortgage
  AIG report about, 166
  Ameriquest loans compared with those of,
    154*n*
  assets of, 58
  audits of, 166, 167
  California regulation of, 66
  change from thrift to mortgage company of,
    64–65
  Chapman (Craig) as manager of, 66, 78, 101
  Chapman (Craig)-Rotella relationship and,
    128
  Chapman's (Fay) concerns about, 56–58,
    60–61, 62, 63, 72, 75–78
  compensation at, 69–70, 78, 129, 166–67
  Countrywide-WaMu competition and, 127
  culture at, 63–64
  Davis (Craig) as head of, 75–76
  defaults and delinquencies at, 137, 153
  expansion of, 78, 136–37
  founding of, 63
  fraud and, 71–73, 76, 93, 154, 166
  funding for mortgage brokers and, 129
  Goldman Sachs relationship with, 121, 131,
    157
  "higher-risk lending strategy" and, 122
  Home Loans Group and problems at, 167
  Justice Department accusation against, 60
  Killinger and, 57, 58, 62–63, 75, 76, 78, 137–38
  Lannoye opposition to, 197–98
  losses at, 66
  mortgage-backed securities sales at, 67,
    73–75
  off-loading of risky loans and, 157
  OTS concerns about, 223–24
  oversight of, 65, 66, 137
  paperwork problems at, 332
  privatization of, 66
  profits of, 64, 65, 71
  proposal to shut down, 76, 78
  public offering for, 65
  repurchase of mortgage-backed securities
    by, 137
  reputation of, 157, 176
  Rotella and, 109–10, 128, 137–38
  subprime mortgages at, 63, 69, 71, 75,
    167–68
  underwriting guidelines for, 56, 65–66, 67,
    78, 125, 137–38, 167
  WaMu acquisition of, 58, 59–60, 62, 63
  WaMu reviews of, 57, 76–78
  See also Jiminez (Ramona and Gerardo)
    family: mortgage loan to
Longbrake, Bill
  end of savings and loan banks comment of,
    318
  hiring of, 18
  housing market warnings of, 161–63
  junk bond incident and, 28
  Killinger as Pepper successor and, 28
  NYSE bell ringing and, 54
  Pepper appointment as temporary CEO
    and, 10–11
  personal and professional background of,
    28, 98
  as potential Pepper successor, 27, 29, 205
  WaMu departure of, 98
  WaMu responsibilities of, 98
Los Angeles Times, 71, 242–43

Mad Money (TV show), 246–47
Magleby, Alan, 297
Maher, John, 40, 42, 43–44, 45, 60
Market Research Department, WaMu, 192
  See also Jenne, Kevin
Martinez, Melissa, 126
Matthews, Phillip, 164
McCain, John, 264, 301
McGee, Liam, 255
McKinsey Group, 241–42
McMurray, John, 186–87, 186*n*, 201–2,
    260–61, 264, 266, 269, 270, 288, 301
media
  bailout reports by, 2
  bank runs and, 2, 201, 207–8, 209, 211–12,
    214, 215, 243, 279, 282
  criticisms of Killinger by, 102, 308–9
  Dimon's Seattle address and, 326–27
  end of modern Wall Street proclaimed by,
    288

FDIC seizure of WaMu and, 300–301, 302, 303

Fishman appointment announced in, 258

IndyMac failure and, 207–8, 209, 242–43

JPM merger offer to WaMu and, 237–38

Kido interview with, 281

Killinger firing reported in, 254

Lehman problems and, 270

Paulson interview with, 284–85

Pepper and, 309–10

sale of WaMu rumors and, 279, 288, 289, 298–99, 300–301, 302

and WaMu failure as nonevent, 314

WaMu final hours and, 267–68, 272, 276, 279, 281, 282, 288, 289, 292, 298–99, 300–301, 302

WaMu information lockdown and, 281

WaMu layoffs and, 321

WaMu shareholder meetings and, 189

See also specific media organization

Meola, Tony, 75, 76, 142, 144, 145

"Merge with Washington Mutual!" ad campaign, 39

mergers and acquisitions, WaMu

corporate cultures and, 52

interest in subprime lenders and, 59

process for absorbing, 50–51

See also specific merger or acquisition

Meridian Capital Group, 255

Merrill Lynch & Co., 153, 270

Microsoft, 91, 164

Miller, Tom, 83, 84

minorities, 59, 60, 64, 142–44

See also Community Fulfillment Centers, WaMu

money laundering, 192

See also Bank Secrecy Act

Montebello, California: Community Fulfillment Center in, 144–45, 144n, 166

Monthly Treasury Average (MTA), 115n

Montoya, Regina, 164

Moody's Investors Service, 61–62, 237, 261, 264–66, 264n, 267–68, 286, 290–91, 292

Morgan Stanley, 3, 269, 287, 288

mortgage-backed securities

defaults and, 173

early problems with, 152

Goldman Sachs relationship with WaMu and, 121

increase in subprime, 57, 70

investment banks bundling of, 120

layoffs of people working with, 188

Long Beach Mortgage repurchase of, 137

off-loading of, 154, 157, 158, 173

Pepper's concerns about, 17

popularity of, 75

ratings of, 120, 158, 173

representations and warranties of, 74

reputation of Long Beach Mortgage, 157

risk and, 74, 75, 120

secondary market demand for, 63, 70, 75

WaMu as bundling own, 120

WaMu pressures to sell, 153–54

WAMU Series 2007-HE4, 156

WaMu volume of, 120

writedowns of, 187

See also Long Beach Mortgage; secondary market

mortgage brokers/lenders

collapse of subprime market and, 168

failures of, 187

First Magnus bankruptcy and kickbacks to, 168

increase in number of, 70–71

Jenne's Option ARMs focus groups and, 116–17

Killinger's comment about "irrational," 163, 170, 240

Perrin's fish analogy and, 130

Reich views about regulation of, 223

as short-term lenders, 119–20

underwriting guidelines and, 137

WaMu acquisition of, 84–85, 93, 97

WaMu funding for, 129

See also specific broker or lender

mortgage servicing rights (MSRs), 101, 158

mortgages

as collateral for raising liquidity, 210

as collateral on WaMu credit lines, 271, 286, 300

decrease in volume of WaMu, 158

JPM profits on WaMu acquisition and, 328–29

tracking of complex data about, 165–66

as "underwater," 153

See also type of mortgage

Moving Forward (WaMu internal newsletter), 201

Mozilo, Angelo, 127, 165n, 186n, 332–33

Mueller, Brian, 212–13, 263, 268–69, 276–77, 278, 292, 320, 323–24

Murphey Favre, 18–19, 29, 37, 38

Murray, Patty, 275

Mutual Travel, 27

naked short selling, 247–48, 330

Naroff Economic Advisors, 152

National Association of Realtors, 136, 151, 152, 152*n*
National Australia Bank Limited, 97
negatively amortizing mortgage, 112, 113–14, 138
NetJets, 89, 97, 301, 303
New Century Financial, 71, 152, 166, 176, 329
New York State
 WaMu acquisitions in, 85
 See also Cuomo, Andrew
New York Stock Exchange, 54, 308, 322
The New York Sun, 269
The New York Times, 88, 125, 126, 129, 187, 189, 279, 298, 300–301, 318
The New Yorker: Bair interview in, 218
Newshour (PBS), 136
NINA loans (No Income, No Assets), 69
Norwest Bank, 27, 41, 42
Nova-Star, 72

Oak Hill Capital Partners, 235
Obama, Barack, 264
Occasio branches, 85–86, 106, 325
Office of the Comptroller of the Currency, 219, 222, 232, 233, 246, 317
Office of Thrift Supervision (OTS)
 closing of small banks and, 319–20
 Countrywide Financial and, 222, 222*n*, 227
 criticisms of, 319–20
 defense of oversight responsibilities by, 317–18
 demise of, 317–18
 expansion of, 221–22
 FDIC relationship with, 220, 224–28, 233, 242, 244–45, 248–52, 260, 262, 266–67, 270, 274, 275, 281–82, 287
 formation of, 220, 221
 IndyMac Bank and, 207, 208, 243–44, 274
 Levin's committee and, 318
 mission of, 220
 power of, 244
 reputation of, 274
 Schumer's IndyMac letter to media and, 208
 Superior Bank case and, 225
 Treasury Department oversight of, 233
 See also Office of Thrift Supervision (OTS), WaMu and; Reich, John
Office of Thrift Supervision (OTS), WaMu and
 bank run and, 281–82
 Bank Secrecy Act and, 192, 224
 blame for WaMu failure and, 317
 capital raise and, 228, 229, 234, 237, 258, 270, 294

closure of WaMu and, 299–300, 315–17
deadline for WaMu of, 274
enforcement order and, 258–59, 267, 270
Fishman/WaMu meeting at, 273–74
JPM acquisition of WaMu and, 304–5
JPM-WaMu direct negotiations and, 233–35, 236
Killinger-FDIC meeting with, 244–45
Killinger's defense of WaMu and, 239
liquidity of WaMu and, 286, 299, 300*n*
Long Beach Mortgage oversight by, 65, 66
OTS early concerns about WaMu and, 122, 224, 228, 229
political importance of WaMu to, 227, 244
pressures to replace Killinger from, 255
ratings for WaMu and, 176, 228, 248–50, 262, 263, 267, 274, 281–82
relationship between, 4–5, 6, 222, 244, 249, 263
Rotella and, 180
S report on WaMu by, 293, 299, 300
sale of WaMu concerns of OTS and, 250–52, 251*n*, 282, 293
seizure of WaMu and, 303–4
WaMu board's lack of information and, 192
WaMu daily reports to, 299, 300
WaMu ignoring of, 223–24
WaMu reviews by, 223–24, 225–27
Old Stone Bank, 38
Olympus Bank, 39
online data room, WaMu, 271–72, 284, 291, 322
Oppenheimer, Deanna, 20, 54, 85–86, 94, 101, 106, 107
Option ARMs
 bank-borrower relationship and, 118
 benefits of, 117, 118
 borrowers' lack of understanding about, 113–18, 138–39, 171
 compensation and, 117, 128, 129, 160, 197
 Countrywide-WaMu competition and, 127, 160
 decline of housing prices and, 153
 decrease in lending for, 158
 defaults and delinquencies on, 157, 161, 186
 documentation for, 126
 in Downey, 154
 FDIC alert about WaMu and, 262
 at Golden West Financial, 120*n*
 as high-margin product, 150
 increase in sales of, 118–20
 at IndyMac, 207
 interest rates and, 111, 112*n*, 114–15, 116–17, 156

investment properties and, 114
Jenne's assignment concerning, 112–18
Jenne's study of delinquencies and, 171, 172
JPM-WaMu negotiations and, 236, 246
Killinger's congressional testimony about, 331
Killinger's views about, 122, 241, 331
marketing of, 116
minimum amounts payments on, 138
off-loading of, 154, 157, 158, 159
OTS-FDIC views about, 266
OTS review of WaMu and, 224
Perrin and, 132
plans to save WaMu and, 228
President's Club awards and, 142–43
pushing of sales of, 196
refinancing of mortgages and, 114, 116, 266
Reich and, 222–23
risk of, 138, 139
Rotella and, 143, 197n
secondary market and, 112, 120
shareholder criticisms and, 194, 196
as underwater loans, 197
underwriting guidelines concerning, 126, 222–23
Vasquez loan as, 156
WaMu assets and, 232
WaMu commitment to sale of, 158–59
WaMu culture/values and, 132
WaMu profits from, 170
Option One Mortgage (H&R Block unit), 153
Optis software program, 100–101
"originate-to-sell" concept, 112
Orman, Suze, 243, 278
Osorio, Ada and Luis, 5–7, 313

Pacific First Bank, 39, 183
Paulson, Henry "Hank"
  Bair and, 219
  Bair-Reich relationship and, 251
  Cantwell conversation with, 293
  closure of WaMu comments of, 315
  congressional testimony of, 293
  Dimon's discussions with, 231
  Fannie Mae and Freddie Mac takeover announced by, 254
  financial market concerns of, 216
  Fishman's comments about saving WaMu and, 318
  JPM acquisition of WaMu and, 301
  Killinger and, 247–48
  Lehman Brothers bailout and, 269
  TARP and, 284–85, 288, 291, 293, 301, 314, 315, 328

Penn Square Bank, 26
pension funds, 73, 173, 194
Pepper, Lou
  anniversary celebrations for, 54–55
  assets/size of WaMu and, 54
  birthday parties for, 23–24
  as board/trustee member, 9–10, 30
  book by, 148–49
  commercial real estate loans and, 26–27
  Dimon's Seattle address and, 328
  dislike of WaMu name by, 203n
  failure of WaMu and, 309–10
  as general counsel for WaMu, 10, 12, 22
  hedging views of, 101
  housing market decline concerns of, 133–35
  Killinger CD gift from, 30–31
  Killinger views of, 87, 102–4
  Killinger's advice from, 102–4, 133–35, 133n
  Killinger's relationship with, 149, 309
  leadership style of, 17–18, 20–21, 27–28
  management philosophy of, 22–23
  media and, 309–10
  Murphey Favre merger and, 18–19
  NYSE bell ringing and, 54
  personal and professional background of, 9, 12–14, 21–22
  personality and character of, 12, 15, 17–18, 27–28, 29, 205
  reputation of, 10
  retirement of, 30
  Rotella's relationship with, 149
  as "savior" of WaMu, 14, 22
  Seattle office of, 148
  selling of WaMu headquarters by, 32
  speeches to WaMu employees by, 9, 11, 12, 54–55
  staff hiring by, 17–20, 55, 95, 103, 163
  successors to, 25–31, 205
  as temporary CEO of WaMu, 9–16
  "too big to fail" idea and, 309–10
  WaMu Alumni Fund and, 310–11
  WaMu culture/values and, 20–21, 23–24, 147–48, 163
  at WaMu reunion, 309
  WaMu visits of, 148
  in The WaMu Way video, 147–48
Pepper, Mollie, 9, 11, 30, 133, 309, 310
Pepper, Ruth, 13–14
Permanent Subcommittee on Investigations, U.S. Senate, 318, 329–31, 334
Perrin, Michele, 130–33, 146, 168–70
Perry, Michael, 207
Pioneer Savings Bank, 38
PNC Bank, 84, 282n

Polakoff, Scott, 4, 5, 250, 263, 273–74, 282
"The Power of Yes" campaign, 68–69, 73, 85, 100, 111, 125
prepayment penalties, 74
President's Club, 68–69, 139–44, 145, 159–61, 188
Project West, JPM's, 231–38, 246, 266, 283, 291, 292, 298
  See also Scharf, Charlie
Providian Bank, 154
Puget Sound Business Journal, 20, 159, 193
Puget Sound Savings and Loan Association, 211
Pugh Capital Management, 163
Pugh, Mary, 20, 163, 188, 191–93, 194

Ramirez, Tom, 142–44, 145, 154, 332
ratings, WaMu
  Bair and, 249, 250–52, 262, 263
  CAMELS, 176, 228, 248, 262, 300
  FDIC and, 248–50, 262, 274, 281–82
  liquidity and, 286
  Moody's, 237, 261, 264–66, 264n, 286, 290–91, 292
  OTS and, 176, 228, 248–50, 262, 263, 267, 274, 281–82
real estate agents, 143, 152
redlining, 64
Reed, William, 164
refinancing of mortgages, 85, 99, 101, 114, 116, 145, 153, 156, 162, 266
regulators/regulation
  Fishman-Frank meeting with, 254
  guidelines for high-risk loans and, 151
  JPM meetings with, 232–34
  liquidity ratio and, 215
  of mortgage brokers, 223
  Reich's views about, 222
  Rotella and, 255
  run on WaMu and, 213
  Schumer's IndyMac letter to media and, 207–8
  and underwriting guidelines for Option ARMs, 222–23
  WaMu liquidity and, 210, 215
  See also specific regulator
Reich, John
  appointment as OTC director of, 221
  Bair and, 222–23, 248, 249, 250–52, 263, 270, 275, 287
  Citigroup case and, 318
  closure of WaMu and, 299, 300
  congressional testimonies of, 318
  criticisms of, 221
  expansion of OTS by, 221–22

and Fishman-Frank letter to save WaMu, 295–96
Fishman/WaMu meeting with, 273–74
JPM and, 233–34, 283
Killinger discussions with, 227, 235, 245, 247
Killinger-FDIC meeting with, 244–45
liquidity of WaMu and, 287
Option ARMs and, 222–23
OTS-FDIC relationship and, 227–28, 248
personal and professional background of, 221
personality and character of, 221
politics and, 221
ratings for WaMu and, 249, 263
regulation views of, 222
retirement of, 317
sale of WaMu and, 282
Schumer's IndyMac letter to media and, 208
self-image of, 221
subprime mortgages and, 223–24
views about WaMu of, 227–28
WaMu capital raise and, 294
WaMu enforcement order and, 258–59
WaMu-OTS relationship and, 222
WaMu as political threat to, 227, 244
  See also Office of Thrift Services
representations, 74
reunions, WaMu, 307–9, 311
Rinehart, Charlie, 42, 46–47, 48, 51, 53
risk
  analysts' pressures on WaMu and, 122
  banking industry and, 122n
  CAMELS ratings and, 176
  decline in housing market and, 138
  fixed-rate mortgages and, 122n
  Killinger's "higher-risk lending strategy" and, 122–23
  Longbrake's warnings about housing market and, 162
  of mortgage-backed securities, 74, 75, 120
  and off-loading of risky loans, 154, 157–58, 161, 173
  of Option ARMs, 138, 139
  Pepper's concerns about, 134
  of subprime mortgages, 153–54
  Vanasek concerns about, 150
  WaMu pressures to sell mortgages and, 153–54
  WaMu purchasing of subprime mortgages and, 129–30
  See also Risk Management Group, WaMu
Risk Management Group, WaMu
  Cathcart as head of, 150

Killinger-Rotella relationship and, 202
Longbrake and, 98
organization and structure of WaMu and, 98, 150–51
problems facing, 135
tracking of complex data and, 165–66
turnover in, 200
underwriting guidelines and, 126
WaMu five-year plans and, 126
See also Vanasek, Jim
Robinson, John, 4–5, 272, 273–74, 301–2
The Rocky Horror Picture Show, 68–69
Rotary Club (Seattle): Killinger at, 238–41
Rotella, Esther, 1, 287, 333
Rotella, Steve
  appearance of, 105
  appraisals issue and, 180, 181*n*
  Baker e-mail about housing to, 152
  bank run and, 2, 213, 280
  Bank Secrecy Act and, 202
  blog of, 280, 302, 305
  branch tour by, 109
  Casey's relationship with, 107
  Chapman (Craig) and, 128
  Chapman (Fay)-Killinger relationship and, 181, 182
  Chapman's (Fay) relationship with, 180
  closure/seizure of WaMu and, 5, 301–2, 303, 305
  compensation for, 174
  congressional testimonies of, 144*n*, 329–30, 331
  demands for resignation of, 205
  FDIC lawsuit against, 333–34
  Fishman's appointment as successor to Killinger and, 255
  Fishman's attempts to sell WaMu and, 1–5, 287
  Fishman's relationship with, 259
  Golon comments about, 197, 197*n*
  high-risk loans and, 331
  higher-risk marketing strategy and, 180
  hiring of JPM people by, 107, 128
  home equity loans and, 331
  Home Loans Group and, 109–10, 128, 137, 180, 192, 255
  JPM departure of, 105, 197, 197*n*
  JPM severance of, 321
  JPM-WaMu direct negotiations and, 232–33
  Killinger concerns of, 201–2
  Killinger defended by, 195–96
  Killinger hiring of, 104–5, 106
  as Killinger's potential successor, 175, 202, 239

Killinger's relationship with, 106, 137–38, 175, 180, 202, 205, 241–42, 329–30
  liquidity of WaMu and, 286
  Long Beach Mortgage concerns of, 109–10, 128, 137–38
  management style of, 107–8
  McKinsey review and, 241–42
  minority lending and, 143
  Moody's meeting and, 265
  off-loading of risky loans and, 157
  Option ARMs and, 143, 197*n*
  OTS and, 180
  Pepper's relationship with, 149
  personal and professional backgroud of, 104, 105
  personality of, 105
  as president and COO, 106
  at President's Club meetings, 141–42, 143
  regulators and, 255
  reputation of, 104, 255
  resentment against, 107
  responsibilities of, 175, 202, 280
  as "savior," 107
  shareholder lawsuits against, 178
  shareholders and, 193, 195–96, 197
  subprime loans and, 197*n*, 331
  tensions within WaMu and, 107, 180
  underwriting standards and, 192
  WaMu board and, 202, 239
  WaMu future of, 175
  in *The WaMu Way* video, 147
Russia: debt crisis in, 62
Ryder, Lynn
  hiring of, 19
  Killinger–five emissaries meeting and, 203–6
  at WaMu reunion, 307

sale of WaMu
  bid-rigging allegations concerning, 282*n*
  employees reactions to, 302–3, 305
  FDIC approval of JPM bid for, 300
  FDIC bidding process for, 290, 316–17
  Fishman's attempts to sell WaMu, 2–5, 262, 269–73, 279–80, 282–83, 284, 287–88, 293–97, 301
  as "government assistance" transaction, 246
  impact on Seattle of, 324
  and JPM acquisition of WaMu, 3, 4, 6, 7, 300, 321–22
  JPM first buyout offer for, 189
  JPM profits on, 328–29
  JPM-WaMu direct negotiations for, 189, 195, 229–38, 238*n*

sale of WaMu (*cont.*)
  official reviews of, 315–17
  Pepper's consideration of, 25, 27
  shareholders and, 283, 290
  and WaMu as distressed asset, 273, 284
  See also Federal Deposit Insurance
    Corporation, WaMu and; JPMorgan
    Chase, WaMu and; Office of Thrift
    Services, WaMu and; *specific person*
salespeople/managers
  compensation for, 140, 166–67
  competition among banks and lenders for,
    139–40
  at Long Beach Mortgage, 166
  Option ARMs and, 116–18
  at President's Club, 139–44
  pressures on, 129
  underwriting guidelines and, 137
  WaMu purchasing of subprime mortgages
    and, 129–30
Salomon Brothers, 25–26
Sanchez, Alberto, 288
Santander Bank, 3, 229, 271, 282–83, 282*n*,
  287, 288, 290, 297
savings and loan banks
  end of, 318
  regulators of, 220–21
Savings and Loan Crisis (1989), 6, 25, 30, 39,
  199, 220, 221, 248–49
Scharf, Charlie
  Bair's meeting with, 266, 316
  FDIC sale of WaMu and, 274, 283–84,
    289–90, 290*n*
  FDIC sharing in losses of WaMu Option
    ARMs and, 246, 266
  and government-assisted acquisition of
    WaMu, 266
  independent examination of WaMu failure
    and, 316
  JPM conversion of WaMu and, 320–21, 325
  JPM lack of interest in acquisition of WaMu
    and, 271–72
  JPM-WaMu direct negotiations and,
    231–33, 234, 235, 236–37, 246, 271–72
  Moody's downgrade of WaMu and, 290*n*
  proposals for JPM acquisition of WaMu and,
    235–38, 295
  report to JPM board of, 283–84
  Rotella at JPM and, 105
  WaMu online data room and, 271–72, 291
Schneider, David
  Baker e-mail about housing to, 152
  Chapman's (Fay) concerns about housing
    market and, 179

Community Fulfillment Centers and, 159
  Cuomo investigation and, 180–81
  FDIC lawsuit against, 333–34
  fraud reports and, 144, 144*n*, 180–81
  high-margin products strategy of, 150, 151
  hiring of, 128
  as Home Loans Group head, 128
  Jenne documentary on high-risk lending
    and, 172
  JPM conversion of WaMu and, 321
  Long Beach Management and, 137, 166
  off-loading of risky loans and, 157
  personality and character of, 128
  at President's Club, 140–41
  professional background of, 128
  Ramirez sales and, 143
  reputation of, 128
  shareholder lawsuits against, 178
  shareholder relations and, 186
  subprime commitment of, 159
  underwriting standards and, 192
Schumer, Chuck, 207–8, 260
Seattle Art Museum, 2, 95, 324, 327–28
Seattle Post-Intelligencer, 247–48
The Seattle Times, 197*n*, 256, 281, 309
Seattle, Washington
  Dimon's speech in, 325, 326–28
  fireworks in, 326–27
  impact of WaMu sale on, 324, 326–27
second-home buyers, 134
second lien investors, 157
secondary market
  blame for WaMu problems and, 241
  Killinger's views about, 330
  losses in, 173
  Option ARMs and, 112, 120
  "originate-to-sell" concept and, 112
  Perrin's views about, 132
  selling of subprime mortgage-backed
    securities to, 57, 58, 63, 73–75, 120
Securities and Exchange Commission (SEC),
  186*n*, 247
Senate Banking Committee
  Bernanke testimony before, 167
  Gaspard discussion with, 284 Paulson-TARP
    discussion at, 293
September 11, 2001, 264
shareholders/investors, WaMu
  ads concerning, 88
  capital raise and, 188–90, 191, 199, 202, 205,
    245–46
  closure of WaMu and, 5–7, 317
  concerns and upset of, 176–77, 187, 188,
    193–200, 206

Dimon's comments about, 326
dividend cuts and, 175, 178, 185, 199
executive compensation and, 187–88
FDIC calls about WaMu failure from,
    311–14
Glaze's relations with, 176–77
Great Western acquisition and, 44
happiness of, 88
institutional, 206
JPM buyout offers and, 189, 245–46
Killinger's relationship with, 47, 55, 81–82,
    102, 173, 188, 189–91, 193–200
lawsuits against WaMu by, 102, 177–78, 195
and Pepper taking WaMu public, 16
Pugh and, 193
Rotella and, 193, 195–96, 197
sale of WaMu and, 283, 290
2008 meeting of, 184–86, 187, 189–91,
    193–200, 206
WaMu board concerns of, 188, 194
short selling, maked, 247–48, 330
Silver Lake State Bank, 13–14
Simpson, Thacher & Bartlett: WaMu
    executives' meetings at, 269–70, 287–88,
    293–94, 295, 301
Smith Barney, 47
Smith, Orin, 163, 252
soccer field meeting, Dunnell-Baker, 124–25
software programs
    layoff monitoring and, 323
    problems with mortgage data, 99, 101, 108,
        164–65, 165n
    WaMu bank run and, 213
    Y2K technology conversion and, 96
Sovereign Bancorp, 255, 283
Standard & Poor's, 264n, 290
State of the Group meetings, WaMu, 146–48,
    162
Steel, Bob, 233, 234, 265
Stever, James, 188
subprime lenders
    Bair's concerns about, 218
    expansion of, 58–59
    fraud and, 71–73
    Russian debt crisis and, 62
    WaMu interest in acquisition of, 58, 59
    See also Long Beach Mortgage
subprime loans/mortgages
    Bair's concerns about, 218, 223
    Baker e-mail about housing and, 152
    benefits of, 61
    Chapman's (Fay) concerns about, 179
    collapse of market for, 167
    compensation and, 128, 197

criticisms and warnings about, 64
decline in housing prices and, 153–54
defaults and delinquencies on, 161, 173, 225
definition of, 179
Dimon and, 230–31
early problems with, 152, 153
exit strategy for selling, 167–68
expansion of offerings of, 64, 70–71
foreclosures and, 77, 161
fraud and, 71–73, 164
as high-margin product, 150
"higher-risk lending strategy" and, 122
increase in sales of, 136–37
at IndyMac, 207
interest rates for, 58, 63, 66, 121–22
Jenne-Home Loans Group meeting about,
    167–68
JPM losses on, 325
Killinger's views about, 122, 137–38, 159,
    241
lack of documentation for, 126
Lannoye opposition to, 197–98
Long Beach Mortgage reputation and, 176
losses from, 153, 161, 167
marketing of, 167–68
minorities and, 64
off-loading of, 154, 161
OTS criticism of WaMu for lending on, 122
OTS review of WaMu and, 224
ownership of, 77
plans to save WaMu and, 228
ratings on, 167
rebranding of, 167
risk and, 58, 153–54
Rotella and, 137–38, 197n, 331
secondary market and, 120
shareholder criticisms of WaMu board and,
    194
at Superior Bank, 225
underwriting guidelines and, 126
Vanasek's views about, 123
WaMu commitment to sale of, 158–59
WaMu goals and, 150
WaMu purchasing of, 129–30
WaMu stops making, 176 See also Long Beach
    Mortgage; mortgage-backed securities
Summit Savings Bank, 39
Suntrust, 282n
Superior Bank, 225
"systemic risk" exceptions, 314, 318

Tall, Craig
    Ahmanson acquisition and, 53
    Chapman (Craig) hiring by, 61

Tall, Craig (*cont.*)
and concerns about mortgage company acquisitions, 97
Countrywide-WaMu competition and, 127
Great Western acquisition and, 32, 33, 40, 41–42, 48
health of, 96–97
hiring of, 27
Killinger management style defended by, 55
Killinger's appearance comment of, 88
Killinger's relationship with, 97, 98, 203
Long Beach Mortgage acquisition and, 58, 59
merger and acquisitions responsibilities of, 38, 48, 49, 58, 59
NYSE bell ringing and, 54
personality and character of, 38
resignation of, 98
role at WaMu of, 97
TARP (Troubled Asset Relief Program), 2, 285, 288, 291, 295, 313, 314–15, 319, 328
Taylor, Bean & Whitaker, 130
TD Bank, 271, 283, 289, 292, 294
Term Auction Facility (TAF), 285–86, 300
Texas: complaints against WaMu in, 99–100
Thousand Oaks, California: WaMu branch in, 6
too big to fail, 26, 309–10
Toscafund Asset Management, 297
Towers, Mike: Killinger–five emissaries meeting and, 203–6
TPG, 6, 189, 235, 237, 238, 245, 246, 257, 265–66, 279, 290, 319
tranches, 74
Treasury Department, U.S., 217, 218, 220, 225, 233, 234, 285, 288, 291, 294, 317
Troubled Asset Relief Program (TARP), 2, 285, 288, 291, 295, 313, 314–15, 319, 328
troubled bank list, FDIC, 3, 248–49, 262, 273
21st Century Mortgage, 72

UBS, 152
U.S. Bancorp, 247, 285

Vanasek, Jim, 73, 98, 123–24, 135, 149–50
Vasquez, Sara, 156–57, 172, 173

Wachovia Bank, 187, 265, 282*n*, 314
Wal-Mart, 217
Wall Street
buying of mortgage-backed securities by, 130
decline in housing prices and, 152
media proclaims end of modern, 288
See also hedge funds; investment banks/houses; secondary market; *specific firm or person*

The Wall Street Journal
Baker e-mail about subprime loans and, 152–53
and Eisinger comment about Option ARMs, 139
Fannie Mae and Freddie Mac takeover announcement in, 254
FDIC-JPM sale of WaMu and, 300–301, 302
Great Western acquisition and, 47–48
Greenspan 30-year mortgage statement in, 119*n*
JPM direct offer to WaMu and, 237–38
JPM initial buyout offer for WaMu in, 189
Lereah optimism and, 152*n*
rumors of JPM-WaMu sale in, 299, 300–301
Scharf comment about WaMu branches to, 325
and settlement of FDIC lawsuit against WaMu executives, 334
Vanasek suggestion to Killinger about responsible lending practices ad in, 123
WaMu Action Teller Doll story in, 86
WaMu stock ads in, 88
WaMu
assets of, 14, 15, 30, 39, 47, 54, 82, 88, 108, 232, 257, 258, 258*n*, 295
blame for problems at, 193–200, 241, 262, 317, 330
borrower-friendly mortgages at, 22–23
as "category killer," 91, 92
charters for, 271, 302
closure/seizure of, 5–7, 294, 296, 299–305, 315
consumer as focus of, 87
cost-cutting at, 102, 103–4, 123
culture/values at, 20–21, 23–25, 38, 44–45, 51, 52, 90–91, 94–95, 98, 107, 131–33, 146–48, 149, 163, 177, 203, 259, 330
customers of, 14–15
expansion/growth of, 17, 25, 30, 39, 40, 54, 55, 71, 85, 86, 88, 108, 109
five-year plans for, 96, 108, 122–23, 126
losses at, 12, 108, 122, 153, 161, 170, 185, 191, 192, 198, 215, 220, 232, 239, 240, 244, 246, 260, 262, 280, 304, 305
market capitalization of, 48–49
mission of, 12
naming of, 90*n*, 203*n*
organization and structure of, 67, 96, 101, 108, 150–51
philanthropy of, 326–27
profits/earnings of, 75, 82, 88, 121–23, 145, 164, 170, 224
public offering for, 16, 183

reputation of, 15, 30, 43
rumors about, 214, 239, 267–68
Seattle headquarters of, 2, 15–16, 32–33, 94–95, 148, 203–4
size of, 54, 67, 88, 100
stock price for, 5, 22, 47, 48–49, 81, 82, 88, 121, 134, 164, 176, 185, 189, 199, 206, 232, 235–36, 237–38, 239, 245–46, 247, 254, 259, 263, 264, 270, 272, 275, 326
See also specific person, acquisition, or topic
WAMU Series 2007-HE4 securities, 156
The WaMu Way (video), 146–48
WaMulians, 90
WaMurabilia, 322
Warehouse Lending Division, WaMu, 130–32, 168–70
See also Perrin, Michele
warranties, 74
Washington Roundtable, 83
Weill, Sanford "Sandy," 87, 230
Welch, Jack, 96
Wells Fargo Bank, 40, 49–50, 53, 158, 229, 251, 271, 283, 289, 290, 297, 314
Western Bank, 39
Whiz (WaMu internal communication system), 44

Who Moved My Cheese? (book), 131
Wholesale Division, WaMu, 129–30, 170
Wigand, Jim, 284, 289–90, 290n, 291
Williams, Robert, 175, 178, 244, 245, 265
Wilson, Liane
   acquisitions of WaMu and, 44
   hiring of, 17–18, 19
   Killinger–five emissaries meeting and, 203–6
   Killinger's marital problems and, 80–81
   Long Beach Mortgage acquisition and, 60
   mergers and acquisitions and, 49, 50–51
   NYSE bell ringing and, 54
   personality of, 50
   resignation of, 95–96, 108
   responsibilities of, 49, 95–96
   software programs at WaMu and, 99
   structure and organization of WaMu and, 96
   at WaMu reunion, 307
Wisdorf, Doug, 206, 308, 309, 310, 319
women: Pepper's hiring of, 19–20
World Economic Forum (Davos, Switzerland), 174
World Savings Bank, 119
Worldcom, 91

Y2K technology conversion, 96